Postmodern Climate Change

International responses to the crisis of climate change have been controversial, contentious, and, to date, largely unsuccessful. Despite concern and action for over two decades, the global rise in greenhouse gas emissions has yet to be arrested.

Leigh Glover argues that efforts by the international community to control climate change using modernity's usual scientific, economic, and governmental tools are inherently flawed, so that the problem of climate change defines modernity's end in ecological terms. This book offers a new way to understand the climate change problem and is concerned with problems of modernity and postmodernity in the context of contemporary environmental thought. Focussing on the international politics surrounding the UN agreement on climate change, the Framework Convention on Climate Change and its Kyoto Protocol, the author examines this important issue using the key aspects of climate change science, global environmental politics, and global environmental management.

This book will be of interest to students and researchers in fields of environmental politics, environmental theory, political science, and international relations, with an interest in climate change. It will also appeal to those in environmental studies, geography, cultural studies, and other relevant aspects of the social sciences dealing with global environmental governance, global environmental problems, ecological justice, and environmentalism.

Leigh Glover is Policy Fellow at the Center for Energy and Environmental Policy, University of Delaware, USA.

Environmental Politics/Routledge Research in Environmental Politics
Edited by Matthew Paterson, University of Ottawa and Graham Smith, University of Southampton

Over recent years environmental politics has moved from a peripheral interest to a central concern within the discipline of politics. This series aims to reinforce this trend through the publication of books that investigate the nature of contemporary environmental politics and show the centrality of environmental politics to the study of politics per se. The series understands politics in a broad sense and books will focus on mainstream issues such as the policy process and new social movements as well as emerging areas such as cultural politics and political economy. Books in the series will analyse contemporary political practices with regards to the environment and/or explore possible future directions for the 'greening' of contemporary politics. The series will be of interest not only to academics and students working in the environmental field, but will also demand to be read within the broader discipline.

The series consists of two strands:

Environmental Politics addresses the needs of students and teachers, and the titles will be published in paperback and hardback. Titles include:

Global Warming and Global Politics
Matthew Paterson

Politics and the Environment
James Connelly and Graham Smith

International Relations Theory and Ecological Thought
Towards Synthesis
Eric Laferrière and Peter Stoett

Planning Sustainability
Edited by Michael Kenny and James Meadowcroft

Deliberative Democracy and the Environment
Graham Smith

EU Enlargement and the Environment
Institutional change and environmental policy in Central and Eastern Europe
Edited by JoAnn Carmin and Stacy D. VanDeveer

Routledge Research in Environmental Politics presents innovative new research intended for high-level specialist readership. These titles are published in hardback only and include:

The Emergence of Ecological Modernisation
Integrating the environment and the economy?
Stephen C. Young

Ideas and Actions in the Green Movement
Brian Doherty

Russia and the West
Environmental Cooperation and Conflict
Geir Hønneland

Global Warming and East Asia
The domestic and international politics of climate change
Edited by Paul G. Harris

Europe, Globalization and Sustainable Development
Edited by John Barry, Brian Baxter and Richard Dunphy

The Politics of GM Food
A comparative study of the UK, USA and EU
Dave Toke

Environmental Policy in Europe
The Europeanization of national environmental policy
Edited by Andrew Jordan and Duncan Liefferink

A Theory of Ecological Justice
Brian Baxter

Security and Climate Change
International relations and the limits of realism
Mark J. Lacy

The Environment and International Politics
International fisheries, Heidegger and social method
Hakan Seckinelgin

Postmodern Climate Change
Leigh Glover

Contemporary Environmental Politics
From margins to mainstream
Edited by Piers H.G. Stephens, with John Barry and Andrew Dobson

Postmodern Climate Change

Leigh Glover

Routledge
Taylor & Francis Group

LONDON AND NEW YORK

First published 2006
by Routledge
270 Madison Avenue, New York, NY 10016

Simultaneously published in the UK
by Routledge
2 Park Square, Milton Park, Abingdon, Oxon OX14 4RN

Routledge is an imprint of the Taylor & Francis Group, an informa business

© 2006 Leigh Glover

Typeset in Times by
Taylor & Francis Books
Printed and bound in Great Britain by
Biddles Ltd, King's Lynn

British Library Cataloguing in Publication Data
A catalogue record for this book is available from the British Library

Library of Congress Cataloging-in-Publication Data
Glover, Leigh.
    Postmodern climate change / Leigh Glover.
        p. cm. – (Routledge research in environmental politics ; 11)
    Includes bibliographical references and index.
    ISBN 0-415-35734-9 (alk. paper)
        1. Climatic changes–Environmental aspects. 2. Climatic changes
–International cooperation.   I. Title. II. Series.
QC981.8.C5G6648 2006
363.738'74526–dc22

                                                                            2006002250

ISBN10 0-415-35734-9   ISBN13 978-0-415-35734-0 (hbk)
ISBN10 0-203-00332-2   ISBN13 978-0-203-00332-9 (ebk)

Rather than put an explanation into words, I'll just say this work is for my wife, Anne Austin.

Contents

Preface

Two widely disparate conditions – that of a warming world and the spread of modernization now under the impetus of globalization – are now clearly causally linked. Industrialization produces global ecological change. Yet, realization of this relationship has resisted translation into effective political action to reverse the trend of declining global ecological conditions. Such is the extent of this malaise is that the solutions to arresting this decline are apparently well understood and have been so for many years, but have not yet produced significant social change. Many rival explanations compete, but none seem to capture the problem in its entirety and give rise to incomplete renditions of the problem of climate change. Here we attempt to consider the problem afresh and, with all due humility, set our sights on nothing less than describing climate change politics in their entirety for the first time.

This project began as a dissertation in the University of Delaware's Center for Energy and Environmental Policy's program in environmental and energy policy, under a committee led by Professor John Byrne, and comprising Professors Michael Buxton, Paul Durbin, and Bob Warren. It includes and reflects collaborative work over a number of years, primarily with John Byrne, and other Center colleagues, with invaluable the input from the dissertation committee.

Having been involved in these issues for many years in several different capacities covering both the science and policy aspects, including being a public servant working on climate change science and impacts policy and administration, a researcher, and a commentator, there have many opportunities for interaction with many others on this issue. No complete account of this assistance and support is possible, but I wish to thank the following particularly, in addition to those named above, whose connections now stretch across the globe and through the decades: Paul Baer, Peter Christoff, Robyn Eckersley, Suraje Dessai, Clive Hamilton, Venkatesh Iyer, and Chris Mitchell. All my colleagues at the Center for Energy and Environmental Policy over these years are sincerely thanked. New York City's General Library and its Science and Business Branch in Manhattan and the University of Delaware's Morris Library, and their staff, proved invaluable resources.

Heidi Bagtazo, Harriet Brinton, Marianne Bulman and Grace McInnes of Routledge have been a pleasure to work with and the Series Editor, Matthew Paterson, has my profound thanks.

On a personal note, I must acknowledge a profound early intellectual debt to Profs. Alistair Davidson and the late Herb Feith when both were in Monash University's politics department and to Prof. David Evans when at Melbourne University for my education, in its broadest sense. For the opportunities in my first career in the public service, I am indebted to Peter Cheng, the late Dr. John Patterson, and David Scott.

Abbreviations

AEC	(United States) Atomic Energy Commission
AIJ	Activities Implemented Jointly
AOSIS	Alliance of Small States
b	billion
bp	before present
c	centigrade
CANZ	Canada, Australia, and New Zealand
CDM	Clean Development Mechanism
CIA	(United States) Central Intelligence Agency
COP	Conference of the Parties
cm	centimeter
EE	Eastern Europe
EKC	environmental Kuznets curve
EIT	Economies in Transition
EPA	(United States) Environmental Protection Agency
EU	European Union
FCCC	Framework Convention on Climate Change
FSU	former Soviet Union
GARP	Global Atmospheric Research Program
GATT	General Agreement on Tariffs and Trade
GCC	Global Climate Coalition
GCM	Global Circulation Model
GCRP	(United States) Global Change Research Program
GDP	gross domestic product
GFDL	Geophysical Fluid Dynamics Laboratory
GHG	greenhouse gas(es)
G-77	Group of 77
IMF	International Monetary Fund
INC	Intergovernmental Negotiating Committee
IPCC	Intergovernmental Panel on Climate Change
JI	joint implementation
JUSSCANNZ	Japan, United States, Switzerland, Canada, Australia, Norway, and New Zealand

m	million
mmtce	million metric tons of carbon equivalent
mmtco2e	million metric tons of carbon dioxide equivalent
NAS	(United States) National Academy of Sciences
NASA	(United States) National Aeronautics and Space Administration
NGGIP	National Greenhouse Gas Inventory Program
NGO	non-governmental organization
NRC	(United States) National Research Council
OECD	Organization for Economic Co-operation and Development
ONR	(United States) Office of Naval Research
OPEC	Organization of the Petroleum Exporting Countries
ppmv	parts per million by volume
ppbv	parts per billion by volume
PSAC	(United States) President's Science Advisory Committee
SMIC	Report on the Study of Man's Impact on Climate
UK	United Kingdom
UN	United Nations
UNCED	United Nations Conference on Environment and Development
UNDP	United Nations Development Program
UNEP	United Nations Environment Program
US	United States
USCANZ	United States, Canada, Australia, and New Zealand
USSR	Union of Soviet Socialist Republics (now Russian Federation)
WCC	World Climate Conference
WCED	World Conference on Environment and Development
WCP	World Climate Program
WMO	World Meteorological Organization
WTO	World Trade Organization
WWI	World War One
WWII	World War Two

1 Climate change and modernity

Introduction

Climate change, as a product of cumulative anthropogenic releases of heat-trapping gases, is warming the global climate, and is popularly described as a 'crisis.' By any reasonable understanding of 'crisis,' this is undoubtedly true. Losses to ecological values and human societies due to climate change are potentially catastrophic, and will be long-lived, largely irreversible, and remain for the most part unpredictable. Indeed, in recent years a great array of social and ecological losses from changes and extremes in climate and weather has been linked to a warming world, from heat-related mortality to a great swath of ecological impacts from the polar realms to the tropics. So far, nearly all of the scholarship, research, and conceptual development behind the international response to climate change is premised on a particular understanding of society and ecology, especially the presumption of the continuation, integrity, and consistency of modernity.

To identify climate change as an outcome of modernity is, at one level, a statement of the obvious – it is a contemporary issue born of industrial society. Pre-modern societies did not possess the technological capacity to alter the global climate or to recognize any association between climate and human activity. Simply put, anthropogenic climate change (hereafter, 'climate change') is largely an outcome of the energy systems essential to industrialized and industrializing societies, namely those based on fossil fuel consumption with their concomitant greenhouse gas emissions. Karl and Tremberth (2003), for example, call this domination of climate change by human influences 'modern global climate change.' Our ability to detect this relationship and to devise a means of response is similarly a distinguishing feature of the contemporary.

Viewed in this way, climate change is but another – albeit global – outcome of 'normal' pollution, with greenhouse gases emissions to the atmosphere constituting the pollutant. Logically and sensibly, it follows that curtailing emissions would largely resolve the problem, making the enabling tasks those of discerning a means of reducing emissions, undertaking the necessary pollution abatement measures, and responding adaptively to the impacts of those climate changes now inevitable. Under such thinking, climate change is certainly a problem of the current era, but one that fits comfortably within the framework of normal activity and perceptions of society and nature in the modern world.

Framed in this rational manner, the problem itself suggests the solution. Initially, a goal for an acceptable level of future global warming (and therefore an acceptable level of climate change impacts) is established. Scientific knowledge is applied to understand the relationship between greenhouse emissions and climate change, science and policy are both used to set emission reduction targets, and institutions are formed to undertake the functions of governance. All nations are threatened by climate change and all contribute some level of emissions, so that governance mechanisms are required at the national and global scales. Climate change is seen as necessitating modification of routine industrial pollution through management by the dictates set by an emerging system of global environmental governance. Scholarship founded on the basis of this formulation of the problem can comfortably place climate change within the context of conventional political analysis, which is indeed what has occurred.

Now is the time to challenge the conventional view of climate change. Climate change represents a problem more fundamental and intractable than pollution, which manifests a deeper and more elemental set of social organization, values, and philosophies. Fundamentally and essentially, climate change is a product of modernity and is being subject to the scientific knowledge systems, approaches to governance, and environmental management goals that comprise modernity's characteristic responses to environmental issues. To date, few have questioned the premises of modernity when analyzing the international response to climate change. Yet, there are vital and urgent reasons for posing such an inquiry. Climate change portends greater social change than the matters of turbulent international relations, interminable discussions of complex policy choices, and vexing scientific questions that dominate climate change's contemporary scholarship. Consider, for example, the following issues that challenge the existing response to climate change:

- effectiveness of reducing future atmospheric greenhouse gas concentrations on future climate is unknown;
- climate change impacts will produce great global redistributions of wealth and welfare that remain highly uncertain;
- reducing global greenhouse gas emissions to achieve the so-called 'stable climate' requires a re-organization of the energy systems of developed nations that cannot occur without great social change, the transition to which remains largely unknown;
- efforts to organize an effective means to reduce global greenhouse gas emissions have conspicuously failed and emissions continue to increase; and

- national economic development has usually occurred through industrialization based on fossil fuel energy systems, yet any efforts to curtail global emissions will probably fail if developing nations continue to follow the historical high emissions path to economic development.

Addressing climate change has proved not only to be difficult, but presents difficulties in ways and in places where the greatest confidence in the human capacities has been exhibited; not only is it not amenable to conventional national approaches to environmental problems, but poses challenges to existing systems of knowledge and environmental problem resolution. In this work we respond to this challenge by examining climate change not as a problem of managing complex social and natural systems, but as a problem of modernity itself. Oriented thus, more original issues emerge as we switch from the conventional fixation on remedy to the more radical issue of cause, considering climate change as a matter of the legitimacy of modern systems of knowledge, social organization, and environmental management. Only through understanding the social causes of climate change and recognizing the limits of the modernity can there be much hope for generating effective alternative responses in the future. Globally, the response of the international community of nations to climate change is organized under the auspices of the UN Framework Convention on Climate Change (FCCC). Studying the international response to climate change involves examining the processes, activities, and politics surrounding this institution, as it involves climate change science, the formulation of international policy initiatives, and the setting of management goals. Analysis of the international response concentrates on the period beginning with the international negotiations leading up to the 1992 UN Conference on Environment and Development, covering the formulation of the FCCC at that event, and extending to the ratification of the Kyoto Protocol in early 2005.

This analysis is organized around three themes essential to, and therefore defining (at least in part), modernity:

- scientific knowledge as a means of understanding the natural and social worlds and the only reliable tool for their management;
- liberal-democratic (global) governance as the coalescence of capitalist economics and representative government; and
- managing the natural world for human ends.

No particular theoretical approach lends itself to a thorough critique of these diverse themes and so we must consider the international response from several perspectives, beginning with the premise that the FCCC exemplifies 'ecological modernization.' Two broad critical approaches have been directed against the FCCC, namely the more familiar political economy and the emerging postmodern of political ecology (see Table 1.1).

Table 1.1 Climate change discourses: challenges of the conventional by modern and postmodern critiques, arranged thematically.

Theme	Ecological modernization	Political economy	Postmodernism
Science	Conventional science studies based on rationalism[1]	Studies of the influence of capital, nation state interests, and corporations[4]	Constructivism and 'post-normal' science.[7] Little support for 'postmodern science'
Liberal-democratic governance	International Relations studies, notably regime theory, liberal institutionalism, and neo-realism.[2] Full embrace of market-based policies. Accepts scientific rationality	Critiques of nation states, developed nations, corporations, globalization, and capital in general.[5] Accepts conventional science, rejects climate change economics	Political ecology takes varying positions on governance, much acceptance of principles but seek alternative policies[8] Skeptical of mainstream science
Global environmental management	Treated as global governance and science issue[3]	Acceptance as goal, skeptical of conventional policy approach[6]	Skeptical or critical of goal and disputes construction of the 'global'[9]

Notes
1 E.g., Bolin (1994) and IPCC (various).
2 E.g., Molitor (1999), Oberthur and Ott (1999), and Soroos (1997).
3 E.g., Beck (1995), Hempel (1996), and Young (1997).
4 E.g., Beder (1997), Boehmer-Christianson (1997), Hart and Victor (1993), and Gelbspan (1997).
5 E.g., Grubb et al. (1999), Paterson (1996), and Saurin (2001).
6 E.g., Newell and Paterson (1999).
7 E.g., Demeritt (2001), Shackley (1997), and Wynne (1994).
8 E.g., Agarwal and Narain (1991), Byrne (1997), Gupta (2001), and Shue (1999).
9 E.g., Byrne and Glover (2000), Ross (1991), and Sachs (1994).

Ecological modernization describes how environmental protection is made possible by restructuring and reorienting (capitalist) economic activity and is exemplified by the national environmental performance of Germany, Japan, the Netherlands, Norway, and Sweden. Germans Martin Jänicke and Joseph Huber are usually credited with the concept's early development, both of who sought to identify a revised modernity that responded to ecological problems (Hajer 1995). Emphasizing how natural systems link with social activity, ecological modernization identifies the environment as systemically integrated into the social realm. Rendering social and natural phenomena into systems enables ecological modernization to resolve environmental issues as the new integration of previously conflicting systems, and concepts such as material and energy flows, sustainability, efficiency, and naturalness are hallmarks of the discourse. Rather than continuing industrial society's general disregard of natural values, ecological modernization seeks to have ecological values recognized in the production and consumption cycles. Political commitment to a longer-term outlook is necessary, and the discourse embraces business, government, science, and environmental NGOs as partners in an enterprise of mutual benefit.

Advocates of ecological modernization, therefore, reject such thinking as economic rationality that recognize environmental values only through pricing or taxation as exemplifying the rationality of an environment essentially external to society. Instead of adopting adversarial approaches to making business respond to environmental values, states seek policy approaches that offer economic gains from environmental protection, such as increased energy efficiency, pollution prevention, and meeting consumer preferences for 'green' products.

Although the term enjoys relatively little recognition and use outside Europe, the concept of ecological modernization captures well those positive outcomes of environmentalism since the 1970s. Reforms under the general banner of environmentalism, notably in developed nations, driven by environmental policies can be broadly described as ecological modernization, often occurring under the rubric of 'sustainable development' (see, e.g., Lafferty 1996, 1999). Ecological modernization reconciles environmentalism with the normal functioning of the state (Hajer 1995) and strengthens its legitimacy. Essential features and activities of the capitalist economy are undisturbed in this process of having industry and state cooperate in policy initiatives that are profitable and ecologically benign.

Critics of ecological modernization attack its conservatism as "ecological modernization is a form of societal behavior which responds to the perceived necessity to preserve the myths of modernity" (Blühdorn 2000: 209). Blühdorn (2000) identifies five criticisms of the concept, several of which were earlier raised by Hajer (1995): 1) it is an economic and technology based concept that writes problems into these discourses, thereby assisting its acceptance into the existing decision-making processes without contradiction; 2) environmental problems are held to be managerial, thereby placing power in the technological and political elites, whose goal is the 'mastery of Nature;' 3) economic growth is considered reconcilable with resolving ecological problems; 4) no changes are required to the existing economic, political, and social orders to resolve any environmental problem; and 5) ecological modernization offers a new form of rationality within society that will transcend that of economic rationality, while leaving the central tenets of modernity intact.

Although ecological modernization has been largely restricted to national and sub-national activity and not to international issues, the concept applies to the international response to climate change, wherein governance takes an international form. Both the nation state and capitalist economic systems are an integral component of the FCCC, an international agreement that assumes the atmosphere is a complex system capable of 'absorbing' atmospheric pollutants within limits determined by scientific research. Central to the FCCC is the belief that cooperation between states, corporations, and interested groups can devise policy approaches that resolve the problem and generate economic wealth, and that cooperation between involved parties shares the common goal of atmospheric protection. Scholarship into the FCCC and climate change politics has occurred largely within International Relations, where the approach of ecological modernization has been largely matched by studies featuring liberal-institutionalism, neo-realism and, pre-dominantly, regime theory. Regime theory has offered few critical insights into environmental issues, as these are treated routine matters of global governance (Lipschutz 1996; Paterson 1999b). For Saurin (1996, 2001), Paterson (1995), and others, regime theory and similar scholarship supports and provides legitimacy for extensions of state and corporate power over environmental values and powerless communities.

Political economy has proved to be a valuable approach for describing and analyzing the international interactions of states, corporations, and capital in shaping international agreements on climate change and at the nation-state scale, examining domestic climate change policies, including foreign policy decisions regarding international agreements. Several scholars have usefully applied political economy, usually focussing on international relations, notably Grubb et al. (1999), Paterson (1996), and Newell and Paterson 1999). To a lesser extent, many descriptions and analyses of the influences on climate change science evoke political economy, as critics of the IPCC (e.g., Boehmer-Cristianson 1993, 1994a, 1994b, and 1997) and of corporations (e.g., Beder 1997; Gelbspan 1997, 2004; and Leggett 2000) cite the influence of political power and capital as shaping climate change science outcomes.

Key features of the international response to climate change fit neatly into political economy explanations. Major corporations involved in the fossil fuel, automobile, and related industries were successful in shaping government policy, public opinion, and international processes in ways to minimize the potential financial impacts on their corporate interests (e.g., Gelbspan 2004, Leggett 2000). Further, the selection of market-based policy tools for implementing the FCCC, the concept of greenhouse gas emissions trading, and global trading relations have been critiqued from a political economy perspective (e.g., Grubb et al. 1999). Political economy highlighted the limitations of the conventional liberal-institutionalist and free-market environmentalism by highlighting the motivations and tactics of states and corporations to protect their perceived interests (Newell and Paterson 1999; Paterson 1996).

An alternative critique with an overt interest in ecological values is 'political ecology.' Hempel (1996) offers that political ecology is concerned with interdependence among political units and with the environment, primarily dealing with the effects of environmental change on political activity. For some of its proponents, political ecology is the outgrowth of political economy and ecological analysis, in which the relationships between power and production are joined with an understanding of 'bio-environmental relationships' (Greenberg and Park 1994). In this sense, its proponents seek to mutually inform the inadequacies of these two approaches to environmental problems which can exist at virtually any scale, and range from predominantly cultural systems to predominantly natural systems, making political ecology a 'conversation' between political economy and ecology. Introducing the *Journal of Political Ecology*, Greenberg and Park (1994) refer to the multidisciplinary character of this approach and express some skepticism at positivist approaches, but demur from offering a fixed definition.

Advocates of political ecology endorse many of the assessments raised by political economy, but additionally offer a wider range of responses and criticisms. Distinguishing features of political ecology include its general commitment to 'ecological justice,' which seeks to extend concepts of justice to natural entities and processes and to future generations. Further, political ecology deals with basic issues of environmentalism in ways that are usually outside the ambit of political economy. Examples of these concerns over existing beliefs and practices include the human domination of nature, human alienation from nature, instrumental valuations of nature, and denial of nature's agency. Political ecology does not deny a role to science, but tends to regard its outputs as the result of particular 'social constructions.' As for the phenomenon of globalization and the goal of global environmental management, advocates of political ecology usually adopt a skeptical or oppositional attitude.

Particular issues raised by political ecology include ethical issues linked to considering the atmosphere as a global commons and this group have promulgated varying types of political and policy responses that such a recognition might entail. Additionally, political ecology is concerned about the project of global environmental management, both on philosophical and practical grounds. Much of the critique has focussed on the fairness of the UN processes and outcomes, the use of economic policy instruments under the FCCC, and the implications of weak greenhouse gas abatement targets for vulnerable communities, such as the small island developing states (see, e.g., Agarwal et al. 1999; Byrne 1997; and Gupta 2001).

Political economy and political ecology are distinguished also by their response to modernity and the environment, as the former is compatible with a largely materialist conception of environmental goods and services, whereas political ecology recognizes wider social and ecological interests. However, this distinctiveness is taken further and it is suggested that political ecology is a critique whose implications are in opposition to modernity. Political ecology contains implications that modernity is incapable of resolving, namely its challenges to the accepted positions on science, liberal democracy, and global environmental management. Accordingly, political ecology contains insights that can be understood as being 'postmodern.' In making such a claim, it is necessary to simultaneously depart from the conventional formulation of the climate change 'problem' and also to proffer a revised understanding of the postmodern by investing the term with a distinctive ecological meaning and implication.

Postmodernity's major proponents – namely the four French authors most closely associated with its theory and philosophy: Jean Baudrillard, Jacques Derrida, Michel Foucault, and Jean-François Lyotard – did not consider ecology or environmentalism as having any major implications or relevance for contemporary social conditions. Nor have the majority of its scholars and promoters done much to alter this situation, as postmodernity scholarship has focussed on culture as expressed in architecture, art, language, literature, politics, and urban life (see, e.g., the reviews of Bauman 1991; Best and Kellner 1991, 1997, and 2001; Harvey 1992; and Kumar 1995). Postmodernity has, however, been considered in ecological terms in political and cultural studies, although often it has often been regarded negatively (see, e.g., Borgmann 1992, 1995; Castree and Braun 2001; Conley 1997; Gare 1995; Soulé and Lease 1995; Spretnak 1991, 1997; and Zimmerman 1994). Where environment and postmodernity have been examined most thoroughly is environmental ethics (see, e.g., Cheney 1989a, 1989b; Oelschlaeger 1995), and increasingly in environmental discourse (see, e.g., Bennett and Chaloupka 1993; Cantrill and Oravec 1996). Many well-regarded reviews of ecological and environmental thought still seemingly have no place for postmodernity, such as those of Dryzek (1997) and Guha (2000). What makes this uneven general mutual regard somewhat surprising is the vast scholarship on both subjects in recent years.

Despite its own contention of the illusionary, ambiguous, and 'constructed' character of contemporary life, postmodernism has become commonly defined by its own cliché, namely that it rejects any 'grand narrative.' Postmodernists often deny any fixed concepts of space, time, and boundaries by arguing that all depends on social construction. Insights into the social condition are derived from analysis of how particular understandings are assembled, an activity often known as 'deconstruction.' For many environmentalists, such sentiments court the obvious risks that environmental values and specific environmental problems can be dismissed as merely another set of social views, or that only discourse itself is of value, making postmodern concepts an anathema to those engaged in political struggles with corporations, states, and international bodies. Opposition to such postmodern approaches is usually based in realist terms, fearing that excessive constructionism will lead to 'paralysis by analysis' or worse, the denial of the reality of ecological problems (e.g., Cronon 1994; Soulé 1995; and Starke 1995). Environmentalism has also supplied its own case for constructionism, however, such as Evernden's (1992) influential *Social Creation of Nature*.

Scientific knowledge is essential to the climate change issue but there is debate as to the character, and indeed to the necessity, of making science the dominant source of knowledge of climate change. One type of criticism of the mainstream effort to confine the problem of climate change to the realms of science is represented by Tainter, who points to the broader routine neglect of history in the consideration of contemporary problems. He argues that such approaches are "inimical to sustainability" and deny that previous peoples have faced such challenges of global changes in climate, so that (Tainter 2000: 331): "Historical research should be considered in policy decisions as routinely as are the findings of climatologists and biologists." Other social scientists have also questioned the dominance of the physical sciences in the describing the causes of climate change, in describing its potential impacts, and in guiding and formulating policy responses and political action.

Ultimately and unavoidably, environmental problems are 'social constructs' of concrete natural phenomena reflected by social choices by which problems are identified, given priorities, and are addressed. Social constructivists, such as Demeritt (1994, 2000, and 2001), often put the case that even the most scientifically-oriented programs to address environmental issues reflect social preferences, so that scientific rationality is directed by processes explicable by politics. That phenomena might be interpreted in widely differing ways is not necessarily to deny the reality of environmental problems, but to suggest that what constitutes facts and features may differ according to perspective. Concerns that postmodernist thinking may undermine efforts at environmental protection seem misplaced, at least at present, when the greatest source of environmental concerns lies in such problems as the continued disregard of ecological values in national and global economic decision-making. Furthermore, even environmental advocates sympathetic to constructionism, such as the aforementioned Demeritt and Zimmerman (1994), similarly fear approaches to environmental problems lacking in recognition of ecological values. These writers have rejected scientific rationality as offering the only way to understand environmental issues, but do not go so far as the anti-rationality of some prominent postmodernists (see, e.g., Lyotard 1984).

Ross (1991) interpreted the climate change issue in the context of cultural studies, producing an account both prescient and insightful, and exemplifying the possibilities offered by a critical approach that could extend beyond the confines of political economy. Ross's work, however, has proved to be singular and few others have followed his lead. While clearly informed by postmodernity and political economy, Ross's work didn't conform to any obvious methodological dictates and, accordingly, there are no unequivocal means by which to build on his contribution.

It follows that the 'postmodern' label is a loose one and may even be detrimental to those concerned with rejecting modernity on environmental grounds; certainly, many in the 'political ecology' group reject what they understand as postmodernism. Yet, political ecologists and others are explicitly examining at least some concepts 'beyond modernity,' such as Escobar (1996, 1999). Expressions of these concepts include a skepticism

that scientific results represent the only possible form of rationally understanding environmental problems, a belief that individual and community
experience constitutes valid forms of knowledge, a rejection that governance
of environmental problems needs to be premised on capitalist economics
and nation-state authority, and a skepticism towards technical elites and
state/corporate entities' efforts to manage the global environment. An
immediate implication of these approaches is that the resolution of environmental problems based on these values cannot be legitimately restricted
to the domain of science and technology.

Whether political ecology is part of postmodern phenomena may be open
to question, despite the brief arguments presented here, but at least two
conclusions seem inescapable. Firstly, political ecology has questioned the
international response to climate change in ways that challenge many premises about the role of science, the effectiveness and legitimacy of liberal-
democratic institutions to manage the global climate, and the plausibility of
global climate management. Secondly, political ecology has raised issues
and questions of the existing response to climate change that have not yet
been addressed, such as the recognition of a global commons and the
'sacrifice' of small island states to rising sea levels, and which seem unans-
werable under the premises and processes of the FCCC.

Climate change as crisis

Climate change as a conventional environmental crisis

Vital to the rationale for the international response to climate change is its
depiction as an environmental crisis. Oral traditions, history, and scientific
research tell of the associations between climatic conditions and social well-
being, a subject of long and active debate. Although the linkage can easily
be exaggerated, such as in the hands of nineteenth- and early twentieth-
century climatic and geographic determinists (of whom Elsworth Hunting-
ton is perhaps the most notorious – see Fleming 1998), climate has shaped
human life on earth, from the evolution of our species to development of
cultures (Schneider and Londer 1984). Brief or extended periods of extreme
climatic conditions have wrecked havoc on many civilizations throughout
history and pre-history. Conversely, there appear to be strong associations
in the pre-modern era between human development and benign, stable climate (Lamb 1982). Yet, a cautionary note must be sounded here: "It would
seem that many students of history have invoked too easily the dues ex
machina of climate change and resource depletion to account for cultural
explanations" (Tainter, 2000: 336). As history reveals, there are conditions
of cultural change that climatic deterioration have caused "great cities to
grow and polities to become complex and yet also cause these systems to
collapse" (Tainter 2000: 336–337). Into these differences over the relative
importance of climate change, it is worth considering the prospects for the

disruption of human affairs produced by a full-blown ice age or greatly warmed world will be more extreme than those arising from the perturbations during the Holocene that has provided 10,000 years of relatively stable climate.

Up to the advent of the Industrial Revolution, changes in global climate were regarded as natural or supernatural events shaping the fortunes of human and other species alike – climate change was another of the natural world's variations. Pre-modern explanations of human activity as an agent of climate change abound; Glacken describes numerous theories, including those of Theophrastus in Ancient Greece (1967). Advancing scientific and traditional knowledge revealed patterns and predictive explanations in climate change, such as the Milankovitch cycles (see, e.g., Gribbin and Gribbin 2001), emerging through climate's chaos and complexity, and theory and speculation abounded over the last two centuries.

Through the scientific era to recent times, climate was considered as entirely independent of human activity. With the association drawn between atmospheric pollution and global warming confirmed in contemporary times, the innocent view of independent nature was lost (as in McKibben's (1989) 'end of Nature'). Realization that the global climate bore the accidental imprint of industrial ingenuity triggered a series of events to address the issue, giving rise to the contemporary era of 'climate politics.'

Briefly, the complexities of climate change can be reduced as follows: as a consequence of the Industrial Revolution, large-scale deliberate combustion of fossil fuels, notably coal, natural gas, and oil products, carbon dioxide and other gases are released to the atmosphere. Abundant, inexpensive, and available fossil fuels supply the bulk of the energy for the world's industrialized economies; some refer to this as the 'carbon economy' (Leggett 2000). By the addition of the so-called 'greenhouse gases' (primarily carbon dioxide, methane, and nitrous oxide) to the atmosphere, the world's retention of heat from solar radiation becomes more efficient, increasing the extent of warming through the (somewhat misleadingly labeled) 'greenhouse effect.' As the planet retains greater heat, the world warms and global climate is affected, sea levels rise, and other changes occur. Global climate is still subject to the processes of natural variation over different timescales, but the effects of human intervention overlay the natural processes of changing climate. Because it is likely that the human effects on climate will predominate in the immediate centuries if not millennia, climate change in this period will be shaped by the consequences of human activity.

Greenhouse gases released by human activity remain resident in the atmosphere for varying lengths of time, the longest of which is carbon dioxide that can remain for several centuries (IPCC 1996a). It follows that the current greenhouse gas concentrations in the atmosphere reach back to James Watt and the early days of coal as an industrial fuel in the age of steam power and that today's fossil fuel combustion will exert a future atmospheric influence on those some eight generations removed from us.

Actions to cut emissions are designed to lessen the future impacts of climate change caused by global warming from future greenhouse gas concentrations in the atmosphere. Despite a variety of research projects on the subject, there are no current feasible technological means to reverse the level of greenhouse gases (IPCC 1996a, 2001a). Consequently, extensive fossil fuel combustion has altered the distributional loads of the global 'carbon cycle,' so that centurial to millennial periods are needed to return conditions to an equilibrium that existed before the anthropocentric carbon additions to the atmospheric.

Until recent times, the major fluctuations in global climate were assumed to be gradual or reasonably so. Past climate has now been shown to be volatile through analysis of analogue climate data, revealing past climate changes of great rapidity, interspersed with periods of both stable, and highly unstable, climate (IPCC, 1996a, 2001a). (Changes in outlook, such as these, may reflect a more general scientific trend in perceiving the natural world, in which 'steady state' concepts have been superseded by views of complex adaptive systems and 'chaotic' system characteristics.) To prompt climate change is risk-taking, in which 'surprising' outcomes may occur. Because of the lag between greenhouse gases release and resultant climate change, management can only now influence the extent and magnitude of these changes – but not prevent them. And as differentiating between natural climate change and anthropocentric climate forcing may remain an impossible quandary, whatever response actions are taken with the goal of mitigating climate change impacts, humanity has initiated a process of irreversible ecological change whose degree of 'managability' cannot ever be properly known.

With the emergent 'new global economy' being characterized as possessed of a 'post-industrial' character with a dominant tertiary sector, some argue that economic ties to natural systems, such as resource demands, are being weakened (known as the 'de-materialization' thesis) (von Weizsacker et al. 1997). Critics claim that national improvements in energy and material efficiency are illusionary and misleading, being the product of the illusionary character of GDP, changes in energy forms, and neglect of import/ export mixes in critical products (see, e.g., Trainer 2001). Evidence exists of trends of greater resource and energy efficiency in developed nations, but globally such gains are overwhelmed by increases in total consumption (as shown in the International Energy Agency's annual statistics on production, consumption, and economic output) (WEA 2000). Globalization is in fact driving global natural resource harvesting, material consumption, and waste generation to unprecedented levels (see, e.g., the UN Development Index) (UNDP 2000; UNDP et al. 2000, 2001). Global industrial growth is not lessening its reliance on ecology, but instead rapidly increasing its dependencies on diminishing natural resource bases and weakened ecological services.

Increasing economic activity has caused global ecological conditions generally to continue to deteriorate and patterns national economic development marked by growing social inequalities (UNDP 2000; UNDP et al. 2001). Ecological losses under climate change will increase under economic globalization, as human disruption to natural systems and the landscape have diminished the adaptive options for species and ecosystems (IPCC 1996b, 2001b). Growing world population has found the absolute number of the world's poor increasing (UNDP 2000; World Bank 2000a). For this unfortunate group, their association with the natural world is absolute and immediate. Survival, for many, is linked to highly stressed local systems of food gathering, agriculture, and water production. Furthermore, the world's poor remain highly vulnerable to climate-related diseases and to climate-related natural hazards (IPCC 1990b, 1996b, and 2001b).

Developed nations have the opportunity to react adaptively to many of the potential climate impacts simply by virtue of being developed; research, education, governance, infrastructure development, technology, and other factors can assist in reducing the harm of effects. But even so, the economic damage of these impacts could be enormous (IPCC 1990b, 1990c, 1996b, 1996c, 2001b, and 2001c). Coastal urban development, for example, will require protection from the associated effects of sea level rise. Natural disasters, such drought, flooding, and severe weather, cannot be dismissed even by the wealthiest of nations. Small island states have been identified as being particularly vulnerable, with human habitation already being diminished in a process that can now only intensify and worsen (IPCC 2001b). Climate change is both conceptually amorphous and elusive, yet climate events can be manifested as cataclysmically as the Asian and Northern African droughts and the floods of Bangladesh during the last century. Potentially, climate change impacts could claim hundreds of millions of human lives (see, e.g., IPCC 2001b). It is in this context that potential climate change impacts must be considered.

Ecologically, climate change will produce a wide array of changes that will be added to other impacts of human activity. At the species level, climate change will increase extinction rates and act as an evolutionary force to alter species distribution, range, and abundance (Midgley et al. 2002; Root et al. 2003; and Thomas et al. 2004). Species loss at this scale could be without precedent in terms of natural losses from human cause. For example, Thomas et al. (2004) modeled the effect of changes in 1103 species' ranges in response to three climate models to 2050 for six sample regions covering 20 percent of the earth's surface. Thomas et al. found that the extinction rate was 15–37 percent. Ecosystem processes will also be affected, such as hydrological systems under altered precipitation regimes and coastal ecosystems by accelerated sea level rise. Another potentially very serious but highly uncertain issue now receiving increased research attention is the increased oceanic acidification resulting from the increased uptake of atmospheric carbon dioxide.

Environmentalists and those concerned with protecting ecological values have been at the forefront of efforts to promote social responses to the climate change crisis. At least two separate streams of thought have contributed to this awareness. Firstly, there are those general concerns raised by environmental ethics, which express a human responsibility for nature; prominent in this effort have been Passmore (1974), Callicott (1994, 1999), Rolston (1988), Stone (1987), and Zimmerman (1987, 1994). Low and Gleeson (1998) draw together many of these themes in their description of 'ecological justice,' which embraces a conception of justice that extends to future generations and to many aspects of nature. These issues have found resonance in the climate change debate. Shue (1993, 1995, and 1999), for example, has identified a number of ethical dimensions for the need to respond to climate change, and more specifically identified ethical aspects of the choices of response.

Secondly, are those writers and activists dealing with environmental issues and economic development, prominently from developing nation NGOs. Their concern over the global and local environmental impacts emanating from developed nations and local industrial activities has promoted awareness of these issues as constituting 'environmental injustice.' Prominent members of this diverse and numerous group have include Agarwal (Agarwal and Narain 1991; Agarwal et al. 2002), Bello (Bello and Rosenfeld 1990; Bello 1992), Escobar (1995, 1996), Khor (1993), Sachs (1991, 1992, 1993a, 1993b, 1994, 1996, 1999a, 1999b), and Shiva (1993, 1997, 1998, and 1999), many of whom have addressed the climate change issue. Environmentalist NGOs were highly influential in the development of national climate policies and the FCCC process, and it was these conceptualizations and arguments that formed the basis of the prominent campaigns by such groups as the Climate Action Network, the Centre for Science and Environment, Friends of the Earth, Greenpeace, Third World Network, and the Worldwide Fund for Nature (see, e.g., Agarwal et al. 1999; Grubb et al. 1999; Gupta 2001; Leggett 2000; and Paterson 1996).

Further, we might now add the issue of security as an emerging motivation to respond to climate change, although oddly enough little systemic work has been done in this field. Part of this concern emerges from the growing field of environmental security (see, e.g., Barnett 2001; Dalby 2002). Many authors refer to climate change's security implications, although frequently in a compilation of global environmental problems. Part of the attention given to climate change also derives from more traditional national security concerns, especially as emerging in the wake of contemporary terrorist activity and the geo-political significance of the September 11 attack on the U.S. Perhaps there has been no more surprising expression of this latter dimension than a report to the U.S. Defense Department (Schwartz and Randall 2003) contemplating the implications of abrupt climate change for U.S. national security. Schwartz and Randall's report is alarmist, if not apocalyptic, and is not dissimilar from the type that drew criticism when expressed by conservationists. Barnett (2003) establishes some potential foundations in this field by tracing out the idea's history and laying out several broad themes for future investigation. Bennett also identifies a number of potential advantages of a climate change security discourse for motivating an effective climate change response. Taking it as axiomatic that environmental degradation leads to violent conflict is, as Barnett explains (2000, 2003), a dubious proposition and one likely grounded on a political defense of the status quo.

In short, there is a compelling rationale for considering climate change as an environmental problem deserving of attention and a sizable and widespread NGO community is now devoted specifically to climate change issues, while established environmental NGOs have added climate change to their political and activist agendas. Newell (2000) provided an extensive account of the NGOs' role in international climate change politics (see also Carpenter 2001; Gough and Shackley 2001; and Grundbransen and Andressen 2004). Climate change is global in scale and will produce highly differentiated impacts of permanent losses to social and ecological values. While future global warming now cannot be avoided due to the irreversibility of the climate system, reducing the level of global greenhouse gas emissions may lessen the magnitude of these impacts.

Managing climate change

Climate change is an environmental crisis because it presents a range of hazardous impacts, but additional to this depiction of a natural hazard is the complicity of human agency as a causative factor. Understanding climate change as a crisis, therefore, involves assessing the extent to which society can alter or meliorate the human role in determining the magnitude of climate change impacts. Essential to the social construction of this 'crisis' is not only an assessment of the potential losses that might be incurred, but additionally a determination of the extent to which social action can shape these impacts. Both the magnitude of the risks and dangers depend on the degree to which they can be managed, implying the necessity of controlling both the social and natural aspects of the problem.

Climate change will produce global impacts, in theory affecting all nations and peoples to differing extents, and is an outcome of greenhouse gases emissions emanating largely from the world's industrial economies. Reducing greenhouse gases emissions therefore requires emission reductions by a majority of the world's industrial nations and in accordance with a coordinated or agreed approach. Yet, because of scientific uncertainty, it is largely unknown what associations exist between the level of climate change impacts and the rate of greenhouse gas emissions. Action, therefore, involves national efforts and international agreements, which must be contentious, controversial, and difficult. While climate change is far from unique in being the subject of an international environmental system, there are few precedents for a regime with this difficult combination of characteristics.

Greenhouse gases are normal pollutants in one sense, but possess a number of unusual and possibly unique characteristics. Few pollutants produce globally dispersed effects, are as ubiquitous with the routine operation of industrial societies, or tied to the basic source of energy on which industrial society traditionally depends. In addition to having a multiplicity of diffuse and point sources, greenhouse gases are emitted by effectively every major sector of an industrialized economy (agriculture, industry, energy utilities, transport, residential, and commercial), and in great quantities. Without exaggeration, curbing greenhouse gas emissions engages every citizen in the industrialized world in everyday life. Curtailing such pollutants has no recourse to ready emissions limits, technological innovations, or voluntary agreement.

Further, emissions vary greatly between and within nations. Great national differences in greenhouse gas emissions exist in comparisons such as between gross totals, per capita totals, historical accumulated totals, and per capita accumulated totals (see, e.g., Byrne et al. 1998; Gupta 2001; and IPCC 2001a). OECD nations dominate global emissions, particularly from the largest economies, and while India and China also have substantial emissions, nearly all developing nations have low emissions and very low per capita rates. Within nations, further differentiation is apparent at the scale of the firm, household, and individual up to industrial sectors and regions. Emissions reductions, therefore, present many complex choices within and between nations.

Climate change impacts present further difficulties for a policy response. Potential climate change impacts threaten human and natural systems, but their global and social impacts will be unevenly distributed, so that few generalizations can be made. Since there is a general absence of regional or local estimates of future climate and other conditions, predictions of climate change impacts at the scale where households, communities, and local government could make adaptive decisions through planning are generally unavailable (IPCC 2001b). As a result, adaptation policies to anticipate these impacts are needed, but until these impacts have relatively clear definition, adaptation measures are highly circumscribed. Calls for increased efforts on adaptation issues come from many quarters, but adaptation policy remains the most neglected field within the existing policy landscape (IPCC 1990b, 1996b, and 2001b).

Politically and ethically, a number of implications flow from these characteristics. Present generations must take action on behalf of future generations because of the consequences of decisions made by past generations. Climate change impacts will tend to bear most heavily on poor nations, who, by and large bear little responsibility for greenhouse emissions. Curtailing fossil fuel combustion has clear economic implications, not least of which may be the potential for inhibiting economic growth in developing nations. Corporations involved in the fossil fuel and transport industries are amongst the world's largest and whose commercial interests are closely tied to the consumption of their products that entail the release of greenhouse gases (NRDC et al. 1999). Actions to reduce emissions by one nation can be rendered useless by another increasing emissions, so that many argue that international cooperation is essential for achieving overall reductions. Greenhouse gas emissions have grown continually, more or less, through the last century; reducing global emissions first requires stabilization, which in itself is difficult at best (see, e.g., IPCC 2000a).

Because of the asymmetry between the impacts and human action, climate change does not generate local sites of political resistance as most issues of environmental injustice. As a global problem, despite the highly differentiated specificity of forecast impacts, the site of political contestation is not local but largely within the institutional settings of international processes and the national fora that formulate foreign and domestic policy. International political activity concerns the actions of nation states, so that policy outcomes are the result of national positions and international negotiations. Vested national interests are a major influence in international climate change negotiations because the implications for the world's major corporations are so high and their association with nation states so close, as well as the interests of states' own enterprises. Local passions rarely come into play in these processes. International climate change policies greatly reflect national interests. Scientific information plays a prominent role in this problem, making control over the production and distribution of knowledge highly politicized and the implications of scientific findings being of great political importance.

Developing a rational policy response typically builds on a relatively clear articulation of the relationships between the actions proposed and their anticipated effects. For climate change, science has attempted to develop an understanding of a highly complex system from which policy responses can be developed. Despite large strides in scientific progress, great uncertainties remain of the identification, location, timing, extent, and seriousness of climate change impacts. Contrasting with many pollution problems, climate change is a real time and singular issue (i.e., there is only one global climate), so that the ultimate effectiveness of actions taken is difficult to assess.

However it is viewed, whether ethically, technically, or politically, climate change is a complex problem. Both extant and future generation's interests are involved, in which present actions determine future values to an extent beyond smaller-scale pollution issues. Ecologically, the implications of climate change policies have permanent effects, with the survival of extant ecosystems in many locations being at stake. Other than large-scale nuclear warfare, few other disturbances of human origin have the potential for such large-scale ecological change. Competing preferences and values between social groups, nations, corporations, and with non-human entities and interests must be resolved, but whatever policy decisions are taken, these will necessarily produce great redistributions of utility, for want of a better term.

Actions to significantly curtail greenhouse gas emissions will entail expenditure, although cost estimates of the transition to a 'low carbon or no-carbon' future vary greatly. Cheap, abundant, and secure supplies of fossil fuels underpin industrial economies and the export of which is the mainstay of several developing nations. Renewable energy use by industrial nations remains low (see, e.g., the *World Energy Assessment* (WEA 2000); UNDP et al. 2000), a large portion of which, furthermore, are the ecologically harmful technologies of large-scale hydro electricity and waste combustion. Energy efficiency and energy conservation offer low-cost approaches to greenhouse gases abatement; however, reaching a low-emission condition additionally necessitates widespread application of renewable energy. Economically, socially, and environmentally, the benefits of the transition away from conventional energy systems to their ecologically more sensitive alternatives are well established (see, e.g., IPCC 1996c, 2001c), and the case for widespread use of renewable energy, compelling. Barriers to the greater implementation of these energy system alternatives are increasingly less technical and more financial, political, and cultural. Framed in this manner, the rationale for understanding climate change as a major ecological problem is clear, and equally so is the difficulty of the task of devising an appropriate international response.

Forming a contrary view of the crisis

Clearly the conventional view of climate change is deficient. Climate change is a product of the routine functioning of industrial society and the international (and national) responses to date are confined within this system of its constituent forms of knowledge, governance, economic relations, nature–society relations, and other factors. Understanding of the climate change problem has generally been identical with these restraints. Breaking out from these limits requires developing a critique of industrial society, that is, a critique of modernity. In the following chapter, a foundation is provided for understanding the development and composition of modern society. Industrial society has been challenged on terms of its nature–society relations, by ecologism and environmentalism, and by postmodernity, which has critically examined the cultural premises of modernity. These critiques have been forged, after a fashion, by environmentalists into something akin to a 'postmodern environmentalism,' an effort that will also be explained and scrutinized for its relevance to the task of addressing the problem of climate change.

2 Modernity and postmodernity

Two contesting views vie to describe contemporary conditions in the industrial world – modernity and postmodernity. Change and, indeed, transformation characterize social life and culture in societies embedded in the globalized, industrial, and capitalist experience. Attributing significance to contemporary developments is fraught with disputes over whether any particular cultural change constitutes the normal or whether the normal is being re-fashioned. When postmodernity offers that modernity has expired, its opponents claim that the alleged break with modernity is illusionary, countering that recent developments are variations in modernity. Into this conflicted realm, which finds expression throughout social science scholarship and in popular culture in such phenomena as the so-called 'culture wars,' enters environmentalism with a unique (albeit varied) critique of contemporary nature–society relations. Environmentalism sits uncomfortably atop the modernity–postmodernity dispute, yet despite the complexities and contradictions there has emerged a distinct set of responses to the concepts of postmodernity giving rise to a postmodern environmentalism.

Modernity

For a condition that embodies contemporary life in developed nations, modernity is a contentious and elusive concept subject to much sociological inquiry and philosophical contemplation. From the beginning of the industrial era, elements of the 'modern life' emerged and were duly considered by thinkers as diverse as Emile Durkheim, Karl Marx, Adam Smith, and Max Weber in an effort that has continued ever since. Scholars differ over what precisely characterizes modernization and the functioning of the societies produced by these processes. Traditional societies exhibit a unity between what modern societies define as identifiable components, such as economy, politics, religion, social relations, education, medicine, and so forth. Modern societies are characterized by urbanity, industrial production, social stratification, social roles taken by professional groups, bureaucracy, and the nation state. Technology is usually taken as a major, if not primary, determinant of the social transformation that culminates in a modern society, wherein all facets of life are technologized.

Modernity is distinguished from 'pre-modern' or traditional social forms, so that modernity embraces the character or essence of an entire society, seeking generalities beyond the immediate dynamics and lingering traditions. Dichotomies between the modern and the pre-modern disturb some scholars who fear that modern society be seen as internally uniform, without its own traditions and those remnants of its precursor social forms not be properly acknowledged. Recognizing social and cultural continuities and appreciating local differences with modern society can be valuable in accounting for certain ambiguities and persistent traits, but overwhelmingly modern societies bear little relation to their pre-modern forms, although clearly there are degrees of modernity.

As Toulmin (1990) remarks, given that modernity can refer to the 'new,' to consider 'the end of modernity' is a contemplation of modernity as an historical era. Yet while the interpretations of modernity's beginnings vary, depending on whether one considers the rise of science and technology, architecture, or of politics and philosophy, Toulmin (1990) notes that for most critics the chronology of modernism begins in the early decades of the seventeenth century.

However, the issue of social transformation to modernity cannot be readily reduced to nostrums about 'modern' technology, as the answers to questions of identifying the social and economic conditions necessary for the transition to modernity, or identifying 'modernizing' technology, assume no universal form. For some scholars, modernity is marked by the rise of modern science, widespread numeracy and literacy, the formation of particular social institutions (e.g., Emile Durkheim), especially bureaucracy (e.g., Max Weber); for others it is the formation of particular class relations within capitalism (e.g., Karl Marx) or the emergence of capitalism itself, industrialism (e.g., Krishan Kumar), the rise of the factory system (Fordism and Taylorism), the pursuit of (secular) efficiency (e.g., Jacques Ellul), scale of organization, urban form and function (e.g., Lewis Mumford), the applications of inanimate energy forms (e.g., Mumford), or the regard of nature and of women (e.g., Carolyn Merchant). Berger et al. (1974) distinguish within modernity both structural and psychological dimensions, arguing that social organization shapes institutions and ways of thinking, distinguished by particular values, outlooks, and expectations. In other words, Berger et al. recognize a modern consciousness, so that modern societies contain 'modern' people whose outlook is peculiar to contemporary times.

Sociologists and historians have identified the following features of modern society (Berger 1977; Berger and Luckman 1966; Berger et al.1974; Briggs 1959; Durkheim 1950, 1984; Hobsbawm 1969; Kumar 1978, 1988; Marx 1906; Mumford 1934, 1967, 1970; and Weber 1930):

- specialized social functions, with birth, death, education, medicine, religion, the production of food, shelter, and clothing, and income-generation typically occurring outside the home; social institutions and a professional cadre provide key social functions;
- pluralism and the operation of a social web that organizes and manages the multiplicity of functions and activities; economic interdependencies link elements of a fractured society of diverse activities; society itself is diverse;
- social relations and activities are discontinuous and temporary, mobility is high, social change is rapid, and social networks fluid and dynamic;
- rationality, efficiency, planning, and future-orientation in individual decisions, social institutions, and bureaucracy;
- individuation and the cultivation of individuality as the basic social element in which personal liberty and individual rights assume the highest status, so that self-expression and achievement are primary goals;
- abstraction marks many social relations, state and corporate structures are large-scale and remote from individuals, power relationships are often indirect, communication uses abstractions and much specialized terminology; and
- society seeks and takes decisions at many scales to shape the future to its design and pursues an escape from a destiny determined by natural forces.

Underpinning these social conditions is the role of scientific knowledge for the operation of social institutions, the functioning of industrial economies and bureaucracies, for the design and operating principles of the major systems to support life, and so forth. Few aspects of modern life do not bear the imprint of scientific knowledge. Concomitant with the modern era is the modern nation state subject to the evolving condition of liberal democratic governance. Environmentalists, as described below, identify modernity with a particular set of attitudes and practices towards the natural world.

Toulmin and the history of modernity

Under the conventional view of the rise of modernity, developments in seventeenth century brought forward a revolution in social organization, technology, knowledge, production, consumption, and the rise of new and distinct organizations and institutions in politics and other realms of life. Essentially, this view of modernity emphasizes the following features. By 1600, growing cities and trade-generated prosperity and the growing educated laity were able to question medieval doctrines. Empiricism allowed the natural sciences to recognize intellectual progress and the understanding of the natural world became increasingly more rational. Concurrently, philosophy became separate from theology, with self-critical thinkers able to reason free of its prejudices. And the European nations were able to generate a sovereign authority over social and political activity with the institution of the papacy no longer able to exert such a power. This was coincident with the rise of the secular culture; churches had no monopoly once scholars could evaluate doctrinal matters through their own reading and contemplation. Accordingly, modern life was superior to medieval life, and the changes initiated at the birth of modernity bore the fruits enjoyed by contemporary society. Fundamental to this view is the role attributed to the power of rationality as a force that reshaped European life and culture, which eventually spread across the globe.

There have been various challenges to such formulations. Mumford (1934), for instance, rejected the view that modern European life was the outcome of a sudden flowering of technological development, emphasizing the long gestation of key technological developments and highlighting the technological innovations of the medieval that underlay subsequent developments during the Industrial Revolution. Many technological innovations of the era came from outside Europe, such as from the Islamic East, and whose adoption in Europe formed part of the transformation towards the modern.

One of the more comprehensive accounts is Toulmin's (1990) *Cosmopolis*, an alternative to the received view of modernity. Two features of the origins of modernity and the modern era characterize the conventional view according to Toulmin (1990: 13):

> [T]hat the modern age began in the 17th century, and that the transition from the medieval to modern modes of thought and practice rested on the adoption of rational methods in all serious fields of inquiry – by Galileo Galilei in physics, by René Descartes in epistemology – with their example soon being followed in political theory by Thomas Hobbes.

Toulmin rejects this view, beginning with the assertion that crisis and turbulence in the first half of the seventeenth century that gave rise to modernity, not prosperity and leisure. It is in sixteenth-century Europe that Toulmin locates the schism with the medieval, for this is when the spoils of colonialism swelled domestic prosperity to unprecedented heights. When this phase of prosperity ends, after the 1620s, Europe descends into turmoil. Spain's political dominance fades, France is divided religiously, the German states are in conflict, and Britain moves towards civil war. Food production is reduced through the impact of the Little Ice Age and Britain and France suffer large outbreaks of the plague.

Literacy and the printed word helped displace the authority of the Church in the seventtenth century, Toulmin argues, but this was a continuation of an activity that had been well under way for the preceding century. Printed works had been available for over a hundred years prior to

1600 and it does not hold that literature only becomes influential after 1600 (Toulmin points to the humanist writers in the sixteenth century: Shakespeare, Bacon, Rabelais, and Montaigne). As Toulmin writes (1990: 19): "Galileo and Descartes were late products of changes that were well under way in Western Europe by 1520, and in Italy a good time before." Therefore, the seventeenth century was not the first time that European scholars were "prosperous, comfortable, and free enough from ecclesiastical pressure to have original ideas."

Also rejected is the common view that the seventeenth century was an era marked by its "original concern for rationality and the claims of Reason," by asserting that scientists and philosophers narrowed the scope of reasonable debate by restricting rationality "to theoretical arguments that achieve a quasi-geometrical certainty or necessity" (1990: 20–21). Additionally, Toulmin suggests that the founders of modern science were far from being atheists and their inquiries remained steeped in metaphysical and theological traditions.

Modernity, therefore, has two sources, not one: 1) a literary or humanistic (note that this term does not mean or imply secularism) phase in sixteenth-century northern Europe; and 2) a scientific and philosophical phase from 1630 onward. Humanism's rise in the fifteenth and sixteenth centuries occurs within Christianity; it was not a secular movement, despite skepticism and open-mindedness. Humanist writers' consideration of questions of religion was that it should be limited by the bounds of human intelligence; they discouraged dogmatism and disparaged doctrinal disputes that could be carried into political action (considering Erasmus, Montaigne, and others). In effect, theirs was a belated effort to forestall religious warfare; human modesty should constrain any Christian's ability to grasp greater Truths.

A clear break with the medieval comes with the humanist's interest in the variety of human life and of the conditions of difference (Toulmin 1990: 127): "Renaissance scholars were quite as concerned with circumstantial questions of practice in medicine, law, or morals, as with any timeless, universal matters in philosophical theory." No clear view of nature could emerge from such confusion, a condition that some welcomed as profusion, so it seemed best to leave matters about general theories to some later time. While the Renaissance humanists were alive to the rich possibilities within human experience, reflecting on "the variety of conduct and motive," this was tempered by a respect for the limits of experience. There was also an interest in the exotic, in foreign cultures, and alternative ways of life.

Skepticism about the possibilities of science abounded; theories circulated and multiplied about basic questions in physics and explanations were little removed from the presumptions of the observer. Here 'skeptical' assumes an earlier pre-Descartes meaning: for the humanists it referred to an acceptance of the possibility of rival explanations because competing philosophical questions could not be resolved beyond the scope of experience; your proofs can't demonstrate the falsity of others.' Humanist skeptics did not aim for certainty beyond experience, which necessarily limited their expressions of certainty or generality (1990: 30): "Tolerating the resulting plurality, ambiguity, or lack of certainty is no error, let alone a sin. Honest reflection shows it is part of the price that we inevitably pay for being human beings, not gods."

As Toulmin succinctly states (1990: 30): "During the 17th century, these humanist insights were lost." He identifies four changes in which these insights were eliminated by the seventeenth-century philosophers, namely transitions from: 1) the oral to the written; 2) the particular to the universal; 3) the local to the general; and 4) the timely to the timeless. For the humanists, rhetorical argument shared equal philosophical validity with logic, a position changed after Descartes, in which the validity of argument referred to text and its internal coherence. Argumentation was replaced by written proof in modern philosophy; formal logic took over from rhetoric, so that whatever arose from particular places, peoples, specific cases, and the things at stake was irrelevant.

In the Middle Ages and Renaissance, philosophers and theologians considered issues as cases, taking it that goodness assumed no universal form and moral judgment necessitated an understanding of the circumstantial. From the seventeenth century (Toulmin 1990: 32): "Casuistry met with the same comprehensive scorn from the moral philosophers as rhetoric did from the logicians." It was after Thomas More and the Cambridge Platonists that philosophy took up an interest in general abstract theory in the 1650s, and that modern philosophers continue to consider the good and just to be timeless and universal principles.

Similarly, the modern philosophers generally had little interest in ethnography and history in their search for the general and universal principles. Those sixteenth-century humanists' interests in geography, history, and ethnography were of little use (1990: 32) "in none of which geometrical methods of analysis have much power." Philosophical understanding to Descartes could never come from studying individuals and particular cases, as this could generate no axioms. Hence, the abstract subsumed the concrete, and the local gave way to the general. After 1630, philosophy has little interest in practical matters and concerns itself with theoretical abstractions. Particular, concrete, and timely aspects of local affairs gave way to the universal, general, and abstract.

Modernity's humanities derive from the secular humanists, while philosophy and science have their source in the seventeenth-century natural philosophers. If Montaigne was 'skeptical' and open to ambiguity, uncertainty, and experience, then Descartes' reaction was the quest for certainty through the rational reasoning of the mind. Furthermore, the intellectual quest for certainty in the seventeentth century was a "timely response to a specific historical challenge – the political, social, and theological chaos embodied in the Thirty Years War" (Toulmin 1990: 70).

With the end of the Thirty Years War in 1648, Europe faced the task of reconstruction. Peace was secured through negotiation – because, in spite of all the slaughter entailed, the conflict essentially proved unproductive – in the Treaties of Westphalia. A new world of European sovereign states with secular rulers was initiated in Westphalia, a world in which the medieval primacy of religious authority ended. Achieving national stability involved resolving internal religious difference, and having nation-state rulers determining and enforcing the national religion gave rise to intolerance and persecution in many places. Assuming the place of the ecclesiastic leaders in these nation states was a growing educated and literate laity, whose rise in authority matched that of the rising nation states. Social relations too assumed new forms: the medieval local feudalism was superseded by an emerging class structure in which traders and merchants could share that status previously exclusive to the landed gentry.

Intellectually, the new era demanded new understandings, most pressing of which was that of transcending doctrinal differences, in which Descartes sought a universal method of understanding and Leibniz, a universal language. A third aspect to this quest was that of a unified science. Toulmin identifies two persistent contesting elements in this latter quest, that of empiricism (the humanist legacy of Francis Bacon) and of mathematical explanation (as Newtonian rationalism), which vie for dominance. At the beginning of the 1700s there were a number of scientific explanations available for many natural phenomena. Despite these differences, Toulmin explains, they were underpinned by a common belief that extended to the social world, namely the possibility that society might be understood along the same systematic lines as the understanding of nature. Social order, therefore, might be understood as constituting logical and mathematical systems.

For Toulmin, the foundation of modernity is Descartes' epistemology, the Cartesian division, that "of matter from mind, causes from reasons, and nature from humanity" (1990: 107), noting that "[t]he sharpness of this separation was new" (1990: 108). Moral reasoning became essentially the product of unbounded rationalism, whereas the natural was the outcome of immutable laws of causal necessity. Human affairs and the natural world are divorced, and indeed, Toulmin notes that in further extending the application of mechanical reasoning to natural problems – "the cosmic clockwork" – the greater the extent to which human affairs were placed in a separate sphere.

From this fundamental dichotomy, others were immediately recognized: "mental *vs* material, actions *vs* phenomena, performances *vs* happenings, thoughts *vs* objects, voluntary *vs* mechanical, active *vs* passive, creative *vs* repetitive" (Toulmin 1990: 109). Interdependencies and relationships between the human and natural worlds were not entirely dismissed in this duality, but rather their "scale and significance" was minimized. Such thinking became 'accepted knowledge' for the next 200 or so years after 1660, shaping social, political, and scientific thought.

Toulmin lists the elements of modernity arising from this division between nature and humanity as "basic doctrines" (1990: 109):

Nature is governed by fixed laws set up at the creation;
The basic structure of Nature was established only a few thousand years back;
The objects of physical nature are composed of inert matter;
So physical objects and processes do not think;
At the creation, God combined natural objects into stable and hierarchical systems of "higher" and "lower" things;
Like "action" in society, "motion" in nature flows downward, from the "higher" creatures to the "lower" ones."
The "human" thing about humanity is its capacity for rational thought or action;
Rationality and causality follow different rules;
Since thought and action do not take place causally, actions cannot be explained by any causal science of psychology;
Human beings can establish stable systems in society, like the physical systems in nature;
So, humans live mixed lives, part rational and causal: as creatures of Reason; their lives are intellectual or spiritual, as creatures of Emotion, they are bodily or carnal;
Emotion typically frustrates and distorts the work of Reason; so the human reason is to be trusted and encouraged, while the emotions are to be distrusted and restrained.

Whilst the validity of such axioms could not have withstood empirical observations during their own time, they were sufficiently general so as not to interfere with scientific progress. In other words, their place was not secured on a factual basis; in effect they were not axioms but presuppositions that directed and shaped thought and inquiry. Redundancy was inevitable however; in the progress of science after 1800, "modern science outgrew its framework" (Toulmin 1990: 116).

Descartes' reasoning and Newton's physics were accepted as common sense for reasons other than empirical support. Toulmin makes clear that it was not the content of Newton's reasoning that fomented its place as accepted knowledge, but because it matched a social resonance in England and Europe during the late seventeenth and early eighteenth centuries. Who adopted these views? Decrying its universalism, Toulmin notes that it was the centralized nation states with their developed classes and institutions that the modern viewpoint was acceptable and 'official:' it was readily adopted by England and France's "educated oligarchy" with their powers over public education and book publishing. But away from the cities, among the literate 'underclass,' there were parallel theologies and social organizations of a nonconformist stripe. Maverick intellectuals, such as

England's Joseph Priestley and France's Julian de la Mettrie, rejected Descartes and therefore enjoyed popular censure. Acceptance of modernity's framework was accordingly differentiated broadly by nation, location, class, and other factors, and individually by temperament and intellectual disposition. New scientific thoughts were best developed in the provinces where the strictures of conformity were less.

Although attacked on theological grounds, Newton's science was within the confines of orthodoxy – as Newton explicitly intended: the natural order is as God intended; mathematics reveals the rationality of this order; and there is stability and hierarchy; indeed, there is stability because there is hierarchy. As to God's dominion over nature, it is as the king's to his subjects, and a husband's to a wife, notes Toulmin of the place of this scientific knowledge (1990). Modernity then, for this era, finds in the natural order the laws that similarly govern social order. Order premised stability within the state, and without in relations with others, a quality prized so highly by the generations haunted by the effects of the Thirty Years War. And order was the product of a hierarchy, replicated successively through the taxonomy of the nation state, from lofty king and state to lowly father and family. Emotions are necessarily held in check, for in their irrationality lies the neglect of order. As Toulmin summates (1990: 128):

> The comprehensive system of ideas about nature and humanity that formed the scaffolding of Modernity was thus a social and political, as well as a scientific device: it was seen as conferring Divine legitimacy on the political order of the nation-state. In this respect, the world view of modern science – *as it actually came into existence* – won public support around 1700 for the legitimacy it apparently gave to the political system of nation states as much for its power to explain the motions of planets, or the rise and fall of the tides.

Cartesian bounds on science were not burst with Darwin's (1859) *Origin of the Species*, as some suggest, but their failure was inevitable, being sprung individually and sporadically. Darwin's landmark was but the loftiest peak in a vast range of scientific developments past which classical modernity could not travel. In the nineteenth century these contradictions arrived with increasing frequency and persistence, notably in the fields of natural history and geology. Empirical findings were irreconcilable with biblical accounts and its scholars had increasingly little to contribute to factual accounts of the natural world. Science created entirely new fields of inquiry, such as psychology, which had no place in the Cartesian plan.

All of the major shibboleths of Descartes' reasoning were shaken in this period, although some persisted well into the twentieth century and a few hold persuasive power today. Still, it was no longer axiomatic that nature's stability was assumed or that matter was always inert and the study of mental activity could acknowledge the irrational and the unconscious. And as the tenet of scientific objectivity being equivalent to non-involvement dissolved, so too did the distinction between 'reasons' and 'causes' as being that which provided for that between humanity and nature. However, not until the advent of environmentalism can it be said that the role of humanity as an ecological force was widely accepted.

Modernity and progress

In Toulmin's account, great emphasis is placed on stability as a social goal in the development of modernity. Desirable as stability may be, it is something of a meta-social goal; stability being that platform that allows social goals to be realized, such as in knowledge, health, comfort, the accumulation of wealth, and so on. Stability was prized in the 1700s onwards because in its loss the Enlightenment offered only the stuff of dreams, knowledge had no purchase, and the sense of doctrinal war was as good as any other. If there is a pulse to the Enlightenment, it is that of progress. Progress was a tautology, a self-justifying ideal with the strength to capture social imagination but, as the Thirty Years War demonstrated, one easily overwhelmed by worldly aspirations.

Central to modernity is the 'doctrine of progress.' Modernization is premised on the belief that through modernity society improves upon its predecessors and, as such, manifests the ideals (and unintentionally, some of the fears) of the Enlightenment movement. For much of the period since the Enlightenment, Western society has taken the doctrine of progress as a social norm and form of meta-narrative: the concept of progress is embedded in the cultural rubric of modern society.

Pollard (1971: 28) describes how the ideas of progress took hold because the results of their application, wherein the "connection between rationalism and the capitalist economy" was forged: progress was manifest in social and economic development. During the height of England's Industrial Revolution, historian Briggs (1959) recognizes a 'cult of progress' – such were the benefits of material growth and national power. Progress was, of course, hardly a uniform depiction of social transformation, given the social and environmental price that it exacted. Key political and ideological struggles of the modern idea have contested progress. At a minimum, adherents of modernity believe that accumulation of knowledge and technologically driven improvements in standards of living are continuous (Thiele 1997). Progress was not confined to 'mastering and possessing nature' (after Descartes), but since the Enlightenment "Rational capacities were increasingly applied not only to the conquest of the natural world but also to the control of the social and political world, duplicating in culture the mastery achieved over nature" (Thiele 1997: 72). Reason could thereby constantly improve humanity materially and morally.

Progress is the theme within modernity that ties together these elements of rational forms of knowledge (i.e., scientific), their application, and the purpose of such efforts. Leo Marx states that belief in progress "derives *from* (and refers to) that distinctively modern kind of social change made possible by acquiring from the realm of nature the unprecedented power to establish a steadily increasing domination *of* nature" (1996: 203). A modern conceptualization of progress has been justified on this belief, of which Marx (1996: 202) observes:

> The socioeconomic motor of this triumphant expansion of human power has been industrial capitalism; its primary intellectual resource has been science, and the equipment required to achieve the kind of serial improvement called Progress has been provided by technology, that is, innovations in the technical arts.

As Marx expounds, the opportunities within these forms of power enabled Western societies to create great wealth, generate improvements in daily life for much of society, achieve political institutions of republican character, and effect "something like global geopolitical hegemony" (1996: 204).

Many scholars argue that progress is a relatively new concept (e.g., Pollard 1971), arising with the age of science, made central to the Enlightenment, and taking a mature form in the Industrial Revolution. It may be that the original conception of progress (as expressed by Bacon, and later by Saint-Simon) was that of a finite process, culminating in a Utopian condition. Progress was embraced by all manner of thinkers in the seventeenth, eighteenth, and nineteenth centuries, from the French Enlightenment, the Scottish and English Enlightenments, Karl Marx and other socialists, to Herbert Spencer and other Victorian idealists (Pollard 1971).

Following the dissemination of Darwin's scheme of evolution, argues Stent (1978), progress assumed an open-ended prospect. Yet the genesis may be slightly earlier as Glacken (1967: 634–635) quotes Condorcet's *Sketch for a Historical Picture of the Progress of the Human Mind*, who believed (1793: 4–5):

> [T]hat nature has set no term to the perfection of the human faculties; that the perfectability of man is truly indefinite; and that the progress of this perfectability, from now onwards independent of any power that might wish to halt it ... but it will never be reversed as long as the earth occupies its present place in the system of the universe ...

Several themes emerge in the history of the idea of progress. Firstly, that progress is identical with modern society, with an ever-receding ideal of modernity effectively the goal of progress, and that progress is a fundamental ideology of such societies. Secondly, progress is bound with scientific knowledge and rational social organization, and associated with industrial means of production (and in developed nations, linked with mass consumption). Thirdly, progress is infinite and deterministic.

This isn't to argue that the Western notion of progress has universal acceptance; critics have abounded. There have been pessimists as to the possibility of progress, such as Thomas Malthus in the nineteenth century and Arnold Toynbee and Oswald Spengler in the twentieth. As Kumar (1978) describes, the first flowering of industrialization aroused rejection. Spengler's (1937) *Decline of the West*, for example, expressed doubt that science would continue to ensure progress, as during periods of its declining performance, other belief systems arise to dominate social activity. These authors' doubts about progress are based in interpretations of history; they tend to doubt that the past can be read as providing predictive ability, and certainly not towards 'progress.' Doubts over 'progress' certainly took hold in the 1914–1945 period, as the West's confidence in its ability to be the torchbearer for the greater project of civilization faltered.

In more contemporary times, environmentalism as a body of thought that may be best understood as a critique of industrial society. Concern over the ecological and associated social harms wrought by modern society has taken a great variety of forms and occupied many intellectuals, especially since the 1960s. Even a broad sweep of the better-known critics of industrial society would run to several dozen, including in its number Carson (1962), Ellul (1964), Illich (1973a, 1973b, 1977a, and 1977b), Marcuse (1972), Mumford (1934, 1967, and 1970), Noble (1977), Postman (1993), Roszak (1972, 1978, 1992, and 1995), Sale (1985), Schumacher (1974), and Winner (1977). To this group of well-known western writers should be added the voices from the developing world, whose critiques of modern society also embrace the burdens of colonialism, racism, and economic exploitation, such as Mohandas Ghandi, Radhakamal Mukerjee, and Ken Saro-Wiwa (see Guha 2000).

As White comments, by the late 1950s 'progress' acquired ironic meaning and in the 1960s and 1970s there were local and global revelations of the environmental costs of progress, so that "Progress, so dependent on technological mastery, became in a duel sense a victim of its own success." (1996: 130). Reviewing contemporary debate on the subject, White summates (1996: 133) that the issue verges towards the religious, evoking matters of faith–not in deities–but in "that science and technology will provide a solution to whatever dangers the manipulation of nature and the exhaustion of resources present." For as the Romantic Movement made explicit, progress is not about technological choice but is a matter of values and aspirations.

Adherents of environmentalism have held that the environmental crisis also threatens social progress, and for this group, climate change is but another manifestation of modernity's environmental assault. Environmentalists lay the blame for climate change at the feet of industrial society's pursuit of progress and find no place for the characteristic optimism of the cult of progress that today's problems will be solved by tomorrow's advances. Instead, they hold the opposite to be true, namely that yesterday's decisions have produced permanent harm to the global climate for which there are no scientific or technological solutions. Climate change suggests that not only has progress come to an end, but for those concerned with the loss of the natural climate system, progress is a largely meaningless term.

Modernity and ecologism

Today, it seems, everybody claims to be an environmentalist. In some senses, the widespread claim is reasonable, as few wish to publicly favor wholesale environmental destruction or allow environmental threats to human welfare to be enhanced by vested interests. On the other hand, if every citizen, corporation, institution, and government in the industrialized world comprises environmentalists, then the concept of environmentalism as one implying protection of environmental values and requiring a re-orientation of routine activity is completely corrupted. 'Environmentalism' has, of course, always been a fairly wooly term, such that its recent transition from having pejorative meaning in the mainstream to a generally positive connotation has aroused little comment. Within the panoply of environmentalism have been proponents seeking radical social change, and applying ecology as a critique of modernity. From this group has arisen the ideology of 'ecologism.' Dobson (2000), Baxter (1999), and others have drawn a useful distinction, suggesting that while 'environmentalism' recognizes environmental values in social activity, no social change is implied, whereas 'ecologism' requires radical changes to accommodate environmental values in social and political activity. Of all the modern social movements within modernity, ecologism has arguably produced one of its most extensive and considered critiques.

Contrasting with the depiction of the social aspects of modernity, where the fathers of modern social thought (notably Emile Durkheim, Thomas Hobbes, Karl Marx, and Max Weber) laid the foundations and anticipated much of the contemporary understandings of modern society, social theory offered little on what we now regard as society–environment relationships. Several scholars have sought to emphasize Karl Marx's recognition of ecological values, especially those working in the stream of eco-Marxism (e.g., Benton 1996; James O'Connor 1988, 1998; and Martin O'Connor 1994), but these readings of Marx as social ecologist are a recent development in the Marxist canon, and are efforts to revise the long-standing regard of Marx as viewing nature as essentially a source of instrumental values. (Much eco-Marxist writing has worked to add Marx's social insights to contemporary environmental problems, rather than depicting Marx as a progenitor of environmentalism.) Many environmentalists consider resolving significant environmental problems impossible under capitalism without necessarily being Marxist or socialist, such as Luke Martell (1994) and the eco-anarchist Bookchin (e.g., 1971, 1986, and 1995).

Environmentalism and ecologism are derived from a wide variety of sources and reflect many cultural and ideological influences, extending to the classic civilizations (see, e.g., Glacken 1967; Pepper 1996; Wall 1994; and Worster 1994). Partly, there are origins in the writings of Thomas Malthus and in the scientific foundations of ecology established by Darwin and Ernst Haeckel. Environmental thought also reflects the eighteenth- and nineteenth-century English and American Romantics with their quest for the liberated imagination, individualism, and celebration of nature, such as expressed by English poets William Blake, Percy Bysshe Shelley, and William Wordsworth and American writers Ralph Waldo Emerson, John Muir, and Henry Thoreau (Pepper 1996). Utopian socialists, such as William Morris, were highly influential, especially in such concepts as communal living and rural socialism as alternatives to urbanized industrialism. Furthermore, environmental philosophy and politics has been shaped by spiritual awareness in Eastern beliefs, such as Buddhism, and has intersected with the great social movements in socialism and feminism to produce eco-socialism and eco-feminism.

So what defines ecologism? Ecologism's critique of modernity, despite variations in opinion, has at its core several distinctive and defining concerns. Ecologism has its roots at least partly in the development of environmental ethics, wherein ethical grounds were established for recognizing and responding to values in future generations, non-human species, and ecological processes (as expressed by writers such as Holmes Rolston, John Passmore, Peter Singer, and Christopher Stone). There appear to be at least three defining characteristics of ecologism based on ecological limits, intrinsic environmental values, and concern over social alienation from nature (see, e.g., Baxter 1999; Dobson 2000).

Firstly, ecologism recognizes that the finite character of natural resources and ecological services necessitates limiting social choices, especially those pertaining to resource consumption and waste generation by industrial systems. Modern societies are industrial, marked by mass consumption of goods and services largely derived from industrial processes of resource extraction, production, fabrication, distribution, consumption, and disposal. Normal operation of industrial systems of production incurs great ecological costs as the indices of global resource consumption, industrial production, ecological damage, and waste generation attests (UNDP et al. 2001). Under industrial society these ecological changes and losses become global in scale and effect. As Vitousek et al. (1997) describe, large portions of global chemical cycles (notably carbon and nitrogen), water, fisheries, and other biotic systems that are now driven by human activities. For example, around one-third of terrestrial net primary productivity is co-opted by human activity (Vitousek et al. 1986). Although society and nature have long influenced each other in dynamic ways (Norgaard 1994), society's recent acquisition of the capacity to shape global evolutionary forces is a novel development (O'Neil and Kahn 2000).

Science and technology are seen as essential for the functioning of modern society, yet far from being neutral forces, ecologism finds this knowledge contains an array of social values. One such value is the positive role of such knowledge in fostering and enabling resource consumption. A variety of methods and approaches to assess the ecological demands of societies are available, such as the 'ecological footprint' (Wackernagel and Rees 1996). Results from these assessments quantify what is readily apparent in the ecological impacts of industrial societies, namely that industrialization greatly increases the extent, scale, and reach of the human environmental impacts (Wackernagel and Rees 1996). In terms of their environmental demands, the industrialized nations are 'overdeveloped,' a condition made possible by science.

Industrialization is integrative, linking resources to commodities to increasingly dispersed points of consumption. Integration involves physical, economic, and cultural connections manifested in ecological impacts. And under globalization, such industrial features as commodity chains and the extent of trade are growing (Held et al. 1999). Globalization facilitates the expansionary dynamic of economic relations towards economic integration: natural resources and processes are assessed for their potential contribution to the industrial system of production and consumption. Creating utility from nature extends to the scale of genetic material to the global, such as in the case of atmospheric pollution by greenhouse gas emissions. Modernity's ecological impacts extend through time, with the capacity for permanent alteration of ecological entities, features, and ecological processes.

Modern society is committed to continually expanding economic activity. Economic growth occurs with little regard for ecological limits or the implications of such growth for environmental values (Daly 1996). Social systems are embedded and bounded by ecological systems, so that problems such as pollution signify that a natural boundary or threshold has been exceeded. Decisions about operating the social system must therefore be cognizant of these ecological limits if social life is to be reconciled with natural values. Natural resources and values may be renewable or extinguishable, but in either case there is an explicit 'carrying capacity' for humanity which industrial society either characteristically ignores or is ignorant about. Ecologism's perspective on limits is not without its complexities and possible inconsistencies, however. Although often negatively associated with the controversial school of 'survivalism' (cf. Garret Hardin, William Ophuls), and the widely read *Limits to Growth* (Meadows et al. 1972), ecologism remains wedded to the necessity of limiting the scale and rate of resource consumption and material production. Importantly, however, no unambiguous political program can be derived from this goal and ecologism itself is divided over determining and imposing limits on economic growth and consumption. Nevertheless, there remains a common belief that protecting environmental values implies limiting human ecological demands at all scales.

Secondly, ecologism explicitly recognizes intrinsic values in ecology. Ecologism identifies how modernity's instrumentalist perspective routinely causes the neglect of ecological values through its assumption of anthropocentrism, a line of reasoning directly from environmental philosophy. In practice, having identified the environment as a medium by which social costs and benefits can be allocated in industrial society, ecologism often pursues solutions whereby socially normative goals are compatible with the promotion of ecological values. Ecologism is at least partially responsible for identifying how the normal activities of states and corporations have generated harm and risk to human health through their environmental impacts, giving rise to 'environmental injustice' (see, e.g., the reviews by Byrne et al. 2002; Hofricher 1993). Industrial activity creates environmental hazards to society and it follows that questions of justice are created when, either through neglect or active decisions, these social harms are distributed. 'Ecological justice' extends the realm of ethical concern to incorporate future generations, ecological entities, and ecological processes so as to match the extent to which industrial activity can affect the future and ecological values (see Low and Gleeson 1998).

Thirdly, ecologism finds that modernity alienates modern society and its members from nature. Again, we find this concern expressed by environmental philosophy, a part of which is rooted in the Romantic Movement. Largely, modernity creates a series of artificial divisions between the social and the natural realms (as does indeed the very distinction between the 'social' and the 'natural'), such that modern religion is divorced from nature, modern food production is according to industrial techniques, modern education is premised on anthropocentrism, and so on. Here the contrast is firmly made against pre-modern societies where social life lies close to the natural world, whereas modern life has transformed both the natural and social into artificial forms. Ecologism often takes recourse in empirical evidence in support of this position, citing the physical transformation of nature by human activity, so that the 'natural' is no more. In the global ecology, it is no longer possible to experience the environment without the influence of modern society (e.g., human changes to global climate). Many proponents of ecologism mourn the loss of 'pristine' nature and, despite varying interpretations as to the significance of this change, they are unified by seeking to prevent its further diminution by the outcomes of modernity. Although social and natural values may be presented as possessed of an irreconcilable character, ecological justice is skeptical of such dichotomies and is drawn towards views of environmental problems that recognize human interests as part of ecological interests. Environmental justice rejects normal presumptions by industrial society of the primacy of human interests over all others.

Ecologism offers a distinctive critique of modernity, although not necessarily comprising unique or original positions. While ecologism does not portend an unequivocal resolution to modernity, there may be several social forms that satisfy its goals, and, alternatively, it may simply be utopian. Part of this problem may lie in the ambiguities arising from its origins, for although ecologism offers a critique of modernity, it is also its offspring. Ecologism draws on modernity in at least two major ways. Much of ecologism adheres to Enlightenment concepts of justice, such as recognizing basic human rights, a commitment to social equality, and the role of free speech. Explicitly, 'environmental justice' and 'ecological justice' are extensions of the ideals of justice to environmental issues and to ecological values (Low and Gleeson 1998). Not only the ends of ecologism reminiscent of modernity, but a good deal of its means are similarly derived. As a critique prompted by environmental degradation and environmental risks, ecologism is promoted and dependent on detection and assessment by scientific knowledge and methods of investigation. Resolving environmental problems usually involves science and technology in some way, which ties at least part of ecologism to roots in systems of scientific knowledge.

Efforts by states and corporations using environmentalism as a rationale for the continuation of modernity receive little sympathy from proponents of ecologism. Within state and corporate powers are various environmentalist strategies and approaches that can be evoked with little disturbance to the status quo, such as administrative initiatives, democratic actions, and ecological modernization. Many environmental NGOs and much of environmental activism has been concerned with acquiring political power with which to influence governments and to combat corporate activity. States have largely reacted to local environmental problems through incremental institutional changes, bringing these problems into customary management practices by engaging professionals in planning, engineering, biology, and other relevant fields of expertise (Hajer 1995). State responses include environmental protection laws, regulations, and agencies in planning and approval activities that restrain or repair ecologically damaging aspects of modern societies. Rational assessment techniques are used to guide policy choices, including economic tools, such as cost–benefit analysis. Given these approaches leave the systemic causes of environmental damage in place, ecologism is unconvinced that these efforts address little more than the symptoms of a deeper malaise.

Ecologism identifies amongst modernity's prominent failings its neglect of ecological limits and commitment to ecologically unsustainable practices, its anthropocentrism, and the erosion of the 'conviviality' between the social and natural realms. As a critique of modernity, however, ecologism is highly divided on several key issues, including its regard of science and technology and its view of governance and the nation state. In one sense, although ecologism may not provide a consistent critique of modernity or escaped several of its key technical means and social ends, its rejection of key ecological aspects of the modern program arguably places the critique in the company of 'postmodernity.'

Postmodernity

Even within the social sciences, where the most-oft applied concepts and terms remain permanently contested, *postmodern* is particularly difficult and controversial. And, in the wider world, as Cahoone wryly commented (1996: 1):

> For some, postmodernism connotes the final escape from the stultifying legacy of modern European theology, metaphysics, authoritarianism, colonialism, racism, and domination. To others it represents the attempt by disgruntled left-wing intellectuals to destroy Western civilization. To yet others it labels a goofy collection of hermetically obscure writers who are really talking about nothing at all.

Entomologically, the 'postmodern' succeeds modernity and is defined by not being modernity. But this inverse or negation of a definition leaves open postmodernism's identity: it can be the outcome of modernity, the refusal of modernity, the latest stage of modernity, the remnants of modernity, a rejection of modernity, and so on. Postmodernism conflates at least two possibilities: firstly, an attack on the understanding and condition of modernity; and secondly, to sketch out a future different from the present. Many applications of the term have used more than one version of these possibilities.

That the postmodern usually resists definition or presents itself as possessed of qualities that, if defined, are lost expresses an intention that postmodernism be understood as an exchange, a discourse, a fragmentation, and abstract. Postmodernity has been given different theoretical meanings, academic applications, and discerned in many aspects of contemporary Western life. There are, therefore, at least three dimensions in which postmodernity can be understood: 1) by its principal exponents or associated schools (e.g., poststructuralism); 2) as applied by different disciples (e.g., literature, art, and architecture); and 3) as expressed cultural practices. Additionally, Best and Kellner see these expressions as constituents of a whole (1997: xi):

> As we conceptualize it, the "postmodern paradigm" signifies *both* specific shifts within virtually every contemporary theoretical discipline and artistic field and the coalescing of these changes into a larger worldview that influences culture and society in general, as well as the values and practices of everyday life.

Not unexpectedly, postmodernity has generated considerable mystery, confusion, and contestation as to its meaning.

Early uses and meaning

Certainly "postmodernism" has been in use, if sporadically, for some time. Applications of the 'post' prefix appear to begin with art critic John Watkins Chapman's comments on French Impressionist art in the 1870s (Cahoone 1996). In 1917, the German philosopher Rudolf Pannwitz used 'postmodern' to describe nihilism of Western culture and the Spaniard Federico de Onis applied the term in 1934 to describe the rejection of literary modernism (Anderson 1998). British theologian Bernard Iddings Bell labeled the return to religion in the face of secular modernity 'postmodern' in 1939, with the more significant deployment by Arnold Toynbee in describing the formation of mass-society following WWI (Anderson 1998).

By the middle of the last century, the term began to acquire more frequent use in artistic criticism, albeit in a period dominated by the artistic 'moderns,' including James Joyce, T.S. Eliot, and Le Corbusier. In the 1950s and 1960s, many intellectuals concerned with art and literature rejected the style known as 'modernism,' a reaction known as 'postmodern,' and in the 1960s and 1970s, architecture criticism followed suit (Anderson 1998). During this period, modernism was fading out as the dominant artistic and cultural form, marked by several developments, including the erosion of an elite avant-garde when 'high' and 'low' culture became indistinguishable in pop art, with pastiche replacing uniform style, and musical forms celebrating chaos and discontinuity (Harvey 1992). In literature, many critics thought that irony and camp captured better the sense of the times than the high-minded pursuits written for the alienated soul. Architecture, however, was the creative realm where postmodernism was arguably most effective in capturing a burgeoning movement intent on replacing high modernism. Jacobs's (1961) *Life and Death of Great American Cities* described how modernist urban planning by the welfare state produced profoundly inhuman urban living, and Venturi's *Complexity and Contradiction in Architecture* (1966) and later *Learning from Las Vegas* (Venturi et al. 1972) celebrated those virtues that protested against the dictates of modernist styling, became seminal works in a gathering groundswell against modernist designs for living and technocratic and authoritarian planning approaches.

Contemporary developments

In the 1970s, 'postmodern' became a more widely used term. Hassan collected literary, philosophical, and social developments under the 'postmodern' label in the early 1970s (see Hassan 1975), as did Charles Jencks for architecture in 1975. Three key works established postmodernity more widely: Lyotard's (1984) *The Postmodern Condition*, Jencks' (1984) *The Language of Post-Modern Architecture*, while Rorty's (1979) *Philosophy and the Mirror and Nature* expressed developments in philosophy that caused U.S. philosophers to take up postmodernism with interest in the 1980s.

Philosophically, postmodern became widely used in the 1980s to refer to the French poststructuralists in a specific sense, and also to describe a more general reaction against 'foundationalism.' Other disciplines in social sciences also took up the term, assuming something of the more general interpretation applied in philosophy, albeit with considerable latitude. During the 1980s arose several articulations of a positive postmodernity, sometimes known as 'constructive,' 'restructive,' or 'grounded' post-modernism. And in the next decade, the 1990s, postmodern entered fully into popular culture, where it could be taken to imply social change, confusion, or the merely contemporary, as the earlier quotation suggests.

Conceptually, many of the roots of postmodernity's key concepts lie with thinkers who rarely or never used the term. Smart (1996: 386–387), for example, identifies a number of authors who questioned modern reasoning and its effects and whose work directly influenced the postmodernists: Theodor Adorno, Martin Heidegger, Friedrich Nietzsche, Georg Simmel, and Max Weber. Simmel has been called the first postmodern sociologist for analyzing the crisis of modern culture, and Nietzsche and Heidegger challenged modernity's understanding of progress. Indeed, modernism has featured a critical self-reflection, in which modernity has examined its own goals, assumptions, and performance.

Within the sweep of the cultural, economic, and technological changes that have marked the world during this period of disenchantment with modernity, or at least many of its features, Cahoone (1996) makes special mention of the decline of Marxism and its effect within the intelligentsia of the Western world. Cahoone marks the decline's onset with the revelations in the 1970s of Russian life under and following Stalin's regime, after which the enthusiasm for Marxism, and for socialism more generally, waned (nowhere more so than for those living under 'actually existing socialism'). For many in the Western intelligentsia, Marxism provided an acceptable form of modernity and the potential for social progress. With its loss as an alternative to capitalism, for many in Western societies, social life had been deprived of its *telos* (Cahoone 1996: 10): "Postmodernism, a wayward step-child of Marxism, is in this sense a generation's realization that it is orphaned." However, as Smart points out, the concerns over the limits of modernity are longstanding, so that "the current preoccupation with the limits and limitations of modern reason can not be dismissed or explained away as simply a symptom of a 'disillusionist' generation of contemporary intellectuals" (1996: 397).

Harvey (1992) is amongst those who fix at least part of the postmodern experience within the social and economic changes occurring in contemporary global economic relationships under the emerging global economy. In this sense, postmodernity is the outcome of the so-called 'post-industrial' experience of the world's developed nations. As an economic transformation, this change is characterized by the transition to service-based economies, the impacts of new communication and information technologies, increased international competition for markets for primary and secondary goods, privatization of public corporations, and the rise of corporate influence over social dominions. Indeed, we can find something of a dichotomy in the observations of the same global transformations of the

postmodernity perceived by cultural observers and the phenomena of globalization examined by socio-economic analysis.

Towards a common understanding

Exponents of the postmodern, including several of its key figures, have
resisted defining the concept, arguing that it cannot and should not be
constrained, so the concept has been broadly interpreted. Notwithstanding
these efforts to foster and promote variation and elusiveness, there are in
fact many common features and agreement as to the place of key historical
thinkers and of modern exponents. Now that postmodernism has passed
into common usage, the majority of its commentators share a set of
common understandings, of which the 'loss of belief in grand narratives' is
usually a part. Key aspects of postmodernism are founded in what are perceived as the failures or inadequacies of modernity, of which a lessening of
the essential rationality of modernity is essential. From this position, postmodernists reject any certain interpretations of meaning, which produces a
'crisis' in representation and a lessening of any foundations to knowledge.
In these uncertain conditions, the Enlightenment's assumptions about the
autonomy of subject and object are lost. Something of these implications
can be grasped from Hassan's (1987: 91–92) contrasts between modernism
and postmodernism: purpose vs. play, design vs. chance, hierarchy vs. anar-
chy, centering vs. dispersal, genre/boundary vs. text/intertext, and root/
depth vs. rhizome/surface.

Postmodernism, then, has rediscovered the vernacular in architecture,
stressed history as being discontinuous, and views economic development as
being beyond the Fordism models of centralized accumulation and the Taylorism of scientific management in industry, replaced by 'flexible accumulation' and globally disaggregated production. Indeterminacy, as represented
by chaos theory, is stressed in science over old certainties. Objectivity, dualism,
and the distinction between subject and object have become discredited
modes of thought. In ethics, as in politics and culture, all views are accorded
equal values. For some, postmodernity has produced a global culture concerned with the surficial and the superficial, mass consumption and concern
with status. It is a fragmented world without unifying themes or social goals.

For a brief moment, 'postmodernism' formed part of the 'culture wars' of
the 1990s and became fashionable as a topic of cultural notoriety, loaded
with pretension and intellectualism. With the passing of this moment, the
term lapsed into popular obsolescence, yet also seemed to have acquired a
kind of legitimacy as a term of widespread (if uncertain) use. Along with
this linguistic familiarity is a broader acceptance that some form of global
cultural transformation is under way, in which the understanding of time,
space, social organization, and culture were being altered, and that postmodernity captured something of this change. Myerson's observation that
(2001: 9): "To many of us, there seemed something intuitively right about

the postmodern view, the theory that modern society and thought had come upon their limits" typifies this awareness.

Academically, postmodernism has been taken up by social science, with each discipline producing its own applications and meaning. Postmodernism, therefore, is not a school of thought, and appears in no immediate danger of becoming unified and productive in this fashion. Yet, the very profusion of interpretations and elusiveness of meaning ensures that postmodernism will continue to generate opponents and skeptics. As explored below, some postmodern theorists reject efforts to catalogue phenomena as 'postmodern,' for this act is restrictive and denies any true understanding of the qualities being examined.

Postmodernists understand modernity as exhibiting a faith in the Enlightenment ideals of reason and rationality, progress, absolute scientific knowledge, and the other attributes sought in the Age of Reason by Voltaire, Kant, and Hegel. Postmodernism, in some accounts, records the negative consequences of modernity, such assumptions of European superiority and associated racism and colonization of the New World. In other accounts, postmodernism is the failure to reach or continue to strive for the Enlightenment ideals, so that contemporary times are marked by exhaustion, pessimism, failures of reason, and abandoning the quest for absolute knowledge. Postmodernism is, at the least, the most recent criticism that modernity and critique of the Enlightenment that modernity has leveled against itself.

Whatever social changes mark the onset or recognition of the onset of the postmodern, the Western world is still operates under the ideas, assumptions, and goals of the Enlightenment, with its scientific rationality, universalism, and the pursuit of progress. Furthermore, many of its key institutions in liberal-democracy and the nation state persist, although views differ as to their current health and prognosis for the future. Declining faith in modernity's assumptions and objectives is also evident, because they cannot be realized or fulfilled (Smart 1996: 396) "on technical grounds (the epistemological problem) or worse, are deemed to be inappropriate, if not unacceptable, on moral-political grounds (the ethical problem)." Through this confusion, some broad shapes of the postmodern may be discerned. Postmodernism contests much of modern social thought that takes knowledge as being cumulative, progressive, rational, and unified. In thought, postmodernism rejects key aspects of Western thought through an acceptance of pluralism, indeterminacy, complexity, and incompleteness. And in culture, great emphasis is given to representation and signs and forms of information, and for a preference of play and fiction over realism and the quest for eternal truths.

Postmodern philosophers and key ideas

Four French authors in particular, Baudrillard, Derrida, Foucault, and Lyotard, are closely associated with postmodern theory and philosophy.

Postmodern philosophy arises from developments in the 1960s under way in French philosophy, where a radical movement rejected the conditions of modern, industrial, capitalist society. Essentially, the radical position centered on Marxism, Freud, existentialism, and phenomenology, which Jean-Paul Sartre, Maurice Merleau-Ponty, and others had co-joined into formulations rejecting what contemporary society wrought on its members (and their consciousnesses). Capitalism, scientific naturalism, psychological repression, mass culture, bureaucracy, and religion had alienated people from the authentic experiences and being, they argued. Behaviorism and naturalism of the conventional sciences were held to be inadequate for understanding the human condition in modern societies and were rejected for approaches focussed on individual experience from the individual's perspective. Resolving these perceived failures of the existing social system, radical thought sought to locate individuals at the 'center' of social life by changing social structures (such as class relations), culture and social mores (to eliminate excessive repression), and allowing for new access to lived experiences. Importantly, such changes did not necessitate any changes to technology, industrialization, or secularism.

A concurrent intellectual development was based on Ferdinand de Saussure's theories on linguistics in the latter nineteenth century, which rejected Marxism, phenomenology, existentialism, and psychoanalysis with their attention on the self and its historical development. Saussure's studies of how language structure confers meaning as a functioning system gave rise to the 'structuralist' school of linguistics. Under what became 'structuralism,' culture can be interpreted as the decisions that give social action their meaning (and thereby become 'signs'). It follows that the meaning of any action can only be understood as the outcome of a shared convention, so that thinkers in this tradition focus on the cultural roots that shape individuals through language, kinship, and ritual.

Human existence, under structuralism theories, can only be understood through a study of cultural signs. Within the systems of signs are the abstract social relations expressed in words, language, kinship, and so on. Structuralism offered a means to chart scholarship in the social sciences around the reductionism of the natural sciences, while retaining the possibility of objective study, which is impossible to approaches such as phenomenology or psychoanalysis. Importantly, structuralism had no place for a singular understanding of the individual for assessing culture. While structuralism was taken up within philosophy and linguistics after WWII, it was anthropology that provided its most famous manifestation with Claude Lévi-Strauss's 'structural anthropology.'

Thinkers sympathetic to the general approach of structuralism struggled with its limitations, especially where the approach removed or overlooked many key aspects of material life. Structuralist explanations recognize the 'surface' of stable and permanent binary relations, where meaning is the product of convention, but they overlook individual motivation and cannot explain causes that are unrelated to expressions of language. Critics of structuralism considered that the theory 'formalized' humanity. Structuralism was criticized for its 'ahistoricism,' as it seeks, assumes, and relies upon a universality of social relations through time. Those seeking to identify and modify structuralism, the 'post-structuralists,' provided many foundations for postmodern thought and several are identified with postmodernity.

Interestingly from an environmental perspective, while many commentators note the importance and prominence of Lévi-Strauss's influence on postmodern thought almost no mention is made of his general attack on modernity's destructive impact on ecology and native peoples and the subsequent neglect of this vital aspect of his work by the poststructuralists. Belated recognition has come through the work of those interested in ecological problems, such as Michael Zimmerman (whose work is discussed below).

Baudrillard and 'simulation'

Baudrillard's writings addressed the ways that the contemporary world is obsessed by images, to the extent, he believes, that the idea of what is real has been altered. In such works as *The Mirror of Production* (1975), *For a Critique of the Political Economy of the Sign* (1981a), *Simulations* (1981b), and *Cool Memories* (1990), Baudrillard created a number of terms and concepts describing the postmodern condition, but perhaps the central theme is 'simulation,' used in a wide range of applications. For example, in *Simulations,* the concept is realized in such diverse phenomena as Disneyland, the Watergate affair, and psychosomatic illness. While the term retains its conventional meanings, Baudrillard invests the word with a far more complicated interpretation, so that it embraces both the real and the copy, and the authentic and its duplicate.

Baudrillard argues that the contemporary world has become so saturated with images that no authentic reference point is available for identifying reality. In effect, the understanding of all phenomena becomes infused with imagery to the point that no 'pure' reality remains: the original and its reproductions cannot be distinguished. In the case of computer-generated images, 'virtual reality' need not refer to the real world at all. Taking this concept to its conclusion, Baudrillard argues that images in the modern world are completely 'detached' from the world, understandable not in terms of reality but only by using an understanding of other images. Doubt must always exist, therefore, about the authenticity of images. Representations of the world no longer represent the world. Many postmodern critics concur, arguing that the contemporary world is without depth and ephemeral, so that much of culture has become a 'cutting and pasting' of existing styles and images. Critic Jameson (1991), for instance, found postmodern architecture, art, film, and other media recycling images detached from their original meanings and trivialized for mass consumption in a capitalist world.

Reality and representation in the postmodern world, Baudrillard proposes, are inverted, so that simulation now shapes and influences reality. This more radical proposition holds that we are responding to simulation of the real rather than the real; images now precede and anticipate the real, assimilate the real, and produce it. Advertising exemplifies the power of simulation to produce the real through influencing purchasing decisions, as do media reports of vote-counts sway voter intentions. Moreover, Baudrillard points not just to political and market manipulations, but to a more fundamental condition that contemporary society cannot be free of the influence of imagery. Simulation, code, and representation govern everyday life. Caught in the world where nothing is authentic has created social panic, he surmises, and society responds by looking for the authentic and the genuine. Such a social need for escape from a world of simulation is manifested in the *creation* of the real, hence the 'hyperreal.' An immediate ecological implication is that any pursuit of the authentic or natural is misguided if that goal embodies a natural world independent of the social; that distinction is now unavailable, and that it's the representation of nature that that's become independent of the original. Doubtless nature will continue to provide a fecund source of images, and through these socially mediated sources postmodern society will understand, manage, and use Nature.

Derrida and 'deconstruction'

An effort to resolve the dilemma of structuralism is through 'deconstruction.' Its most famous exponent is Derrida (e.g., 1976) who has directed this critique against that bulwark of Western thought – reason. Western philosophy has made logocentricism its central quest, namely the search for rational language that portrays the world perfectly: words should represent thought without distortion. Essential to Derrida's attack on reason is that assuming its superiority excludes all that does not fit with it, making reason indifferent to the claims of the different, the contradictory, and the ill-fitting, in other words, to the claims of the 'other.'

Within all Western thought there is a center, which can take many forms, such as an ideal, an essence, a God, a truth, and so on, from which meaning is derived, argues Derrida. All is then assessed in terms of its relationship with the center, establishing a view of the world bound by binary relationships between a privileged 'center' and a marginalized 'other.' Deconstruction subverts the established center by substituting the 'other,' and is thereby a political act of subversion of the orthodox, dogmatic, and authoritarian. Reversing this hierarchy creates an opposite meaning to the original, but this new meaning is as unstable as its predecessor, so that all texts under deconstruction have no central construction, with neither privileged or marginal states. Deconstruction returns to the origins structuralism's origins, namely the construction of signs, wherein meaning derives from the relationships between signs, and not what they signify or from any of the signs' inherent qualities. Derrida takes this observation further than the structuralists by positing that the meaning of signs cannot be independent of the observer, thereby denying the structuralist's, and all other rationalist's, claims of 'scientific' neutrality.

Reason cannot be timeless and universal and, therefore, meaning and identity must be relative and provisional. Constructed meanings can be always be successively retraced to reveal further differences, with deconstruction showing the provisional character of meaning in any instance, so that meaning is in flux according to prevailing circumstances. Political and economic forces are required to exercise power to suppress certain meanings and interpretations in order to shape the world to their needs. Here we find Derrida not so much rejecting reason per se, but that part that presumes universal and permanent certainty because a multiplicity of meanings are always present.

Foucault and power and knowledge

Although grouped with his contemporaries as either a poststructuralist or postmodernist, Foucault's interests were not directed at language and text, but towards power within society and its institutions. Much of his work focusses on modernity's establishment, examining the birth of modern medicine and the clinic, mental illness and asylums, crime and prisons, and sexuality (1973a, 1973b, 1977, and 1978). Foucault refutes the Renaissance's notion of the autonomous individual possessed of a 'human nature' free of historical and cultural influences and demonstrates how subjects are shaped by social and institutional forces so that the self is only defined by extant social relations, and is, therefore, politically constructed. Humanism, according to Foucault, is plagued by the errors of taking the intentions of free-acting individuals as the basis for social theory.

Power within society is not monolithic to Foucault, but local and specific, making efforts to describe power in totalizing terms an abstraction that misses the way power is used and controlled in individual circumstances. No particular qualities bestow influence on an individual, institution, or state, as power can only be constructed and exerted contextually; power is not an attribute, but a relationship between entities. Meaningful resistance to power is therefore always local directed against local oppression. Subjects, in Foucault's view, are not rational, unified, or autonomous. Foucault extended this theory to social science by arguing that 'totalizing' theories are to be avoided, as dominant theories or all-encompassing accounts close off the possibility of considering alternatives. Such 'total' theories colonize areas of knowledge and experience, allowing only for those alternatives capable of being fashioned to conform to the dominant theory.

Having rejected social theorizing based around humanism and structural approaches, Foucault concentrates on explaining social life as the result of the power relations arising from constantly shifting alliances of discourse, knowledge, and practice. In this way, a middle ground emerges between the abstractions of meta-theories only dealing with social and economic entities (such as the state and class relations) and those small-scale theoretical approaches that ignore power relationships. One implication and source of difficulty is the effect individuals can exert over their circumstances, an omission that Foucault attempts to correct in latter works by examining the effect of personal initiatives.

Lyotard and the postmodern condition

Lyotard's *The Postmodern Condition: A Report on Knowledge* (1984) is a seminal work in postmodern accounts. Commissioned by the Council of Universities of the Quebec Government, its survey of scientific knowledge concluded that that knowledge had become the main force of economic production and society is best understood as a web of communication. Science, in this world, became just another 'language,' losing its special privilege. Lyotard concluded that science was increasingly more engaged in language, communications, computing, computer science and computer languages, and data storage, so that only knowledge capable of being rendered into these forms of information could be preserved. Information will become a commodity in the future, fought over by nations, bought and sold internationally, and corporations will use information in gaining ascendancy over the nation state. Such forecasts are unremarkable in contemporary times, yet Lyotard's interpretation of this phenomenon remains controversial.

Lyotard's interest in science extends to the fundamental question of how such knowledge is legitimized and the ways in which scientific discourse differs from narrative discourse. For Lyotard, narrative is the stuff of myth shared amongst a community, the telling of which supplies its own legitimacy and legitimizes the community. Narratives connect with a mythic notion of time, with the myth, its teller, and the audience formed into a cohesive group that supplies its own legitimacy and authority. Science, on the other hand, must supply its own legitimacy. Scientific statements must pass the tests of falsification (or verification) through proving affirmative statements and disproving contrary claims. But because science and narrative are different, science cannot assess narrative and it cannot answer questions of its own legitimacy (such as why should there be science?). Paradoxically then, science must turn to narrative to supply its legitimacy. Lyotard identifies two supporting narratives for science: politics and philosophy. It is from the Enlightenment that the first supporting narrative derives, in which political freedom is the product of science and reason. For the second narrative, Hegel's vision of a unified knowledge in which all knowledge would come together in a self-conscious spirit defines science's philosophical basis. These grand narratives or 'metanarratives,' as Lyotard dubs them, in reference to their intention to provide fulsome explanations and to subsume all minor narratives.

Science's problem is, that since WWII, according to Lyotard, societies lost faith in the grand narratives of reason and science to produce progress. And scientific discoveries suggested that a unified body of knowledge was growing increasingly less likely. Accordingly, science's gallant role to ensure freedom and progress could no longer be supported by its underpinning narratives. Faced by these difficulties, science retreats to a 'performativity,' in which it no longer searches for absolute truths, but concentrates on validating its performance. Science is therefore legitimizing itself, not through its former promises, but by virtue of self-referential justifications based on its own activities.

Whereas traditional societies function under a single myth, postmodern societies operate in a world of multiple and competing stories, according to Lyotard; there are no metanarratives, but many micro-narratives. By definition, no micronarrative is dominant, nor do any offer explanations of other micronarratives. Lyotard's understanding of postmodernity constituting 'a disinclination towards metanarratives' forms one of its defining attributes, despite its evident paradoxical formulation (i.e., the authority of no authorities, the metanarrative of no metanarratives, and so on). Questions of legitimation are at the center of such thinking, in which modern society has developed a rationale on which social changes could be justified. Such a worldview legitimized the modern state, institutional, economic, and technological changes taking place. Erosion of the widespread belief in this explanation of the modern world formed a 'delegitimation' of the modern world. Delegitimation could make many forms, but the most prominent of these has been the loss of acceptance of the 'grand narrative.'

Postmodernity and environmentalism

Postmodernity has been controversial, drawing attacks from socialists, liberals, and conservatives. Postmodern politics are controversial as a means to understand contemporary politics (i.e., as critique), as a condition (i.e., the positive), and as a goal (i.e., the normative). Critics from the right find in postmodernity an effort to re-invigorate the socialist program following the demise of actually existing socialism. Socialist critics locate in postmodernity an enthusiasm for capitalism and an indifference to free-market failures. Progressives have considered postmodernity as enshrining a moral indifference and a social apathy that abandons any commitment to social progress. And conservatives reject postmodernity for questioning and abandoning traditional values and social relationships. Although these simple characterizations appear to embody an incompatible set of criticisms, nearly all contain internally valid responses to postmodernity. And although rooted in basic differences in political philosophy, at least some of the debate over postmodernity has been at cross-purposes. A source of difference arises from whether postmodernity is considered as a condition (simply put, as that which succeeds modernity or defines the contemporary), or perhaps more specifically, as a way to understand contemporary social conditions, or alternatively, as a social and cultural objective.

Postmodernity recognizes that capitalism is the world's dominant economic system in which capitalism only supports cultures to the extent that they support it. Hence, the postmodern condition in an economic and political sense offers no immediate support for those seeking values contrary to market interests, thereby providing grounds to draw the opprobrium of conservatives and progressives. Advocates of modernist political creeds, especially communism and socialism, have been particularly upset by postmodernism, as have those seeking specific social values in political activity; this latter group find postmodernism as relativistic, nihilistic, cynical, and morally ambivalent, if not immoral.

Environmentalists and social scholars covering a range of political perspectives, such as Borgmann (1992, 1995, and 1999), Cheney (1989a, 1989b), Gare (1995), Harvey (1992), Kuehls (1996), Luke (1997), and Zimmerman (1994), accept the *prima facie* argument that contemporary life is distinct from the modern phase, and many hold that the postmodern condition is ecologically or socially undesirable. Distaste for conventional economic reasoning and a denunciation of unfettered capitalism is common to nearly all environmentalists, almost by definition, including those specifically discarding postmodernity. If the current circumstances actually represent the 'end of history,' to employ Fukuyama's (1992) aphorism, then environmentalists would consider future ecological prospects as very dim indeed. Such a perspective acknowledges but contests the social and ecological features of a postmodern condition. This acknowledgement that can be mistaken for, or assumed to be identical with, advocacy of the political, social, economic, and environmental implications of postmodernity as advanced by some postmodernists. Yet, this charge is consistently rejected by those scholars highlighting the differences between the normative and positive dimensions to their reaction to postmodernity, namely those between 'what is' and 'what ought to be.'

Environmentalism and postmodernity

Postmodernity has made a critique of modernity central to much thinking about society–nature relations in modern society by environmental scholars possible, yet opinion as to whether postmodernity can or should prove useful to environmental thinking is quite varied, as are views as to whether postmodernity and environmentalism are connected. Postmodernism arose from philosophical concerns with language, meaning, and representation, largely from thinkers in structuralism, post-structuralism, and semiotics. Its exponents and debates have assumed center stage in contemporary discussions over culture and society in academic fields. Postmodern philosophy, as

expounded by those most associated with its development, offered no association between environmental concerns and contemporary culture. Best
and Kellner offer (1997: 268):

> Key postmodern theorists analyze language, discourse, and significa-
> tion as ideal worlds of meaning divorced from social and natural
> environments. Derrida, Lyotard, Foucault, Rorty, and others focus
> strictly on critiques of Western philosophy while failing to engage its
> core anthropocentric outlook. ... Postmodern theorists are helpful in
> showing how we are enmeshed deeply in sociological and technologi-
> cal, social, and semiotic systems, but, unlike the Frankfurt School and
> postmodern science, they fail to analyze our embeddedness in the
> natural world.

Unfortunately, Best and Kellner are consistent with the failing they identify
and offer only a few pages on the environment in their wide-ranging works
on postmodernity (1991, 1997, and 2001).

Nature's absence from most of the seminal postmodern writings is cur-
ious, as postmodernity has some roots in a critique of modernity's distan-
cing from nature in the theories of Max Horkheimer, Theodor Adorno,
Martin Heidegger, and Herbert Marcuse, according to Zimmerman (1994).
Although many of the social themes raised by this group found their way
into postmodern theory, their critiques of the social relationship with the
natural world and associated role of science did not. As Best and Kellner
state (1997: 269): "No major postmodern philosopher or social theorist, in
other words, has explored the connections between the deification of the
Western rational self, the alienation from the natural world, and the modern
project of the domination of nature." This state of affairs may reflect more
of the construction of the identity of the so-called 'major' theorists than it
does about the contributions emerging from environmental ethics. Conley,
who goes some way to addressing this schism herself, observes in the state
of postmodern theory that (1997: 2): "[w]e are witnessing in debates surrounding cultural theory an edginess, even evidence of timorousness, about
'what to do' with ecology."

A few postmodernists have considered ecological questions and have
directly contributed to the environmental debate, although these contributions have frequently gone unnoticed, as Conley (1997) makes clear in her
thorough account. Guattari's (2000) 1989 essay *The Three Ecologies* offers
that the three ecologies, namely the environment, society, and the psychological, are being destroyed by technology and science and by the global
capitalist system. In expressing the "paradox" of this condition, whereby
the instruments of modernity cannot resolve the problems they have created, Guattari arrives as the conclusion that defines much of the postmodern
response to the environmental crisis. What is required is an "ecosophy" praxis
to guide the way through the misinformation and deception created by

global capitalism and the mass media in order to establish a new relationship with nature. Such an approach will break down the barriers between these ecologies that capitalism has fostered through its production of subjectivity and quest for semiotic conquest of the world. Paul Verilio also produced several works that evoke ideas of nature and environmental conditions and the cultural conditions of postmodernity, such as in *Open Sky* (2002), when he writes of the ever-accelerating world that that reduces the colors of the natural world increasingly into a monochromatic gray.

Not that the scholars within environmentalism were necessarily concerned with building bridges to postmodernism either; many leading environmentalists were uninterested in, or generally unaware of, developments in Continental philosophy. Reviews of the development and varieties of environment thought (largely in a political context), such as those of Dobson (2000), Dryzek (1997), and Pepper (1996), indicate that postmodernist thought was of no relevance to its development or major forms of social expression. Similarly, prominent works in environmental philosophy and ethics from Passmore (1974), Rolston (1988), and Stone (1987) dealt largely with contemporary environmental problems and conceptions of ethics. Partly, this may be explained by the absence of any obvious intellectual lineage between environmental ethics and structuralism/semiotics or to Marxism. Further, the primary interests of environmentalism concerned human ecology in a broad sense, both in terms of the relationship of indigenous peoples with their environment and with contemporary society and the natural world, such as Bookchin (1971, 1986, and 1995), Callicott (1994, 1999), Næss (1973), and Roszak (1972, 1978, 1992, and 1995).

Postmodernity has, however, exerted a great influence over a large swath of the academic disciplines interested in questions of environmental politics, with inquires considering discourses of power, the role of contemporary culture, the representation of ideas and the role of symbols, and so forth. Scholars have employed and questioned postmodernity in environmental issues in geography (e.g., Marcus A. Doel, Harvey), eco-feminism (e.g., Spretnak, Donna Haraway, and Val Plumwood), environmental politics (e.g., Escobar, Gare, and Ross), philosophy (e.g., Cheney, Zimmerman), international relations (e.g., Kuehls, Gearóid O'Tuathail), science studies (e.g., Bruno Latour, Oreskes, and Kristen Shrader-Frechette), spirituality (e.g., Griffin), and many other fields and scholars. Despite this range and depth of scholarship, there is much in postmodernity that environmentalism finds controversial.

In many ways, postmodern politics rejects interpretations of political activity based on fixed actions and interests of defined sets of actors, such as in Marxism's class-differentiated interests and the struggle for control over the economic means of production. Alternatively, postmodernists suggest that political outcomes in contemporary times are less governed by these traditional actors and concerns, and are better characterized through fluid, dynamic, and reciprocal relationships between all relevant actors. For a start, much political conflict is now generated by the desire for greater consumption of goods and services, giving rise to new social movements. Change can occur not only through class actions, but also through ideologically diverse groups working individually, or in concert, on specific issues. Eco-socialist Pepper explains (1993: 136): "Postmodernism tends to place all social conflict in the cultural, not political domain. Its struggle is not to *control* state bureaucracy, but *against* the state." Conventional political views of the left and right are made redundant, according to Pepper, because the state is depicted as inefficient, unresponsive, and oppressive and the private sector as its opposite. Indeed, many developed nation's environmental causes are actively promoted as being beyond the stultifying dichotomies of established political parties and limits of left/right ideologies.

Postmodern politics takes up the themes of "fragmentation, ephemerality, discontinuity, and chaotic change" (Harvey 1992: 44), and express skepticism for major political reform through any singular alternative subverting the mainstream. Environmentalists often interpret this stance as a relativism that denies the objective reality of environmental problems and dismiss postmodernity as dangerous and misleading. Certainly, postmodern politics appears to have no transcendent political causes and no singular history of political struggles; each group pursues its own cause and writes its own history.

For some environmentalists, the association between postmodernity and environmental critiques is disastrous. Pepper considers that the critiques share some undesirable characteristics (1993: 57):

> Green politics often lack structure and coherence, reject authority and embrace cultural relativism – paradoxically despite their desire to see *all* societies conforming to meta-theories of ecology, i.e. the laws of nature like carrying capacity. Therefore green politics have much in common with postmodernism.

Starke (1995) is disturbed by the parallels between postmodernity and the philosophy of deep ecology, stating of the latter (1995: 275):

> [It] can build foundations for no science of humanity in the natural context, no eco-democratic, bioregional model of society, no possible conception of rights (either individual or natural), no philosophical justification for the existence of political community and no meaningful framework for practical politics.

If such theorists as Beck, Dobson, Hajer, and Lafferty for example, are correct in identifying environmentalism as a major and influential social force, then its difficult to reconcile green politics as deficient in structure and coherence, and simultaneously successfully defiant of the industrial project's authority. In practice, green politics have been both highly influential and inconsequential according to circumstances, as examples of success and failure abound. At least some of this variety in appraisal depends on our expectations, and therefore on what we understand as constituting green politics. 'Green politics' assumes a multiplicity of forms offering widely differing positions on specific issues; for example, one of its most successful manifestations, that of ecological modernization, seems not to reject authority, nor do those favoring democratic or administrative approaches that are some distance from deep ecology's radicalism.

Indeed, it seems that much of the contemporary response to environmental problems runs counter to postmodern thinking. Environmentalists, national and international institutions, and governments consider environmental issues, especially at large scales, as matters of science and opportunities for liberal democratic governance. Such 'metanarratives' commonly supply the environmental concepts and political tools fundamental to environmental policy formulation and planning. Professionals, researchers, government officials, and others have roles defined as the designated arbiters of environmental and social knowledge within a fixed social and economic structure. Such responses seem anchored in universal formulations of nature–society relations and official views of the causes of ecological change. Postmodern thought rejects this role by claiming that such professionals do not possess an exclusive knowledge or authority in interpreting the world for the application of management and governance, especially in relation to scientific knowledge. Rather, postmodernists insist that scientific knowledge is a social construct, and that there are no single truths about the environment, but a multiplicity of views.

An immediate political implication of this postmodern view is that the authority and privilege of science is taken as being identical to the interests of societies' centers of power. Knowledge vested in indigenous and local peoples has been deemed irrelevant to environmental issues as defined by modern societies which rely on scientific analysis; postmodern thought challenges scientific knowledge by asserting other forms of knowledge as having equal or greater validity. Examples of indigenous knowledge of land and biodiversity providing more effective responses to issues of biodiversity protection and land restoration than scientific reasoning validate postmodernist claims that science cannot provide a complete response and can even be a force for increased ecological loss.

Postmodernists reject the positivism of conventional science, especially its claims of a correspondence between the outcomes of the empirical scientific method and identifying an objective reality. In the place of the objective causal models of environment and society, postmodernism offers subjective accounts of discourse that explicitly derive from actor's perceptions. For environmental management, the co-existence of such different ways of understanding issues creates particular and novel problems for decision-making such as reconciling differing views, of deciding whether truths can be established, of determining criteria to identify efficacious policy choices.

Environmentalism expresses postmodern politics as a form of resistance, based on environmentalism's critique of industrialism with its attendant social and environmental failures, and suggestion that unlimited economic growth is undermining the future of modernity, so that sustainable modernity is an ecological impossibility. Yet prominent environmental thinkers are divided over the implications and prospects of postmodernity. Cheney (1989a), for example, wants to use postmodernity for pursuing the goals of bioregionalism and to replace the centrality of science in understanding the natural world with an 'ethical vernacular' based on the individual, community, and the land (1989a: 134): "The fractured identities of postmodernism ... I suggest, can build health and well-being by means of a bioregional contextualization of self and community."

Luke's (1997) *Ecocritique* canvasses the (developed world's) landscape of social movements, activists, and theorists in environmental politics, ranging from green consumerism and the managerialism of the U.S. NGO the World-watch Institute, to the Biosphere 2 experiment and the eco-village of Paolo Soleri, to deep ecology, Herbert Marcuse, and Murray Bookchin. He suggests that from these ecocritiques an alternative modernity can be erected. Luke offers a closely observed account of these alternatives, and although much of the material necessary for sorting out where these critiques sit in regard to modernity is provided, such a task is left to the reader.

No single guide exists for identifying which aspects or schools of environmentalism can be considered postmodernist and those that are not. In lieu of this assistance, the following categorization is suggested, based on Dryzek's (1997) system of environmental 'discourses.' There can be no definitive categorization of environmentalism and Dryzek's also has its share of problems, but it has the virtue of covering a wide spectrum of thought and employs straightforward categories. Each discourse can be evaluated according to the extent that its theory and (intended or actual) practice can be accommodated with the use of scientific rationality, liberal-democratic governance, and environmental management as currently practiced by the world's developed and industrializing nations (see Table 2.1). Environmentalism, as a collection of discourses concerned with environmental protection, cannot be collectively identified as postmodern. Many environmental schools don't seek revolutionary change, but follow programs for a 'reformed' modernity. Deep ecology, eco-feminism, bioregionalism, eco-theology, eco-communalism, social ecology, environmental justice, and animal liberation reject the tenets of modernity, are generally irreconcilable with modernity's practices, and can be considered as postmodern responses to modernity.

Escobar and the opportunities of the postmodern condition

Escobar (1996) offers a 'discourse analysis' of political ecology that he calls a "poststructural political ecology," which is essentially a political analysis

Table 2.1 Environmental discourses and their relationship with modernity.

Environmental discourse	Accept and or reconcilable with modernity?	Defining characteristics
Green romanticism (deep ecology, eco-feminism, bioregionalism, eco-theology, eco-communalism)	No	Revised nature–society relations. Social 'reconnecting' with nature impossible under modernity.
Administrative rationalism	Yes	Reform through existing state institutions of governance; assumes modernity.
Democratic pragmatism	Yes	Citizen activism in liberal democratic states using existing institutions.
Ecological modernization (as practiced)	Yes	Alignment of interests of capitalist economy, states, community, and environmental protection.
Green rationalism:		Various.
A. European Greens, Left Greens	Yes	
B. Social ecology, environmental justice, and animal liberation	No	
Market rationalism	Yes	Use of existing markets with market-based instruments.
Sustainable development	Yes	Constrained capitalism and institutional reform in the cause of economic growth, environmental protection, and social justice.
Radical political ecology	No	Ecologically driven political economy.

based on an "articulation of knowledge and power" and of the processes that realize "social reality." In common with many of political ecology's practitioners, Escobar views contemporary economic and social changes responsible for ecological decline as the outcome of global capitalism and draws directly on two prominent eco-Marxists, James O'Connor and Martin O'Connor. Under the postmodern condition, Escobar identifies a crucial transition in Nature-society relations. James O'Connor (1988, see also 1998) and Martin O'Connor (1994) argue that capitalism is riven by an ecological contradiction in which the productive capacities of nature, space, and labor are diminished over time. Capitalism responds to this condition, which produces a falling rate of profit, by finding new fields for exploitation, thereby staving off these contradictions' effects. This 'postmodern' form of capitalistic response, supplemental to the first, finds its apotheosis in sustainable management. In this transformation, capitalism is not restricted to exploitation, but extends its interests to ecological management and conservation under the rubric of 'sustainable development.'

Four assumptions underlay sustainable development, according to Escobar, and each with distinct ecological implications: 1) a 'saving the world mentality,' which promotes the global at the expense of the local; 2) a belief that the word's poor create environmental problems, but which ignores how capitalism creates poverty in the first place; 3) a faith that capitalism's market structures can resolve ecological problems, so that ways must be found to consider ecological issues economically, which necessitates the 'capitalization' of nature; and 4) that the concept of 'environment' can replace that of nature. Sustainable development seeks to reconcile capitalism and economic growth by leaving the market in place. In identifying global environmental problems, sustainable development seeks global management solutions. Escobar uses Foucault's concept that scientific management and the worldview of science involves a particular association between its language, words, and the entities it depicts, identifying the earth's ecology as a ailing patient in need of the medicine of scientific environmental management. Such a perspective amounts to a zeal for controlling nature, argues Escobar. He finds sustainable development unable to critique the forces of capital giving rise to ecological harm and claims that sustainable development will worsen the prospects for environmental restoration and protection by requiring an increasing level of nature's commodification.

In depicting capital's modern form, Escobar follows an eco-Marxist reasoning. Economic activity retains its vitality through a concern with production and the necessity of constant restructuring. Escobar refers to Polanyi's (1944) depictions of the failure of the self-regulating economy in the Great Depression, a crisis created by shortages in land, labor, and resources that forced nation states to intervene on the part of capital. Environmentally, the state's entry into the business of saving the economy evokes its essential role in capitalizing production conditions, in the widest sense. Modern history is marked by capital's continual expansion into social life and science (sometimes referred to as the 'colonization of the lifeworld').

Capital's postmodern form finds capitalism extending into new realms of the natural world and operating in new ways. Whereas modern capitalism is simply interested in accessing nature's material bounty in relatively immediate ways and without regard to the social and ecological implications, postmodern capital seeks to capture the processes and capacities of nature that create natural goods and services, as well as their outputs. To control these social and ecological sources of value, capital must embrace such ephemeral qualities as knowledge, culture, codes, and processes in nature and related social and symbolic systems with roles in creating potential economic value.

Escobar follows a postmodernist approach to understanding and describing nature, holding that it is 'construction.' Nature, humanity, and organisms are all actors in the drama of life (thereby evoking the post-modern 'death of the subject' and anti-foundationalism) made possible because the boundaries between culture and nature are not fixed or permanent, but are pliable and permeable. Accordingly, as the Western view of nature has constantly shifted according to cultural/historical factors, our prejudices have been written into Nature's identity, such as those on issues of race, gender, nation, family, and class. Creating 'postmodern nature' reinvents the understanding and role of nature under the demands of post-modern capital that sweeps away the last vestiges of organic nature with the logic of command and control. In doing so, the postmodern condition also surpasses modernity's view of nature that is rational, realistic, and organic. Escobar endorses Donna Haraway's concept that modern science's view of organisms and individuals has been replaced by 'cyborgs' that depicts entities that are simultaneously organic and mechanical. Cyberculture offers, therefore, cultural promises for more equitable social relations and the demise of the ideology of naturalism. Depictions of an independent, autonomous, and separate nature are rendered obsolete, so that the post-modern's nature is the antithesis of the Romantic ideologies' pre-modern 'back to nature' or revised modernity 'preservationalist' modes of protection.

Escobar promotes strategies of resistance based in postmodern thought that oppose modernity and he quotes Enrique Leff with approval. Seeking strategies that are ecologically sustainable, culturally defined, and that oppose sustainable development, Escobar hopes to circumvent prevent conventional development and create complex, balanced, and sustainable approaches to the social relationships with the environment. Culture must displace economic exploitation at the center of the social relationship with Nature, thereby creating a new productive rationality. It follows that the Leff/Escobar formulation is concerned with 'environmental democracy,' economic decentralization, and cultural and political pluralism. Although the postmodern condition offers a revised social relationship with nature and ways to build new global relations, Escobar leaves open the questions of implementation and the forms this ecologically informed world would assume. A few environmentalists have taken up this challenge with characteristically diverse results.

Gare's "postmodernism and the environmental crisis"

One of the more substantial efforts to locate ecology in the politics of the postmodern condition is Gare's *Postmodernism and the Environmental Crisis* (1995). Contemporary environmental crises result from philosophical and political failures that Gare posits with modernist, postmodern, and Marxist theories' inability to fully capture the relationships between the postmodern condition, globalizing capitalism, and the ecological crisis. In response, he creates a 'postmodern ecology' to generate a new ethics, politics, and economics within a new 'grand narrative.' Gare notes that while postmodernism has been largely concerned with 'narratives,' environmentalism has been aligned with 'science,' so that postmodernism has said much about oppression, but that Marxism and opponents of the mainstream have generated a far more effective critique on the environmental crisis.

A strength of Gare's analysis of the ecological crisis and the postmodern is its recognition of key social and economic changes in the late twentieth century, especially those impacts of the information and communications technology innovations and globalization as felt by the developed nations. Changes in the international economy have been re-ordering social and economic conditions within the Western world, re-shaping the character of national economies, changing production patterns, the prospects and composition of social classes, technology, culture, and knowledge. Former tenets of economic and political control within nations states have been diminished, accompanied by a weakening of the Western bourgeoisie (including salary earners, the working class, farmers, and those tied to domestic markets) and the rise of new service sector sub-classes and an emerging international bourgeoisie. Accompanying these economic and social changes are several cultural changes. Interestingly, he suggests that the emerging postmodernity and decline of grand narratives had the greatest impact on intellectuals who lost their place as the arbiters of culture. Commercial factors came to guide the value of knowledge, with market rationality being applied to the functioning of universities and the directions of science alike. Accordingly, the public intellectual is a role of the past and experts on popular culture share status with their counterparts on high culture, whilst economics is the dominant social science, and those disciplines without direct economic value have diminished.

Of the world's environmental troubles, Gare states (1995: 73): "As yet, there is no definitive social construct of the environmental crisis." He notes that the mainstream, Marxist, and poststructuralists all view the problem differently. His treatment of the mainstream is, broadly, a critique of political economy emphasizing capitalism's harmful effects and of economic rationality in environmental policy based firmly in a Marxist tradition. Whilst noting the developments in environmental economics and ecological economics have brought only limited success, he considers their future possibilities as inadequate for the task of addressing major environmental problems. Within ecologism, at least, Gare's analysis is a conventional attack on conventional economics.

Given this orientation, it follows that Gare concentrates on the contributions of eco-Marxism. Marxism's insights into capitalism provide a critique of the world's dominant socio-cultural order which is, at its core, the 'fetishism of commodities.' Commodification, whereby natural goods, services, information, and life itself are brought into the sphere of market relations, makes opaque the relations between society and nature. This system produces many results: power relationships within society are obscured, people and nature are exploited, goods are produced for profit and not for use, economic growth is fostered that further degrades the environment, and social relations are marked by greatly unequal power and wealth. When introduced into new realms, the ecologically destructive character of capitalism is revealed. Eco-Marxism makes clear that the growth imperative of capitalism drives both natural resource consumption and polluting wastes, and under globalization, the reach and extent of this destruction accelerates.

Not that Gare fully endorses Marxism; he describes the general disinterest in environmental matters by traditional Marxist scholars, such as represented by the Frankfurt School, noting André Gorz, Richard England, and Barry Bluestone as exceptions. Amongst these failings is that while Marxist scholars reject the centrally planned economies of the former Soviet Union and Eastern Europe, it is far from clear what a socialist state might comprise and how it would adopt a benign relationship with the environment. In effect, Gare applies the broader perceived failing of contemporary socialism, namely the difficulty of depicting a vision of the future untainted by the practice of former existing socialism, to the narrower problem of depicting environmentalism under socialism, given the generally appalling environmental record of former actually-existing socialism. Marx's writings, Gare states, are unhelpful on this point, having "conceived the future in terms of a mode of production which will be even more successful in terms of dominating nature."

Gare's interest in environmental postmodernism is with its theoretical ideas, and less with its exponents, who he briefly identifies (1995: 87):

> Postmodern environmentalists, that is, the 'deep ecologists' and associated movements (ecosophy, deep green and eco-feminism) are those who reject Euro-, anthropo- and andro-centrism, and the grand narratives of progress formulated in these terms.

Postmodern thinking exposes the repressive character of progress under Western civilization, and further, that the forces of opposition tend to reproduce the forms of thinking that produce such oppression in the first place. Gare states that while Nietzsche, Heidegger, the poststructuralists, and some postmodernists offer insights into this domination, they offer few guidelines for solutions. With their emphasis on language and discourse, postmodernists offer little in the way of praxis. Further, Gare argues, from the influence of Derrida it is possible to retreat into relativism, making any concerted social response to environmental problems impossible. Foucault too, offers little support for grappling with global environmental problems, according to Gare, for his position is ultimately ambivalent about widespread resistance to power, and of the sources and reasons for resistance. And while Deleuze and Guattari (1988) offer a Nietzschean approach to realizing individual freedoms against state oppression, Gare notes that greater satisfaction of desires in the U.S. in the last 30 years has not produced socially optimal outcomes.

A major liability of postmodernity's contribution to environmentalism is its inability to construct political programs based on firm critiques of society's dominant power relationships. In this sense, Gare draws a contrast between postmodernity and what he regards as the useful and insightful critique of political economy. Global environmental destruction has involved far more than individual power relationships and 'discursive formations,' he argues, as they result from the power of market institutions, corporations, and nations states operating at the global scale, and various power relationships between groups within societies. It is these latter forms of power that postmodernity must inform if it is to assist in addressing ecological problems. Yet postmodernity cannot do so, being (1995: 98) "simply committed to the defense of local knowledge and local power against global knowledge and global power." Not only do poststructuralists "fail to reveal the interconnectedness of environmental problems" but also "invalidate the efforts of those who are striving to reveal them" (Gare 1995: 99).

Because of the way postmodernists (and poststructuralists) have developed an ambivalence over any simple relationship between object and language (especially in the hands of Baudrillard), discourse becomes inwardly focused on discourse itself. If theories are increasingly defined and developed in relation to other theories, environmental destruction becomes "incomprehensible;" then, in a telling phrase (1995: 99): "This inability to deal with the phenomenon of a global environmental crisis manifests the loss of contact with the world." Environmentalism is popular in the postmodern era, matching with a general skepticism towards the concept of progress and concomitant with an acceptance of diverse cultures and beliefs, with special sympathies towards those diminished by progress. Although postmodernism fosters alterative perspectives, so that deep ecology, ecofeminism, and New Age thinking offer greater respect for nature and opportunities for alternative values (Gare 1995: 100), "hardly any of this support has translated into effective action, into changing the way people live and the way the economy is organized to make society less environmentally destructive."

In one of the most forceful attacks on postmodernity from an environmentalist perspective, Gare states (1995: 99):

In their failure to orient people for action, their attack on rationality *per se* as an act of oppression, their efforts to liberate suppressed desires, their rejection of perspective and finally their lack of contact with any reality beyond language and texts, poststructuralists are expressing the spirit of postmodern culture, and the failures of the poststructuralists are revelations of the defects of this culture. It is these defects which account for the career of the environmentalist cause in the affluent West.

Responding to these failings, Gare proposes a revised environmental post-modernity based on a new 'grand narrative.' Gare's proposals have three bases: 1) Heidegger's "project" and the complex theology of 'being' (following Nietzsche) as an antidote to modernity; 2) postmodern science; and 3) components of eco-Marxism. Needless to add, the resulting amalgam is complex and theoretically dense. This narrative must connect individuals to the global environmental crisis, revealing the history and character of these issues, how they can be resolved, and the role of individuals in that activity. Such a narrative must operate alongside those revealing the links between individuals and the global political and economic order. Existing narratives that result in environmental destruction must be overturned and replaced by one that is revelatory about power relationships within society, yet also connect with existing narratives while comprehending the failures of existing narratives.

That tendency to oppression by previous grand narratives can be avoided by ensuring a "polyphonic grand narrative in the form of a dialogic discourse," that gives voice to a diversity of cultures and "local stories," and "any totalizing perspective utilized to give coherence to the narrative must only be accepted provisionally" (Gare 1995: 140–141). At its core, this new narrative is an alternative cosmology entailing a philosophy of process, namely a postmodern science. This science is based on the notion of the world being 'a process of creative becoming,' wherein people create themselves by constructing narratives and from which environmentally sensitive narratives are formed. Meaning in the world, therefore, escapes the reductionism of modernity, wherein ends determine value, and the nihilism that Nietzsche identified as the ultimate outcome of modern society, is avoided. Gare appears to argue for an 'intrinsic' perception of entities in the world to replace the mechanistic and 'instrumental' perception characteristic of modernity or, at least, of Cartesian reasoning. Intrinsic value, therefore, is based on recognizing the realization of creativity, i.e., the 'process of creative becoming.'

Unsurprisingly, this narrative will be diverse, and deliberately so, in replacing the "linear" narrative of modernity although humanity certainly faces a considerable task to conduct this narrative (1995: 143): "For any individual, whether this be a person, an institution, a movement, a class, a nation, a civilization or humanity as a whole, what is required is a multi-dimensional narrative of at least acknowledging thousands of different temporal and spatial orders, both within the becoming of humanity and within the rest of nature." In this way, Gare responds to the failures of modernity with its conceptions of the 'self' and the 'other' as described by the poststructuralists.

While the philosophy behind the preceding summary is dense, especially its 'new cosmology,' the rationale for the future is relatively straightforward. There are two sides to Gare's proposals, an 'environmentalist' nationalism and revised socio-economic policies. Gare is critical of postmodernists who deride the nation state, claiming that the erosion of nations has fostered expansion of exploitative capitalistic practices. Because Gare posits the global environmental crisis as an outcome of capitalism, existing international responses are destined to fail, and only reconstituted nations committed to resisting capitalism can succeed. One form of resistance Gare favors is national isolationism oriented towards ecological goals, which disarms transnational corporations and the harmful effects of globalization. Environmentalism harnessed by the nation state can serve as a means to attack capitalism. Revitalization of the nation state also enables the fragmentation under postmodernism to be reversed, he argues. Gare considers that nations essential for effective global action and they can serve as a means of facilitating discourses at every level, from local to national.

Existing state policies are oriented towards the needs of capitalist economies, a condition that environmentalism and environmental justice must engage and overcome, argues Gare. Managerialism has replaced democracy in the current response to environmental problems, he writes, in clear reference to contemporary ecological modernization. Applying the concept of 'retrospective path analysis,' Gare finds a means to overcome these problems (1995: 154): "which accords with the conception of people as creating themselves through constructing narratives within which they can situate themselves, and which tends to democratize decision-making." Through this technique of setting future goals and examining alternative 'pathways' to these ends, an open discourse about these possibilities is established. Social science's role in such a setting is greatly altered, being shifted away from cost–benefit analysis and towards identifying and comprehending the dynamics and interrelationships of society and the natural world.

Spretnak's postmodern ecology

Spretnak's ecocentric proposals are developed through a number of works (e.g., 1991, Spretnak and Capra 1984) and perhaps most thoroughly in *The Resurgence of the Real* (1997). Spretnak is unequivocal in identifying the features and failures of modernity and its worldview; describing how the environmental and social 'contradictions' in the nineteenth century became its outright failures in the twentieth, not least being "the goal of the perfectability of the human by means of rationally designed institutions" (1997: 41). Key to understanding modernity's limitations, states Spretnak, is that the Enlightenment, scientific revolution, Renaissance humanism, and the Reformation were all reactions to the preceding order that attempted to sweep away all traces of the past. Modernity discarded much of value of the pre-modern era and its formation was "a radical break *from* all perceptions of organicism, holism, and interrelatedness and *toward* any discoveries that fit in the neoclassical, mechanistic worldview" (1997: 44). Spretnak's account of the rise and subsequent development of modernism reaches back to identify the Socratic break with nascent philosophies, whereby the classical division between humanity and nature was established.

Spretnak's account of modernity conforms to those above in many respects, especially Toulmin's *Cosmopolis*. However, Spretnak acknowledges the emergence of the postmodern era, but is critical of the poststructuralist's philosophy and several postmodernists. Her critique takes deconstruction as a starting point and refutes its claim that reality can only be understood as a social construction mediated by power relationships, finding deconstructionism to be reconstituted modernity (1997: 66–67):

> They uphold the modern body–mind split by asserting an inner version of social construction whereby culture (mind) projects assumptions and other concepts onto dumb matter (the body) – the usual one-way construction of meaning, according to both Cartesian and deconstructionist thought. The inauthentic individual, trapped by the language games and power plays of his or her culture, feels more acutely than ever the radical discontinuity between self and the rest of the world.

Spretnak notes that much of what the deconstructionists produced was not as original as its promulgators suggested, and that many failed to identify such precursors as the nineteenth-century critics of scientific positivism, the sociology of knowledge, the works of Wittgenstein and Nietzsche, and the contributions of 1960s grassroots groups on racism, patriarchy, and the like. Although support for deconstruction has diminished, it persists in those believing that: "human interaction with nature is a one-way process of projecting concepts, that any talk of coherence in the biosphere is a projection, and that beliefs and values are merely relative and have no validity other than their own invention" (1997: 69). Not surprisingly, Spretnak's 'ecological postmodernism' is the mirror opposite of this perspective, in which 'ecology' assumes the broadest interpretation. Encapsulating these views, the author writes (1997: 72):

> Foremost, "ecological postmodernism" changes the essential gesalt. Instead of perceiving ourselves as social "atoms," colliding and combining with other discrete "atoms" in a human society that uses and projects concepts onto its background matter (nature), we perceive an unbroken continuity of cosmos/Earth/continent/nation/bioregion/ community/neighborhood/family/person. These are the extended boundaries of the self. Our field, our grounding, our belief is the cosmos. Moreover, we finally slough off the modern obsession with escaping from nature and realize that all human endeavor is derivative of the Earth community, not the other way round.

While moderns seek objective truths and deconstructionists engage in extreme relativism, Spretnak's ecological postmoderns pursue experientialism, and where deconstructionists see the world as an aggregate of fragments, the ecological postmoderns see a community of subjects. Nature is an opponent to moderns, she writes, a wronged object to deconstructionists, but a subject to ecological postmodernity. This ecological postmodernity represents radical social change counters modernity with a philosophy and social construction that features ecological justice, eco-feminism, and an eco-theology. Accordingly, its central themes deal with worldviews, personal values, personal relationships and community realization, spirituality and the natural world. Spretnak is concerned with the experience of living in the world and evokes aspects of the Romantic Movement in her consideration of both the regard of nature and of the impacts of industrialization. Tied into this view are her concerns with the ways in which modernity disrupted familial relationships and fostered the subjugation of women, especially those relationships that existed between women and nature.

A future rendered in these terms opposes modernity's familiar themes: rationalism, conventional economics, mass production industrialism, objectivism, scientism, the mechanistic worldview, anthropocentrism, bureaucracy, opposition to nature, comparmentalisation, escape from religion, and 'hypermasculinity.' Spretnak, as an eco-feminist concerned with spirituality, gives special attention to the 'sacred.' While less explicit in defining spirituality in a postmodern world than Borgmann (see, e.g., *Crossing the Postmodern Divide* (1992)) or Griffin (1998a, 1998b), Spretnak firmly ties her postmodern ecology to an appreciation of the cosmos, and specifically states that modernity "shrunk" religion down to concern with ethics and morals from its larger appreciation of the creative cosmos.

Rather than asserting an overt and isolationist eco-feminism, Spretnak pursues a social goal of inclusiveness of all peoples, subverting a perceived masculine bias in much of the writings on modernity and postmodernity. Postmodern ecology here concerns questions of knowledge and awareness, tracking both developments in science, economics, and the understanding consciousness, with Theodore Roszac quoted with much approval. By defining many contemporary developments in (Western) society as extensions of modernity, referring to Giddens's "radical modernity" and Griffin's "mostmodern" concepts, Spretnak seeks a positive version of postmodernity, suggesting this would be a "constructive modernity" (1997: 223). Much of Spretnak's argument closely resembles those of the religious philosopher Griffin, with the added dimension of eco-feminism.

Zimmerman's "radical ecology and postmodernity"

Zimmerman's (1994) *Contesting Earth's Future* proposes that drawing uncritically on Heidegger's antimodernity critique can lead the postmodernists to some politically undesirable outcomes. When postmodernity refuses the totalizing explanations of modernity for discarding "uncertainty, ambiguity, difference, and otherness," it runs the risk of totally rejecting modernity, including its emancipatory goals, argues Zimmerman. Marxists and liberal democrats have attacked deep ecology and radical ecology as reactionary antimodernism, contending that this inclination of 'cultural despair' opens the way to oppressive government. Evoked here are concerns that radical ecologists seek a degree of social control only available under authoritarian rule. Many supporters of radical ecology "envision the emergence on nonauthoritarian, nonoppressive, nonhierachial, "postmodern" societies in which free, playful, decentered, heterogeneious people live in small, bioregionally oriented, technically efficient, democratic, ecologically sound communities" (1994: 6). Of such "grand proposals," Zimmerman is skeptical and wishes to reconcile radical ecology and the dangers of an environmental totalitarianism.

Zimmerman explores the relationship between postmodernism and deep ecology, social ecology, radical ecology, and eco-feminism, and he recognizes the antipathy between deep ecology and postmodernism, despite their mutual criticism of modernity. While noting that postmodernism and counterculturalism have exchanged some influences, antagonisms remain (Zimmerman 1994: 92): "[P]ostmodern theory fearing that New Paradigm and deep ecology are naively utopian, whereas the latter two accuse postmodern theory of anthropocentrism, ecological ignorance, and nihilism." Deep ecology holds that, in contrast with postmodernity, "this dark side can either be discarded or transformed in a maturation process that will lead to an ecologically sound society" (1994: 91). French postmodern theory turned away from the concerns of Lévi-Strauss and Heidegger's criticism of modernity's impacts on the natural world, while adopting many of their "antihumanist attitudes." Contrasting with conventional views, Zimmerman argues that postmodern theory has influenced deep ecology in several ways and lists the characteristics of postmodernism as critiques of representational reality; representationalist concepts of language; foundational metaphysics; self-grounding, self-present, self-centered, patriarchal, anthropocentric subject; and of 'master' narratives. Although deep ecologists disallow any 'master' narrative along with the postmodernists (under which progress involves dominating the 'other'), they consider that postmodernists only regard the 'other' as human and ignore the non-human. Similarly, while both object to modernity's dualisms, deep ecologists deem that postmodernity goes too far in its quest to eliminate distinctions ('de-differentiate') essential to deep ecology, such as between wild nature and technology or between nature and its representation.

For followers of Baudrillard, the argument would run along the lines that with the invention of ecology, which created a scientific scheme for interpreting the natural world, the first step had been taken in Heidegger's reduction of the world to a 'represented' state for the "technological human subject." With ecology being central to deep ecology's philosophy, nature was removed from a realm of independence and began the process of being taken up in electronic media. Postmodernity's defense, writes

Zimmerman, is that it doesn't seek "de-differentiation," but the pursuit of difference, and that it is modernity that forces the destructive application of universal categories. Postmodernists are here referring to the manner in which modernity effaces cultural differences and marginalizes those who don't fit with its universal categories (that were "abstracted from white, property-owning males"). They are also concerned that deep ecologists' ecocentrism contributes to a 'de-differentiation' that erases human/nonhuman differences and endorses a "totalizing worldview that reflects a problematic yearning for a lost origin or ground" (1994: 98–99). To which deep ecologists responds that ecocentrism seeks not only the interests of deep ecologists.

Zimmerman suggests that many deep ecologists take no account of postmodern critiques of representation, taking for granted their own claims about society and the environment "correctly disclose these phenomena," and this neglect of the role of language in "shaping and defining" experience makes their writings often seem "philosophically naive" (1994: 99). Deep ecologists 'reply' that postmodernity's deconstruction promotes relativism that constrains the search for truths and represents another aspect of modernity, namely that it "amounts to a linguistic idealism that recapitulates modernity's anthropocentirism." And if there is only relativistic anthropocentrism, Zimmerman reasons (1994: 99): "Deep ecologists ask: if everything, including species, is a linguistic construct, on what basis are we to justify preserving species?"

Deep ecology, along with most of environmentalism, has much invested in science. For this reason, its followers only reluctantly concede its social construction, with problems arising when scientific theory changes, especially when reflecting its practitioner's ideologies and interests. Much ecological theory has been underpinned by preconceptions subsequently proved false, such as the belief that ecosystems tended towards 'climax' or 'mature' communities. 'Postmodern' ecologists have suggested that ecosystem succession is without direction and, further, that no 'stability' is ever reached with nature being in constant flux. Traditional views of ecology emphasizing ecosystem order, balance, and cooperation have been replaced by those emphasizing ecosystem disturbance, difference, and competition. Augmenting this change has been the advent of chaos theory, adding further reasoning for departing from explanations featuring regularity and equilibrium. While chaos theory supports the claims of postmodernists about the fallacy of totalizing explanations, there are attendant risks.

Deconstructive postmodernism (à la Derrida) further challenges deep ecology. Derrida holds that all is 'text' in which there is an "endlessly differentiating play of signifiers" and without origin or foundation, there can be no ultimate closure with the 'referent.' Zimmerman (1994: 138) states that Derrida takes from Heidegger the notion of the history of metaphysics posits a stable ("transcendantal") referent which grounds knowledge and experience, but finds Heidegger's search for the "ontological primal" the same as philosophy's search for the transcendental signifier. For deep ecology to make nature as a transcendental signifier, therefore, makes it no different from other metaphysical systems underpinning political beliefs seeking to create universal norms. Derrida argues that Lévi-Strauss's structuralism shares with Heidegger and Rousseau the nostalgia for myths and culture's origins. Deep ecologists agree with Derrida's deconstruction of anthropocentrism, but baulk at its extension to a deconstructed nature, which necessarily undermines ecocentrism. For Derrida, nature would be as any other social construction, so that ecocentrism becomes prey to the same impulse that generates all political quests for totality (i.e., closure with the origin). Derrida denies Heidegger and others holding to beliefs that Ancient Greeks or even traditional societies ever lived in harmony with nature. In this respect, the gap between Derrrida and deep ecology becomes very wide.

Climate change's challenge to modernity

Environmental philosophy and politics can be tested by their relationship with modernity, which roughly hews the discourse into those set against it and those more or less reconciled to reforming modernity from within. Only a small number of environmental thinkers have directly taken up postmodernity as offering a response to the ecological crisis, which necessarily entails interpreting the works of its seminal thinkers, who offered no thoughts on the environmental condition per se. Researchers and scholars of environmental problems concerned with postmodernity, including those interested in constructivism, and those several environmentalist discourses set against modernity, have applied postmodern concepts to the broader conceptualization of these issues in several ways.

Any views based an all-encompassing or universal formulation of nature–society relations, of the causes of ecological change, or any other phenomena are incompatible with postmodern thought following the concepts of Derrida. Gare and Spretnak come close to offering 'universalist' visions in some respects, with the former's view of the spreading environmental crisis and the latter's notion of an all-embracing cosmos. Their views for the future offer and promote relationships with the natural world shaped by its multitudinous variations temporally, spatially, ecologically, and locally. National and international institutions and governments have a tendency to consider environmental issues, especially at large scales, as problems that they are best equipped to resolve. Professionals and others implicated in these metanarratives often have their positions and roles defined in terms of being the designated arbiters of knowledge of the environment and society. Rational science and rational policy have been made essential to the modern state's response to environmental problems. Postmodern thought rejects such singular and authoritarian formulation by claiming that such professionals and their institutions of science and state governance do not possess an exclusive knowledge or authority in interpreting the world.

Challenges to scientific knowledge are critical because of the central role of science in environmental issues and policy responses. Postmodernists insist that scientific knowledge is a social construct, and that there are no single truths about the environment, but a multiplicity of views. State authoritarianism or exclusivity is also inimical to the full representation of the interests of nature and society as a whole.

An immediate political implication of this postmodern view is that the authority and privilege of science is taken as being identical to the interests of societies' centers of power, and that scientific knowledge, corporate influence, and state political power are reciprocally reinforcing. Knowledge vested in indigenous and local peoples has been deemed irrelevant to environmental issues as defined by modern societies who chose to rely on scientific analysis. Postmodern thought challenges scientific knowledge by asserting other forms of knowledge as having equal or greater validity. While this may seemingly invite superstition, pseudo-science, and social prejudice to assume the role of rationality, the alternatives to science simply acknowledge that there are valid competing forms of knowledge that have their own form of empirical support and rationality. Indigenous knowledge of land and biodiversity, for example, have provided more effective responses to issues of biodiversity protection and land restoration than scientific reasoning. Added to this these claims are the politics of scientific knowledge, in which the use of science by states and corporations has produced outcomes coincident with their interests, and with the interests of science's practitioners.

Postmodernists reject the positivism of conventional science, especially its claims of a correspondence between the outcomes of the empirical scientific method and identifying an objective reality. In the place of the objective causal models of environment and society, postmodernism offers subjective accounts of discourse that explicitly derive from actor's perceptions. For environmental management, the co-existence of such different ways of understanding issues creates particular and novel problems for decision-making such as reconciling differing views, of deciding whether truths can be established, of determining criteria to identify efficacious policy choices. Assumptions of clear distinctions between the natural and social world's that underlie conventional depictions of environmental problems have been shown to be increasingly problematic where many natural systems, even those at the global scale, involve human activity. Environmental management, even at global scales, now appears less concerned with determining what to do about the natural world and more with how to manage a system of nature–society relations. These conditions, in sum, have provided environmentalists with a new framing for perceiving environmental problems, complete with both opportunities and new difficulties for this task.

Three basic components of modernity are essential to understanding the climate change issue. As *knowledge*, the response to climate change is based on a scientific understanding of the problem. In developing an appropriate form of action, policies are being developed around the *social organization* of liberal democracy at the international level. And the *social goal* of responding to climate change is to manage the global environment in ways according to human objectives. These elements are, in effect, the *what, how,* and *why* of the international response to climate change.

Scientific knowledge is the basis for progress in the modern era. Here we mean 'modern' science, namely that output of the 'scientific method' as practiced by modern scientists, featuring empirical observations, testable hypotheses, independent verification, and experimental repeatability. Technology is the expression of such knowledge and provides the means for organizing economic activity and addressing social needs, such as providing food, housing, clothing, medicine, transport, education, commerce, manufacture, and so on. Modern life is so interwoven with science and technology that arguably no aspect is free, or could be free, of its involvement or influence. Furthermore, modern life is characterized by the pervasiveness of scientific rationality, a mode of thinking through which society and its institutions are organized, evaluated, and reproduced. A crucial application for science is environmental management.

Although rendered synonymous with modernity by some advocates of liberal democracy, the history of modernity reveals that quite a variety of social organizations are possible under modernity, ranging from planned economies under dictatorships, to capitalist economies under dictatorships, to capitalism under both weak and strong democratic governance. One consistent feature of modernity in this respect has been the dominance of the nation state as the fundamental political unit.

Since the demise of the Cold War, nations with capitalist economies (usually with both private and public enterprise elements, i.e., a 'mixed' economy) and democratic governance through representative government have become the dominant ideological goal of social organization. There is a correspondence between representative national governance and capitalist economies, as evidenced by the composition of the OECD (although a few OECD parties' democratic achievements are arguably relatively recent). However, at this point of history, only liberal democracy enjoys widespread favor as the desirable form of political economy, promoted as the ideal by such bodies as the UN and the World Bank. Therefore, it has become the basic feature of the international policy response to climate change.

As to whether liberal democracy is necessarily modernist or whether capitalism is a precursor to democracy, these remain open questions. Some scholars argue that modernity and liberal democracy are synonymous (e.g., Grey 1986). At this point in history it does appear safe to say that capitalism is an ascendant force, however uneven, faltering, or truncated this has been. Much the same is claimed of democracy (e.g., Dahl 1998), but this is far more contentious, if only because, for some, representative governance as practiced by the developed world fails the test of democracy. History seemingly offers comfort to many divergent views on these points, but if anything is clear, it is the contrast between democracy's relative fragility and capitalism's tenacity, in which the latter has at least occasionally (if not systematically) directed itself against the former.

Global environmental management implies much, but here refers to the unique ecological capacity of human beings to determine global environmental conditions according to pre-determined objectives. Deliberate action is central to this management; it does not refer to the effects of greenhouse gases emissions that are not intended – one hundred and fifty years of historic emissions occurred without a purposive goal. Into this realm we admit those actions to control human activity in order to ensure particular ecological goals; controlling current and future greenhouse gases emissions to avert climate change is clearly global environmental management. Management is the result of the understanding of the world through science and the organization of collective action through social institutions.

3 Climate change science
Modern knowledge of a decreasingly natural world

Scientific knowledge is the basis on which the entire response to the climate change issue rests. Without science, detection of small changes in climate cannot be discerned at scales beyond the local and forecasts of the rate and direction of future changes are impossible. Global data collection, data analysis, and climate modeling are essential in the efforts to gather knowledge about climate processes and to build scenarios of future climate. Identifying future impacts and resultant risks to human and natural systems is a function of contemporary scientific knowledge allied to other social assessments. Put simply, without contemporary science operating on a global scale there would be no recognition of the climate change problem and, hence, no dedicated response.

Environmental issues in the modern era are characterized by the role of scientific knowledge through its factual basis and their organization and integration through ecology, and climate change is unremarkable in this sense. However, the facts of climate change are not as objective, certain, and progressive as conventional accounts assert. Climate change knowledge reflects a range of values, interests, and assumptions and in turn influences the direction, values, interests, and priorities of climate change governance and politics. Capturing the character of the climate change science discourse is far from straightforward; it is a sprawling, multi-disciplinary, and inter-disciplinary exercise without clear boundaries. Public controversy brought climate change science into the realm of the popular media where corporate and environmental interests contested the outputs of scientific institutions. Further, there is its scale of the research programs involved and the complexity of the science itself to add to the burden of explanation.

A history of climate change science

Nineteenth-century foundations

Accounts of terrestrial warming reach back to ancient times, and many speculated as to how human actions could produce such an effect. By the nineteenth century, there was great interest in geological and biophysical changes from earlier times. For example, Agassiz's theory of glaciation gained scientific acceptance by the mid-1860s, although Croll's 1875 *Climate and Time* offered a comprehensive geophysical account of climate change that proved controversial (Gribbin and Gribbin 2001). Despite lively debates over these issues, Victorian science generally believed in global climatic stability, which allowed for gradual oscillations between glacial and non-glacial epochs.

Through the course of the nineteenth century, experimentation and observation eventually identified water vapor and carbon dioxide as the principal gases in the 'greenhouse effect;' notably in Tyndall's 1863 paper. Prominent Swedish scientist Svante Arrhenius (1896) calculated the effect on global temperatures of changes in the concentrations of atmospheric carbon dioxide, leading to his contemporary acclamation as the 'father of the greenhouse effect.' Such claims are, however, somewhat overstated. Arrhenius' research was not directed at understanding the greenhouse effect or motivated by any environmental concern; Fleming (1998) quotes Elisabeth Crawford's biography of Arrhenius and concurs that Arrhenius' contribution was neither especially prophetic nor original. Indeed, Arrhenius (1908) speculated in *Worlds in the Making* that coal combustion would elevate atmospheric carbon dioxide concentrations leading to a favorable global climatic warming. Papers published around the turn of the century by T.C. Chamberlain conjectured that volcanic eruptions and rock weathering were responsible for changes in atmospheric carbon dioxide levels and played a role in the cycles of glaciation (Hart and Victor 1993).

In this, the first phase of modern scientific inquiry into climate change, Arrhenius's theories "made no institutional or intellectual impact on the atmospheric sciences at the time" (Demeritt 2001: 314) or indeed, for the next five decades. Kellogg (1987) notes the trivial energy contribution to planetary energy flows as grounds for complacency over potential anthropogenic climate change and Fleming (1998) quotes C.E.P. Brooks' catalogue of climate change causes that include changes in the earth's orbit, changes in solar radiation, elevation of land masses, changes in ocean circulation, changes in atmospheric circulation, volcanic dust, cosmic dust, sunspots, and polar migration and continental drift.

While it appears that Arrhenius' work lay dormant for many decades, scientific curiously was not inactive in theorizing over climate change. Further, Arrhenius' claim was refuted by conventional science, even in the 1950s by Roger Revelle and Hans Suess, who held that the ocean's absorptive capacity would counter the possibility of increasing atmospheric concentrations of carbon dioxide (see Fleming 1998). As a phenomenon, climate change was deemed essentially geological in its pace, gradual, and, of course, entirely natural.

Twentieth-century threats to climate and the era of global measurement

There arose two camps that were to direct the course of climate change science that worked almost separately for some time: one dealing with the carbon cycle and causes of carbon dioxide increase; the other with atmospheric modeling, which included an interest in the effects of higher carbon dioxide levels on climate (Hart and Victor 1993). Both groups benefited from U.S. military patronage, a fact omitted from nearly all historical accounts of the science.

As Hart and Victor state (1993: 647): "The invention of nuclear weapons appears to have raised the legitimacy of the idea that humans could change the climate, and Federal nuclear programs supported the first institutionalized research on the topic." Scientist von Newman (1955 in Ausbel 1983) linked the threats of climate change and nuclear war as threats to civilization in the 1950s, a theme subsequently taken up by others. During this period (Fleming 1998: 118): "Many people were certain that atmospheric nuclear testing was changing the earth's weather." Nuclear fallout was widely believed to be an agent of climate change and the U.S. Congress Joint Committee on Atomic Energy convened a hearing in 1955 to placate public concern. Fallout research was conducted by U.S. agencies, the Atomic Energy Commission (AEC), the Office of Naval Research (ONR), and Department of Commerce, and while scientists came to dismiss any fallout–climate linkage, this federal support effectively culminated with the two interests being "fused into a coherent greenhouse research program: the carbon cycle and a global atmospheric circulation" (Hart and Victor 1993: 648).

English engineer Guy Callender revived interest in anthropogenic carbon dioxide in warming the climate in the late 1930s onward, establishing the basic theories of global warming based on infrared radiation and carbon dioxide, although the contribution of this meteorological amateur has often been downplayed (Fleming 1998). Callender argued that the bulk of carbon dioxide from fossil fuel combustion remained in the atmosphere. Until the 1970s, carbon cycle research was the domain of oceanography. Research using atmospheric radioactive tracer studies by the U.S. AEC provided a basis for subsequent research by Suess into carbon levels in the ocean (Hart and Victor 1993). In the 1950s, Suess established that a portion of fossil fuel-derived carbon dioxide was being dissolved in the ocean, so that with a portion remaining in the atmosphere, an anthropogenically-enhanced greenhouse effect was possible (Hart and Victor 1993).

Suess and Revelle of the Scripps Institute of Oceanography carried out a more thorough investigation of these ocean atmosphere exchanges (Revelle and Suess 1957) using AEC and ONR funding (Hart and Victor 1993: 648). Many accounts of climate change science place the Revelle and Seuss 1957 article as the turning point in research (as does Revelle (1985) himself) and proclaim Revelle as scientist of almost singular prescience in warning of global warming (see Fleming 1998). However, the article held that the oceans were absorbing most carbon dioxide released since the Industrial Revolution. "Clearly their work was not the dramatic turning point in our awareness of the risk of global warming that later authors perceived it to be" (Fleming 1998: 128). Further, it is from the Revelle and Suess (1957) that the oft-used line derives, namely, that humanity is "conducting a great geophysical experiment," although as Hart and Victor (1993: footnote 31) state: "The rhetoric of the 'geophysical experiment' was not alarmist. Early students of climate change welcomed higher temperatures and considered cooling a 'deterioration' of climate." Fleming similarly rejects elevating the statement to iconic status (which, he suggests, very closely resembled earlier words of Callender and influential researcher Gilbert Pass), in stating (1998: 127): "It was not a clarion call to the dangers of global warming."

At this time, an American chemist, the late Charles Keeling, undertook an individual program of precision measuring of atmospheric carbon dioxide using an instrument of his own invention, enabling an unprecedented degree of accuracy (Christianson 1999). Keeling's sampling of unpolluted airs confirmed Callender's theoretical work of the 1920s and 1930s, which established a theoretical association between rising global temperature and increasing atmospheric carbon dioxide (Christianson 1999). Resolving Revelle and Suess's theoretical proposition required empirical observation of atmospheric carbon dioxide, a task for which Keeling was newly equipped. Collaborative efforts between Keeling and Revelle were instrumental in establishing the first permanent carbon dioxide monitoring at Mauna Loa, Hawaii and at the South Pole in 1957 under the support of the International Geophysical Year (Christianson 1999). Subsequent analysis of the Mauna Loa data confirmed the thesis of rising atmospheric carbon dioxide concentrations and inability of the oceans to quickly absorb this gas. Over the next twenty years, Keeling continued monitoring at Mauna Loa, producing the 'Keeling Curve' of rising carbon dioxide concentrations from 1958 to the present (which Christianson (1999: 167) notes is "arguably the most famous graph in all of Earth science.") Such was the clarity of Keeling's findings that Hart and Victor (1993: 651) quote a 1961 report from the *New York Times* describing the sources of these increasing pollutants.

Monitoring of carbon dioxide and the other greenhouse gases related to human activity now identified is undertaken in a comprehensive global program. Carbon dioxide has been increasing in the atmosphere steadily since the Industrial Revolution when it was around 287 parts per million by volume (ppmv) to its current level of ~375 ppmv (note, it was 315 ppmv in 1958 at the bottom of the Keeling Curve). To put this change onto perspective, carbon dioxide was last at this level in the Pliocene, three million years ago (and *if* stabilized in the future at 500 ppmv, then the most recent precedent is the Eocene climate of 35–57 million years before the present).

Global climate modeling and the global carbon cycle

Mathematical meteorology provided the other major contribution to the development of climate change forecasting, and this too had a foundation in U.S. military support in atmospheric modeling in prominent projects, such as the Geophysical Fluid Dynamics Laboratory (GFDL) (founded in 1955) (Hart and Victor 1993). But as Hart and Victor (1993) describe, because of the costs, modeling research was only conducted at two sites until the late 1970s (GFDL and the National Center for Atmospheric Research) and climate change was a minor theme and largely of 'experimental' interest. Researchers at the GFDL authored a paper in 1961 on the radiative balance of the atmosphere, which led to experiments to model atmospheric carbon dioxide changes and a refined paper in 1963 (Hart and Victor 1993).

Uncovering the workings of the global carbon cycle had to be correlated with a reckoning of global temperatures if the speculations of Arrhenius were to be determined, the latter of which necessitates worldwide meteorological data collection, coordination, assessment, and analysis. International cooperation on meteorological observation increased after WWII with the formation of the World Meteorological Organization (WMO) in 1951, which officially replaced its predecessor, the International Meteorological Organization (Cain 1983).

Technological innovation in this period extended the realms of meteorological knowledge, reflecting increasing demands for its applications in the era of jet aviation and nuclear bomb development. Through the late 1950s and 1960s, the International Geophysical Year (in 1957), the World Weather Watch (started in 1968), and the Global Atmospheric Research Program (a 1967 initiative) marked advances in the global collection, sharing, processing, and distribution of climate data. Although directed at meeting increasingly globalized demands for weather forecasting, these advances enabled more rigorous and creative investigations into global climate. Paterson (1996) notes that these 'early' developments in the science and early international meteorological cooperation were "necessary preconditions" for global warming to become a political issue in the 1980s.

During the 1960s there was "a broad discursive shift in the general understanding of climate as a problem" (Paterson 1996: 24), when an interest in how humans might alter climate to their advantage was overtaken by inquiries as to whether such a change was already under way in an uncontrolled fashion. In 1965, the U.S. President's Science Advisory Committee noted that human activities on global climate could be environmentally harmful (the first official recognition, according to Agrawala 1998a). Kellogg (1987: 119) writes that, of this period "a handful of scientists on both sides of the Atlantic were beginning to develop a physical theory to explain the behavior of the complex system that determines climate." However, Hart and Victor (1993: 657) note of the Committee's report (whose atmosphere chapter was penned by Revelle): "It seems to have made little substantive impression on policymakers."

Against the usual historical narrative of steady progress, the mid-1960s were not highly productive. Despite all the basic elements for a theory of anthropocentric global warming being in place, there was simply little institutional or elite interest in the problem of global warming. For example, Keeling's carbon dioxide monitoring program struggled for funding (Hart and Victor 1993). Hart and Victor discount claims that skepticism over the greenhouse effect prompted cautious progress, rather they note the strong support of the concept by reknown climate researchers Roger Revelle and Bert Bolin. As Hart and Victor (1993: 653) state: "Like carbon-cycle researchers, atmospheric modelers adopted the view of the greenhouse effect as a geophysical experiment." Atmospheric modelers ignored available carbon cycle information that would have proved critical to understanding climate change, because their interest lay in climate equilibria – indeed, it was not until after 1965 that the U.S. atmospheric modelers and carbon cycle researchers joined forces (Hart and Victor 1993).

Climate as an environment issue

While much of the scientific understanding of the greenhouse effect was established, the general tide of environmentalism of the late 1960s did much to carry the issue forward. Against the backdrop of waning military funding, general environmental concerns, and specific issues prompted greater support for climate change research. A specific concern was the possible climate effects of possible supersonic air travel (Hart and Victor 1993). Further discoveries of the radiative properties of the chloroflurocarbons and sulfate aerosols brought atmospheric chemists more strongly into atmospheric modeling activity (Demeritt 2001). Although meteorologists came to consider atmospheric pollutants as possible determinants of weather, it took two reports from 'outside' the established institutions with approaches that were interdisciplinary and openly environmentalist in intent.

Cain (1983), Kellogg (1987), and other commentators identify two studies in 1970 and 1971 as re-shaping the attitudes towards global climate: *Man's Impact on the Global Climate: Report of the Study of Critical Environmental Problems* (SCEP 1970) and the *Study on Man's Impact on the Climate* (SMIC 1971). In the former study, the problem was considered of low likelihood but of large consequences, while the latter, the output of a conference, became the major background paper on climate change issues at the 1972 UN Conference on the Human Environment (Paterson 1996). Uncertainty was high in the SMIC study; atmospheric aerosols released as a consequence of human activity might counter or outweigh the potential warming due to enhanced carbon dioxide levels – the authors recommended the issue of scientific uncertainty be addressed by further data collection and theoretical developments (SMIC 1971). "Neither SCEP nor SMIC was technically novel" Hart and Victor (1993: 662) concluded.

One result of the 1972 UN Conference was the elevation of climate to the status of an international issue. Cain (1983) suggests that one manifestation was the series of climate-related UN conferences in the 1970s, including the 1974 World Food Conference, 1976 Water Conference, and the 1977 Desertification Conference. Meteorological research underwent a change in this period, broadening the scope of its interests from that of weather to embrace questions of climate and climatic change. A conference organized by Global Atmosphere Research Program in 1974 and a WMO experts' workshop in 1976 extended the state of knowledge slightly (Paterson 1996), but perhaps more importantly, established the possibility of greenhouse-enhanced climate change as an issue of legitimate concern. Another Stockholm outcome were new funding opportunities for climate change research. Extreme weather events in the early 1970s extending from Peru to the Soviet Union caught wide attention. U.S. Secretary of State Henry Kissinger addressed the UN General Assembly in 1974 on the need for greater international research into such disasters, which the U.S. was willing to lead (Hart and Victor 1993). This new momentum in climate change research reflected these factors, in which actual scientific advances played virtually no role.

Theories that tropospheric accumulation of aerosols and particles from human sources could act to cool that part of the atmosphere were rejected at a 1975 WMO International Symposium on Long-Term Climate fluctuations, adding support for carbon dioxide to exert a warming influence on the atmosphere. Later in the decade further scientific developments added credence to the global warming theories, particularly the improved global circulation models utilizing increased observational data. Studies by the U.S. National Academy of Sciences in 1975, 1977, and 1979 finally concluded that there was little reason to doubt the calculations that doubling of carbon dioxide would lead to a 1.5–4.5°C global temperature warming in the twenty-first century (Paterson 1996). Increased monitoring of carbon dioxide occurred in response to WMO wishes in 1977, as part of a set of directives that also led to establishing a broader climate research program.

Around this time, contrary speculations on future climate arose. Theories that the climate was exhibiting signs of a global cooling were popular in the 1970s – there was talk of another Ice Age, rather than of global warming (e.g., Calder 1974; Ponte 1976; Gribbin 1976; Halacy 1978; Bryson and Murray 1977; and SMIC 1971). Global temperatures did cool some 0.25°C between 1940 and 1970, contrary to the correlation of rising temperatures and rising carbon dioxide as widely believed, and giving rise to theories of cooling based on accumulating atmospheric aerosols. As Demeritt (2001: 315) notes: "Scientific evidence for these fears came primarily not from the theoretical and physics-based atmospheric sciences, but from the empirical-descriptive traditions of glacial geology and cognitive disciplines concerned with the changing history of the earth's climate." Ross (1991) suggests that it was the public prospect of another Ice Age that first generated widespread interest in the subject of climate change.

Adherence to such beliefs in mainstream science was relatively short-lived, refuted partially by empirical evidence of a contemporary warming trend. While these cooling theories doubtless drew greater community attention to climate issues, much skepticism and doubt greeted the theories of global warming, which came on the heels of the concerns over an imminent ice age. That some of the proponents of the cooling theories appeared as global warming advocates fueled public doubts over the possibilities of catastrophic warming. However, Kellogg (1978: 205) began a 1978 article on global climate thus: "Whether mankind has the *capability* of altering the climate of the earth is no longer a debatable topic." Debate, however, was not yet over. During the next two decades identifying and quantifying land-based sources and sinks of greenhouse gases was to prove one of the most testing aspects of the science and one with great policy implications.

Concern over climate change formed one of the reasons for holding the First World Climate Conference in Geneva in early 1979, primarily under the auspices of the WMO, and organized by prominent scientists and government officials from the U.S. and Europe (Agrawala 1998a). Although guarded, the Conference Declaration expressed a belief that global warming due to increasing amounts of carbon dioxide was likely, although future impacts were poorly understood. Consequently, later in 1979, the WMO established the first international program of research into climate, the World Climate Programme. And although the Conference offered no climate change policy recommendations, it was instrumental in fostering several conferences on the issue in Villach, Austria in 1980, 1983, and 1985, and Bellagio, Italy in 1987.

Knowledge as advocacy

By the early 1980s several works had already appeared urging a political response to climate change, such as Tickell's (1977) *Climatic Change and World Affairs*, Schneider's (1976) *The Genesis Strategy*, and Lovins et al.'s (1981) *Least-Cost Energy: Solving the CO_2 Problem*. These accounts, as indeed is part of the Villach Conference outputs, are not restricted to issues normally classified as 'science,' but extend into policy advocacy. Although Brenton suggests (1994: 165): "At this stage, even after the Villach and Bellagio meetings, the climate issue was still scientific rather than private property," at least part of the scientific discourse has an unambiguously political character.

Bolin (1994), Hecht and Tirpak (1995), and others refer to a paper by Ramanathan et al. (1985) that identified the potential greenhouse contributions from non-carbon dioxide greenhouse gases. This significant finding made the climate change issue was more pressing than previously thought (Bolin 1994: 26): "The radiative forcing of the atmosphere, corresponding to doubling of the CO_2 concentration, was anticipated by about 2030 rather than during the latter part of the century." As Hecht and Tirpak state (1995: 380), this development "accelerated interest in the need for policy actions." Subsequently, this advance became part of an assessment conducted by Bolin and others and supported by UNEP and WHO, published as Bolin et al. (1986), and presented at Villach in 1985 (Bolin 1994).

Outcomes from the 1985 Villach conference became pivotal in the future direction of greenhouse science. Villach offered a science program designed to meet an anticipated political need for any scientifically-based policy response to climate change. Scientific advances in the preceding decade underlay the 1985 Villach conclusions: atmospheric modeling had advanced, and the radiative properties of other anthropogenic gases had been assessed and incorporated into the climate models. Entitled the 'International Conference on the Assessment of the Role of Carbon Dioxide and other Greenhouse Gases in Climate Variations and Associated Impacts,' it aimed to establish the state of knowledge on climate change, to form a consensus on the warming capacity of the different greenhouse gases, and to forecast possible future global warming resulting from the effect of these gases (WMO 1985).

Villach's findings were more confident than the World Climate Conference; the participants (scientists attending in a personal capacity) reached a consensus that contemporary experiments showed global mean temperature would increase by 1.5–4.5°C for a doubling of atmospheric carbon dioxide (or equivalent) (WMO 1985). Other important findings included that temperature rises in first half of next century could cause a mean rise greater than any in human history, could cause sea levels one meter higher, and that greenhouse gases other than carbon dioxide will also contribute to global warming. Critically, the Villach/Bellagio meetings suggested the use of an international treaty to reduce the rate of greenhouse gas production to slow the expected rate of global warming.

Responding to a range of atmospheric issues (most prominently climate change, acid rain, and ozone depletion), the Toronto 1988 Conference 'The Changing Atmosphere: Implications for Global Security' invited politicians, government officials, NGOs, and scientists. Although the attendance was not as high-level as later climate change conferences, as Brenton (1994: 166) states that "the conclusions on climate change (which were of course not binding on governments) were eye-catching." Global carbon dioxide emissions were to be cut 20 percent from their 1988 levels by 2005, deforestation curbed, and a World Atmosphere Fund established using fossil fuel levies in developed nations. Both the concepts for policy action and the timing of their release proved highly influential.

Organizing global science in a warmer world

Dominance of the global warming theory within the greater scientific community occurred in the 1980s and its popular acceptance was doubtless aided by the global prevalence of unusual weather events in that decade. During this time, the trend of global warming was unequivocal: 1987 becomes the warmest year on record, with the decade of the 1980s on its way to being the warmest on record, containing seven of the eight warmest years on record. Climate made the headlines of the world's papers: the globally hottest years on record, the effects of the strong 1982/83 El Nino/ Southern Oscillation, a 1987 freak hurricane in the English Channel, the separation of a particularly large piece of the Antarctic ice shelf, a severe U.S. drought, a devastating Bangladesh flood in 1988, and other events. Scientists connecting these events to global warming were widely publicized and criticized, but the connections met with great public interest (Ross 1991).

Something of a coalescence of research and policy attention emerges in this period (see Brenton 1994, Kellogg 1987). Outcomes from the 1990 Second World Climate Conference reinforced those of the first world conference in 1979. In the U.S., the National Research Council (NRC) (1983) and the U.S. Environmental Protection Agency (EPA) (EPA 1983) produced major studies of climate change. Interest in atmospheric protection produced the UN Montreal Protocol on Substances that Deplete the Ozone Layer in 1985 (for the protection of stratospheric ozone). NASA climate scientist James Hansen's testimony to the U.S. Senate Energy and Natural Resources Committee in 1988 that he was "99 percent sure" that global warming was occurring as a result of anthropogenic greenhouse gas releases (Hansen 1988) drew media and public attention (and appears in many accounts of climate change as being a pivotal event), especially his remark that it was "time to stop waffling so much and say the evidence is pretty strong that the greenhouse effect is here." Empirical research by Hansen and others (e.g., Hansen et al. 1981) indicated a global warming trend, confirmed by subsequent monitoring reportage (e.g., Jones et al. 1988).

When, also in 1988, the Intergovernmental Panel on Climate Change (IPCC) was formed, it became from this time onwards the main interface between climate change scientists and the general public and is the preeminent authority ("hegemonic" to quote Agrawala 1998a) on climate change science. With the formation of the IPCC, climate change receives a further impetus and a great scientific enterprise emerges. New climate change research programs are initiated by international organizations, by OECD and some non-OECD national governments, together with those under various research and educational institutions. A major institutional development was the creation of the U.S. Global Change Research Program (GCRP) in 1989, one of the largest science projects ever funded by the U.S. Congress. Pielke (2000a) reports that the Program had received over

US$16.5b by the year 2000. Through this period, the basic tool of climate change science, the general circulation model, underwent considerable development and refinement.

Findings of the first assessment report on climate change science by the IPCC in 1990 concluded that global warming has taken place and UN negotiations on the FCCC draw upon, and indeed are premised upon, the IPCC report. Scientific activity through the 1990s saw a great deepening and broadening of knowledge that had a robust core; none of the major principles or findings of the first IPCC assessment report on science were overturned. Refinement and increasing sophistication of the general circulation models, together with improved resolution of the warming potential of the major greenhouse gases and representation of more complex ocean-atmosphere phenomena enabled the production of global warming scenarios of greater confidence and finer spatial resolution.

Portending climatic catastrophe

At the time of the formation of the IPCC, some basic uncertainties about the carbon cycle and global temperature existed: the 'missing' part of the carbon cycle, the effect of aerosol masking, finer resolution of the global warming potentials of individual greenhouse gases, and the effect of various potential feedback effects, such as cloud formation under the enhanced greenhouse effect. In addition to the 'routine' task of resolving these cutting-edge problems, continued examination of historic and paleoclimate data altered the basic conception of the character of climate change.

Climatic evidence from sources such as ice cores, sediment analyses from the sea floor and lakebeds, and tree rings reflected a basic instability in the global climate system with data confirming unexpected and abrupt changes in global climate (see, e.g., Dansgaard et al. 1989). Rather than gradually sliding between glacial and inter-glacial states according to the dictates of the Milankovitch cycles (generated by variations in the earth's orbital effects) and other factors, it appeared that climatic epochs could begin and finish with astonishing speed, and that during glacial periods climate changed frequently and quickly. Instead of climate change taking tens of millennia or longer, local sites have experienced changes of up to $10^{0}C$ over decades or years (NRC 2001). Although persistent for over a century, the belief in the basic stability of the climate system was laid to rest. Such a re-evaluation prompted closer attention to the influences of abrupt climate change on human history, especially on the effects of catastrophic demises of favorable conditions, such as the Younger Dryas (11, 600 years bp) and the so-called 'Little Ice Age' of medieval Europe.

In effect, these developments revived interest in earlier aspects of climate change, namely the identification of causal factors in climate change. Prominent in this research agenda was the investigation of links between atmospheric conditions and 'drivers' of global climate, especially ocean-atmosphere interactions. Research has been directed towards those dynamic phenomena central to global climate activity whose persistence has been called into question, notably the thermohaline and the 'northern conveyor belt,' (see, e.g., Broecker 1987, 1997 and Broecker et al. 1985). Rapid changes in the earth's carbon dioxide levels appear attributable to modifications to ocean circulations, yet the last 10,000 years have been a period of stable and warm global climate, prompting the question of whether rises in greenhouse gases will change the ocean-atmospheric system from its existing mode. Broecker (1987: 123), whose research on ocean currents has been seminal in this debate, likened humanity's position to playing "Russian roulette with climate." While the IPCC had duly acknowledged the possibility of climate 'surprises' under global warming, to which the portend of possible rapid shifts in ocean-atmosphere phenomena gave substance, the notion of 'dangerous interference in the climate system' presaged risk-taking of a greater magnitude than previously envisaged.

Indices of a warming world and of atmospheric enrichment by carbon dioxide were identified in the scientific research journals with increasing frequency across the realm of the natural sciences, from thinning of polar ice and retreating glaciers, coral reef bleaching, shifting ranges and changing abundance of certain species, to effects on vegetative and animal growth and activity (see, e.g., the literature reviews in IPCC 1996b and 2000b). Investigations into a wide variety of biological phenomena revealed the effects of warming trends across the globe and in many ecosystems.

Record-breaking global temperatures become the norm during the 1990s, slowed only by the effects of the 1991 volcanic explosion of the Philippines' Mt. Pinatubo. By the decade's end, it had become the hottest on record, with the 1998 the hottest year. In its most recent assessment report, the IPCC (2001a) stated that the 1990s were highly likely to be the warmest decade since the 1860s and in the northern hemisphere, the warmest for the last 1000 years. As reported by the WMO, 2001 became the second warmest year for 140 years and, including 2001, eight of the ten warmest years of the last 40 years occurred since 1990 (Waple et al. 2002: 1). This warming was of the general magnitude forecast by the climate models of the late 1980s and early 1990s. Additional to atmospheric warming, studies reported in *Science* (Levitus et al. 2000, 2001, Barnett et al. 2001) showed that rising ocean temperatures replicated model forecasts, with Hansen et al. (2005) empirically confirming the warming hypothesis based on the earth's energy budget, adding further confidence to the case for anthropogenic global warming.

Contemporary climate change science has resolved many of the uncertainties that persisted about global climate since classical times. Using the IPCC's third assessment report series (2001a, 2001b, and 2001c) the following claims can be made with high confidence. Firstly, global surface temperatures have increased noticeably, by about 0.6°C, over the twentieth century and precipitation has increased in the mid–high latitudes (including more heavy rainfall), with less rainfall in the sub-tropics. Snow and ice cover has diminished across most of the world and sea level, globally averaged, rose 10–20 cm during the last century. There are no significant changes in the frequency of extreme weather events. All the principle greenhouse gases have increased since the Industrial Revolution, but their warming effect on the global climate has been partially offset by the influence of stratospheric aerosols associated with sulfur dioxide emissions. Ecologically, there is abundant evidence of a warming world, with a large number of studies providing evidence of its effects on individuals and communities of plants and animals (IPCC 2001c), and studies detecting the 'fingerprint' of global warming across these studies of species density, location, phenology, morphology, and genetics (Parmesan and Yohe 2003, Root et al. 2003, Thomas et al. 2004, and Walther et al. 2002).

Global climate models and scenarios of future climate

Understanding how the global climate system works and monitoring its changes comprise only part of the mission of climate change science, for these elements are essential to the task of building a predictive capacity to forecast the rate, magnitude, and direction of future climate change. Without this capacity, climate change would occupy only a minor role in climate change politics and the formulation of an international policy response. International climate change policies and their attendant politics rest atop climate research as represented by the outputs of models of the global climate and the scenarios of future climate they produce. And since the estimation of climate change impacts has been based on scenarios of future climate, nearly all the research into potential impacts of climate change has relied on climate model outputs, as have the early efforts at adaptation policy.

Building this understanding of the greenhouse effect was the culmination of a long, varied, and interactive process between changes in the environmental world and the evolution of knowledge, involving rising global temperatures, increasing greenhouse gases, terrestrial climatic and greenhouse gas monitoring, determining the radiative properties of these gases, and models of the earth's heat budget and global carbon cycle. Integral in developing contemporary scientific understanding of climate change has been the need to understand the interactions between great numbers of variables and enormous quantities of data that comprise global climate models (which share an acronym with its major form, that of general circulation models), which depended greatly on the continued development of the computer (McGuffie and Henderson-Sellers 1997: 4): "Without the recent growth in computational power and the reduction in computing costs most of the developments in computer modeling which have taken place over the last three decades could not have happened."

Global climate models represent a major achievement in the physical sciences and posses immense complexity; some 25–30 person-years are required to code a single full atmospheric global climate model (McGuffie and Henderson-Sellers 1997: 4). Supercomputer runs of several hundred hours can be required for single experiments. By necessity, these models have been developed in large research institutions, after which the major models are known. Major models include those of the GFDL, National Center for Atmospheric Research, Goddard Institute of Space Studies, Hadley Center, and the Max Planck Institute. These groups, amongst others, produce these models for use in various applications and produce the results for the IPCC process.

Climate models are derived from weather forecasting models, using similar representations of atmospheric phenomena in physical and chemical derivations, but necessarily dealing with greater time periods and complicating factors. These models incorporate the major global climate variables in the relevant physical, chemical, and biological parameters, including ocean currents, ice cover, and atmospheric effects. Ocean processes must be included in climate models, whereas weather models can employ fairly simple renditions of ocean surface temperatures. Computational demands are also far higher for global climate models that for weather models, which necessitates operating the models at a coarser scale than weather models and making the time intervals far longer. Grid size in a weather model will typically represent tens of kilometers and a climate model grid will typically be of several hundred kilometers a side and of around ten atmospheric vertical layers. Each grid cell represents several thousand square kilometers, which restricts the type and size of climatic phenomena that can be reproduced. Global temperature changes can be accounted for, but regional and local changes are within the grid scale of the models. One technique to produce scenarios at these finer scales is through 'nested models,' in which finer grid scales are embedded in the lager grid cells and driven by the larger model. Notwithstanding these advances, some phenomena remain difficult to represent in global climate models, such as clouds.

Global climate models are used to generate scenarios of different climate in response to greenhouse gas emissions scenarios. Much has been made of what to name these prognostications; many climate scientists have rejected the label of 'forecasts,' while others consider that any description of the future is a forecast. Wigley (2001: 13) calls a scenario "a plausible picture of the future that, in this case, defines future emissions for a range of gasses," which is derived from a set of socioeconomic scenarios of socioeconomic variables. Scientific depictions of global warming necessarily and unavoidably mix recorded data of past events with speculative data of future human activity that is expected to give rise to particular levels of greenhouse gas emissions and other related decisions.

International attention has focussed on the model results produced by the IPCC, especially the scenarios of future warming. Despite great public attention and controversy over the IPCC's scenarios, the values of these increases has been quite stable through the three rounds of IPCC assessments, namely a global average warming in the vicinity of 1.5–4.5°C when the carbon dioxide concentrations are double their pre-Industrial Revolution levels. (It should be noted that the warming range is just that and there are no probabilities determined within this range.) Each scenario is driven by models of the socio-economic influences on greenhouse gas emissions. Six scenarios were used, known collectively as 92a-f. Of these scenarios, IS92a represents the Business-as-Usual case, based on an economic growth rate of 1.68 percent per annum. At either end of the range are the high emissions case (IS92c based on a 0.56 percent economic growth rate) and the low rate (IS92e based on a 2.39 percent rate). However, all these scenarios are basically versions of the BAU case. New IPCC scenarios supersede the six IPCC IS92 scenarios from 1992, grouped into four 'storylines' (IPCC 2000a). These new scenarios incorporate projections of declining sulfur dioxide emissions, which reduce the atmospheric concentrations and allow greater radiative forcing and therefore increased warming. More recent research has suggested that warming will be at or exceed the IPCC's upper forecasts following revisions to the effects of declining atmospheric aerosols (Andreae et al. 2005).

IPCC's (2001a) third assessment report provided scenarios of future greenhouse gases that without intervention, showed carbon dioxide concentrations rising to 540–970 ppmv by 2100 and producing a global average warming of 1.4–5.8°C (which would be the greatest rate of warming for 10,000 years). Such a warming would be concentrated in the northern high latitudes in winter. Sea level rise would be 9–88 cm. Although the emissions scenarios produce differing warming forecasts over the next century, for the next few decades, all the IPCC scenarios for climate warming and sea level rise are effectively identical.

Institutional science: the Intergovernmental Panel on Climate Change

When the WMO and the United Nations Environment Programme established the IPCC, whose membership is open to all WMO and UNEP member countries, it was described thus (IPCC 1998):

> The role of the IPCC is to assess on a comprehensive, objective, open and transparent basis the scientific, technical and socio-economic information relevant to understanding the scientific basis of risk of human-induced climate change, its potential impacts and options for adaptation and mitigation. IPCC reports should be neutral with respect to policy, although they may need to deal objectively with scientific, technical and socio-economic factors relevant to the application of particular policies.

Direction is provided through the Secretariat and its Bureau, with a staff of around 50, which is institutionally located within the WMO in Geneva.

Meeting approximately once a year, the IPCC's major activities involves releasing IPCC reports, determining the organization's work plans, the structure and outline of reports, as well as organizational matters, such as the election of the Chairman and Bureau, setting principles and procedures, and tending to the budget. A task force oversees the National Greenhouse Gas Inventory Programme.

While the IPCC serves as an organizing agent for climate change research, generally it does not produce its own research for the major assessments. Research centers, universities, and government science bodies produce most of the research on climate change, generally independently of the IPCC. An important exception is the production of the emission scenarios that underlie the global climate model projections, which are in response to IPCC needs. National public funding provides the bulk of the financial support for research used by the IPCC. A great deal of research, especially that in the early stages of the IPCC, was not the result of new initiatives directed at the climate change problem, but was drawn from existing research activity. Indeed, much of the participation of researchers in the IPCC review processes hasn't been funded and the participation of many researchers has been voluntary. Despite the size of the largest national and international programs on climate change, it is largely unrecognized that a considerable amount of research activity has occurred without direct financial support.

Climate change science is a collection of findings drawn from many disciplines and places and isn't project-based, such as the U.S. government's response to cancer, the Manhattan Project, or the space missions. Although the research is a response to a policy problem, it combines the full range of research, from monitoring, model-building, basic process research, through to the variety of impacts, and then to mitigation and adaptation measures. Overall, this is a sprawling, complex, and differentiated type of research effort, one capable of great dynamism, creativity, and flexibility, but which has simultaneously focussed its greatest efforts on resolving a relatively small number of uncertainties in order to improve the performance of the global climate models.

IPCC divides climate change science and technical issues into three components for its major assessments, each handled by a working group: climate change science, impacts of climate change, and economic and social issues. Three assessments have been produced so far (1990, 1996, and 2001), with the fourth scheduled for 2007. Working groups two and three have had their thematic responsibilities altered between assessments; in 1992, Working Group III gained the so-called 'cross-cutting issues' of emission scenarios, integrated assessments, decision-making, and a selection of social issues, but for the third assessment round, the arrangements returned to something closer to the original configurations. A number of IPCC Special Reports, Methodological Reports, and Technical Papers have also been produced (e.g., IPCC 1992, 1994, 1997a, 1997b, 2001a, and 2001b) as a way to deal with particular issues, especially the need to update emission scenarios in light of new information (IPCC 1994, 2001a) and to resolve persistent problems with quantifying carbon sinks (IPCC 2001b).

Each assessment report comprises a full report and a policy-maker summary, and the work of between one and around a dozen lead authors for each chapter, nearly all of whom are internationally-recognized scientists in their fields. As to their selection, Shackley notes (1997: 77): "Although formally nominated by national governments, the selection of the LAs [lead authors] is heavily influenced by the coterie of scientists and policy makers who in practice constitute the active core of the IPCC."

Whilst experts review the chapters of the main reports, government representatives approve the summaries line-by-line. Considerable effort goes into these processes. Agrawala (1998b: 624) reports that the 1995 Working Group II second assessment report was reviewed twice, beginning with 20–60 reviewers per chapter, totaling 700 experts from 58 countries, and then with all IPCC member governments and those reviewers who contributed in the first round. Lead authors determine the final contents of the main reports. While Working Group I, and much of Working Group II, are concerned with the physical sciences, Working Group III has been predominantly concerned with economic inquiry. Some caution is therefore needed in describing 'the science of the IPCC,' because many of the comments and commentaries on the IPCC tend to describe its activities as if all were 'natural sciences,' when this is not the case.

IPCC processes are quite open to NGOs and outside observers during peer review and consultation processes in plenary sessions and workshops. National delegations can be quite influential during the drafting of assessment text and nations, such as Saudi Arabia and Kuwait who have been openly critical of IPCC findings during such sessions. However, the IPCC has used this aspect of its processes to create "a continuing forum for mutual understanding and learning between scientists and policy makers in a stable and trustworthy context" (Shackley 1997: 78).

An innovation in the third assessment report was the Synthesis Report (IPCC 2001d), which more explicitly addressed policy questions than the usual three-volume assessment reports and their summaries. Several issues raised in the Synthesis Report are of great importance. Firstly, the finding that stabilizing greenhouse gas emissions at a level around that of present will never result in stabilization of atmospheric greenhouse gas concentrations. Stabilization of atmospheric greenhouse gas concentrations requires substantial emissions reductions. Secondly, after stabilization of atmospheric concentrations is achieved, therefore, climatic equilibrium will take several hundred years. If stabilization occurs at twice the pre-industrial level (550 carbon dioxide ppmv), average global temperatures will find equilibrium at 2–5°C higher than present, at which the likelihood of harmful change cannot be avoided. Holding concentrations at 450 ppmv, for example, requires significant emissions abatement and critically, must be achieved within the next few decades. By implication, the absence of such abatement commits the globe to high levels of warming and the possibility of having set train global climatic changes of great significance.

IPCC assessments have improved since the first. During the first assessment, Working Group I outputs were unavailable to Working Group II, making the latter's effort thin in detail and broadly descriptive. Subsequent Working Group II full assessment reports better reflected the depth of research conducted in the field and contained the results from modeling using global climate models outputs of future climate scenarios. Forecasts from Working Group I have varied between assessments, but skeptics exaggerated these differences: the basic findings of Working Group I have been broadly consistent from 1992 through to 2001.

Climate change science and modernity

Modernity is indivisible from the discourse of science; science shapes and enables modern society and is a marker that distinguishes the pre-modern from the modern (Thiele 1997: 69): "Modernity largely developed in the Western world owing to the growing power of science." Science is held as a special knowledge in modernity and holds the status of a 'meta-myth.' Positive science holds that reliance on empiricism – observation, experimentation, and independent replication of results – separates science from pre-modern forms of knowledge, such as religion, magic, and astrology. Pre-modern knowledge systems, by contrast, are grounded in metaphysics or religious creeds, notions of authority and faith that were subsequently overthrown by the rise of science in modern societies.

Under a structural view, science provides a form of knowledge through reasoning that is both universal and stable. Its most ardent supporters hold that scientific rationality is inherently superior to alternative forms of reasoning and experience. In this manner, the 'Scientific Revolution' refers not merely to a wave of technological innovation and discoveries, but to a novel way of understanding and interpreting all that may be perceived. Thiele offered (1997: 71):

> Modernism was grounded in the assumption that that the order of the universe is natural, accessible to reason and observation, and describable in impersonal, materialistic, mechanical, and mathematical terms. ... For the last four centuries, modernism has flourished in the power accumulated through scientific knowledge and technical engineering. With this in mind, we might say that the first characteristic of modernity is scientism, that is, a belief in the preeminent power and prerogatives of science.

Belief in science, however, may be faltering. Pubic skepticism is mounting, evidenced by such phenomena as the rise of 'anti-science' movements in aspects of postmodernism, resurgent mysticism, and New Age beliefs. Winner (1977) analyzed the fear of autonomous technology, wherein technology deterministically exceeds any human capacity to limit its reach, control its effects, or ensure its efficacious use. German social theorist Ulrich Beck (see, e.g., 1992, 1995, and 1997) has described how science creates problems for which it has no solutions. Science's lack of public accountability, its allegiances to elite interests and corporations, and its inconsistent responsibilities towards social and ecological values have all proved fertile sources for questioning science, not only over its methods and outputs, but as a social enterprise.

In the twentieth century, science was deeply mistrusted on two fronts: the applications of technology to warfare (expressed most strongly about WWI and later over atomic weapons) and by environmentalism. For example, Carson's (1962) *Silent Spring* publicized the ecological destructiveness and social risks of synthetic pesticides and is frequently held as heralding the environmental movement. Commoner's (1966) *Science and Survival* placed environmental destruction and the risks of nuclear annihilation as both consequences of unchecked science. Later, Sagan and Turco's *A Path No Man Thought* (1990) and Sagan (1983) highlighted the risk of a cataclysmic 'nuclear winter' in the wake of an international conflict using nuclear weapons. Such complaints were essentially pleas for science to be socially responsible, and explicitly so. From such pioneering works, environmentalism has flowered and diversified, but retaining much its core critique of science.

Climate science has been placed in a frame of rational policy formulation where science is linked to policy: knowledge gaps are identified, scientific programs are devised to meet this need, uncertainties are resolved, and policy-makers proceed with policy-making suitably equipped with appropriate knowledge. Institutions have been created for this role and public funding allocated. Under the guiding premise of this model, global change is best understood through identifying and analyzing natural and social causal factors, integrating these inputs in large-scale models, and using these outputs for policy creation (Jasanoff and Wynne 1998: 2). Accordingly, global biophysical systems are studied by natural sciences, while social scientists examine social forces giving rise to these environmental problems.

This model, however, has failed in many ways. As Jasanoff and Wynne (1998: 2) state: "The scale, complexity, and interconnectedness of the causes of climate change – and the fundamental links between climate change and other global changes – tested science's incremental and discipline-based approaches to investigating nature." Consequently, the ability of the model to assist institutions in formulating effective policy responses at international, national, and sub-national levels is in doubt through the failure of the approach to deal with the "contested, open-ended, and geographically dispersed" character of climate change. Further to these challenges is the erosion of the positive model of science, which is how conventional analyses characterize climate change science. Views that science reflects a range of values and interests and that its outcomes are not 'objective,' but ultimately the negotiated outcomes of a social practice is at odds with the conventional view of climate change research. Science is thus considered as a political process that is both shaped and shapes, social action. Several studies have examined the ways in climate change research has been influenced by its social setting, of the effect of those influences on scientific practices and results, and of how scientific findings are used to reflect the political circumstances of climate change policy-makers.

Positive science and ecological modernization

Science conventionally presents itself as neutral and independent (operating in the world of 'facts'), whose task is to inform an equally independent world of decision makers, who operate in the realm of 'values.' Vannevar Bush (1945) famously described these as the distinctions between science based either in research or development. (Sometimes characterized as 'speaking truth to power.') Other labels have been applied to this cleavage, such as *pure* vs. *applied* and *needs-driven* vs. *opportunity-driven* (Jasanoff and Wynne 1998: 7). Common to this nomenclature of bifurcated science is the differentiation between the impartiality of a science untainted by political influence and its opposite.

Whatever the theoretical appeal of this ordering, it was long apparent to scientific practitioners and policy-makers that mutual exclusivity of influences was honored more in the breach than in observance. One well-known development to this 'independent spheres' model is Alvin Weinberg's zone of overlap, 'trans-science,' in which social questions asked of science cannot yield 'scientific' answers (1972 in Jasanoff and Wynne 1998: 7). Trans-science contains the concession that science is not without political power and nor is politics without 'truths' of its own. Pure science is not disrupted by policy in this concept, but the concession for the need for science to respond to social influences is made. Decisions about science are acknowledged as being shaped by policy needs, with the result that scientific authority is bestowed on policy decisions. Such a conception has deep social implications, for within the realm of trans-science lies a series of social questions deemed amenable to scientific resolution over which the two interests vie. Notions of trans-science seem also to apply to quite a broad array of accounts of the climate change issue, including those concerned explicitly with its political dimensions, which are content to accept the findings of climate change as objective research.

Helpful as this notion of a hybrid science might be, there appears to be a constant force to retain the concept of science as essentially beyond the social domain (and to simply treat trans-science as science) and for science to retain its role as the interpreter of nature and thereby remain the exclusive arbiter of truth. Both science and policy interests have a mutual benefit in the legitimacy conferred on the appearance of mutual exclusivity, wherein activity in the co-production of knowledge is effectively denied, a tendency that social studies of science have attempted to describe and discredit.

One perspective of climate change science that draws on the positivist tradition is that its practitioners form an 'epistemic community.' Developed by international relations scholar Haas (1992) this concept holds that networks of experts can claim authority in a particular field and that they hold a set of normative beliefs and values. Several features of the scientific community conform to the general identity of an epistemic community, including its legitimacy derived from the international community of national governments comprising the parties to the FCCC, its accountability to this international community, the integral (essential) role of climate change science in the issue, and the role of the natural sciences. Certainly, the scientific community's outputs have received wide acceptance. Within international relations scholarship, those of quite different theoretical positions assume a similar view on climate change science. Political economists (such as Paterson 1996), realists and neo-realists, and liberal institutionalists (such as Young 1994, Sell 1996, and Soroos 1997) perceive climate change science as effectively incontrovertible. Advocates of epistemic approaches are less interested in consensus within the scientific community than that among the community of nations and their decisions to respond to global warming (Demeritt 2001).

Attitudes towards science, technological development and its applications are in flux, as described above, and are so fundamental as to be questioning of modernity itself. In the views of Giddens, and Beck (1992, 1995, and 1997, Beck et al. 1994), modernity is undergoing a transformation from its (traditional) industrial form to that of 'reflexive modernity.' All aspects of contemporary life can be questioned and re-evaluated in contemporary times, a process driven by new forms of knowledge that precipitate changes in social outlooks and values. Science and technology are viewed with critical regard in contemporary society, argue Giddens and Beck, being both resolver and creator of social and environmental problems. As Beck remarked of science in contemporary society (1997: 23): "It is the success of science, not its failures, which have called it into question and taken away its monopoly." Such thinking that underlies Beck's (1992) identification of contemporary western communities in *Risk Society: Towards a New Modernity*, in which the dominant principle of social organization is shifting towards the understanding and distribution of risk and away from the allocation of goods. Industrial society's production and distribution of goods, that is reliant upon science, is a risky activity according to Beck. Continuation of modernity concerns, therefore, allowing and facilitating greater social 'reflexivity' to risk, a role that extends to the realm of science itself.

Understood in conventional terms, climate change science and the IPCC in particular, have characteristics of both traditional science and of a form of knowledge production that appears distinctly unscientific (being an overtly politicized science that includes non-scientists). Some of these developments can be understood if science is placed in the social context where risk and uncertainty assume different roles. But even with this change in setting, institutions like the IPCC are the source of much confusion and controversy.

Environmental problems require a decision-making based on available knowledge and yet there is often an absence or insufficiency of scientific certainty about the issues involved. Part of this problem is attributed to the limitations of reductionism in understanding complex (and chaotic) ecological systems. Scientific uncertainty in the face of social urgency seemingly undermines the role of science and disarms its utility. Invocation of the precautionary principle offers a means by which decision-makers can proceed without the certainty of a scientifically resolved outcome when circumstances or outcomes are sufficiently pressing. But this is an incomplete solution as the precautionary principle employs scientific rationality in identifying risk, and the ecological challenge to science remains.

Basing social policy on scientific findings carries the implication that knowledge identified as scientific should assume a primacy in decisions involving human affairs. Recourse to claims of the neutrality or independence of science has, therefore, political significance for the control and use of science. One critique of the traditional view of science concerns the dangers of 'scientism,' defined by Habermas (1971: 4 as quoted in Proctor, 1991: 162): "[S]cience's belief in itself – or the conviction that we can no longer understand science as one form of possible knowledge but rather must identify knowledge with science." Ellul's (1964) 'technological society' is entirely the outcome of 'technique,' albeit an effect that is as much unconscious and structural, as it is deliberate and planned. Effectively, the exceptional aspirations of the Enlightenment's leaders for a science-guided society have become the fabric of everyday modernity. Along with other 'critical theorists,' Habermas was concerned with the conflicting circumstances in which participatory opportunities for communities in democracies are squeezed out by scientific and technical rationality; with legitimate authority vested in the 'technocrat.'

Yearly considers that Habermas's speculations of excessive state intervention haven't been realized, but in reference to global environmental problems (1996: 118): "It seems that in this case what Habermas feared of the state has, in significant respects, become true of the international policy community." Even though science has the role 'establishing facts,' what concerns Yearly are those various values and assumptions are already established before research gets under way. Scientism seems to cover many aspects of the criticism made of this science, and despite the depth of the Habermas thesis on this subject, there are several other critiques that raise other associated points that appear to lie outside of 'scientism' that need to be covered.

Whenever there is a lack of a self-reflective awareness, scientism remains a constant possibility in social fields where scientific problems are being resolved. For example, while Zygmunt Bauman (1991) considers uncertainty as essential to maintain the rationale of the scientific enterprise, there is a second form of ignorance that challenges science, namely that uncertainty over whether scientific knowledge is optimal on any specific point thereby endorsing "the creed of the superiority of scientific knowledge over any other knowledge." Science's ability to determine the legitimacy of knowledge, its ability "to draw the line between knowledge and ignorance, transparency and legitimacy and obscurity, logic and congruity" (Bauman 1991: 243) is questioned. For Bauman, acceptance of this doubt marks a division between the modern and the postmodern, so that science, for all its powers, is but one 'story' or knowledge form, amongst many.

Climate change science as positive science

Enormous effort has been devoted to climate change science. There may be no comparable peacetime research endeavor or single issue that has received the worldwide participation and involvement of the scientific community. Atmospheric physics, climate modeling, climate paleohistory oceanography, and related scientific fields were characterized by what were considered largely academic goals until the advent of climate change issue, which transformed their public profile, research goals, and research funding. Policy initiatives and other actions to lower energy use and reduce emissions in industrial societies have largely been known since at least the mid-1970s (see, e.g., Lovins 1977) and arguably earlier. World fossil fuel supply crises of 1970s provided the impetus for improved energy efficiency, energy conservation, and initiated the majority of renewable energy research and development. Although forecasting the rate and extent of global warming has seen climate research pushed to its limits of available knowledge, the immediate techniques of how to reduce emissions through energy efficiency, energy conservation, and the application of renewable energy are without scientific controversy (as opposed to discourse over the choices over policy tools to achieve such ends). In this manner, climate change research cojoined with existing energy research and development.

Science occupies its place in the broader climate change discourse because the governmental response to climate change is managerial. From this simple proposition, we can discern between those critiques that are basically empirical and those that reject the managerial response, some of which seek promote alternative perspectives, such as pluralist/behavioralist approaches or socialist/class-based approaches. Further, we can discern that broad critique that arises from 'scientism' and of the broader discussions about science, and of modernity itself.

Climate change science supplies its own framing for the narrative of the linear unfolding of knowledge. This frame constitutes science as essentially independent, wherein it defines, identifies, and resolves problems, and whose findings become available for the waiting world. Yet this story is seemingly riddled with misrepresentations, omissions, and instances of outright error. It is not clear from the orthodox accounts of science how social forces shaped the evolution of knowledge, nor is there great interest in this question. Within this narrative is the creation of the IPCC, an institution that necessarily tangled science with politics, a development that sits uneasily in orthodox scientific accounts (to the extent that some overlook its creation).

Orthodox approaches to science have also been problematic when dealing with climate change science as a controversial public issue, as vested interests undermined scientific processes and results, in attempts to forestall the inevitable questioning of the world's fossil fuel system. Conventional science accounts indicate little of how diverse and specialized knowledge was brought together, how knowledge and certainty became standardized and globalized, how particular claims to knowledge were produced, and how problems were framed. Social, economic, and bureaucratic influences on agenda setting, prioritizing, directing, legitimizing of science have been neglected. There are also social dimensions to science community itself as furnished by vocation, training, and activities and political dimensions through the interactions of its participants, and the values evoked in research, the competition for resources and influence. In an overarching sense, climate change science's self-history has struggled to distinguish between influences internal and external to its activities, undermining science's claim that it's an independent narrative and should be treated as such.

A political economy of knowledge

Climate change science history as shaped by capital and politics

Accounts of climate change science by its practitioners (e.g., William Kellogg) and by historians (e.g., Gale Christianson) taking a strongly positivist approach tend to form the 'official' history, sanctioned by prominent research institutes and official funding agencies. Following the inclinations of professional exclusion, science practitioners sometimes adopt a territorial attitude by claiming that the intricacies and scientific difficulties of comprehension prohibit the unqualified from properly appreciating how the science developed. Doubtless, only experienced scientists can understand the scientific issues, but this ability hasn't seemingly prevented simple historical errors. More problematic has been the treatment of social influences on the scientific enterprise: the influence of Cold War politics, extreme weather events, institutional rivalries, and public opinion. Furthermore, the positivistic accounts have climate change science unfolding as a progressive and rational process in which the overriding goal is the reduction of uncertainty and the satisfaction of scientific curiosity. Absent from the inspiring story of great scientific achievement on a vital environmental issue is the role of the decidedly less heroic elements of neglected scientific findings, self-interest, happenstance, rivalry, and sheer disinterest in identifying and protecting ecological values.

An alternative way to organize an understanding of climate change science's development is to examine the influences of political and economic power. Through the early part of the twentieth century the phenomenon was largely neglected; it offered neither a source of riches nor military advantage. Gaining control over the climate, however, proffered obvious rewards for the economies and political powers to those who could employ scientific knowledge for such a goal once such possibilities were realized. Such a motivation underpinned state investments in understanding weather and it was a short step to its broader application to climate research, an endeavor promoted by the Cold War and the possibilities for the superpowers to gain strategic advantages. Hart and Victor (1993) state that the U.S. Federal weather modification program that was the main way in which global warming was considered in basic research and which effectively prevented broader effective research inquiries. Meteorology in Canada, U.K., U.S., and elsewhere has its roots in military programs (Demeritt 2001: Note 11), and carbon cycle research and atmospheric modeling arose from Cold War motives. Of these circumstances, Demeritt (2001: 315) concludes that both the environmental objective and the military shared a "consistent rationalty" of the Cold War's "closed world discourse" (after Edwards 1996) of "a language of integrated systems, an image of global containment (of communism and environmental problems) and apocalypse, and a practice of technologically centralized management, communication, and command-and-control."

Throughout this period, the possibility of increasing greenhouse gas concentrations altering the global climate was known, but remained of little interest to science. National funding provided both the technological developments in the form of institutional support, computing power, research programs, data collection, and other elements of large science programs. But climate research was unconnected from any concerns for environmental protection. Hart and Victor (1993: 656) who quote Revelle (1966): "Our attitude toward the changing content of carbon dioxide in the atmosphere that is being brought about by our own actions should probably contain more curiosity than apprehension."

Hecht and Tirpak's (1995) account of the development of the U.S. national climate program in the 1970s is instructive. In 1970, the National Science Foundation cut its support of the Rand Corporation's climate modeling program, forcing Rand to canvas other federal agencies to fill this void. Fatefully, around this time the Defense Advanced Research Projects Agency was searching for additional users for its underutilized (the first) large parallel processing computer (the ILLIAC IV). Rand successfully argued that deliberate or inadvertent climate modification by the USSR (such as caused by its Arctic river diversion project and a proposal to dam the Bering Strait) necessitated investigation by the Agency, who classified the project secret and named it 'Nile Blue.' Experiments were carried out using pioneering research in climate modeling on changed sea surface temperatures, increased atmospheric dust, and statistical analysis using controlled runs in global climate models. At the conclusion of the Agency project, it was transferred (back) to the National Science Foundation in 1975 and re-named the Climate Dynamics Research Program.

Waning military interest in the planet's environmental fate saw their support for climate modeling decline in the late 1960s (Hart and Victor 1993, Demeritt 2000), and climate scientists began to receive institutional funding in response to environmental concerns from the WMO's GARP initiative and elsewhere (Hecht and Tirpak 1995). Similar circumstances of the climate change issue arriving propitiously for a large agency facing declining funding also occurred in the case of the U.S. GCRP in the late 1980s. In this instance, the U.S. space agency, NASA, was facing a reversal in its fortunes following declining political interest when several Congressional committees were hearing about the impending crisis of climate change and a seeming onset of extreme weather events around the globe. NASA parlayed the need for increased scientific research into climate change into one of the largest scientific programs of all time, based on a rationale that only it uniquely possessed the requisite combination of technology and expertise (Pielke 2000a).

Climate change science is the product of a wide array of political and economic factors, largely unconnected to scientific discovery. Conventional accounts of this history that refer to these influences dismiss them as being coincident to a process that was destined to arrive at the present. But these accounts struggle to explain the controversy that has plagued their subject since the time it became clear that that the UN intended to create an international agreement on climate change. Only by admitting the entry of explanations of political and economic power can the story of the 'greenhouse skeptics' be told.

Doubters, skeptics, and dissenters: organizing dissent

Around the time of the first IPCC Assessment Report, and notably following its release, there was a welter of popular works on global warming describing the basic mechanics of climate change and outlining the potential impacts of a warmer world (e.g., Gribbin 1990; Oppenheimer and Boyle 1990; Pearce 1989; and Schneider 1990). While the IPCC results represented a relatively cautious consensus, climate change became one of the greatest public controversies in contemporary science. Self-described greenhouse 'skeptics' questioned essential aspects of the research presented by the IPCC and its supporters, including its climate data (notably the instrumental record), data interpretation, modeling techniques (especially the global climate models), model outputs, emission scenarios, warming scenarios, and climate change impacts scenarios (e.g., Balling 1992; Michaels 1992; and Singer 1989). Many of these 'skeptics' had backgrounds in the "empirical-descriptive," rather than the theoretical and physics-based parts of the atmospheric sciences (Demeritt 2001: 315).

Most skeptics were based in the U.S. and this was the locus of most of the controversy, although there were parallel debates in Australia, Canada, England, Europe, and elsewhere, usually orchestrated by conservative think tanks (such as Canada's Fraser Institute and Australia's Institute of Public Affairs). As the orthodox science exhibited a globalization and standardization, so did the arguments of the skeptics, producing largely identical and parallel public disputes over the same points of contention. Originally, the 'skeptics' included the merely skeptical, namely those scientists who rejected climate change on scientific grounds within the confines of the scientific community. Soon after the conservative political groups sought to discredit the mainstream science, 'skeptics' were identified with those with a vested interest in refuting climate change science in the public and policymaking realms (i.e., 'hired antagonists'). Scientific skepticism was legitimate and remains so; indeed, the extent of doubt expressed within the IPCC's First Assessment Report is considerable (IPCC 1990a). Any scientists who considered that these differences could be, and would be, settled within the halls of science, couldn't have been more wrong.

In the early days of the bid to win the general public's hearts and minds and to provoke national government policy-makers, several prominent environmental groups fell prey to temptation and used eye-catching public images and catastrophic messages of climate change impacts. An enthusiastic media conveyed these images of allegedly imminent danger from rising seas and severe storms to the dismay of many scientists. After this initial activity and a rebuke from science, all the prominent environmental NGOs fell in with the orthodoxies of the IPCC. This early tactical error on the part of the NGOs furnished some corporations with a rationale for responding in kind, enabling them to claim that they sponsored the skeptics to counter environmental NGOs 'extremism.' Scientists became wary of accusations of alarmism and irresponsibility raised in public fora. Throughout much of the 1980s and 1990s, there was a contest over climate change science that was determined in the public theatre, where the rules of scientific engagement intermingled with those of campaigns by corporations, environmental groups, politicians, and sundry other actors. Seemingly the notions of scientific problem-solving were lost, or least obscured; facts and speculations mingled, experts vied with lay persons, motives and qualifications were questioned, partisan publishers vied with established journals of science, and radio and television became mediums for discourse. As a result, the outcomes were as uneven, fragmented, confusing, and at times as bizarre, as can only be produced by contemporary popular culture.

While scientific 'truth' might have been the self-proclaimed object of scientific endeavor, winning public and political support necessitated use and manipulation of the mass media. For the dominant industry interests and environmental antipathy of the U.S.'s Reagan/George Bush and England's Thatcher administrations, a 'skeptical' view of climate change science was politically valuable, and as a market commodity such information was readily manufactured. In the U.S., energy-related corporations and conservative research centers invested heavily to discredit climate change science, which entailed creating organizations for this purpose. Most notable of these organizations was the Global Climate Coalition (GCC), funded by a large number of corporations with direct interests in producing and consuming fossil fuels, and the Global Climate Council (whose membership list is secret).

Assessing the political effects of the 'alternative climate science' are hard to gauge but easy to identify. Certainly its advocates enjoyed access to the highest levels of U.S. federal policy-making. For example, under the auspices of the conservative think-tank, the George C. Marshall Institute, a group of skeptics produced a report discrediting climate models (Seitz et al. 1989) that was widely read in the George Bush White House (Hecht and Tirpak 1995). Overlapping membership and close ties existed between the conservative think tanks, conservative media outlets (such as talkback radio), the Republican Party, the oil and energy industries, and the climate skeptics, that facilitated and coordinated Congressional, media, and lobbying campaigns on energy and climate change issues (Gelbspan 1997; Leggett 2000; and Levy and Egan 1998). Congressional lobbying, advertising, free education kits for schools (including videos, books, games, and posters), establishing 'front groups' of experts and scientific advisory panels, and research and public polling projects were all used in these campaigns. Orchestrating the campaigns were several organizations with names mimicking those of government and environmental NGOs and belying their corporate ownership, including the American Energy Alliance, Climate Council, Information Council for the Environment, International Climate Change Partnership, Kyoto Earth Summit Information Center, and Greening Earth Society (Helvarg 1994; Gelbspan 1997; Levy and Egan 1998; and Rowell 1996).

Gelbspan's (1997) *The Heat is On* gave account of corporate activity, largely by fossil fuel and automotive companies, to undermine climate change science (and to influence national and UN and U.S. policy-making), later extended in a subsequent work (2004). Levy and Egan (1998), Passacantando, (1999), Beder (1997), and others identified other examples of corporations and interest groups using science, or its imprimatur, as one element in sophisticated public relations and political lobbying campaigns. Conservative political groups, such as the Cato Institute, Atlas Economic Research Foundation, and Frontiers of Freedom, directed funds from ExxonMobil and other firms to the institutes run by prominent skeptics.

These campaigns combined science within larger strategies and activities. Indicative of the scale of these operations is their funding – although obviously much corporate information is withheld from public scrutiny. Corporations that belonged to the GCC certainly invested in the U.S. political process; from 1989 to 1999 its members contributed over US$63m to the major parties (commoncause 2002). Gelbspan states that the GCC spent over US$1m (in 1994 and 1995), the National Coal Association some US$700,000 (in 1992 and 1993), and the American Petroleum Institute allocated US$1.8m for public relations in 1993 alone in its efforts to defeat a proposed carbon tax in the U.S. (1997: 55–56). Journalists Bob Burton and Sheldon Rampton (2002) claimed that GCC expenditure was US$1m a year to combat climate change science and quoted the *Los Angeles Times* on 7 December 1997 as writing that the Coalition had spent US$13m on its 1997 'anti-Kyoto Protocol' campaign.

Such was the success of the skeptics approach that the discourse took on the public appearance of a legitimate dispute within the scientific establishment, rather than the orchestrated views of a relatively small number of opponents (the principal skeptics included the scientists Robert Balling, Sherwood Idso, Richard Lindzen, Patrick Michaels, and S. Fred Singer). Greenhouse skeptics did not generally attempt to obscure their linkages with greenhouse gas industries, but rather emphasized that economic harm to corporate interests from the implications of reducing greenhouse gas emissions was identical with a broader risk of national economic decline. There was a substantial research output to support their economic claims, but the skeptics' efforts to conflate the science of global warming with the costs of response actions ultimately foundered.

Boehmer-Christiansen proffered an explanation that implicated the self-interest of established scientists in garnering research funds, that when combined with other interests, had promoted the climate change issue (1993, 1994a, and 1994b), although Boehmer-Christiansen herself received coal industry funding. Further, having sought identification as 'skeptics' and being openly critical of the motive and science of their colleagues, these self-styled renegades increasingly found the fora of legitimate science being increasingly denied to them. Bolin, then IPCC Chairman, dismissed the skeptics thus (Bolin 1994: 27):

> In reality, there are few articles in the scientific literature that support the view that the IPCC has overestimated the response of the climate system to increasing greenhouse-gas concentrations. Instead, this controversy rather been presented in special reports and the popular press. Key scientific issues cannot be resolved this way.

While the skeptics could gain little purchase on the legitimate scientific debate, they enjoyed popularity on conservative talk radio and had regular access to influential Republican members of the U.S. Congress, who held control of the House through this time. Under the pretext of 'balance,' the skeptics testified regularly before U.S. Congressional committees and sub-committees dealing with science, technology, energy, environment, and inter-national relations issues. Of this situation, Levy and Egan state (1998: 351):

> Nevertheless, the "climate skeptics" have succeeded in turning climate change into an apparently balanced "debate" in the American mass media. Moreover, they have played a key role in a number of state and Congressional hearings by providing some cover for politicians who, because of their ideological inclination or allegiance to certain busi-ness interests, want to delay any action on greenhouse gas emissions.

Boykoff and Boykoff (2004) analyze the U.S. 'newspapers of record' and conclude that their efforts at achieving 'balance' between the two sides of the debate distorts the weight of scientific evidence.

Despite these campaigns, Levy and Egan conclude that (1998: 351): "Industry associations have enjoyed much less influence over the scientific and policy discourse in the international negotiations." In a direct sense, this has become more correct with passing time (see, e.g., Leggett 2000), but by exerting strong influence over the U.S., which has played such a major role in the international negotiations, arguably the lobbyists have been highly influential in at least supporting U.S. negotiators at the FCCC meetings, especially in the early Conference of the Parties. Losing the sci-ence debate and eventually losing the public debate hasn't undermined the skeptic's ability to continue providing a rationale for U.S. policy-makers seeking to reject the prospect of taking meaningful action on climate change. Co-joined thus, government authority drew upon the views of openly partisan science in devising policy on U.S. responses on climate change and for related domestic policy. Generally dismissed as routine par-tisan politics, few considered the implications of marrying legitimate state power with 'illegitimate' science.

Environmental controversy was nothing new for many scientists engaged in biology, forestry, ecology, agriculture, and other fields. At least a part of the scale and intensity of the climate change controversy reflected the accumulated experience of corporations and environmental groups in public environmental disputation, but more so, the economic and environmental stakes were (and are) unusually high – perhaps uniquely so. For many sci-entists accustomed in the quieter waters of meteorology, encounters with the storm of a fully-fledged and often personally-directed campaign of 'skepti-cism' was particularly bruising (see, e.g., Schneider 1990).

Between the publication of the IPCC's second and third assessments, debate over the legitimacy of climate change science in the public realm broadly resembled the conditions reached within science many years earlier: recognition of the IPCC as an orthodox belief, with a small group of opposing contrarians and corporate agents. With the election of George W.

Bush as U.S. President in late 2000, much of U.S. climate change policy from the Clinton administration underwent review, revision, and reversal, coincident with President Bush's doubts over orthodox climate change science (Bush 2001a). These scientific doubts were of a general character and expressed in support of the President's case against ratification of the Kyoto Protocol and curtailing electricity utility greenhouse gas emissions. Because of the prominence of the protocol and coming after the November, 2000 collapse of the Sixth Conference of the Parties meeting in the Hague and before its July 2001 resumption in Bonn, world attention was focussed on the implications of the Bush administration's position on the protocol, not on its opinion of the science.

As for the timing of the Bush administration's skepticism, it could have scarcely been worse. For a start, it followed the release of the IPCC Third Assessment Report (Working Group I) (IPCC 2001a) which had received reasonable publicity, no doubt partly because its findings were alarming, and most journals and papers of repute presented its findings factually (e.g., Global warming was *Time* magazine's cover story of April 9, 2001). An article in *Nature* on the need for action attracted broad attention, as did the National Academy of Science's *Climate Change Impact on the United States* (NAS 2001).

In scenes reminiscent of the former U.S. Presidential administrations of Ronald Reagan and George Bush, once again climate change science was a public controversy. A schism between the G.W. Bush administration's position and that of its government agencies was apparent, wherein the administration's position was advanced publicly by members of various conservative think tanks, while relevant government agencies ventured few public opinions. No new arguments were produced by the skeptics and the debate, conducted in a popular media that this time seemed to better grasp the identity of an orthodox science, had little of its earlier excitement. Such too was the timing of this new round of skepticism that the new Presidential administration now oversaw and controlled the world's largest global change research programs (such as the GCRP). Most climate change research emanates from the U.S. and much supported directly by U.S. agencies or research programs indirectly through support of universities. While its agencies supported and endorsed conventional climate change science, the national administration apparently did not.

Reaction from the mainstream scientific community was generally muted, but with some exceptions. For example, *Nature* opined (2001: 499):

But a string of regulatory decisions by George W. Bush and others in recent weeks make it abundantly clear where his administration stands on matters in which scientists would normally play an important advisory role. It stands firmly with employers and polluters who helped pay for Bush's singularly unimpressive election victory last November, and damn the scientific evidence.

In June 2001, the NRC's Committee on the Science of Climate Change responded to a request from the G.W. Bush administration to identify the science's "certainties and uncertainties" with a report (NRC 2001) confirming the IPCC third assessment findings. Whatever confirmation the administration had been seeking, the tactic seemed almost farcical, as the position of the NRC had consistently supported the mainstream science over many years. In any event, the administration now had to reject not only the science of the IPCC, but also that of the NRC. Despite these problems, the G.W. Bush administration has continued in its efforts to undermine climate change science, such as covertly, through doctoring a 2003 EPA report on environmental conditions to emphasize scientific uncertainty (Revkin and Seelye 2003), and overtly, through re-vamping the U.S. Climate Change Science Program (CCSP 2003), under the rationale that further information is required for decision-making.

Mainstream climate change science's relationship with the skeptics may have been more complex than usually described, but ultimately the skeptics' politically motivated campaigns of 'dis-information' failed to move from the discredited margins of science because their work couldn't withstand peer-group scrutiny. Yet, there have been considerable rewards for science, for as Victor (1995: 366) noted, in 1984 the U.S. National Climate Program received US$20m which had risen to US$1.5b by 1995, and concluded: "Climate science is the most successful sales job by scientists since the War on Cancer in the early 1970s or the never-ending space race that began in the 1950s."

Victor continues on a theme we pick up below (1995: 366):

> Remarkably, considering that the policy relevance of climate research has been the engine for greater funding, there remains relatively little attention to the impacts of climate changes and much more on climate modeling and monitoring programs. The skew is changing, but it leads many to wonder whether the scientific research program is delivering adequately on the policy claim that science elites make when they ask for money.

Today, many in the climate change community of policy-makers, researchers, and activists would echo this sentiment, noting that the impacts research remains a lower priority and adaptation research continues to languish behind. For example, when the G.W. Bush administration released a revised version of the U.S. climate change research program in mid-2003 (CCSP 2003), the emphasis remained on data gathering and climate modeling. This is, of course, skepticism about priorities rather than findings.

IPCC controversies

As the official arbiter of climate change science, the IPCC depicts itself as neutral in conducting its work. Such institutional self-perception was insufficient to escape the charges of political interest from both external and internal sources. Boehmer-Christiansen has been widely publicized in journals such as *Energy Policy*, as a staunch critic of the IPCC, arguing that the climate change regime reflects a coalition between research institutions, international bureaucracy, and alternative fuel interests. She concludes that there has been insufficient scientific reduction of climate change uncertainty to justify the FCCC, and that greenhouse gas abatement policies reflect the outcomes of international trade and investment in energy allied against the coal economy. Science plays a particular role here, based on a model that divides knowledge production ("thinks and recommends") from the political decision-making ("politicians accept and implement") (1997: 443). Accordingly, the IPCC is politicized, because it serves it own interests by serving the FCCC (1997: 443–444): "If 'big' research plays its cards right long enough, it may be allowed to research climate change for another decade or so."

There is at least one recent example of attempted covert political intervention in the IPCC. The IPCC chair, the atmospheric scientist Robert Watson, was up for re-appointment in 2002 and was the target of influence by the G.W. Bush White House, if a leaked memorandum is to be believed. Watson was favored for replacement by energy economist Rajendra Pachauri from India's Tata Institute and a Director of the Indian Oil Corporation. Environmental NGOs claimed this change was motivated by the prospect of replacing the high-profile Watson with a leader more likely to be compliant to U.S. interests; certainly the Tata Institute's energy policy positions are not conspicuously reformist, nor is it prominent in climate change research: Pachauri now chairs the IPCC.

A less clandestine and earlier example of political activity in the IPCC occurred over the IPCC findings in the second assessment report that affirmed climate change. This high-profile finding was subject to controversy over whether the summary accurately reflected the views of participants and received great attention by climate change skeptics. In fact, the well-known and contentious phrase that the "balance of evidence suggests that there is discernable human influence on climate" was a watered-down wording brought about from the efforts of delegates from Saudi Arabia and Kuwait, as briefed by a Washington attorney Don Pearlman for unnamed corporate clients (Leggett 2000). Yet, the critics of the IPCC process and the summary finding were from the GCC and other groups whose major complaint was corruption of the scientific process (see, e.g., Michaels and Balling 2000: 18–21), a charge made possible by their (successful) efforts to shape the text of the IPCC in the first place. Reviewing the scientific aspects of the dispute, Edwards and Schneider (2001) thought the IPCC statement was without scientific controversy.

While corporate and conservative NGOs' charges of political bias seem to have little impact, other sources of criticism have been more telling. Environmentalists have generally been the strongest supporters of climate change science; indeed, much of their campaigning comprises promoting IPCC findings. Not all those following environmental values have universally accepted the orthodox knowledge production of climate change science. Agarwal and Narain (see, e.g., Agarwal et al. 1999) of New Delhi's Centre for Science and Environment iterated a number of complaints against the Western bias of the IPCC activities, citing neglect of the values of democracy and ecological sustainability. Social and economic analysis by IPCC's Working Groups II and III have attracted broader criticism, particularly their applications of conventional economic valuation techniques for estimating the potential costs of global arming.

A fissure in the assumptions of the role science has opened around the discourse of political economy in which the IPCC and the regime of which it is a constitutive part, which have been depicted as expressing the interests and strategic goals of the developed world. Wynne surmises (1994: 172): "[T]he critical voices assert a global political, economic, moral and cultural crisis." Although possibly overplayed, there has been at least one widely publicized instance of these claims. Within *The Social Costs of Climate Change: Working Group III Report* from the IPCC (1996c), Chapter 6 contained reference to value of life estimates as determined by conventional economic analysis, which held that poorer lives are worth less than richer ones. Not surprisingly, controversy resulted (Mashood 1995, Mashood and Ochert 1995).

Given that the IPCC deliberations are a relatively open process of a select group, the egregiousness of this example demonstrates the degree that Working Group III findings have not attracted wider attention for their particular valuations of other social and environmental entities. While too much should not be interpreted from a single event, the incident was emblematic of the relative insularity of the IPCC process that allowed the values embedded in orthodox professional methods and practices to pass into publication without apparent awareness of their implications or possible reception by those 'outside' the cadre of practicing economists. Economics has provided social science's only major contribution to the IPCC assessment process and which have held fast to the tenets of orthodox neoliberalism. In this manner, the association of the IPCC with the dominant economic outlooks of the developed nations, and of corporations generally, is unambiguous.

Responding to overall charges that the IPCC reflects 'political' values, Bolin stated (1994: 27):

Although the IPCC was given the task of assessing and presenting available knowledge objectively, there is a danger that political value judgements may also penetrate into the IPCC process. Although such a tendency must be prevented, it probably cannot be completely avoided. This has been noticed in the IPCC plenary sessions, at which workplans and rules for the assessment process are agreed upon.

Scientific credibility of the IPCC process demands, therefore, that scientists and politicians exhibit a mutual awareness of their respective territories and remain within their confines. On the IPCC assessment process, Bolin cautioned (1994: 27):

> Scientists as well as politicians need to recognize their different roles. The former must protect their scientific integrity, but also respect the role of politicians. Scientists must be viewed as honest representatives of their scientific colleagues, to ensure that the assessment process will retain its credibility.

Not only has the leadership of the IPCC extolled the virtues of conventional science, but the most comprehensive account of the IPCC's history to date (Agrawala 1998a, 1998b) perpetuates this belief (1998a: 617):

> An important point which is often overlooked is that the IPCC was the product of an intensely *political* process within the US and the UN system. The specific purpose for setting it up was also political: to engage governments worldwide in climate change decision-making. Thus, it is a paradox that the IPCC has managed to attract and sustain participation of high caliber *scientists* and has consistently produced reports that carry credibility in scientific circles.

A number of assumptions might be inferred from Agrawala's "paradox" about the character of ideal science: its independence from the political realm; only creditable science can be produced by research independent from politics; and only legitimate scientists can produce legitimate science.

IPCC membership is formally determined by the rules set by its founding organizations and its activity is self-organized and effectively self-regulating. Governmental authority determines national involvement (i.e., the selection of national representatives, design of national review processes, and the like), although in effect the major research organizations play a significant role in determining the choice and number of staff they wish to be involved, so that in practice, there is considerable national variation in determining IPCC involvement.

So who is chosen? Given that the great number of those directly participating, observers could be forgiven for thinking that few prominent researchers in relevant fields are excluded, but several factors are involved. Scientists' participation in the IPCC is heavily biased towards wealthier nations because the majority of research on which the IPCC draws is not funded by it, so those working in richer institutions are more likely to be invited to join. Further, with a relatively small number of institutions involved in devising and operating the major global climate models, there is much internal referral. Although the IPCC has been scrupulous in ensuring a broad national representation in the working group leadership positions

(Agrawala 1998a), Agarwal et al. (1999: 31) claimed that U.S. and U.K. researchers made up 209 of the IPCC 1996 Working Group I, whilst there were eight Chinese and Indian researchers, with Working Groups II and III presenting a similar picture. Bouton (1999) found that the vast majority of IPCC lead authors studied in the U.S. or the U.K. and concluded that the IPCC paradigm was one that eschewed diversity. National representation in the working groups in the Third Assessment Report series appears to have a less uneven national representation, but remains dominated by OECD nations and institutions, principally the U.S.

Postmodern science

Postmodernity offers a critique of positivist science, although some interpretations of postmodern science itself appear to embrace an acceptance of the non-rational. Where political economy identifies the interests of capital and political power in influencing the direction, priorities, and applications of scientific activity, postmodern thought is concerned with the rationality of science. Accordingly, postmodern inquiries into science examine how science comes into being, how science is made valid as an issue of legitimacy, and asks whose interests are expressed in science and who has use of the outcomes of science. Several of the critiques of climate change science deal directly with these issues prominently: firstly, the construction of the science; and secondly, the phenomenon of 'post-normal science.'

Postmodern thinkers, such as Foucault and Derrida, stressed that knowledge cannot exist free of the institutions that led to its creation, and therefore the values and interests of the latter are embodied in (and ultimately confined by) the former. In this sense, science is not understood procedurally or methodologically, but as a form of rationality that is itself socially conditioned. While Kuhn (1970) demonstrated that scientific truths represented collective decisions by practicing scientists (embodied in 'paradigms'), and which evolve by 'revolutions,' he did not endorse the relativism seemingly inherent in such a view. Strong constructivism became a logical extension of this position, in which scientific knowledge is wholly the product of the beliefs of scientists. Postmodernism can be fitted to this general scheme, it being a more general rejection that knowledge follows a "unique and natural" course of development that provides for the improvement of the human lot. Some postmodern thinkers in effect argue that scientific truths are as relativistic any other and furthermore, are a direct product of their institutional settings.

Lyotard (1984) offered an explanation for abandoning the notion of scientific neutrality by stating that science, as a discourse, is itself legitimized on two failing philosophical and political 'metanarratives.' Philosophically, Lyotard identifies the works of Hegel and his belief in the unification of all knowledge and the teleology of total being, wherein human ignorance is superseded. Politically, the goals of the French

Enlightenment form the other prop beneath science, wherein reason provides the key to human liberation from the oppression of religion, traditional social hierarchies, and political orders. Lyotard argues that modern society itself no longer believes in these narratives, as absolute knowledge and freedom based on reason remain elusive and questionable. Social faith in science has declined as a consequence of its applications in anti-social and destructive forces. Furthermore, he asserts that the progress of science hasn't been towards unification of knowledge, but consistently becomes more fractured and specialized, so that science itself no longer constitutes a metanarrative.

Lyotard's philosophical premise of the search for instabilities is supported by his claim of the world's uncertainty, so that perfect control over any natural or social system is impossible. In this reasoning, Lyotard (1984: 55–58) uses quantum theory, microphysics, and other scientific phenomena and then applies the problem of persistent uncertainty to social issues, concluding that society is discontinuous and uncontrollable. Illustrating this point, Lyotard refers to a dog's behavior when poised between two conditions, fear and aggressiveness, which if both are increased produces an unpredictable state – its response can either be fright or to fight. Hence, Lyotard concludes (1984: 59): "This provides us with an answer in the debate between stable and unstable systems, determinism and non-determinism."

Proponents of postmodern science need not go as far as Lyotard, and indeed the more familiar declarations of its manifestations refer to a series of developments with science that portend a number of basic changes in its project. Best and Kellner (1997: 195–251), for example, describe chaos theory, entropy, and evolutionary theory as scientific expressions of postmodern non-linearity, change, and indeterminacy. These developments were only possible, they argue, by science loosening and abandoning a number of cherished beliefs about the physical and biological world. Best and Kellner (1997, 2001) hold that postmodern science describes a set of new developments and outlooks as part of science's expanding and vigorous enterprise. For these writers, postmodernism reflects a change in science's circumstances, rather than its demise.

Postmodern science has its critics, primarily either opponents defending traditional science or anti-modernists pursuing a different agenda. Lyotard's postmodernist take on science and its adherents became part of a larger controversy culminating in the so-called 'science wars.' With the publication of Gross and Levitt's (1994) *Higher Superstition: The Academic Left and its Quarrel with Science*, debate within the science and technology studies community spilled into the mainstream, in which traditional (realist) approaches to science were set against its 'opponents' in constructivism, postmodernity, and post-normal science. Physicist Sokal notoriously published a hoax paper in the leading cultural studies journal *Social Text*, purportedly on 'postmodern physics,' to highlight the scientific credulity of postmodernity – which generated much publicity and debate. Combining accusations of left-wing academic bias in the social sciences with attacks on postmodern science, widespread publicity of these reactionary developments from conservative political groups inevitably followed. As it happened, the 'science wars' became part of the U.S. so-called populist 'cultural wars' of the time (Ross 1996).

Defenders of the conventional view of science considered that equating the outcomes of science with those of 'irrational' systems of knowledge was to abandon the human prospect to irrationality, placing the health of society and nature in the hands of faith healers, astrologers, and witch-doctors, as it were. Questioning rationality's role in science isn't necessarily an embrace of the irrational; for example, Feyeraband questioned whether the advance of scientific knowledge was in anyway attributable to demonstration of improved explanation and rejected the 'domination' of rationality in science (see *Against Method*). Sokal – the science wars warrior – criticizes Lyotard for drawing together a set of pseudo-scientific rationales. such as Gödels's undecidability theorum, Heisenberg's uncertainty principle, and fractal geometry, which he holds to be ambiguous in their implications (Sokal and Bricmont 1998). Some commentators remarked that Sokal, Gross, and Levitt's commitment to positive science is of a particularly narrow cast, adopting a position that Karl Popper had debunked some time ago. Within the community of science and technology studies, the vaunted re-assertion of positivism met with a cool reception (see, e.g., Hilgartner 1997; Ihde 2002; and Ross 1996).

Smith (2001) places Lyotard's postmodernism into a lineage of twentieth-century anti-modern thinkers, albeit with a distinct rhetoric and identity. Smith identifies Lyotard's 'anti-causalism' as a form of irrationalist conventional wisdom, at one with the century that produced Spengler and Ludwig Klages (2001: 170). He paraphrased Lyotard as follows (Smith 2001: 177):

> Society is unmanageable, in other words, because causal reason is powerless in the face of indeterminacy and "objects on the human scale" are indeterminate in most cases. We know this, Lyotard says, by the mathematical inference from the alleged ambivalence of a dog faced with a fight or flight decision.

As for its political implications of such reasoning, Smith draws the conclusion that Lyotard's declaration of the impossibility of social control is paramount to endorsement of laissez-faire politics.

Much of the postmodern interest in science is united by a perception of new dimensions of scientific uncertainty and unpredictability, and variously interpreted as breaking down traditional science's defining characteristics of linearity, rationality, and other positivist attributes. A limitation of this claim is the revolution in science seems to have left its major institutions, practitioners, funding sources, government relationships, modes of science education, and other basic features of the activity entirely intact. What quantum physics, Mandelbrot sets, chaos theory, and the like have so far produced appears to be a conventional form of scientific progress that fits with even fairly positivist accounts of scientific development. If the revolutionary impact of these developments were as significant as has been claimed, then the scientific establishment should have been greatly altered in the resulting 'paradigm shifts,' yet it appears that the scientific establishment has accommodated these new theories with little disturbance.

Smith's (2001) suggestion is that this collection of new discoveries' appeal is their compatibility with irrationalism. And Smith finds postmodernity's association with irrationality altogether too strong, arguing that Lyotard himself is confused on the matter. Further, Smith detects a circularity in Lyotard's position, suggesting that the postmodernist is committing himself to a scientism worthy of the most ambitious modernist in regard to controlling society by using scientific rationality as an assessment criterion. Lyotard appears to be arguing that science informs us of the impossibility of managing science scientifically, implicitly making science the means by which social control is measured. Smith finds such a claim irrational and argues that Lyotard is further seeking to undermine the rationality of science.

Largely this debate concerns 'realists' and 'constructivists.' Realists hold that the material world corresponds highly with scientific representation, wherein human agency plays but a minor role in such representation. Once developed, argue realists, such scientific representations will appear the same to any user. For constructivists, in contrast, the material world's representation is highly influenced by scientists and science, so that social consensus creates representations. There would appear to some middle ground, however, between full positivism for which there is little contemporary scholarly support, and the full irrationalism of the Lyotardian kind. And here the debate in the science wars is instructive. Gross and Levitt, Sokal, and others hold that the social sciences can tell us nothing about science, and vice versa, thereby staking a claim for science's epistemological authority and methodological autonomy. Defending science studies, Gabriel Stolzenberg succinctly stated (2001: 47): "In the literature of science studies, talk of the science construction is talk about scientific belief formation from a perspective from which rationality appears to have a less decisive role than classical epistemology says it should." This entails, argues Stolzenberg, understanding belief as a differentiation between the strength of this conviction from its support in logic and evidence, even though the latter informs the former. Exemplified by the work conducted under 'constructivism,' rational explanations are sought for the way science produces particular answers. Here, postmodernism has produced a series of insights that have eluded conventional science and the critique of political economy, as valuable as these have been.

Constructivism

Science and technology studies examine the creation of scientific knowledge, within which there are two aforementioned general positions of constructivism and realism, to which can be added that of empiricism (which holds that the real world is unknown and that science makes an interpretation of a world that cannot be revealed). Complex phenomena such as climate change science, these studies suggest, emerge from the interplay of social, economic, and political influences. As Jasanoff and Wynne (1998) state, a variety of approaches have replaced the linear model of policy by drawing upon science that features more interactive relationships, including those examining: the confluence of problems, policies, and politics; power relationships and agenda setting; system uncertainties and decision stakes; policy cultures; and policy interests and competing discourses. Constructivist approaches can include constructionism (studies of practices to construct reality), reflectivism (studies of the ideas and contemplations that build institutions), and interpretive approaches (studies of the significance of local frames of reference) (Jasanoff and Wynne 1998).

Rosa and Dietz (1998) offer a useful system by identifying two approaches to understanding climate change science for social inquiry: neo-realist and interpretive (i.e., constructivist). Neo-realist approaches accept science's findings uncritically or as a means for "extending knowledge of human ecosystems." In effect, such views endorse positivist science, supporting the objectivity of science conferred by the scientific method and the isolation of the scientific domain from direct political influence. Interpretive approaches are a form of neo-idealism and examine climate change as a social problem, focussing on the causes of global climate change and identifying responsible actors. Dividing science into categories, Rosa and Dietz (1998) argue that because climate change science involves research at the verge of existing knowledge, it is more amenable to constructivist investigations. Climate change science involves complex models that cannot be evaluated by checking their forecasts and omits components that cannot be modeled, these authors claim. Most constructivist researchers, however, adopt this mode of inquiry seemingly based on a more general rejection of realist interpretations of science (e.g., David Demeritt, Shelia Jasanoff, Simon Shackley, and Brian Wynne).

Constructivist approaches are concerned with knowledge production as a social representation of reality that can either assess scientific knowledge claims, emphasizing the uncertainty about climate change, or to determine the social construct of science and emphasize social factors in bringing the issue to prominence. On the first approach, Rosa and Dietz (1998) note that global climate models embody considerable uncertainties, but occupy the top tier of knowledge. Researchers following this approach, such as Shackley and Wynne (1995), find that anthropocentric 'drivers' of climate change and the associated social impacts and adaptations become peripheral to an approach dominated by models of natural systems. Demeritt exemplifies this approach when stating (2001: 308): "It is my contention that the demand for and expectation of policy relevance has subtly shaped the formulation of research questions, choice of methods, standards of proof, and the definition of either aspects of 'good' scientific practice." Anthropogenic factors are thus excluded from scientific consideration by being labeled 'policy issues' (Rosa and Dietz 1998). Social science seeking to addresses the social dimensions of climate change is relegated behind the natural sciences in the consideration of climate change. Recourse to a resolution, for this group of constructivist critics, is for greater involvement of the social sciences.

In the second constructivist approach, historical, cultural, and political factors that shaped the rise of the climate change issue are examined. Rosa and Dietz differentiate between those studies of the rise of scientific concern and those examining its elevation in social awareness, using Hart and Victor (1993) to exemplify the former and Mazur and Lee (1993) and Ungar (1992, 1995) the latter. Hart and Victor (1993) portray how the rise of climate change as a public issue resulted from scientific elites taking advantage of other policy arenas, as described above, rather than developments in climate change science. Ungar (1992) depicts climate change coming to public attention through heightened anxiety and media coverage of specific climatic events which then connected with the scientific discourse. Constructivist analysis of this sort is not concerned with establishing the truth claims of science or any other agency, but with what social factors give claims credence.

Objections to constructivism by practicing scientists, including some sympathetic to the general objective of matching climate change science to social and environmental goals, often read in constructivism an accusation that they succumb to political influence, for example, Schneider (2001) and Henderson-Sellers and McGuffie (1999). Complaints such as these do not engage the basic issues of constructivism, which deal with the character of scientific knowledge. For example, Gottfried and Wilson (1997) regard the case brought by Sokal and others against the postmodernists in the 'science wars' as attacking only extremists, whilst ignoring the more widespread and pernicious following of constructivism. Their compliant against the 'Edinburgh Programme' of constructivism is a classic realist formulation of the natural/social science divide, to wit (1997: 545): "No view of the world is sound if it ignores the steadily improving predictions of twentieth century science."

Conservative proponents of positive science in the 'science wars' include those denying any social influence into science's methods and outputs; few researchers into science and technology studies, however, hold that science is purely objective. Outputs from science (such as technology) carry implicit values because they are developed for purpose and "the pursuit of science is always directed by values" (Milbrath 1989: 233), such as reflected by public and private funding choices. There is, however, great variation in the belief to the extent to which social influences shape science, with the positivist view admitting to only a minimal role. Positivism, even in the form of the epistemic community, leaves open the question of how to ideally create, direct, prioritize, and apply climate change science.

Conservative entrants into the discourse about the construction of climate change science have sought to identify within its activity a political bias contrary to their own interests and proclivities. Not that these claims have gone uncontested, and the Left has supplied critics of its own, such as Agarwal and Narain (1991), Shiva (1993), and Redclift and Sage (1998). This group identifies the interests of vested global powers seeking to secure a pattern of environmental exploitation having enlisted science as a means of technological control. Demeritt (2001: 308) finds this approach concedes too much to the "upstream" manner in which science is formed by "cultural understandings, social commitments, and power relations." Objections such as these risk going too far into relativism by treating natural sciences as identical with social sciences, so that science not only involves expressions of social judgment, but is also entirely political.

As a remedy to these limitations, Demeritt offers the approach of 'heterogeneous constructionism' in which nature, society, and science are 'constructed' "through the specific and negotiated articulation of heterogeneous social actors' (2001: 311). Heidegger is credited with the notion that nature and other worldly things are "disclosed to us as objects through practical engagements that configure them in ways that are recognizable *for* us and transforming *of* us." (Demeritt 2001: 311). Demeritt concedes the 'difficulty' of this notion, in which entities are real (ontologically), whilst their conception is socially contingent. Construction of science is not entirely semantic in this scheme, but does involve the input of human perception. Therefore, heterogeneous constructionism lies between the nominalists (where constructions are entirely linguistic) and the idealist (i.e., neo-Kantian) wherein there can be no ontological existence outside our beliefs. Heterogeneous constructionism conceives a world "distinct from and prior to representation" (Demeritt 2001: 311).

So what does this mean for the understanding of climate change? To start with, this form of constructivism accepts the existence of climate and our knowledge of it. Our attention is drawn to specific scientific practices and the way in which our knowledge of climate implicates us in understanding human nature and self-awareness in new ways. Rather than being impotent in the face of climate, its hazards are now amenable to prediction and risk evaluation through science. After Beck (1992), we are able to make (individual) reflexive choices about the future, which as Demeritt (2001: 312) reasons: "In turn, this reflexive subjectivity, with its decision-oriented belief in the possibility of managing life's contingency through rational choice, infuses the science of global climate change with some tacit beliefs about determinacy, prediction, and rational control." Constructivism offers a critique of climate change science that focusses on those social influences shaping its development. As such, key issues are evoked, included scientism, the relationship between policy-making and science, the global perspective generated by climate science, greenhouse gas projections, and the general circulation models utilizing these projections.

Climate change science and 'scientism'

Conventional accounts of recent developments in climate change science's history depicting its role as essential to policy-making are at least partially premised on an climate change problem being amenable to a technical resolution. White and Hooke (2004) support the increased scientific and technological investments and consider that growing policy development in climate change evidence of a solution being guided by such inputs. Policy-making is typically depicted as a rational and linear process based on science. Extending this rationality to decisions in the social realm evokes the risk of 'scientism,' wherein efforts to shape social concerns into matters of science raises the specter of technocentrism. Constructivism suggests that the characteristics of climate change policy formulation must influence the science, giving critics several avenues for inquiry, including those questioning rational policymaking models.

Critically reviewing the 'conventional tools of policy analysis' used in addressing such issues as climate change, Morgan et al. (1999) found them to be built on a number of vital, yet untenable, assumptions. Many, if not all, of these limitations appear to express 'scientism' when applied by policy-makers. For Morgan et al. (1999: 271–272) these conventional policy tools assume: 1) "a single public-sector decision maker who faces a single problem in the context of a single polity;" 2) impacts of decisions made are of "manageable size" and can be marginally valued; 3) values involved are "known, static, and endogenously determined" and decision-makers select policies by maximizing utility; 4) time preferences are captured by economic discounting; 5) uncertainty is both "modest and manageable;" and 6) the systems involved are essentially "linear." Much of the controversy over climate change science could be directly traced to these specific claims and the ensuing debates involved exposing and questioning this underlying scientism.

Pragmatically, one of scientism's major failings is that it effectively resolves problems, but not necessarily those originally posed. Global change research is prone to this problem, as Cohen et al. claim, giving rise to the following issue in climate change research (1998: 342):

> While the reductionism of the dominant natural science approach to CC [climate change] has constructed it as an environmental problem amenable to scientific analysis, this formulation has not been especially helpful in figuring out how to respond politically because it

ignores the human dimension of the problem and the difficult and locally differentiated politics of responding to it.

Three features of the scientific response (and therefore also shaping the political response) to climate change are examined by Cohen et al. (1998): 1) reductionism; 2) instrumental rationality; and 3) alliance to moral-liberal and technocratic politics. Firstly, reductionism, which is the result of the way that climate change science evolved, with its coalescence of two streams of research; of oceanography's concern with carbon cycle fluxes; and of atmospheric science with its modeled atmospheric behavior in the invention of the general circulation model. "The GCMs provide just one of many possible approaches to studying climate change, but they have become far and away the most authoritative." (Cohen et al. 1998: 344). These models are the cornerstone of climate change research as proving the basic scenarios of future climate, which in turn are the basis for impacts research.

Bolin exemplified how scientific authority and political independence are related in orthodox science (1994: 29): "However, scientists must set their own agenda for assessments that can be used in a political context. Only scientists can grasp the intricate interactions that take place in the complex system of the global environment." IPCC and many national climate change research programs follow the hierarchial model of science-impacts-response. Cohen et al. note the "uncertainty trough" phenomenon in this arrangement, whereby the "consumers of model output from one field accord it greater confidence and certainty than practitioner in the originating discipline." Another problem arises in impacts research, namely 'cascading uncertainty,' where the uncertainties in different individual models and data sets may be amplified by their linkage. Scientific reductionism, therefore, carries an array of political implications and over which Cohen et al. are more deeply concerned than the 'technical' implications (1998: 346):

> More troubling, the hierarchical structure constitutes an environmental and technological determinism: the physics of climate change, as represented in the GCMs, set the environmental parameters to which societies must adjust and adapt.

Secondly, there is the technical and instrumental rationality in climate change science, which in its classical Weberian sense is the purposeful and rational application of knowledge to social ends. For Cohen et al. this gives rise to (1998: 347): "In the case of CC [climate change], the social context under which greenhouse gases are produced has been largely ignored, except as technical questions about rates and physical processes." Particularly offensive to Cohen et al. is that the "luxury emissions" of the developed world are treated identically as those "survival emissions" of the developing world. Consequently (1998: 347): "Thus, CC [climate change] science is predicated on the idea that the objective of properties of greenhouse gases can and should be distinguished from their human meanings or any social objectives in managing them."

Reductionism plays into the international and national politics, founded as they are on climate change science. Scientific claims formed the basis for the first calls for action at Toronto in 1988, as they note, "rather than the basis of equity or some other normative criteria." A political agenda was constructed as a scientific endeavor (1998: 348), "advanced as a logical response to an objective and unbiased assessment of the facts of science." And this cleavage persists, with issues of policy being demarcated from those of science, reinforcing the reductionism and the "marginalization of any broadly cultural and social consideration of CC [climate change]." Both the rationale and legitimacy for scientific research appear deeply flawed (Cohen et al. 1998: 348): "By denying the epistemic legitimacy and scientific value of anything that appears remotely political, CC [climate change] discourse has tended to turn its attention away from those dimensions of the problem that are most important for policy purposes."

This paradox produces the following outcomes (Cohen et al. 1998): 1) IPCC scenarios are 'misleading,' by limiting future choices; 2) cost estimates of responding to climate change are built on these scenarios and therefore, the scenarios constrain socio-political choice; and 3) this produces an ironic outcome, whereby their scientific heritage makes confers legitimacy on the scenarios, but this ultimately their neglect of social issues makes them less political useful. Achieving democratic consensus and formulating effective policies (the aforementioned moral-liberal and rational-technocratic objectives of climate change discourse), makes scientific knowledge necessary to overcome the impediment of uncertainty, argue Cohen et al. (1998: 349):

> The moral-liberal formulation depends on communicating scientific knowledge of the objective risks of CC to sway self-serving, naïve, or scientifically ignorant behavior contributing to global warming, while the rational-technocratic relies on science to identify the optimal policy to which individuals must submit.

Perversely, the foundation of a secure positive knowledge is a weakness for devising effective policy (1998: 249):

> The moral-liberal politics of global citizenship and public education to convince individuals to change their lifestyles to avert global climate change has run afoul of public apathy and mistrust (Hinchcliffe, 1996), while the rational technocratic is vulnerable to being discredited, when, as is almost inevitable, the social and political commitments of its science-driven agenda become apparent.

One other aspect that requires brief attention is the prominence of economic advice amongst all the contributions of social science, both within and beyond the IPCC process. There is little doubt that economic studies have played a decisive role in climate change politics (as discussed in Chapter 4). Explanations proffered to explain the policymaker's partiality for economics make frequent reference to its resemblance to the physical sciences, bestowing on it the virtues of reductionism, positivism, and an alleged freedom from social science's uncertainties. Economic predictions carry greater weight than most of the social sciences, leading the latter to frequently adopt the approaches of the former. Bedded in quantification and fixed principles, economics purports to a value neutrality and predictive capacity suited to policy needs, in which the authority and legitimacy of state policy-makers is matched by the appearance of these qualities in economic scholarship.

It follows that if the IPCC were to rely on one discipline for insights into the social condition, it would be conventional economics – which is exactly what has transpired. Policy-makers and the IPCC have accepted the outputs of conventional economics on the same terms as the outputs of climate science, whereby such predictions can provide a means by which divisive debate can be obviated and its findings presented as solutions to technical questions. Scientism is evoked in a straightforward manner: economic prediction has become a substitute for public discourse and its values veiled in the ensuing policy formulation process. 'Scientific' advice of the IPCC promotes conventional economics and advocates political positions in technical language, including the use of market-based policy instruments, cost–benefit analysis as a means of policy evaluation, and so on. While scientific uncertainty about the climate system offers a rationale for taking modest measures to reduce greenhouse gas emissions by conservative stakeholders, certainty about the economic advantages of the FCCC policy choices promote the liberal-democratic approach to policy.

Arguments have been advanced for greater inclusion of the social sciences into the understanding of climate change. Tainter (2000) makes the case for further historical studies into climate change research on the basis of their necessity for the cause of sustainability and certainly Tainter's own works express the complexity of social development and ecological conditions. Causes of environmental problems identified by a society preoccupied with the present will only consider the recent past. He offers that history provides opportunities for two lessons, from the evolution and functioning of problem-solving systems have evolved and from "where we are in history." Frequently neglected in contemporary study of global problems is the longer sweep of events and circumstances, making Tainter's inquiry valuable for re-framing of this knowledge debate. No longer is the issue an immediate inquiry into today's policy needs, but that of a more dynamic and difficult line of self-reflective inquiry, such as whether the rate of knowledge production is sufficient to keep pace with the emergence of new policy issues.

Science and policy development

A widespread interpretation of the role of science is the reduction of uncertainty, so that it's assumed that climate change policy is constrained or inhibited by scientific uncertainty. Such a rationale, in various forms, has been advanced for a large number of climate change research programs, including the IPCC. And, as described, the level of scientific effort and output has been great; expenditure on the U.S. GCRP alone has exceeded US$17b to date. Demonstrating the effectiveness of science in policy-making, given the magnitude of what's involved, should be easy. As with many fundamental questions of the response to climate change there has been comparatively little assessment of the extent that climate change science has assisted in the policy response, or whether it has played any role at all. One explanation might be that such reviews would emanate from, or at least strongly involve, policy-makers, which rarely offer assessments of scientific expenditure simply because they threaten unpleasant political implications. Governmental reviews of publicly funded science activities are more likely to assess performance against the anticipated scientific results, a straightforward procedural comparison, rather than determine the effectiveness of scientific input for policy activities, which involves difficult value judgments and political risk. Oreskes et al. (1994) point out the differences between predictions from traditional reductionist scientific studies and those of integrative earth sciences, such as global climate modeling, of which the latter may be 'unverifiable.' Although climate modelers strongly reject such views. this prompts the conclusion that if the models aren't really predictive, then assessing their policy influence necessarily involves determining the persuasiveness of their message, rather than their veracity.

Suggestive of the problem of linking science to policy is, that despite the enormity of the IPCC assessment process, it has had to institute 'special reports' when specific knowledge needs have been identified, and even then these reports have had a tenuous relationship with specific policy outcomes. Further, the form of IPCC scientific outputs from the natural sciences do not evoke specific policy formulations, nor do they offer reviews or evaluations of different policy options. Social science assessments of the IPCC, however, are a different matter, as the conventional economics of Working Group III do suggest particular policy directions. IPCC outputs in the social sciences have an ambiguous status; scientists do not consider these outputs as 'science' and were largely excluded from the controversies over the validity of climate change science. Environmentalists' response to the IPCC also reflects this schism by supporting IPCC 'science,' while often rejecting the economism of its Working Group III.

Pielke's (2000a, 2000b) review and assessment of the GCRP describes how it was designed to support policy development, concluding that the science hasn't motivated a political consensus, but rather has been used by differing groups to support previously held positions. Pielke (2000a: 9): "As a result the Program has achieved notable bureaucratic and scientific successes while falling short of its ultimate goal to support policy development." Although the program's mission was to develop a predictive understanding of the global climate, it was not structured to provide recommendations or policy alternatives for policymakers, and as a result (Pielke 2000a: 9): "It has not systematically provided information useful to policy makers." By depicting the relationship between science and policy as "linear," whereby policy is built on scientific findings, argues Pielke (2000b), scientific issues precede policy demands. Pielke (2000b) notes, however, some recent emerging signs that policy and science questions are drawing closer together.

Brunner (1996) also opined that the comprehensive and predictive global climate models central to the GCRP were of little assistance to policy formulation, whilst being central to scientific activity. Brunner identified four related problems. Firstly, that the models are poor predictors of the future and the integrated assessment models that link global circulation models with climate change impacts models cannot be verified because they include forecasts containing social variables. Secondly, predictive models do not feature in U.S. policy formulation processes, as this is not how policy is formulated. Thirdly, actual climate change policies are not comprehensive and are unlikely ever to be so, obviating the need for comprehensive models. Fourthly, the comprehensive approaches exclude the regional and local scales. In effect, similar criticisms apply to the IPCC and policymaking under the FCCC process, and to national climate change policymaking by the majority, if not all, of the OECD nations.

Defending both the legitimacy of science's role in meeting policy needs and conceding that the linkage need not imply a rigid correspondence offers a way to re-interpret the rationality of science's role. Edwards's (1996) response to Brunner is that these models "perhaps cannot serve the immediate needs of policymakers," but have been highly influential – just not in the ways that Brunner examines. Models form the center of the epistemic community that includes scientists and policy-makers (after Haas's theory of epistemic communities in international relations), thereby meeting a political need, argues Edwards. In a field where "wholly empirical methods are infeasible," computer models are essential for assessing truth claims and occupy the central position in this epistemic community. These models, according to Edwards, form a public realm in which knowledge, data, and techniques, together with networks of individuals and institutions, can interact.

Climate change models can serve as 'hueristic guides' to complex phenomena and thereby serve a political need (Edwards 1996, Elzinga 1997), meaning that the models are indicative, serving to generate interest or guide further investigation, rather than being 'reality maps.' Conventionally, as revealed by the history of climate change science, uncertainty serves as a rationale for both further research and for delaying policy responses on greenhouse gas emissions and other matters. Edwards interprets this issue differently, arguing that the uncertainty in comprehensive and predictive models can supply a contrary rationale because model uncertainty means their political use can only be hueristical about general tendencies of change, not as predictive forecasts. Further, Edwards suggests that the very global character of the models promotes a "one-world, globalist" approach to climate change policy, in which the absence of regional information forestalls any divisiveness on these grounds. Not that such a revised view of rationality has the support of those with more traditional views of the rational scientific process, and suggestions that the global climate models are heuristic have offended some climate change modellers (e.g., Norton and Suppe 2001).

Dismissing Edward's heuristic case for the rationality of climate change science on the grounds that it appears to concede too much from the conventional model of policy-relevant science may be rash on the part the model's defenders. Following Brunner and Edwards, technical advice is most likely to be well received under the following conditions: when success is likely, its focus is narrow, a stream of short-term benefits or results can be produced, outcomes are economically favorable, and it produces obvious results. Reasoning such as this should be welcomed by the science community for it subtly shifts the rationale for the weaknesses of the rational model entirely into the policy realm, so that the culprit is the limitations of the policy process and policy-makers. As Edwards comments (1996: 155): "These are merely the facts of life in the policy world, where many actors' motives are governed by the election cycle." Given that climate change science arguably doesn't comply well with any of these criteria for success in the policy realm, even that it has heuristic influence appears as a major success.

That the work of the IPCC and climate change science in general has been a heuristic influence does acknowledge that many of the claims of the rational policy model are false. Given the controversy and public expense of climate change science around the world, that the majority of its work has been esoteric and irrelevant to policy is a finding that undermines both notions of science's utility and indispensability and diminishes claims that policy-making has been a rational and science-based process. While neither the reputation of science or policy-making is necessarily diminished by this conclusion, the necessity of their association is shaken. It appears that the actual science produced is secondary to the social consensus that the science has created. One reason why science is weakly connected to policy-making is because the rationality of science cannot be matched clearly to the politically influenced rationality of policy-makers. Further, the concepts embodied in science, such as the global character of a problem, is what makes science so influential, which suggests more about how society responds to science than about science itself.

It seems paradoxical, if not contradictory, that climate change science can both independently follow its own path and also respond to policy needs.

Science and policy may follow separate agendas, but their legitimacy is mutually conferred. In the contentious politics of climate change, politicians seek the solid foundations of science as the basis for political action, which "absolves them of any responsibility to exercise discretion and responsibility," an arrangement offering scientists considerable power and prestige. That science and policy are connected by links of a heuristic character loosens but doesn't dissolve the rational model of policy-making and of positive science. It does, however, admit much to constructivism. Science's connection to policy does not conform tightly to a rational and positivist model and policy-making models based on a detailed understanding of scientific developments appear naive or self-serving. Science has been essential to climate change politics, but primarily in ways best understood as social constructions.

Constructing the IPCC

Scientific knowledge of climate change examined as part of the response to global warming, cannot be divorced from its institutional setting. Not only is the IPCC the frame within which all legitimate climate change science is considered at the international level, but that science produced and/or utilized by the IPCC typifies all mainstream climate change research. Further, climate change science takes a single identity under the IPCC and this institution's outputs constitute a scientific consensus. It could be argued that the IPCC Policymaker Summaries, essentially the work of governments seeking agreement over the findings of the full assessment reports, aren't 'science' by virtue of this production process.

Taking the state of scientific understanding that underpinned the UN Vienna (on ozone depletion) and Long Range Transboundary Air Pollution (on acid rain) Conventions, Agrawala (1998a: 612) suggests that there was a comparable understanding of climate change at Villach 1985, so that "Thus historical precedents would argue for the feasibility of signing at least a 'bare-bones' framework convention on climate change right after the 1985 Villach workshop." Scientific uncertainties were not an impediment to decision-making at the Villach meeting. Victor (1995) notes that UNEP had three "visions" on how to approach the climate convention, and these impinge on the issue of the IPCC: 1) an international scientific assessment be conducted under its auspices; 2) a legally binding framework convention be negotiated; and 3) commitments in the framework be targets and timetable for controlling emissions.

Devising global agreements over acid rain and ozone-depleting substances were essentially large-scale pollution problems, whose resolution required changes to a relatively small number of industrial practices by relatively few nations, involving commodities and services for which technical solutions and substitute compounds were known and considered of reasonable cost (Litfin 1994; Soroos 1997). By way of contrast, climate change requires global action to reform the fossil fuel energy system, the engine of global capitalism, whose effects would reach every corner of the global economy. Prior to the agreements on acid rain and ozone depletion, there had been an effective coalition of national governments in place, but (Agrawala 1998a: 612–613) points out: "Such a governmental coalition *did not exist* in case of climate change in 1985. Therefore, irrespective of the *scientific* credibility, the Villach recommendations were not *politically* sufficient to generate momentum for a climate convention."

Climate change science was accordingly organized into an institutional form to meet with the imperative of governance. As Hecht and Tirpak (1995: 380–381) describe, it may not be widely realized that UNEP's attempt to create a climate convention led to the creation of the IPCC. Responding to the Villach report, UNEP Executive Director Moustafa Tolba formally requested U.S. Secretary of State George Schultz take action on climate change. Based on their personal involvement, the authors state that opinions were divided amongst the relevant U.S. federal agencies: most opposed negotiations on a convention, citing the extent of scientific uncertainty; the Department of Energy rejected the Villach report on the basis of its non-governmental authorship; and the EPA and Department of State supported a convention. Agency motives varied; as Victor succinctly stated (1995: 364): "[A]ctivists saw it as a first step; skeptics saw it as a way to delay. Both were right." Majority view prevailed and the U.S. presented WMO and UNEP with its proposal for a 'government-led' scientific 'mechanism' to assess climate change science, which materialized as the IPCC.

IPCC knowledge is structured according to the relationship between the working groups; science determines the relationship of emissions and climate, which then enables the impacts of climate to be identified and assessed, and then a set of response and adaptation strategies are devised. Redclift evokes an echo of C.P. Snow's 'Two Cultures' debate in discerning the "deeply rooted epistemological differences" between the natural and social sciences within the IPCC working group structure. In the original IPCC conception, the natural science agenda is manifest (Redclift 1998: 177):

> [T]he taxonomy began with scientific 'processes' (Working Group One) and led on to 'impacts' and then, 'responses'. The point about this view of science is that it begins with the physical, and takes on a human character some way down the road ... The etiology of climate change (in this example) is given by its physical characteristics.

Dividing the scientific task according to the IPCC's working group structure produces a hierarchy of knowledge. Shackley describes (1997: 78) that the division of the working groups not only appeared to give primacy to the natural sciences but to treat "knowledge of social dynamics as less 'scientific' and therefore less able to muster political and social consent and support." Further, in reference to the dominance of economic thought in Working Group III, Shackley writes (1997: 78): "Only certain paradigms from the social sciences have become accepted in the IPCC." Redclift continues (1998: 177):

> The forms of investigation that scientists are expected to undertake lend authority to this view of science: science is timeless and placeless, in some sense independent of human intervention, waiting, as it were, to be discovered. Knowledge, according to this view, is a process of gradual accretion, through which we learn 'more', on a linear uni-dimensional basis.

Social sciences, argues Redclift, are pluralist in their acceptance of differences and, rather than having universal character, are situated specifically in time and place.

Explicit to the design of the IPCC has been the prime role of identifying what would constitute a 'stable' or 'sustainable' climate and the ways to realize such a goal, from which (Wynne 1994: 171) "should be derived the necessary social, economic and other policies for survival." Crucial amongst the assumptions underlying the rationale for the application of science is that greater knowledge and the associated reduction of uncertainty will of themselves deliver greater social consensus and enable increased policy efficacy. Social science serves to inform natural science about human perturbations to natural systems and is itself informed by natural science so that the social and economic impacts of these perturbations can be identified. Subsequently and additionally, social science is restricted to a communicative role in this setting, charged with the responsibility of educating the broader public of the risks posed by climate change (Scott et al. 2000).

Clearly the most prominent treatment of social science by the IPCC has been Working Group III's use of conventional economics. Economics is effectively accorded the status of 'science,' sharing with the natural sciences a role in the IPCC's mission. Although environmentalists have generally accepted the IPCC's findings on global warming without qualifications, the IPCC's economic work has been rejected by environmentalists and accepted by conservative NGOs as a rational approach. Decisions on the selection of economic tools involve choices between political and ethical values and for which there can be little debate that the selection of conventional economics is not 'neutral.' Given that developed nations and large corporate interests have supported the use of economics in formulating policy approaches, and many IPCC economic outputs have been rejected by developing nations and environmental NGO's, the IPCC have been criticized for their *political* choices in promoting conventional economics as the best means to analyze and assess climate change policy choices.

Implications of the globalizing perspective

Science has bestowed on the modern world an awareness of climate change hitherto inaccessible. And those at the center of climate change science are confident in the necessity of the approaches taken. Ross observes (1991: 24): "[I]t is a mistake to think that theories of climate change that take the globe as an experimental object can rest simply upon criteria of empirical verifiability or formal coherence." Climate change science is part of the apparatus of groups already dominant in the global economy; as climate change "theories draw their power in the world from an elite culture" (Ross 1991: 24). As does science itself.

Wynne (1994: 169) describes the social and cultural construct of global environment, of which:

> The discipline of scientific knowledge is seen as the one superordinate discourse which can lend coherence to this incipient anarchism, to identify and describe the real natural problems, account for the underlying processes, and to define reliable and realistic options for societal response. Thus the social authority of science becomes a central issue.

Arising from this condition are two features, according to Wynne: firstly, the effort to establish a scientific basis for international policies; and secondly, the integration of social science into this activity. Fulfilling its role of predicting future warming, the IPCC devises projections of future greenhouse gas emissions, which in turn require estimates of future economic and social conditions giving rise to these emissions. IPCC climate models have depended on emission projections reliant on a cluster of business-as-usual scenarios, which Cohen et al. (1998) and Demeritt (2001) find a narrow and constricting conception of future possibilities. This has gesnerated a science discourse marked by its global scale and "universalizing physical abstractions." As Demeritt suggests (2001: 313): "These universalizing abstractions can then be used to legitimate the specific political program of international emissions trading and other climate change mitigation measures in the warm and fuzzy glow of global citizenship." For Demeritt (2001: 313) this construction "appeals to the common and undifferentiated interests of the global citizenry."

IPCC science, therefore, expresses the modern impetus for universality, equality of effort and reward, and the imposition of common management. Demeritt acknowledges that global warming has global dimensions to its causes and effects, but under the construction of the 'global,' other possible conceptions of the problem are lost, "such as the imperatives of the capitalist economy" (2001: 313). Critics of the 'northern' bias in the climate change issue (Demeritt 2001: 313) "contend that the threat of future climate change holds little meaning for developing nations," in which climate change is another global environmental problem relevant only to the developed nations, such as Shiva (1993); Redclift and Sage (1998); and Sachs (1999).

There is a risk that the 'highly technical and undifferentiatedly global basis of its appeal' will come to be rejected as elitist or obscurantist. Appeals to the interests of a global citizenry are founded on scientific certainty about the problem at hand, rather than the more difficult task of making the problem meaningful to the differentiated interests of the world's population. Hence (Demeritt 2001: 329): "As a result, continued scientific uncertainty has become the principal rationale for continued inaction."

Calculating future greenhouse gas emissions

Greenhouse gas emissions present an interesting challenge for climate change science: they are the basic source of a problem that can be analyzed scientifically, but are (predominantly) generated by social activities that are inherently less amenable to strict scientific rationality. Forecasting future emissions scenarios realizes this acute problem for the scientific rationale and method. Scenarios of increasing greenhouse gas emissions drive the changes in radiative forcing in general circulation models, which are in turn the products of models' socio-economic factors. While most attention has been directed at the general circulation models and the findings of increasing global temperatures, comparatively little has been paid to the scenarios of emissions, and consequently public debate has been minor. Yet implicit in these scenarios are a great number of assumptions about social and economic factors which have gone largely unidentified and therefore unexamined in the public sphere. Accordingly, this raises issues about the scientific robustness of these models, to wit Demeritt (2001: 318): "Indeed, given the indeterminacy of future emissions scenarios, the promise of scientific prediction is downright deceptive."

Greenhouse gas emissions uncertainty is rarely mentioned, although the IPCC began to examine this issue more closely (see IPCC 2000b). For Demeritt, this suggests a research priority directed towards the physical sciences and neglect of questioning the issue's social dimensions (Demeritt 2001: 318): "This silence is symptomatic, I would suggest, of a tacit environmental determinism running through global warming discourse." Certainly, most funding and attention is overwhelmingly directed towards resolving physical science uncertainties, evoking the charge of "environmental determinism" of the physical sciences by social scientists.

Because greenhouse gas emissions produce a universal effect this enables researchers to be blind to differences in the anthropogenic sources of these pollutants and therefore amenable to abstraction in calculations of global radiation budgets and nutrient cycles, yet critically, the same universality cannot be assumed over the social relations behind these emissions

(Demeritt 2001). Behind the façade of universality of emissions production is the highly uneven distribution between the nation states, within nations, and between corporations, with the contingent questions of the politics evoked by concept of the differences between 'luxury' and 'survival' emissions (e.g., Agarwal and Narain 1991; Byrne et al. 1998; NRDC et al. 1999; and Shue 1993). Greenhouse gas emissions produced by frivolous, extravagant, and wasteful activities in rich nations are counted as identical to the scant and frugal emissions of the poor necessary for their basic survival, (as explored more fully in Chapter 4).

In 1991 a controversy broke out between the two prominent NGOs, the Washington-based World Resources Institute and New Delhi's Center for Science and Environment, over greenhouse gas emissions. A World Resources Institute Report (WRI 1990) on climate change brought two then-relatively unexamined issues into prominence. Firstly, the report undertook a comprehensive account of each nation's greenhouse gas emissions that included those emanating from land use and from a suite of the major greenhouse gases, not just carbon dioxide. Secondly, the report calculated the extent of greenhouse gas sinks on a national basis, and allocated these according to emission levels, so that each nation's net emissions were estimated. For the first time, an account was provided showing the effect of all greenhouse gas emissions and which treated carbon sinks as a global commons available for regulation. As Lipietz (1995: 134) concluded, the results revealed that not all gases are equally subject to the 'precautionary principle' as 'short-lived' gases such as methane can theoretically be deferred, whilst the 'long-lived' carbon dioxide require precautionary action. Further, the allocation of national sinks provides the many of the greatest polluters with the largest sinks, an arrangement that works against the interests of developing nations.

Agarwal and Narain (1991) rejected the World Resources Institute report's comprehensive approach to emissions because the developing world's production of methane arises principally from agriculture (especially rice paddies), which they classify as 'survival emissions' in contrast with carbon dioxide emissions from the developed world, such as from automobiles, which are 'luxury emissions.' Allocation of the global carbon sink between nations should be on egalitarian grounds, argue Agarwal and Narain (1991), and would be more equitable on national population levels. Several political implications of this debate are discussed below, but our concern here is that any scientific treatment of emissions is shaped by 'upstream' value judgments, even such seemingly routine and innocuous issues as identifying what constitutes a greenhouse gas.

General circulation models

Climate change modelers often concede the influence of social factors from 'upstream' by policy demands and funding sources, and, in turn, models influence 'downstream' applications in policy formulation. For example, the initial choice of models and techniques was socially constructed, as Demeritt states (2001: 327): "Choice was influenced by scientific perceptions of political desirability which had been informed by policy maker's belief in its technical ability." However, the constructivist's suggestions that social factors influence science are, for some scientists, tantamount to suggesting that science is corruptible. From this perspective, science is a sealed box and regardless of its social 'location,' its internal workings are inviolate. Whereas in climate change science there are few objections to constructivist interpretations of economic studies, and impacts and adaptation research where social variables are obvious, 'realists' regard general circulation models as 'real science.'

Several reasons contribute to this interpretation. Firstly, the general circulation models are ostensibly built from knowledge of the natural world and don't involve social variables (which, as described above, is not the case in forecasting the future). Physically abstracted properties of the global climate system are presented in the models as the products of the physical and chemical laws governing the oceanic and atmospheric processes. These models are based in representations of those physical processes deemed the most creditable and rational means of understanding global warming and assumptions that complex ecological systems can be simulated from assemblages of simplified components using models of their first order physical properties. Secondly, these models are of immense complexity, involve a highly specialized group of researchers, are operated by prestigious science institutions, and are very expensive to develop and operate, which places global climate modeling in the league of 'big science.' As a celebrated and high-profile scientific endeavor, there has been much peer review and assessment, making the scientific community confident in the project's scientific merits. Additionally, the very complexity and institutional infrastructures surrounding this modeling prevents the ready 'intrusion' of those not appropriately qualified. Thirdly, within the hierarchy of climate change science, founded on the general circulation models, it follows that scientists with realist views place these models as the natural science 'core' of climate change science and admit to increasing social influences when various other studies utilize the model outputs. Global climate models are held to conform to the goals, methods, tests, and expertise that define positive science. Positivism and traditional conceptions of climate change science account for model development as the progress of normal science, in which all critical decisions are relegated to the realm of the logic of the scientific method and the instruction of empirical findings.

Constructivists have not been satisfied with these explanations and don't regard global climate models as being in any way exceptional exemplars of the positive scientific process, arguing that their design, development, and application exhibit an array of social influences. Starting with an obvious issue, that of global climate stability over time, the critical shaping influence of the social can be demonstrated. Climatic stability at the global scale, as described above from empirical findings of past climate, cannot be assumed even over relatively short periods, such as the next several centuries. Climate change researchers are only too well aware of the risks of assumed stability and the IPCC from its first assessment report onwards has identified future climatic 'surprises' as an issue of concern. Rapid climatic changes have caused great disruption and loss to human societies in the past and constitute one of the major concerns of future climate change. Ecological and social damage expected from climate change is high, as described above, yet catastrophic change would produce an even greater level of harm. Yet the probability of such changes from the current phase of climate stability are unknown, constituting therefore, an event of high uncertainty and high risk. Scenario forecasts of future climate from the general circulation models do not indicate any surprising changes in global climate. These findings are not necessarily indicative of future climate stability, however, but are most likely an artifact of the model outputs.

Shackley and Wynne (1996) argue that the climate modelers have deliberately sought to predict what is most certain. Demeritt (2001: 325) states that the prudence of 'sensible planning' on the part of the modelers (and by the IPCC) embeds a subjective judgment about risk tolerance into climate models. Even if the risk of extreme change is low (itself a matter of judgment), the possibility is potentially of great interest to policy-makers, a suggestion with which at least a few climate scientists agree. Investigations into the anticipated costs of climate change using an integrated assessment model in a study by Mastrandrea and Schneider (2001) produced an abrupt climate change and the authors present a case for considering "non-linear" climate changes as part of a risk management approach. IPCC's Working Group III (IPCC 2001c), in contrast, argued that only modest emission reductions were economically optimal until the probabilities of low-probability high-risk events were better resolved, a strategy which Mastrandrea and Schneider suggest would come undone when such events occurred. Knowledge of such risks is not only of anthropocentric value as rapid and extreme events are critical in assessing potential ecological impacts.

Demonstrated here is a conflict that can be considered in scientific terms, but one in which scientific decisions represent different interpretations about the valuation of social and ecological phenomena. Policy-makers are in many ways beholden to the assumptions in the findings of climate change science, accepting (in all likelihood, unknowingly) the judgments of modelers that the risks of extreme climatic change being low and of lesser importance in the assessment of devising responses to climate change risks. Unknown risks of extreme climate change, therefore, become legitimized by climate change science that is understating that risk and by a science culture that accepts an unacknowledged degree of risk tolerance.

Post-normal science

Postmodern approaches to science recognize a number of recent developments in science and in science/society relations that challenge the beliefs of
conventional, positive science. New institutions and practices have emerged
that feature negotiation over scientific outputs, involving groups from outside the scientific community who are not necessarily qualified in science,
and producing findings whose purpose may not be to advance scientific
knowledge but to inform scientific 'progress' through new insights from
outside the conventional scientific process. Accordingly, a new form of science known as 'post-normal science' has arisen and more critical positions
adopted on science as a social institution (Ravetz 1999: 648): "There is a
consensus on science as a major social institution, with structures of prestige and influence, and possessing the power to initiate, defer, stop or even
suppress research."

Ravetz (1999) describes how post-normal science extends beyond those
traditional assumptions of science's certainty and value neutrality, making
'systems uncertainties' and 'decision stakes' the essential elements of its
analysis. Using an assessment of the extent of these two factors in any scientific investigation, distinctions can be drawn between 'applied science'
where both dimensions are low, 'professional consultancy' where at least
one is salient, and those instances where at least one of these factors is
severe. Funtowitz and Ravetz (1992 in Saloranta 2001, 1993, and 1994)
argue that in these latter instances 'normal' science cannot perform satisfactorily and post-normal science comes into play. Understanding post-
normal science may be clearer from the circumstances giving rise to its
application than in strictly defining its characteristics, it being a response to
the problems of complexity and indeterminacy. As a result, there are many
complex philosophical and epistemological problems associated with post-
normal science, in addition to the usual technical and methodological
questions.

As Ravetz, Funtowicz, and others explain, post-normal science is a
response to particular types of scientific issues and occurs in particular circumstances. Healy considers extended peer communities as pragmatic problem solving borne of political contexts (1999: 655–656):

> Post-normal science was conceptualized as a means of confronting
> increasingly prevalent post-normal situations in which conventional
> distinctions between the spheres of facts, values and politics no longer
> hold sway and which without urgent remedy threaten calamitous out-
> comes.

Perhaps post-normal science's most striking characteristic, and that which
seemingly attracts most attention, is that the participants are not all scientists and often involve people without relevant training in the conventional

sense. Post-normal science is not the product of the scientific community operating in relative isolation as is the case in normal science, but the outcome of the scientific community engaged with others possessed of a legitimate interest in the issue. Thus, post-normal science is formed by an 'extended peer community' who can contribute 'extended facts' into the analysis, which may include anecdotal experiences and reportage. Healy puts the case that an increasing number of environmental issues evoke post-normal science so that (1999: 656): "the post-normal is increasingly normal."

Also distinctive of post-normal science is its approach, which combines aspects of traditional science, such as the scientific method, with other attributes that traditional science has sought to exclude. Post-normal science also differs from normal science in its treatment of uncertainty: normal science takes itself as value-free and considers that uncertainty can be parameterized using technical means. Uncertainty management under post-normal science embraces a broader factual base and recognizes broader forms of uncertainty, including those generated by methodological, ethical, and epistemological sources. Healy (1999: 656): "[A]n arena is revealed in which the limitations and weaknesses of both scientific and lay knowledge may be opened up and examined side by side, so facilitating a dialogue that can be used to effect their reconciliation." Advocates of post-normal science depict it as extending, rather than subverting, normal science. Post-normal science also challenges theoretical aspects of traditional science. Normal science employs established criteria, argues Healy (1999: 657), involving "detachment, objectivity, originality and repeatability," to evaluate its findings, yet the objective/subjective difference so essential to normal science cannot work for post-normal science where value and fact intermingle. Consequently, post-normal science (Healy 1999: 658) "revolves around the resolution, by negotiation, of uncertainty in the context of conflicting values and agendas."

Post-normal science is promoted as a cure for scientism, undoing what Healy (1997: 515) characterized as: "An unrealistic and overblown appreciation of science and its powers is closely linked to the dominance of technocratic outlooks and practices in contemporary institutional culture, and the resultant imperatives of prediction and control." Ravetz and Funtowicz drive to the heart of the scientism debate in making the claim for post-normal science (2001: 641): "Hence the traditional claims to truth and virtue made for science can no longer protect it from the checks and balances that are applied to all other societal institutions." Ravetz (1999) describes post-normal science as both Kuhnian "normal science" and a 'normal' application of expertise to solving policy problems. Yet, as he describes, the usual assumptions about science and policy of "how the framework is set, by whom, and with whose awareness of the process" (1999: 648) are no longer managed "implicitly." Social influences are explicitly admitted through the 'upstream' project shaping and the 'downstream' interpretation and application of results under post-normal science, but also through aspects of the experimentation process. Post-normal science does seemingly produce that 're-enchantment' of science that Griffin (1998a, 1999b), Spretnak (1991, 1997), and others have sought, and as such, is an important development in the discourse over the social applications and social implications of science.

Some commentators embrace post-normal science enthusiastically and envisage a future where scientific inquiry sheds more of its ties to positivism and extends beyond post-normal science. For Cortner (2000), the scientific challenges of ecological sustainability require a more holistic and integrated science, community engagement, collaborative decision-making, and flexible and adaptable institutions. Established scientific culture with its assertions of scientific rationality, value neutrality and objectivity, applications of the scientific method, and preference for technical solutions has kept science separated from citizens and from policy formulation processes. According to Cortner, science, as an institution and a culture, must be changed to better conform to democratic ideals and processes.

'Civic science' involves collaborative activity between scientists and citizens in designing, undertaking, and interpreting research (Cortner 2000). Drawn back into community processes, scientists cannot be distanced from the implications of their research and become accountable and society views science's outputs as the outcomes of choice, not preordainment. Scientists also contribute to defining the issues that science is to address and serve as advocates for particular issues and goals. She concludes (2000: 29): "If liberty is indeed, as Jefferson pointed out, the parent of both science and virtue, it is incumbent upon scientists to promote policies that expand liberty, and to rethink scientific myths and methodologies that foster undemocratic processes and results."

Naturally, traditional science's defenders are contemptuous of post-normal science, whose very name suggests postmodernity, and whose processes, participants, and outputs don't justifying the moniker of 'science.' Rather, it's proposed that the post-normal science activity is better understood as 'post science,' in which scientific outputs are debated and negotiated so as to assume a final form that satisfies various political constituencies. Traditional science is being exploited by political interests, follows one interpretation, to add credence and prestige to political-influenced findings. Embracing these extra-science activities, agendas, and 'nonscientist' actors as part of the scientific process can only result in poor science, goes the argument. Results from post-normal science, it is reasoned, are built on an assumption that socially normative outcomes are somehow equivalent with the natural world, taking away the empirical foundation supporting science and putting in its place a politically approved pretense.

Critical amongst these differences between traditional science and post-normal science is the treatment of skepticism and certainty over standards of proof. While accounting for the sort of 'trans-science' activity, whereby science and politics exchange influences, post-normal science claims that it deals with uncertainty more successfully than orthodox science. Such declarations are tempered by several factors. Research applications can be subject to the 'uncertainty trough,' wherein those producing the science are more uncertain about their findings than those subsequently applying it for further research or policy development. On the other hand, uncertainty about scientific findings can be increased by social factors, notably those alienated from scientific institutions or of contrary political views that will often regard science outputs with greater skepticism. Critically, reducing the uncertainty of the science does not automatically lower the 'decision stakes' (see Jasanoff and Wynne 1998).

Is climate change science post-normal?

Several commentators consider climate change science to be post-normal science (Elzinga 1997; Funtowicz and Ravetz 1990 in Bray and von Storch 1999; and Saloranta 2001). Best exemplifying these claims is the design and operation of the IPCC: it produces science to explicitly resolve stated policy needs, in which science and policy actors exchange influences in a process to produce scientific results. IPCC science is used in a manner akin to producing guidelines or standards, such as a government environment protection agency might do (e.g., Jasanoff 1992), rather than leaving its findings for interpretation completely outside the scientific sphere. Although he does not employ the term, Agrawala's comment on the IPCC's design fits with post-normal science (1998a: 606): "Through this innovative set-up the founding fathers of the IPCC sought to advance what many thought was an oxymoron: quality scientific assessments by democratic consensus." Although the IPCC produces 'science,' its political opponents can charge it for not being 'scientific,' for, in the conventional sense, its outputs are not normal science. Some identify in this approach a failing, especially those who reject its findings. As Senator Charles Hagel (2001) who testified to the U.S. Senate Committee on Commerce, Science and Transportation stated: "The IPCC summaries aren't science, they're UN politics."

Bray and von Storch (1999) examined climate change science for empirical evidence of post-normal science, concluding that the contrast between the relative certainty of the state of knowledge and uncertainty regarding potential climate change impacts suggested that scientific advice contained a normative element and indicated a socioeconomic construction of the issue. Saloranta (2001) finds the IPCC's management of uncertainties conforms to post-normal science, for in addition to the exemplars of the expected technical uncertainty there are also explorations of methodological uncertainties and the ethical uncertainties associated with preventing "dangerous" interference with the climate system. Also Saloranta notes that the IPCC's nomenclature for its climate models outputs are 'projections' of future climate, not 'predictions,' a distinction made so as to dispel any notion that the results didn't anticipate any specific policy response, but were restricted to simulations of a range of forcing scenarios, which he finds consistent with post-normal science. Further, Saloranta found that the membership of the IPCC working groups fitted well with the post-normal science concept of extended peer communities comprising scientists, government representatives, and NGO members.

It might be expected that the IPCC itself would explicitly promote the post-normal science approach to climate change science. Attacks on the IPCC and its findings, however, have produced quite the opposite response from the organization. Questions of the IPCC's scientific credibility have typically caused it to take recourse in stressing its conventional scientific credentials and dismissing charges of undue policy influence as expressions of partisan politics. Adherence to the myth of scientific objectivity made the IPCC more vulnerable to criticism, not less. Climate change 'skeptics' exploited the post-normal science character of climate change science as the grounds for politically-motivated critiques, hence (Demeritt 2001: 309): "[D]isclosure of the social relations through which scientific knowledge is constructed and conceived has become grounds for discrediting both that knowledge and any policy decisions based upon it." Post-normal climate change science, it appears, is not without its difficulties and limitations as both a theoretical explanation and as a practical course of action.

Some commentators recognized the post-normal science dimension of the IPCC without calling it such, describing how the IPCC represented a shift in the manner in which science was brought to the immediate needs of international policy-makers. Brenton (1994: 165) concluded that up to the Montreal Protocol that "the climate issue was still scientific rather than public property" and others have advanced an understanding of climate change science that discerns two stages: initially driven by internalized priorities and interests, then becoming a form of knowledge bound into, and exchanging influences with, broader social and cultural agendas. Accounts of climate change science such as these have the work of Arrhenius as beginning the first stage (e.g., NRC 1983), and the first World Climate Conference and/or the IPCC as marking the onset of the second (e.g., Brenton 1994). Other locations for this suggested transformation (or rather the consolidation of this metamorphosis) have been advanced, such as the changes made to the review process of the IPCC's second assessment report process. NGOs and government officials were officially involved in the review process (essentially reviews of drafts prepared by scientists) and in the drafting the IPCC's policy-makers' summaries, in which science and politics were rendered into a unified position. As a result, the second assessment report carried a certain added legitimacy for national policy-makers, and as Jasanoff and Wynne comment (1998: 21): "Thus, the IPCC came to be regarded as an active participant in the science/policy interface, and not just an advisor."

A great number of 'non-scientific' influences shaped the direction and priorities of climate change science well in advance of the IPCC's creation. Arguably, the IPCC institutionalized a long-standing dialogue between science and its supporters, and if so, then a case exists that post-normal science was functioning over a similar period. Although the case does not seem to have been made yet, the entire post-war history of climate change science exhibits 'post-normality,' such is its interleaving with military, institutional, and political interests. Credence is added to such a proposition by the explicit statements within the scientific discourse, such as in the first World Climate Conference declaration (WMO 1979) and the SMIC (1971) that raised issues associated with the implications of climate change and calling for political/policy responses. From this perspective, the difficulty is identifying when climate change science was ever normal science.

An uncertain climate for post-normal science

Advocates of post-normal science find a synchronicity between issues, their political constituencies, and the fashioning of scientific inquiry, such that prominent issues cannot be confined within the scientific community and to scientific process and be able to retain social credibility. Much is made of the superior treatment of risk and uncertainty by post-normal science, an especially critical and contentious dimension of climate change. In effect, the entire science debate could be framed in terms of the uncertainty about future global climate, so that manifestation of post-normal science has the potential to revelatory.

Climate change science could be thought as having assumed its mature form with the creation of the general circulation models based on the coalescence of relevant components and scientific fields into an approach that offered predictive capacity. Creation of the IPCC was premised on the understanding that anthropocentric global warming was occurring and the IPCC's institutional role was to enhance understanding of an extant discipline and to make it available for impacts and adaptation studies. Although many, if not most, of fundamental scientific uncertainties were resolved prior to the IPCC's creation, this was politically deemed an insufficient foundation for international policies concerning greenhouse gas emissions abatement. In effect, the IPCC's task wasn't to generate knowledge that would vault over a certainty threshold set by policy-makers that would enable policy formulation to proceed, as the conventional science formulation suggests. Rather, the post-normal science role of the IPCC was to lend credence to the idea that such a threshold existed by virtue of its institutional status, elite membership, and research program. Duly, the entirely innocuous IPCC statements that a 'discernible' human imprint on climate had been detected was put under the spotlights of the global media and framed in terms that global warming had now become 'certain.'

Many commentators have explained these circumstances using the role of the precautionary principle on which the FCCC has proceeded, which is entirely consistent with the facts and logically credible proposition. Conventionally, FCCC policy processes proceeded on the basis that the risks of inaction or delay were of such magnitude that waiting for full scientific certainty would be imprudent. Hence, the IPCC findings 'caught up' with the policy process and replaced the newly validated precaution with scientific evidence. However, if the threshold of scientific certainty existed and required routine research to be satisfied, then a body such as the IPCC would be unnecessary. Furthermore, the IPCC drew public attention for addressing the issue of whether human activity was causing global warming, a question that the precautionary principle was meant to obviate.

Evidence that the IPCC, by virtue of being post-normal science, was institutionally well equipped to deal with the political difficulties generated by the uncertainties of climate change is difficult to locate. Some commentators and scientists find the wide error bands on climate change forecasts undermine any efforts to interpret these findings for policy-making. For example, the ability to predict the values of even simple parameters, such as crop yields at specific locations under global warming, as the IPCC repeatedly itself acknowledges, is far from convincing. Ongoing prevalence of such uncertainty demonstrates to some that science faces an almost insurmountable barrier, so that the whole enterprise is discredited by the presence of a limit to its knowledge or that 'immature' knowledge is being pressed into service in a way that discredits science. Hadjilambrinos, for example, stated (1999: 524): "A major issue that has the potential to limit severely the role of science in the GCC [global climate change] policy debate is the considerable uncertainty that remains for virtually all aspects of GCC science."

Conceptually, while the uncertainty of scientific findings can be considered irrelevant to the mission or outputs of science, it assumes great import when applying scientific knowledge, becoming the yardstick of its utility. Shackley and Wynne (1996) consider the management of uncertainty in climate change research as 'boundary-ordering,' by which the science's legitimacy can be maintained for policy-making. Scientists demarcate a boundary (a social world defined by individuals, texts, projects, concepts, and the like) and within that realm their "expertise is autonomous." Connecting the scientific and policy communities are the advisory scientists, and it is their (Shackley and Wynne 1996: 280): "representation of uncertainty in semi-public and policy context facilitate interaction, translation, and cooperation between science and policy worlds while still ordering the relations between science and policy so as to sustain the special cultural authority of science." By managing the rhetoric of uncertainty as it "impinges on the public policy world," the authors suggest that scientific community increases the "ordering and interpreting" scientific uncertainty within the scientific domain. Policy-makers can also benefit from these circumstances, being freed of a great reliance on knowledge in someone else's control (Shackley and Wynne 1996). And in this scheme, we can more readily discern a clearer model of the IPCC, which in effect has built a post-normal science storefront onto the factory of conventional science research, and where the orders for scientific output are sent directly to the research community.

Formally, it was not until its third assessment reports that the IPCC indicated the certainty of their predictions, which were based on guidelines to authors seeking determination of the probability of the major parameters, using formal methods where possible. (This development followed an earlier problem, when something of a clash occurred in the second assessment round when Working Group II authors sought, unsuccessfully as it turned out, such advice from Working Group I.) Resulting probabilities in the third assessment reports were qualitatively grouped using common terms, ranging from 'virtually certain' to 'exceptionally unlikely.' However, the IPCC were not able assess uncertainty consistently between different findings, with central issues omitted from evaluation and minor ones included. Most prominently, the temperature forecast (i.e., 1.4–5.8°C mean global warming by 2100 in IPCC 2001a) is without probability assessment. Reilly et al. (2001) refer to the IPCC's revision of the second assessment reports warming estimates (i.e., 1.0–3.5°C in IPCC 1995a) and find the prompted question of whether the third assessment resulted from any new understanding, in terms of probability, unanswered by the IPCC. Schneider (2001) was concerned on this subject, noting that it is difficult to make the case that the IPCC has been well equipped to respond to the problems of uncertainty faced by policy-makers.

Hadjilambrinos places the issue of uncertainty and the institution of the IPCC into a political construct (1999: 524):

> The Panel has, admittedly unwillingly, found itself more interested in maintaining consensus within the diverse scientific community and keeping the issue of scientific uncertainty outside the public policy debate than in promoting scientific investigation of GCC. Although this has allowed the scientific community to maintain its position in the policy debate, it has also become a significant constraint on the role science can play in promoting a just and effective international GHG abatement policy. Maintaining a consensus in the face of high uncertainty implies that science must maintain a conservative position ...

Uncertainty, therefore, may operate dualistically. Within the IPCC, 'control' over uncertainty comprises a core mission necessary to maintain science as essential to the larger policy debate. Paradoxically, as Hadjilambrinos points out, this very approach necessarily disengages the IPCC from entry into wider debate where the critical social issues are being determined.

Creating and maintaining a consensus within the IPCC over uncertainty and other issues also reveals much about the post-normal science condition.

Readers of *Nature* were provided with an insider's insight into this activity by Schneider's (2001) account of the IPCC meeting to develop a series of emission 'storylines' for its special report on emissions, which featured an array of scientists and non-scientists. A wide variety of 'emissions stories' was generated for the next century, ranging from below current levels to a five-fold increase, however, when it came to assessing storyline certainty (Schneider 2001:18): "Because of the divergent views of participants about the likelihood of each storyline, the final report offered no assessment of the relative likelihoods, in an attempt to avoid endless disputes." Schneider reports pressing for some indication of each storylines' probability in order to assist policy-makers without success, reasoning that without such guidance, each storyline might be assumed to be equally likely. Such assessments were to come later from researchers working within 'conventional' science.

Assessing the post-normality of climate change science

Post-normal science seems to capture well central characteristics of the IPCC, yet claims that this institutional design necessarily provides an improved way of meeting public and policy needs for scientific knowledge seem conditional. As a new model for climate change science itself, post-normal science will seemingly have to overcome several hurdles. To begin with, there is the primary claim that the IPCC produces outcomes of increased normative value due to it post-normal science approach to climate change science. Critics of the existing approach to developing knowledge about climate change have faulted the IPCC. Redclift suggests (1995: 15):

> The scientific controversy accompanying global climate change, and the deliberations of the IPCC, have suggested that increasing our knowledge about future climate change and its impacts will enable us to adopt more appropriate values, emphasising long-run sustainability over short-run economic gain. However, the evidence for this assumption is weak.

While part of this failure that Redclift identifies is that of the naïve scientific servant espousing independence while following the dictates of a political master, there are associated questions about the willingness and ability of the IPCC to act as an agent of political reform. Post-normal climate change science has attempted to present itself as a plurality in which competing values are resolved, producing a kind of values consensus. Such a claim is misleading: climate change science has been particularly tame in analyzing the social causes of climate change, fully endorsed conservative economic analyses, and been completely unreflective on the role of science as a causal agent of climate change. Adding the participation of non-scientists to the IPCC negotiations does not seem to have informed the IPCC process of the values of ecological justice in any noticeable way, at least partially because the 'non-scientists' have been public servants following broad directives of national governments and prominent government agencies, usually with strong representation of foreign affairs, trade, and economic development.

Secondly, there is the relationship between conventional science and the IPCC. Post-normal science can only retain any credence by utilizing the findings of conventional research activities, as evidenced by the types of defense that the IPCC has offered when criticized. IPCC has undertaken a juggling act in trying to maintain the credibility of climate change science, while itself being a political interpreter of this science and arguing that its activity is conventional science, which has created confusion among scientists themselves, policy-makers, and the public. Professional climate change skeptics and opponents to the FCCC have not missed this opportunity for political advantage, pointing to the difference between science and post-normal science, and highlighting the disingenuousness of the IPCC in posing as an instrument of conventional science. Critiques from these groups found a place in the public media because at some levels an aspect of their claims rang true to those who associated government-approved research conspiratorially with government malfeasance. Addition of other agents into the science process did not succeed in making climate change more acceptable to the broader public, but presented the science with an additional flank vulnerable to attack. Arguments that post-normal science amounts to 'post-science' have resonance, as the experiments and studies on which IPCC deliberates, assesses, and evaluates are the product of conventional science, so that without conventional science, post-normal science has nothing to evaluate. On these grounds, many of the failures if the IPCC in the public arena and the debacle over the climate change skeptics appear to be rooted in the post-normal science construction of the IPCC.

Thirdly, claims that post-normal science deals better with uncertain policy issues than rational uses of conventional science cannot be substantiated by the IPCC's treatment of climate change uncertainties as knowledge. Schneider's (2001) phrase of needing to "avoid endless disputes" over uncertainty from a post-normal science process and the IPCC's resolution simply to give up in the face of such challenges suggests the pivotal role that internal rules of process may play. Conventional science is holding itself as a site where disputes are professionally resolved, implying scientifically-mandated solutions are beyond the reach of 'non-scientists.' Hence, post-normal science in this instance appears to provide a rationale for confining the scope of post-normal science processes. Nevertheless, as a tool to bestow the legitimacy of science on useful scientific findings, the IPCC has proved to be of great value. IPCC outcomes have increased the depth of knowledge on climate change and proved valuable in forcing a consensus on divergent views, and have been lauded for this difficult and worthy effort, yet the probability of much of its findings is largely unknown.

Fourthly, combining the natural and social sciences within the ambit of the IPCC's role armed it with the scope to offer to policy-makers and the public a comprehensive knowledge base for assessing climate change policy. However, this arrangement seemingly bestows on social science the imprint of the natural sciences, so that in instances where social values are uppermost in policy decisions, the IPCC has made conventional economic rationality 'scientific.' Co-joined thus, widespread support for taking action on climate change, based on the uncontroversial findings of climate change science, is dissipated over widely divergent views over more explicitly value-dependent policy choices (evoking differences over fundamental policy variables as the treatment of developing nations, the protection of endangered species, the rights of corporations, and so on). If post-normal science has offered a path through this tangle of views, it has not yet become apparent to climate change commentators. Post-normal science has not led to widespread internal questioning of the values in either the natural sciences, or that social science masquerading as a natural science which reported that anything but trivial actions to reduce greenhouse gas emissions would be 'uneconomic.'

Post-normal science offers a means of winning legitimacy for science on contentious issues, creates consensus from diverse views, and can potentially package science in ways amenable for policymaking and public discussion. Public confidence in post-normal science outcomes requires careful handling of the participants in the post-science process, yet the greater the dilution of the 'science' contribution, the greater the participants come to reflect usual political differences. To date, the performance of the IPCC does not inspire boundless confidence in post-normal science. Connections between IPCC science and policy seem more symbolic than real; the IPCC has only come closest to offering policy advice where this involves economics, where its credibility is lowest; formal certainty of climate change predictions is largely absent; the activities of the IPCC have created conditions where the legitimacy of climate change science has been lessened; and IPCC analysis of social causes of climate change is missing.

4   Climate change governance

An international liberal-democratic system

Liberal-democratic goals formed the basis for developing the international response to global climate change. Although sometimes considered a relatively new environmental issue, concerns over global warming and the advocacy for reducing greenhouse gas emissions are now over two decades old. Preceding the FCCC were a series of international events, some scientific and others political, that considered options, established positions, and shaped key debates beginning in the late 1970s. Many key issues arose in these early stages, establishing the contours of the ensuing political debate. Liberal-democratic principles were fundamental to the early political events on climate change, shaping specific policies in the FCCC's development, making its values explicit and pervasive. Historical accounts of the development of the FCCC's development have generally paid little attention to these early events, Paterson (1996) and Ross (1991) being important exceptions, and neglecting those factors and circumstances that made the FCCC into an instrument of liberal democracy.

Consistent with the recent trend for UN international environmental agreements, the FCCC is a framework convention. Such agreements are given effect through a two-stage process, whereby basic agreements and broad principles laid down in the framework convention are followed by an on-going process of international deliberations to determine the operational functioning of the convention in the form of protocols. In effect, the framework convention provides the legal and administrative footing on which negotiations between national parties can proceed. Consequently, these agreements can evolve and have the opportunity, in theory, to consider a wide array of policy approaches. Practice reveals, however, that the FCCC's policy response has kept safely within the confines of liberal democracy.

Devising a system for global climate governance

Assumptions of the inevitability of the features of the FCCC's development give many historical accounts a narrative a logical progression. Accepting that history is 'written by its winners,' such teleology is understandable, but such received histories is far from complete. Applying a more open perspective, it is clear that many different possibilities and opportunities were foregone or rejected. Liberal democracy's dominance in the current configuration of the FCCC and Kyoto Protocol expresses the effect of political activity, making assumptions of its superiority on instrumental, rational, and administrative grounds problematic. Equally questionable are those rationales promoting the FCCC policy designs as ethically optimal with the calims that it represents a fair, equitable, and socially optimal approach.

Ross (1991) maintains a prominent role for political influence throughout the process of creating the global governance response to climate change, beginning with the *realpolitik* of the superpowers' Cold War quest for national strategic advantage. Prompted by the 1970s global cooling scare, the U.S. Central Intelligence Agency commissioned several climate change studies. While the first report in 1974 linked U.S. global power and domestic climatic conditions favoring agriculture, a second considered the implications of climate change for the U.S. (Ross 1991). Food production would fall in many parts of the world, a consequence of drought and failed harvests, enhancing the U.S.'s global authority through virtue of the strategic advantage of surplus domestic food production, according to its findings (Ross 1991). Such times, the report speculated, would be politically and economically unstable, producing grave national risks to the U.S. from jealous national rivals (Ross 1991). Throughout the Cold War, as Ross (1991) describes, the U.S. undertook numerous attempts at weather modification for military purposes – until such activity was eventually banned by UN resolution. Food aid became a commodity of national strategic interest through the Cold War and was linked to climate issues. As the concern over climate change shifted from global cooling to global warming, nation states' concerns began to be expressed in global environmental diplomacy. Ross suggests (1991: 12): "One can only guess at the role played in this drama by Washington fantasies of global food supremacy generated by the cooling theory of the seventies."

Conventional accounts of the burgeoning international response to climate change usually stress two linked factors, a rising scientific consensus and institutional formations for global environmental governance based in the UN. Accordingly, the initial impetus for an international agreement has its genesis in a number of 1970s science and environment meetings that raised the issue and its relationship with various phenomena, such as the UN meetings on the human environment (1972), world food (1974), water (1977), and desertification (1977). Then in 1979, the WMO's first World Climate Conference was convened which identified the risks of anthropogenic global warming and called for research into its causes and potential effects. These concerns reached a wider audience following the 1985 Villach meeting of international scientists, which promulgated the possibility of rapid global warming in coming decades.

During the latter years of the 1980s, climate change acquired a rapidly escalating public profile and appeared on the agenda of mainstream political interests. In 1988, there was a ten-fold increase in the number of articles on global warming over the previous year and both U.S. Presidential candidates identified the issue (Soroos 1997). Soroos (1997) reports that a 1989 poll of the U.S. public's awareness of global warming recorded 80 percent, up from the 60 percent in 1988, and that nine committees in the U.S. congress held hearings on 32 bills dealing with the greenhouse effect. Developed nations around the world followed a similar pattern, with growing public awareness and tentative policy initiatives.

Prominently, the Toronto Conference recommended an international framework convention on climate change, to be supplemented by additional and specific protocols. Specifically, it sought a 20 percent reduction in carbon dioxide emissions by developed nations by 2005 as the first phase in reducing global emissions. Also recommended was a 'World Atmosphere Fund' funded by a fossil fuel tax levied in the developed nations (Bodansky 1994). Attended by 340 scientists, government officials, NGOs, and industry representatives from 46 nations (Soroos 1997), the Toronto Conference was not a governmental event as government officials attended in a personal capacity (Bodansky 1994). Furthermore, the Conference Statement did not purport to represent the views of all participants – it was not a negotiated document – and was not binding on participants (Bodansky 1994). As Soroos (1997) and other commentators noted, the Conference was the first major international meeting to formulate policy responses to global warming.

International political activity

Below is a list of the significant events in the international political response to climate change:

First World Climate Conference (Geneva, 1979)
Scientific Conference (Villach, 1980)
Scientific Conference (Villach, 1985)
Changing Atmosphere Conference (Toronto, 1988)
Intergovernmental Panel on Climate Change formed (1988)
Summit on Protecting the Atmosphere (New Delhi, 1989)
Ministerial Conference on Air Pollution and Climate Change (Noordvijk, 1989)
Small Island State Conference on Sea Level Rise (Maldive Islands, 1989)
Action for a Common Future Conference (Bergen, 1990)
Second World Climate Conference (Geneva, 1990)
International Negotiating Committee begins (1991)
UN Conference on Environment and Development, FCCC signed (Rio, 1992)
First FCCC Conference of the Parties (COP-1) and the Berlin Mandate (Berlin, 1995)
COP-3 and the Kyoto Protocol (Kyoto, 1997)
COP-6 and the Bonn Accords (The Hague, 1999 and Bonn, 2000)
COP-7 (Marrakech, 2001)

In many ways, the Toronto Conference stands isolated as a highly influential event without the sanctioning of national governments, but with unofficial government representation. But in its wake, the fledgling intention to internationally govern climate change became one characterized by national government involvement, and dominated by industrialized nations, at least until 1990 (Bodansky 1994), and arguably has continued to the present. Several additional international meetings and conferences followed that year: a meeting of legal experts in Ottawa to discuss potential legal instruments; an international meeting of national representatives in The Hague; and importantly, at Noordwijk where 67 national environment ministers attempted to forge a multilateral agreement on targets and timetables for greenhouse gas emission reductions (Gupta 2001). As Soroos (1997) states, the Noordwijk meeting was the first international attempt to form a governmental agreement on greenhouse gas emissions abatement. Noordwijk also saw the emergence of major areas of disputation between nations. While most participants favored a reduction regime to curb greenhouse emissions at their 1988 levels by 2005, four critical nations opposed such an explicit target (namely England, Japan, U.S., and the U.S.S.R.). Accordingly, the Noordwijk Declaration called for reductions to achieve stabilization of emissions by developed nations at totals to be established by the IPCC at the forthcoming Second World Climate Conference (see Churchill and Freestone 1991: Appendix 24). Eventually, key aspects of the Noordwijk Declaration formed part of the wording of the FCCC.

Partially through their involvement in the conferences in Toronto and Noordwijk, developing nations became aware of the implications of climate change impacts and of the responses being considered by the developed world (Brenton 1994). Developing nations also held their own meetings in this period, such as in New Delhi in 1989 and in the Maldives and Nairobi in 1990 (Brenton 1994). That bifurcation that marked most UN deliberations between the developed and developing nations could now be seen in the climate change issue, driven partially by developing nation concerns that the developed nations' meetings were neglecting developing world interests and issues.

Internationally, climate change was raised at the 1989 Group of Seven meeting in Paris, the communiqué of which called for the urgent creation of an international framework convention on climate change (Soroos 1997). Climate change was raised in the same year at the Malta summit of the U.S.–Soviet Union, at the Commonwealth nations conference in Langkawi, Malaysia, and at the Belgrade Conference of non-aligned nations (Soroos 1997). In 1988 (the same year as the IPCC was established), the government of Malta proposed that the UN respond to climate change, and subsequently UN resolution 43/53 Protection of the Global Climate for Present and Future Generations of Mankind was passed that year.

President Gorbachev called on the UN Conference on Environment and Development to be held in Rio (popularly known, grandiosely, as the 'Earth Summit') to become a summit meeting attended by heads of states during the Global Forum on Environment and Development in Moscow in 1990. In April 1990, the U.S. George Bush White House convened a two-day meeting of representatives of eighteen nations to explain U.S. reluctance to agree to any commitments to abate their greenhouse gas emissions, citing scientific uncertainties. Such an action did not convince many attendees (Soroos 1997), and at the 1990 Economic Commission for Europe Conference on Action for a Common Future in Bergen, Norway, ministers from Europe and North America addressed the climate change issue. Soroos (1997) notes that this meeting produced an informal agreement to stabilize emissions of the major greenhouse gases at their 1990 levels by 2000 and requested that the IPCC examine the issue of a 20 percent cut by 2005.

Climate change policy initiatives by several nations reflected the intention to devote both capital and political activity to the task of reducing emissions and enhancing carbon sinks. Most notably, the Netherlands and the European Community adopted emission reduction targets. Gupta states that the problem had been defined as one of emissions and sinks (2001: 31): "The enthusiasm in Europe stemmed from the optimism that once a problem is defined, technologies can be found to deal with it." There was some momentum developing as within the OECD, Gupta (2001) reports that 24 of the 26 members had national greenhouse gas reduction targets by 1994 (Turkey and the U.S. being the exceptions).

In the complicated interplay between individual nations and international activity, apparent successes in climate policy by progressive nations were not readily replicated internationally, despite what many saw as an encouraging start. Hopes that the Second World Climate Conference might provide a forum for a multilateral agreement on emissions reduction were disappointed. Efforts by the majority of ministers from 144 nations during the Conference's final two days to fix an abatement timetable and targets for industrialized nations were opposed by, prominently, Saudi Arabia, the Soviet Union, and the U.S. However, the Conference did recognize the principle of (Jager and Ferguson 1991) "equity and the common but differentiated responsibility of countries should be the basis of any response to climate change, developed countries must take the lead." Lacking superpower agreement to any quantitative commitments, the meeting could only call for future action in the form of a global convention with appropriate powers. As a result, the Conference produced a statement along similar lines to the existing UN resolution. Subsequently, the UN established an International Negotiating Committee to negotiate a framework convention on climate change for signing at the Rio Earth Summit.

Preparations for the FCCC

Five International Negiotating Committee meetings were held between early 1991 and mid-1992 (the last comprising two parts). Early decisions saw the UN Montreal Protocol on Substances that Deplete the Ozone Layer on stratospheric ozone depleting substances adopted as a model for Committee deliberations, so that an initial 'framework' convention to establish basic issues would be followed by a process that could then determine the issues surrounding emission reductions (Molitor 1999). Many of the aforementioned antagonisms and national allegiances that emerged in the Second World Climate Conference flowed seamlessly into the Committee process, with emission targets and timetables continuing as a major sticking point. Some 135 countries participated in the process, with the major issues producing a wide variety of national positions. Key national blocks were the developing nation's Group of 77 (G-77), the Association of Small Island States (AOSIS), Canada, Australia, and New Zealand (CANZ), and the E.U. (albeit with several factions).

Hecht and Tirpak (1995) report that the White House controlled U.S. climate policy during this period and three senior advisors exerted a critical influence. These officials believed that emissions control would be costly, that the U.S. would have to support developing nations in this endeavor, and considered it unlikely that climate change impacts would economically trouble the U.S. (Hecht and Tirpak 1995). On the crucial debate over 'targets and timetables,' a compromise was brokered between the U.S. and key European nations; the Europeans dropping their call for specific targets in order to secure U.S. support for the convention (Hecht and Tirpak 1995; Soroos 1997). High-level negotiators from the U.K. and the U.S. determined the final wording of the Convention's targets and timetables at a meeting in Washington and submitted these to President George Bush for approval (Hecht and Tirpak 1995). One month after the International Negotiating Committee finished its deliberations, 154 nations signed the FCCC at the 1992 UN Earth Summit. Ratification required 50 nations to participate and this was achieved quickly; by March 1994 180 nations had ratified the agreement and the FCCC came into effect.

Negotiations at Rio were intense over critical aspects and determined the essential features of the FCCC. Designation of the goal for developed nations curb emissions at their 1990 levels as a 'voluntary aim,' resulted from the insistence of the U.S.; such was the leniency of this goal and condition that the U.S. Senate ratified the FCCC on a 'voice vote' and thus became the first industrialized nation to sign. Although the FCCC represented a landmark achievement in environmental agreements, any optimism over the prospects of rapid international cooperation was misplaced. International activity to construct an agreement for specific actions onto the 'framework' was to take most of the next decade and essentially involved an on-going dispute over the issues of the Rio negotiations.

Cutting greenhouse gas emissions

Abating greenhouse gas emissions formed the basis of the emerging agreement, making the provision and verificiation of each nations' emissions of fundamental importance for any international approach to managing climate change along scientific grounds. Scientifically, a number of difficulties remained in measuring emissions from managed biological sources in agriculture and forestry, but measurements of fossil fuel combustion were technically straightforward. Although the FCCC and Kyoto Protocol list those gases subject to their control, some systems of measurement count only the dominant gas, carbon dioxide, while others convert a suite of greenhouse gases to a common unit, the carbon dioxide equivalent. Technical resolutions of greenhouse gas measurement, despite these complications, could be portrayed as neutral science, akin to an inventory and accounting system, and following the lead of the Montreal Protocol and other similar pollution control initiatives.

Suggesting that decisions over what to include as a greenhouse gas, of which nations to count, or what baselines should be used are merely technical matters is to mask contentious political choices with science. Calculations of national greenhouse gas emissions can express an array of political and scientific differences, and in the presentation of data on emissions are embedded a number of political decisions and value judgements. To begin with, annual national emissions vary greatly between nations. Dominated by a handful of major emitters, the international emissions pattern is highly skewed, with the majority of the world's nations having low to very low emissions. Eight nations produce about half the world's emissions of carbon dioxide from fossil fuel combustion: In 2000, the proportions were: U.S.: 24.2 percent; China: 12.8 percent; Russia: 6.4 percent; Japan: 4.9 percent; India: 4 percent; Germany 3.6 percent; U.K. 2.3 percent; and Canada 2.3 percent (IEA 2002). Of the world's remaining nations, none contributes more than two percent (IEA 2002). Adding the non-fossil fuel sources of emissions, for which data collection is more difficult, is unlikely to alter this basic picture.

Despite the large emissions from China and India, greenhouse gases predominantly emanate from developed nations, some forty of which accounted for about 75 percent of global carbon dioxide emissions in 1990 and about 79 percent of carbon dioxide concentrations in the atmosphere (see Gupta 2001). Within the developed nations block, the distribution is also highly skewed, with emissions from four nations – Germany, Japan, Russia, and the U.S. – accounting for nearly 70 percent (IEA 2002), (see Table 4.1). Further exemplifying this differentiation are emissions from the larger U.S. states, such as California and Texas, that exceed those of smaller OECD nations, such as the Netherlands, Belgium, Austria, and Denmark, and obviously greater than the vast majority of developing nations (NET 2002).

Developed nations usually have far higher absolute emissions than developing nations, indicating something of overall levels of economic development and scale of industrial activity. Yet when emissions are calculated on a per capita basis, the association with development becomes stark. Many per capita accounts have been published and display an array of differences in technique and methodology (e.g., Agarwal and Narain 1991; Byrne et al.

Table 4.1 Total carbon dioxide emissions of selected FCCC Annex 1 parties in 1990 (gigagrams).

Party	Emissions (Gg) (1)	Percent of Annex 1 parties (2)
United States	4,957,022	36.1
Russia	2,388,720	17.4
Japan	1,173,360	8.5
Germany	1,012,443	7.4
Sub-total	9,531,545	69.4
All Annex 1 parties total	13,728,306	100

Notes
1 Does not include land use emissions.
2 Annex 1 parties refers to the list of developed nations in Annex 1 of the FCCC, as described in this chapter.

Source: Framework Convention on Climate Change Secretariat (1998). *The Kyoto Protocol to the Convention on Climate Change*. Bonn.

1998; and Meyer 2000). Developed nations, on average, produce five times the per capita emissions as undeveloped nations (see Bolin and Kheshgi 2001). Turton and Hamilton's (2001) calculations differ from most of the earlier estimates by including land use emissions and offset of carbon sinks, thereby presenting a more comprehensive account. Nations such as the U.S., Canada, and Australia expel over 20 (metric) tons of carbon dioxide equivalents per person annually, with Norway (14.1), Germany (11.9), Japan (10.2), Italy (9), France (8.2), and Spain (8.4) indicating the central range for industrial nations, with a small number demonstrating relatively low emissions, such as Switzerland (6.6), Sweden (4.8), Monaco (4.4), and Latvia (0.4) (Turton and Hamilton 2001). Generally, energy consumption. GHG production, and world-system position are tied; energy consumption and GHG output is greatest amongst the 'core' nations and lowest amongst the 'periphery.'

Emissions estimates need not be restricted to nation-state boundaries and some research has been conducted into emissions from corporate entities. Although greenhouse gases are produced by every sector of an industrialized economy, a relatively few corporations are responsible for a large portion of global emissions. Greenhouse gas emissions from global corporate sources were investigated by a group led by the U.S. NGO, the Natural Resources Defense Council, which found that almost 80 percent of carbon emissions came from 122 private and state-owned producers and that almost 47 percent was from only 20 of these producers (NRDC et al. 1999).

Framework convention on climate change and the Kyoto Protocol

Prevailing through negotiations when failure seemed imminent and surviving a potential deadlock in the final sessions, the successful creation the

FCCC was a highlight of the Rio Summit. While for its supporters, the FCCC appeared to usher in a new era of international cooperation on global environmental protection, critics from developing nations and environmental NGOs feared that too much had been negoitiated away in the quest for a successful compromise. Negotiations had produced a relatively weak framework convention, largely following the approach of the successful Montreal Protocol. It was agreed that developed nations would take the lead in greenhouse gas emissions reduction and developing nations would undertake emissions monitoring and reporting. Developed nations accepted a voluntary emissions reduction target that their national emissions at the year 2000 would not exceed those of 1990. Under the Framework Convention design it is left to a negotiating process featuring annual meetings known as the 'Conference of the Parties' (COP), to develop legally binding instruments to bring the Framework Convention into force.

Following the structure typical of such agreements, the FCCC features a preamble, a statement of objectives, a list of principles, defines specific terms, contains specific articles describing policy measures and the obligations of national parties, together with the creation of a number institutions designed to aid implementation. Beginning with the Preamble, the FCCC establishes the character of the climate change problem in a manner that attempts to avoid overt controversy. Reference is made to the difference between the level of emissions from developed and developing nations, to the need for domestic action and need for actions in one nation not prejudice the prospects for another state. As Gupta (2001: 32) notes, the Preamble avoids "references to politically charged terms such as global commons and heritage." As to its objective, the FCCC states that it seeks future stabilization of the atmospheric greenhouse gases that would prevent dangerous interference with global climate, but without specifying quantitatively that level and offering only some general indications of the types of dangers involved.

In some ways, it is the agreement's five principles that most shape the content of the major articles and subsequent policy development in the protocol process. Nations are divided into developed and developing, which must accordingly assume "common but differentiated responsibilities," in which the developed nations are to 'take the lead' in reducing emissions. Developed nations, 24 in all, comprising the (1992) OECD, together with Eastern and Central Europe, Russia, and Ukraine (the so-called 'economies in transition') that are listed in the first annex to the FCCC (and in the jargon of climate change negotiations are known as 'Annex 1 nations,' with the developing nations called 'non-Annex 1 nations').

Importantly, the FCCC adopts the 'precautionary principle' as a basis for action (see, e.g., Freestone 1991). Under the FCCC, this principle means that the threats of climate change are sufficiently serious (and irreversible) that response measures cannot wait for full scientific resolution. This principle directly counters the arguments of the U.S. advanced during and prior to the International Negotiating Committee process, that scientific uncertainty prevented any decisions on measures to reducing emissions. "Economic development" is explicitly identified as another principle, this being necessary for responding to climate change, which is to be undertaken in an open international economic system. These latter principles tie the climate change response to the general 'global free trade' rhetoric as promoted by such bodies as the World Trade Organization and World Bank, effectively placing climate policy into the broader process of economic globalization.

Nations prepare inventories of their greenhouse gas emissions according to a prescribed methodology, with several rounds of 'National Communications' now completed. Six greenhouse gases are included under the agreement (carbon dioxide, methane, nitrous oxide, hydrofluorocarbons, perfluorocarbons, and sulphur hexafluoride), which are converted to carbon dioxide units on the basis of their 'global warming potential.' Of the obligations for developed nations, most crucial are those on emissions reductions in Articles 4.2a and 4.2b. National emissions of "carbon dioxide and other greenhouse gases not controlled by the Montreal Protocol" are to be returned to their 1990 levels by the year 2000. This target is identical to that agreed at the 1989 Noordwijk Ministerial conference.

All nations are to cooperate in many activities, such as in research, sustainable development, education, training, and raising awareness. Developed nations are to assist developing nations, through technology transfer and other means, especially those deemed most vulnerable to climate change. Developing countries obligations depend on the efforts made by developed nations. Specifically, Article 4.7 states:

> The extent to which developing country Parties will effectively implement their commitments under the Convention will depend on effective implementation by developed country parties of their commitments under the Convention related to financial resources and transfer of technology and will take fully into account that economic and social development and poverty eradication are the first and overriding priorities of the developing country Parties. Developed nations are to reduce their emissions and developing nations are allowed to increase emissions, with developing countries to be assisted in their uptake of modern technologies to reduce emissions and adapt to future climate change.

From Rio to Kyoto: preparing the Kyoto Protocol

At the first Conference of the Parties (COP-1), held in Berlin in 1995, negotiators allocated two years for a sub-group to develop proposals specific emissions reduction (known as the Ad-hoc Group on the Berlin Mandate) to replace the FCCC's earlier goal. This decision was taken against the background where arguably no Annex 1 nation successfully lowered their emissions, noting that the 'favorable' emissions profiles of the former Soviet Union and Eastern Europe after their retreat from central economic planning in the early 1990s and subsequent economic collapse. Following the FCCC, negotiators set 1990 as a base year and only sought action from developed nations, extending the 'north–south' division of Annex 1 and non-annex 1 parties.

COP-2 achieved little, except that subsequently the U.S. changed its position (under the Clinton administration) and accepted the concept of emission targets that it had opposed up to this time (Gupta 2001). Agreeing to a target was effectively conditional on acceptance of the U.S. wish that targets be met through implementation measures that offered the 'maximum flexibility' to nations. While the prospects for the success of the Ad Hoc Group were virtually assured once the U.S. position was accepted, other problems developed. That 'policy flexibility' sought by the U.S. was code for preferring market-based tools over 'command and control' approaches, but also a penchant for the fewest fixed requirements for nations under any agreement. From this time forward, Jacoby and Reiner typify the rationale offered by U.S. officials of European economic irrationality (2001:299):

> The storyline of the next five years might be summarized as an effort by Europe to force the United States to accept a fossil emissions target while resisting efforts to enshrine the flexibility that would help reduce the cost of such a commitment and increase the likelihood of ratification.

Continuing negotiations were marked by a consistent division between the E.U. and a group comprising the U.S., Japan, Canada, Australia, Norway, New Zealand, and Iceland, with some support from Russia and the Ukraine. Policies favored by the Europeans were specific, notably the call for carbon taxes, and the opportunity for the E.U. to adopt a collective target under which they would negotiate their own national targets (basically to allow Britain and Germany to carry a greater burden than the poorer Greece and Spain). U.S. negotiators vigorously opposed carbon taxes and sought flexibility for the U.S. and the other 'umbrella group' members to allow emissions reductions undertaken abroad to be counted as their own and to allow credit for carbon sinks in forests and agricultural lands. Activity in the international arena was being influenced by developments in domestic policy, nowhere more so than the U.S. During 1997, the U.S. Senate passed Resolution 98, by a 95–0 vote, known as the Byrd–Hagel resolution opposing any climate agreement that would harm the U.S. economy or didn't include developing countries in emission targets (Paarlberg 1999). A concerted media campaign began in the U.S. in anticipation of COP-3 to discredit climate change science (see Chapter 3) and industry, labor, and agricultural groups campaigned along similar lines to the Senate resolution to influence U.S. government policy.

Annex 1 nations had performed dismally in their efforts to meet the initial greenhouse gas reduction targets, as national greenhouse gas reporting under the FCCC indicates (UNFCCC 2001). By the time of COP-3 in 1997, few Annex 1 nations reduced emissions through climate change policy means; successes were largely driven by factors incidental to climate policy (e.g., economic collapse in the nations of the former Soviet Union and Eastern Europe, notably Russia and the Ukraine, Germany's unification, and Britain's 'dash for gas' under privatization). Emissions growth in this period was greatest in the U.S., although most 'umbrella group' members also increased; growth rates were generally lower in Europe.

COP-3 was most concerned with establishing emissions targets. Tied into these negotiations was the design of policy instruments and it was the admittance of these 'flexibility mechanisms' that enabled the resulting national targets to be relatively close between the major powers, despite the considerable differences in emission rates and national circumstances (Jacoby and Reiner 2001). Although the E.U. argued for a 15 percent emissions cut by 2010 for all developed nations (of the three key gases), the U.S. sought stabilization only. Compromises were reached and accordingly, COP-3 produced the Kyoto Protocol with emission reduction targets between a 5 to 8 percent reduction for most of Annex B nations (as shown in Table 4.2). Of equal difficulty to produce were the Protsocol's policies to assist emission reduction sought by the 'umbrella group.' Agreement at Kyoto was aided by many circumstances, but was doubtless assisted by adopting 'flexible' policy mechanisms at the 'in-principle' level and leaving the details for future meetings. After the manner of the FCCC, the Protocol

Table 4.2 Kyoto Protocol greenhouse gas reduction first-phase commitments for 2008–2012.

Nation	Change from 1990 emissions (%)
European Union (1), Bulgaria, Czech Republic, Estonia, Latvia, Liechtenstein, Monaco, Romania, Slovakia, Slovenia, and Switzerland	–8
United States	–7
Canada, Japan, Poland, and Hungary	–6
Croatia	–5
New Zealand, Ukraine, and Russia	0
Norway	+1
Australia	+8
Iceland	+10
All Annex B Parties	–5.2

Note

1 European Union is a collective target under which member states are allocated individual emission reduction targets.

Source: Framework Convention on Climate Change Secretariat (n.d.). *The Kyoto Protocol to the Convention on Climate Change*. Bonn.

negotiators had again fostered agreement by displacing contentious issues onto future meetings, while establishing essential policy principles. While the Kyoto Protocol represented progress in developing a final international agreement by establishing its basic policy structure, critical operational details remained unresolved.

At Kyoto, individual national greenhouse gas emission targets were set for developed nations for the period 2008–2012 with reference to 1990 as the base year (as listed under the Protocol's Annex B). Developed countries listed under the FCCC (under Annex I) are identical to those under the Protocol, except the Protocol does not include Belarus and Turkey and has the addition of Kazakhstan, who voluntarily joined. (OECD newcomers South Korea and Mexico have not sought inclusion in the Protocol's Annex B parties.)

Collectively, the Annex B nations' emissions abatement task amounts to a 5.2 percent reduction from their 1990 levels. No particular scientific significance should be inferred from the 5.2 percent target figure; it is simply the outcome of negotiations, as are the individual national variations and exceptions. Six greenhouse gases are counted under the Protocol: carbon dioxide, methane, nitrous oxide, hydrofluorocarbons, perfluorocarbons, and sulphur hexafluoride (as listed under the Protocol's Annex A). These gases are not treated individually, but are combined on the basis of their global warming potential, and calculated as carbon dioxide equivalents (according to IPCC formulae). Developing nations are expected to make efforts to curb emissions production, but have no targets for the first commitment phase. Although it subsequently withdrew from the FCCC process (as discussed below) and rejects the Kyoto Protocol, the U.S. negotiated at COP-3 and agreed to a reduction target (though the support of the U.S. Congress was never sought).

Individual national targets range from the extraordinary increases to a few nations (Australia 8 percent, Iceland 10 percent, and Norway 1 percent), stability (New Zealand, Ukraine, and the Russian Federation), to reductions for the majority, ranging from 92–95 per cent of 1990 emissions for the other 32 Annex B nations. Under the Protocol (Article 4), the E.U. was allowanced to redistribute its 8 per cent reduction allocation amongst its 15 member states (known as the 'EU Bubble') within which the Union has differentiated each nation's target (shown in Table 4.3). Within the E.U., the heaviest cuts are likely to be borne by Luxembourg, Denmark, Germany, with Austria, the U.K., Italy, and the Netherlands also making cuts, France stabilizing, and the poorer Spain, Greece, Ireland, and Portugal allowed increases, along with Sweden.

A host of policy options are identified in the Protocol (under Article 2), including the measures of energy efficiency, protection and enhancement of carbon sinks, sustainable agriculture, renewable energy, elimination of market imperfections, and policy development. However, greatest attention and disputation involved the three innovative policy mechanisms designed

Table 4.3 'European bubble:' Kyoto Protocol greenhouse gas reduction first-phase commitments for 2008–2012 for Europe.

European nation	Change from 1990 emissions (%)
Austria	−13
Belgium	−7.5
Denmark	−21
Finland	0
France	0
Germany	−21
Greece	+25
Ireland	+13
Italy	−6.5
Luxembourg	−28
Netherlands	−6
Portugal	+27
Spain	+15
Sweden	+4
United Kingdom	−12.5

Source: European Union, The. Environment Council (1998). *Press Release.* Community Strategy on Climate Change – Council Conclusion. Appendix 1, 16 June, Luxembourg.

to assist developed nations reduce emissions in a cost-effective manner: emissions trading; the Clean Development Mechanism (CDM); and Joint Implementation (known as the 'Kyoto mechanisms). These policies allow the developed nations to obtain credit for emissions reductions taken beyond their borders and allow for international trade of these credits, the most important of which is emissions trading. Annex B nations can also claim credit for carbon sinks, under some restrictions, which are taken as direct offsets to national emissions.

Wild ride: from Kyoto (COP-3) to Marrakech (COP-7)

Following COP-3, the next two Conferences of the Parties saw little, if any, progress. Debate centered on the Kyoto mechanisms and continued with the divisions between the E.U. and the slightly revised 'umbrella group' of Australia Canada, Japan, Russia, and the U.S. and some smaller nations. COP-4 did little more than list existing disagreements and deferred their resolution to COP-6. Differences over in policy preferences and national outlooks over the controversial issues apparent in the original negotiations over the FCCC that had been effectively deferred right through the Kyoto Protocol process. Preparations for the late 2000 COP-6 at The Hague were not propitious and, once under way, negotiations immediately stalled on longstanding disputes: details of the Kyoto mechanisms, especially emissions trading; the treatment of carbon sinks crediting; and funding and technical transfer for developing nations and their possible future inclusion in the Protocol. COP-6 talks duly collapsed before the end of the second week, with open acrimony between representatives drawing wide media coverage; COP-6 President Jan Pronk declared the conference 'suspended.'

Although held responsible for collapse of The Hague conference by some commentators, a deadlock over carbon sinks between the E.U. and the umbrella group was only one of several irresolvable matters. Two of the Protocol's articles were particularly contentious: Article 3.3 on land use and forestry activity since 1990 and Article 3.4 on allowances for nations to include pre-existing 'additional activities' as carbon offsets in their emission reduction activities. Such activities include an array of land management and land use practices, such as planting forests, raising crops, stocking lands, and controlling erosion – and the Protocol left open to negotiation as to exactly how this would be counted. With release of the IPCC's Special Report (IPCC 2000b) on this issue in time for COP-6, the implications of the ambiguity of Article 3.4 were revealed. It transpired that the full potential of these carbon sinks in developed nations exceeded their greenhouse gas reduction targets, so that a generous interpretation of Articles 3.3 and 3.4 would relieve the developed world of the need to reduce emissions growth. Taken together with the potential credits available from emissions trading and the aforementioned carbon sinks and additional activities, it was theoretically possible that no OECD national emissions would be necessary. For example, Hamilton (2001: 141–142) argued that the OECD would be required to reduce emissions by 690 million tons of carbon per annum (mtC) by 2010, of which 'hot air' credits could contribute 170 mtC, forests another 170 mtC, and carbon sinks a further 360 mtC. And it was the issue of the allowable size of the carbon sinks, and predominantly the claims made by the U.S., that was rejected by the E.U., and to a lesser extent the Group of 77 and China.

Opponents of the FCCC from conservative politics were jubilant over The Hague failure. For some, it represented the manifestation of the Kyoto Protocol's flaws: the overly ambitious targets, the exclusion of developing nations from binding commitments, the potential economic damage wrought by emissions reduction, and other reasons (Victor 2001). FCCC supporters were highly concerned by grave doubts over the agreement's very future and, indeed, over the prospects for any future agreement on limiting greenhouse gas emissions (Grubb 2001a; Grubb and Yamin 2001). Developing countries were critical of the overall failure of The Hague, but as the differences between hegemons of the E.U. and the U.S. were never resolved, the developing nations never saw the disputed texts nor were they significantly engaged in the debate (Egenhofer and Cornillie 2001).

COP-6 was reconvened in Bonn in July 2001 as COP-6 *bis*. Several intervening meetings of national representatives in Oslo and Ottawa to resolve matters failed, but one event during this period re-shaped the prospects for Bonn – the results of the U.S. Presidential election. Newly-elected U.S. President G.W. Bush, in whose election campaign commentators had located statements that both support and decry the FCCC (cf. Jacoby and Reiner 2001), despite a campaign promise to limit power station emissions that included carbon dioxide, resolved any ambiguity by opposing any curbing of U.S. carbon dioxide emissions and the Kyoto Protocol in a publicly-released letter to four U.S. senators (Bush 2001a). President G.W. Bush then declared in June 2001 the Protocol to be "fatally flawed in fundamental ways" and announced that that U.S. would not ratify (Bush 2001b). Reaction to the U.S. decision by a large number of foreign governments, especially those of the E.U. and Japan, expressed disappointment and outrage. Arguably, U.S. withdrawal was the most publicized aspect that the FCCC had received in the worldwide media, playing as it did into the global politics of the controversial U.S. leader.

Contrary to predictions of the immanent failure of the entire FCCC process at Bonn and to widespread surprise, in the formal 'absence' of the U.S., COP-6 *bis* produced agreement from 178 nations for a set of agreements over the key provisions of the Kyoto Protocol. Doubtless the attempted unilateralism of the U.S. over climate change had a galvanizing effect on the meeting, creating a determination not to lose the FCCC if nothing else (Vrolijk 2001). Benedict (2001: 72) called President Bush the "unsung hero" of the Bonn Agreements, as in response to his administration's efforts the "European governments closed rank and, along with Green politicians and environment groups around the world, interpreted the stark U.S. position as a moral challenge and an irresponsible repudiation of the seriousness of climate change."

Not unexpectedly, agreement meant compromise. On the key issue of sink allowances, Bonn allowed what had bitterly opposed when driven by the U.S. in the past meeting, for having withdrawn from the Protocol, the U.S. could no longer be the chief beneficiary of such decisions. Further, on the vital issue known in Conference of the Parties jargon as 'supplementarity' (i.e., the amount domestic emissions reduction could be supplemented by using the flexibility mechanisms), over which the U.S. and the E.U. had been intractably opposed, was discarded and emissions trading became effectively unlimited and the CDM minimally restrained. In effect, the U.S. position had prevailed in the two key issues through its formal absence (i.e., it attends but doesn't vote). Those environmental NGOs who consistently pressed for an effective FCCC were quite divided over the COP-6*bis* results between those who found them overly compromised and ineffective (dubbing it "Kyoto-light") and those celebrating the international agreement as a vital first step.

Of the Bonn Accords, no commentator has suggested that the system of emissions accounting, reporting, and control can be readily grasped. Not only did the agreement create a virtually new category of pollutant that poses singular challenges to control, but that the policy remedies are also unique, innovative, and of great complexity. Devising effective governance systems for controlling greenhouse gas emissions is an arduous technical and administrative matter that has generally eluded the nation states, in spite of the fact that energy conservation policiers have been well established for several decades, making their resolution at the international scale through diplomacy a formidable task.

One of Bonn's key outcomes was to allow unlimited emissions trading. Annex B nations are to be unrestrained in their purchase and sell as many emission credits, limited only by the uncertain notion that such purchase must be "supplemental" to domestic activity. In order to prevent nations selling permits to the extent that they fail their own targets, limits were imposed using set reserves to prevent nations 'overselling.' Annex B nations can trade emissions, both purchasing and selling, but to prevent 'gaming,' a credits reserve stipulates a sales limit of 10 percent of their total allowable emissions. Land use, land use management, and forestry activities since 1990 can be counted towards a country's emission reductions, with a limit imposed on forest management activities as established by 'Annex Z.' Under the Annex, most nations have allocations under one million tons of carbon, with the notable exceptions of Canada (12 million tons), Japan (13 million tons), and the Russian Federation (over 17 million tons).

Marrakech was the location for COP-7 in October/November 2001, but being held in the wake of the World Trade Center terrorism attack in the U.S. and many considering that the Bonn accords had resolved many pressing issues, the event had a considerably lower profile than the Bonn meeting. At COP-7, the work continued on eliminating some the remaining uncertainties, generally technical details, to produce the Marrakech Accords. Developing countries were active as the G77/China group of 133 nations, and although most of their issues were resolved at Bonn, they reiterated their refusal against any emissions commitments and highlighted the inadequate leadership of the developed world in effective emissions abatement. Discussions on capacity building and technology transfer in developing countries and economies in transition resulted in the creation of three new funds on adaptation, a special climate change fund, and a least developed nations fund. Although there were no major changes to the Kyoto mechanisms, the conference gave emissions trading, the CDM, and joint implementation their final form. Whether or not the mechanisms would be supplemental to domestic activity was settled in favor of the Umbrella group, with no limit being imposed on the amount that emissions savings obtained through the mechanisms could be counted as domestic reductions. Refinement of the emissions trading rules saw measures introduced to prevent the 'overselling' of emission credits (i.e., the sale of emission credits needed to comply with a nation's own emission reduction targets) through a holding requirement known as a 'commitment period reserve.'

No major carbon sink issue remained after the Bonn Accords and the Marrakech negotiators settled several details. Eligible to be counted as carbon sinks are forest, cropland, and grazing land management, and revegetation, with only forest management limited by a cap. CDM projects are allowed to include afforestation and reforestation in the first commitment period (and limited at 1 per cent of five times the nation's 1990 emission level). One significant change was the increased carbon sink allowance of the Russian Federation, which was granted an additional 15.4 million tons of carbon (under the aforementioned Protocol Article 3.4), which has the effect of increasing the already considerable amount of emissions credits that other Annex B nations can purchase. But the most significant development was establishing a compliance system featuring a penalty for compliance failures. Nations exceeding the emission limits in the first commitment period will be suspended from using the flexibility mechanisms and the amount by which the limits are exceeded will be added to the second commitment period (i.e., 2013–2017) with a penalty of 1.3 times that amount. COP-7 couldn't resolve the handling of re-instating eligible nations or a legal wording for compliance; both issues to be taken up following the Protocol's ratifion.

Remaining Kyoto Protocol issues

With the Marrakech Accords, the international regime on climate change was established, albeit with ratification of the Kyoto Protocol still to occur. Resolving the remaining major uncertainties within the Protocol at COP-7 opened the way for key players to move ahead with ratifying the agreement. Ratification required at least 55 nations to sign on and their collective emissions amounted to 55 percent of the 1990 emissions from nations with emission targets (known as the "55/55" rule). Given the distribution of emissions amongst the developed world, the commitment of the few largest emitters exerted a critical influence on the Protocol's prospects of becoming a functioning legal agreement. Agreement from the E.U. (24 percent of Annex 1 emissions) and Japan (9 percent of Annex 1 emissions) were readily secured along with most of the smaller developed nations, with the U.S. (36 percent of Annex 1 emissions) and Australia maintaining their decisions not to ratify (UN FCCC 2002, 2003). When some 31 Annex I nations had signed giving a cumulative 43.9 percent of the aforementioned 55 percent emissions target (UN FCCC 2003), all depended on Russia, with its 17 percent of Annex 1 emissions, signing.

Waiting for Russia's agreement proved a frustrating experience. Although research by Müller (2004) and others found economic advantages to Russia by signing, Russia didn't rush its decision. In 2002, the FCCC Secretariat's optimism over Russia's expected agreement reflected the general views of observers (UNFCCC 2002). Indeed, Russian confirmation was expected at COP-8, but the temptation to continue to extract further concessions from the negotiation process proved too strong and no Russian accord was achieved in New Delhi. Korppoo (2002) considered the delays to be due to internal Russian politics, not to procedural problems. However, at the World Climate Conference in Moscow in 2003, the Russian delegation questioned the veracity of climate change science, but indicated a national commitment to sign. Months later at COP-9, an aide to Predident Putin, Andrei Illarionov, stated "We shall not ratify" (Myers and Revkin 2003). Ratification of the Protocol eventually occurred in Februrary 2005 when a deal between Russia and the E.U. over Russia's admittance to the WTO proved a sufficient inducement and it duly came into force.

Despite Russian exploitation of the Protocol's ratification procedures, the U.S. has exerted the greatest indididual influence over the FCCC processes and outcomes. Agrawala and Anderson state (1999: 457): "The United States is the single most important national actor in the global climate regime for reasons of both historical and practical significance." Such reasoning takes into account the sheer magnitude of U.S. greenhouse gas emissions, historically and currently. Globally, the U.S. contributes about a quarter of anthropogenic greenhouse gas emissions, while it has about 4 percent of the global population and U.S. per capita emissions are among the world's highest, at around 20 tons of carbon dioxide. Concern over U.S. isolationism in the negotiations increased with the G.W. Bush administration's withdrawal from the Kyoto Protocol, but this issue has been canvassed many times throughout the history of the international climate change negotiations (see, e.g., Paterson and Grubb 1992). Insistence on developing country participation in emissions reductions agreements has been a persistent issue with U.S. negotiators. While in fact, the Byrd–Hagel resolution perpetuates an error in suggesting that developing nations are essentially exempt from emissions reduction, whereas this only formally applies to the Kyoto Protocol's first commitment period, this has made little impact on the U.S. position. Commentators describe U.S. Senate's Byrd–Hagel resolution as effectively preventing the U.S. from ratifying the Kyoto Protocol. Even during the Clinton administration, where there was some sympathy for the FCCC's goals, no attempts were made to test the Senate's resolve. Rather, the Clinton administration proceeded on a range of domestic policy measures as if the U.S. had agreed to its reduction target without attempting to gain Senate approval (Bugnion and Reiner 1999); in any event, the Clinton 1993 U.S. *Climate Action Plan* was a "weak set of voluntary measures" (Paarlberg 1999: 242). U.S. Senate approval of international agreements can be difficult to achieve; for instance, the U.S. shares with the government-less Somalia the distinction of failing to ratify the UN conventions on preventing discrimination against women and supporting children's rights (Jacoby and Reiner 2001).

February 2002 saw the release of the G.W. Bush Administration's *U.S. Global Climate Change Plan* with its aim of an 18 percent reduction in U.S. 'greenhouse gas emissions intensity' by 2012. Although this initiative had many components, the basic policy tools for emissions reduction relied on voluntary measures. Critics of the policy were especially dissatisfied with the measure of greenhouse gas intensity, largely because the historical trend virtually assures the policy's goal would be met without any additional policy initiatives. This target is not far from recent historical trends as the International Energy Agency calculated that from 1990 to 2000, U.S. carbon intensity deceased by 14.9 percent, and using the U.S. Energy Information Administration forecasts of U.S. carbon emissions growth of 1.5 percent, the projected reduction would be 15.5 percent (IEA 2002). Dutch research group RIVM modeled the Bush policy and concluded that its energy efficiency goals were actually below recent historical rates and that, by 2013, U.S. greenhouse gas emissions would be 32 percent above those of 1990, compared with 39 percent higher in the absence of the policy (de Moor et al. 2002; see also Blanchard and Perkaus 2004). Environmental NGOs in the U.S. and abroad were unimpressed with the administration's initiative whose release has now been largely forgotten, seemingly also by the administration itself, which has given the program a low public profile. Additionally, the administration released its *National Energy Plan* (NEPD 2001) proposing a rapid escalation in fossil fuel and nuclear power station construction, oil drilling in the Arctic National Arctic Wildlife Refuge, and other measures incompatible with greenhouse gas emission abatement.

In withdrawing from the Kyoto Protocol, the G.W. Bush administration proposed a new global accord for emissions reduction to replace the Protocol. There are no signs or announcements by the U.S. government that this intention has been transformed into action and the current status of the proposal is uncertain. At least one major U.S. NGO, the Pew Climate Center, has embarked on a project to identify alternative international agreements to the Kyoto Protocol and this might be an early indication of the Bush administration's program to forge a 'Beyond-Kyoto' proposal. With nearly every nation having signed on to the FCCC, to consider its abandonment in favor of an alternative scheme would require considerable U.S. diplomacy, a role for which it seems particularly poorly positioned at this time.

While the Protocol's ratification occurred without U.S. participation, there are obvious concerns over its effectiveness without the world's largest polluter and grounds for considering that the Protocol's modest abatement target can't be reached under these conditions. Producing around a third of the developed world's emissions, the U.S. has one of the stricter targets under the Kyoto Protocol (7 percent as opposed to the average of 5.2 percent) and achieving the 2008–2012 target will require emission reductions of the order of 25–30 percent. Consequently, the overall target of the Protocol of a 5.2 percent reduction from the 1990 baseline is very unlikely to be achieved in the absence of the U.S. Other aspects of the dynamics of the climate change system will also be altered by the U.S. absence, namely the increased bargaining power to those who will supply emission credits, notably Russia and the Ukraine. Investment, research, and development in technologies and policies for the low-carbon economy are unmistakably lower than if the U.S. were facing a major challenge to its fossil fuel-based energy system, and although this issue may not have a high profile, in many respects it may be of the utmost importance for the longer-term prospects of addressing climate change.

Successful ratification in the absence of effective independent action by the U.S. evokes long-standing concerns over the 'free-rider' problem. Under the COP-7-approved compliance system, penalties are triggered for signatories failing to comply with their emissions targets, from which the U.S. is now exempt, although it remains free to participate in the Protocol's global carbon market. A number of nations and NGOs have complained over this 'perverse' reward for the U.S., freed of its emission reduction obligations, it can still profit from participating in emissions trading. Challenges of various types are being mounted against the U.S., including recourse through international law and international trade agreements' protest mechanisms. Regardless of the resolution of these individual cases, however, none are likely to substitute for the necessary repair to the Protocol's own compliance system. Despite all the difficulties of the FCCC negotiations, especially those to conclude COP-6, the withdrawal of the U.S. from the Protocol creates enormous difficulties for its future integrity, legitimacy, and effectiveness.

Emissions and the Kyoto Protocol

Global growth in global greenhouse gas emissions and within the block of developed nations has not diminished significantly with the creation of either the FCCC or the Kyoto Protocol. Overall, the task of reducing emissions has increased significantly since the Kyoto Protocol's creation in 1997. As a group, the developed nations increased their emissions from 2.65 to three gigatons of carbon annually between 1990 and 1999, taking into account the economies in transition reduced emissions due to economic decline (1.25–0.85 gtC/annum) (Bolin and Kheshgi 2001), bringing up global emissions from 6.1–6.55 gtC/annum (Bolin and Kheshgi 2001). IEA (2002a) reports that of the top 15 nations with their 2000 emissions level lower than the 1990 total, only Albania did so with an increase in GDP. Economic decline accounted for the emissions reductions achieved by the other 14 nations, some exceeding 50 percent GDP loss (IEA 2002a). Non-Annex B nations emissions aren't subject to reduction targets and importantly, neither are the so-called 'bunker fuels' emissions used for international sea and air travel. Currently, the FCCC has no proposals for controlling bunker fuels which account for some 3.5 percent of global emissions, a level exceeded by only half a dozen or so individual nations.

Broken down on a national basis, the current emissions situation is as follows. E.U. emission levels are currently close to returning to that of 1990. As a group, USCANZ (U.S., Canada, Australia, and New Zealand) are around 12 percent above their 1990 levels and continue to increase, while Japanese emissions are also increasing, but at about half this rate. Emissions growth in the U.S. is noteworthy: the Energy Information Agency (2000) estimates levels will be around 30 percent above the Kyoto targets by 2010. None of these groups appear able to meet their Kyoto Protocol targets using domestic measures. Combining domestic action with the Kyoto mechanisms, the E.U. may come close.

Reduced emissions in the U.K. and Germany occurred for reasons unrelated to climate policy, due to privatization and conversion to gas in the former and the benefits of reunification in the latter. U.S. policy has relied on voluntary measures (also known as 'no regrets' policies) and its current emissions levels closely resemble forecast trajectories made around the time of the Rio Conference. Europe, despite its rhetorical correctness, has similarly failed to reign in emissions, partially due to the political demise of the proposals for a carbon tax and mandatory efficiency standards. In its Third Assessment Report, the IPCC's Working Group III (2001c) concluded that although technological improvements to energy-saving and alternative energy technologies are available to reduce greenhouse emissions, social, economic, and political barriers are restricting their applications, and that further, rapid economic growth and behavioral changes have nullified any gains. IPCC (2001c) further reported that most nations had done little to further energy efficiency and conservation programs.

Policy architecture of the FCCC and Kyoto Protocol

Both the FCCC and the Kyoto Protocol are complex agreements and ambitious in their scope, if not their goals, covering the complex issues of funding, technology transfer, as well as the policies on greenhouse gas emissions and carbon sinks. Describing and analyzing their policy architecture is a considerable task as Grubb et al. (1999), Oberthür and Ott (1999), Yamin and Depledge (2004), and others have shown. Greatest political and scholarly attention focusses on emissions issues. Ultimately, any international climate change agreements will be assessed on their performance in reducing the profligate combustion of fossil fuels. Notwithstanding that there are many groups involved in the formal and informal processes of designing, negotiating, and implementing these agreements, and new international institutions have been developed to assist this activity, the FCCC is an agreement between nation states as recognized by the UN. Under the FCCC and Kyoto Protocol, emission limits and policy prescriptions are applied to the 'exterior' of national activities and suggestions that the agreement guide or mandate national policies have been unsuccessful, leaving nation-state sovereignty minimally affected by the FCCC and Kyoto Protocol. States are given the responsibility for managing emissions within their borders. Greenhouse gas inventory and reporting requirements are also national responsibilities, but for developed nations pose a minimal burden in manipulating data already collected for other purposes. Climate change impacts are also considered as primarily constituting risks to particular natural and environmental systems within nations, an understanding that makes states responsible for understanding and anticipating these potential changes. Adaptation to future climate change is also the business of states under the agreements. Given this orientation, many global dimensions of emissions production, such as bunker fuel sources, fall outside the ambits of nationally constructed responses.

At least one aspect of national circumstances is considered collectively, namely the differentiation between the more developed nations given emission targets and those less developed nations without targets. This division accords generally present national (per capita) income and historical contribution to global emissions: Annex II is basically the OECD; 'Economies in Transition' includes the former Soviet Union and its eastern and central European satellites; 'Annex I' is these two groups combined; and 'Non-Annex I' are the remaining nations and the poorer nations with economies in transition to capitalism and open markets. Within the E.U. bubble, reduction allocations are broadly proportional to national income.

Long disputed by the U.S., the exclusion of developing nations from emission targets has proved an intractable issue for the U.S. in climate change negotiations. China and India are usually not identified by name in the public FCCC fora, but both have large emissions on an international scale (ranked #2 and #5 in 2000), and the U.S. has been consistently concerned over China. Emissions limitations by the larger developing nations are essential for long-term stabilization but this issue remains highly contentious. National emission reduction targets for future commitment periods, and consideration for developing nation targets, are likely to be based on interpretations of the national 'ability to pay.' Although the national emissions reduction targets under the Kyoto Protocol were subject to intense negotiation, including those who achieved increase allowances, the debate's parameters were established prior to the FCCC. Using 1990 as the common benchmark year for the major gases means that concern is over (relatively) recent emission trends. Further, the economies in transition are allowed to nominate benchmark years other than 1990. No standards or guidelines were used in setting these limits imposed on each Annex I party, rather the individual targets reflected national circumstances and negotiation outcomes, culminating in almost arbitrary emission cuts.

Incrementalism is an essential design element of the emissions reduction strategies with acknowledgements of the long timeframes needed to consider fundamental social change and changes in global climate being addressed by only short-term emission reduction goals. Starting with the FCCC's aim, emissions reduction was set for the target year 2000 and offered no guidance for post-2000. By way of a remedy, the Berlin Mandate called for targets to be set for 2005, 2010, and 2020. Any aspirations for a longer-term approach in the Kyoto Protocol did not come to fruition, as it adopted targets for the first commitment period only, namely 2008–2012. Surety about the target was further diluted by the Protocol adopting a commitment period of five years, rather than a single year, granting nations additional 'room' in which to satisfy their goals.

Ambiguity over emission targets beyond the near term is surpassed by the uncertainty over the level at which the ultimate goal of the FCCC seeks for atmospheric stabilization of greenhouse gases. Currently, this aspect of the policy architecture is open to wide interpretation. At the very location of a complex international agreement where some solidity might be expected, the FCCC has effectively none. Stabilization is impossible in the short term given the atmospheric residency time of carbon dioxide, but the question of the long-term stabilization level remains essentially undefined by the FCCC.

Of all the policy architecture's attributes, the market-based policies of the Kyoto policy mechanisms have generated the greatest debate and controversy. Exclusion of developing nations from the targets and timetables framework of the Protocol may have attracted international media attention following the complaints and the U.S. and its withdrawal from the Protocol, but the issue remains one of broad policy and geopolitics. Greatest negotiating energy, research, and scholarship have been devoted to the intricacies of the Kyoto mechanisms (here taken to include the associated issues of carbon sinks), undoubtedly the central issue of the Kyoto Protocol. In some respects, the Kyoto mechanisms are unifying framework for the policy architecture, providing the connections between different issues, including that of developing country participation.

Designing a market-based climate change policy response

Given that the Kyoto mechanisms represent the application of economic theory to problems of regulating pollutants, in this case from national entities, the governing economic rationale of this central attribute of the policy architecture is essential. Economics was foremost amongst the social sciences in studying the problems of environmental damage and looking to define optimal economic outcomes between the costs and benefits of pollution. In the absence of defined property rights or market for atmospheric services, the climate change problem fulfills the economists' definition of a global open access resource (i.e., a form of common-pool resource), wherein greenhouse gas emitters endeavor to maximize their individual economic gains with the inevitable consequence of a diminished commons resource. Avoiding the 'tragedy of the commons' finds conventional economics taking recourse to property rights for controlling the destructive potential of the 'market failure' of unrestrained consumption.

In the 1980s there was great interest in applying market solutions to an array of environmental and public natural resource issues and giving rise to 'environmental economics.' Economists, under the banner of 'free-market environmentalism,' encouraged states to create and usually administer market institutions to control levels of access and use of public commons resources which were allocated to private and public parties through sales, auctions, tradable permits, quotas, licenses, and the like (see, e.g., Anderson and Leal 1991). Social utility is optimized through economic allocation, environmental economists argue, because resource use is directed towards its highest economic returns. Central to market-based approaches to environmental problems is the necessity to translate all values into marketable forms, which allows economists to determine environmentally-sustainable levels of use using economic theory (Common 1995).

Environmental economics offers a rationale for using market-based approaches to environmental problems. Where costs are uncertain and the rate of marginal damages is greater than the benefits of damage avoidance, then the use of price instruments is favored. If the opposite applies, then the steeper costs requires quantitative restrictions. In other words, if environmental costs are relatively steady over time, then it is economically preferable to carefully assess the costs of actions so as to identify the least-cost solution and the issue becomes one of price setting. Such choices avoid the risk of spending too much for minor environmental gains. If, however, environmental costs rise steeply over time, intervening action becomes more urgent and requires setting a quantitative limit on pollution. Because climate change is the outcome of steady increases in atmospheric greenhouse gas concentrations, the values of which cannot be altered rapidly by changes in annual emissions, environmental economics considers in the shorter term that marginal costs of abatement are greater than the marginal costs of climate change costs.

Climate change was not amongst the issues considered at this time in the growing field of market-based environmental policies, as most policy attention was directed at resource conflicts at the national and state scale. Applications of market-based policies to international issues were inevitable and at least one prescient analyst argued that national emissions limits could not work and options, such as carbon taxes and tradable emission permits, would be necessary for an effective international approach to climate change (Grubb 1990). An early effort that marked the beginning of a flood of similar works was a 1992 UN Conference on Trade and Development report calling for a market approach for climate change (Hempel 1996). Currently, a veritable research industry on market-based approaches to climate change has grown on the basis of the opportunities provided by the Kyoto mechanisms, interestingly because the international experience is driving interest in national market-based policies to reduce greenhouse gas emissions. Several authors have placed the Kyoto mechanisms in the context of a broader trend in developed nations' governments towards 'deregulated' policy settings, their disenchantment with 'command and control' policy approaches, and the corresponding increase of economic policy instruments in environmental and resource management fields. Claims for such a lineage may be exaggerated; environmental regulation and protection involves a shifting matrix of many elements, including technology mandates, performance standards, voluntary agreements, and with limited use of economic tools, such as taxes, subsidies, and pollutant trading schemes. Despite the appeal of market-based policies to nations and states around the world, especially in those with a strong ideological commitment to free market policies such as Australia, Canada, New Zealand, U.K., and the U.S., nearly all successful environmental management in developed nations has been, and remains, essentially regulatory, often combined with allowances and incentives.

Including price instruments in the FCCC architecture fits well with environmental economic theory. There are three critical assumptions in this reasoning and these have support through official climate change science. Firstly, that the relatively low estimated costs of climate change impacts are correct, so that emissions are largely unrelated to damages in the short term and, secondly, that climate change damages have a linear relationship with increases in emissions. Thirdly and linked to the first two, it is assumed that irreversible change can be anticipated. These assumptions appear to be supported by IPCC outputs; rapid or catastrophic future changes in climate are deemed to be of low probability, and conventional economics found that only modest levels of expenditure in emissions reduction is justified.

There are no precedents for an international system of market-based policies to control greenhouse gas emissions, either internationally for similar types of pollutants or nationally to control greenhouse gas emissions. In a very real sense, the Kyoto mechanisms are experimental. Models for the Kyoto mechanisms came from other national and state examples of market-based environmental policy. Most commentators and scholars refer to the U.S. experience in pollution control through its sulfur dioxide emissions trading scheme under its Acid Rain Program and the U.S. role in promoting this system a model for the FCCC. Interestingly, the U.S. sulfur dioxide trading scheme is modest in comparison to a potential international market for carbon emissions and began only in 1995; furthermore, there was little experience with emissions trading outside the U.S. Advocacy for international emissions trading was based on theoretical and ideological reasoning and although the dictates of liberal democracy required many economic attributes of this policy instrument, these did not include evidence that it was a superior policy choice or even that it could work.

'Cap and trade' economic policy approach

Trading of greenhouse gas emissions between developed nations under the Protocol follows the general approach of a 'cap and trade system.' Once limits on total emissions are set, known as a 'cap,' nations are then allocated a set emissions level, and a system can be devised so that parties can trade rights to emit greenhouse gases. In this case, the cap is the Kyoto Protocol first commitment period emission targets for Annex I nations. Each participating nation faces a limit on its emissions that must be met by domestic actions to reduce emissions, an effort that can be supplemented through emission trading. Nations are allowed to attach a market value to a portion of the emissions they have reduced and then sell these notional gases as 'emission credits' to another nation who is able to count these credits as part of their own reduction efforts. Emissions trading is deemed to be 'flexible' because nations can make economic decisions over the relative advantages of domestic emissions reduction, purchased and sold emission credits in the quest for least-cost emission abatement pathways. Internationally, the theory of cap and trade is that the trading system ensures the most efficient determination of emissions reductions by allowing nations access to the cheapest sources of emission credits.

Wealthy nations with high emissions, therefore, can be expected to purchase emission reduction credits from poorer nations on the basis that national income can be an indicator of the costs of cutting emissions. National circumstances will provide for variations in ability to reduce emissions (and count carbon sinks as offsets) and the costs of doing so. Nations with greatest 'market power,' therefore, will be able to purchase emission credits at the lowest prices. Advocates of emissions trading claim that recipient nations (i.e., the sellers of emission credits) will tend to be poorer countries that will be able to invest the resources gained from emissions trading in more efficient and lower greenhouse gas-emitting technologies. Effective technology transfer, especially towards developing nations, is essential for longer-term emissions reduction and arguments have differed over the effects of limits on the Kyoto mechanisms on this trade.

In practice, economists recognize the need to address the 'classic' limitations of market approaches to policy problems that also apply to the greenhouse emissions trading system. Several concerns about the economic efficiency of emission trading have been expressed, such as the risks of potential 'free riders,' who receive the benefits of lower global emissions while deliberately avoid making any contribution. Market-based schemes can also be undermined by the potential for 'leakage,' whereby unrestricted emissions counteract efforts by nations undertaking abatement and undermine the overall performance towards the ultimate goals. For example, lower fossil fuel prices resulting from increased emission controls could stimulate leakage in the short term, whereas a long-term problem could arise from industry relocation to places with lesser emission limits (Wiener 1997). Operation of any trading system incurs transaction costs, and in the case of emissions trading these will include expenditures or losses incurred through monitoring, verification, regulation, and administration, which have to be factored into the overall cost reckoning.

Economic literature on emissions trading has consistently supported the proposition that the unrestricted trading brings the lowest costs of greenhouse gas emission abatement. Several hundred research efforts support conventional economic forecasts of the benefits and efficiencies of future trading. An early study employing 'pessimistic' assumptions about the likelihood of emissions trading, including carbon sinks, and other factors by 2008–2012, estimated the costs of emissions reduction at US$360 ton of carbon (WEFA 1998 in Weyant, 2000). Unlimited trading of emissions offers the lowest global cost of meeting the Kyoto targets and the use of the CDM and Joint Implementation brings the cost still lower (studies suggest US$4–20 ton of carbon). Other model results indicate that unrestricted emissions trading (i.e., without the 'supplementarity' clauses) would lead to a halving or better of the marginal abatement costs (e.g., OECD in Yamin et al. 2001), with Weyant and Hill (1998) reporting a range of reductions of 20–80 percent in 2010 depending on the particular models and countries.

Economic evaluations have been based on key assumptions concerning: energy prices, the extent to which these prices spur innovations and practices to reduce greenhouse gases, future changes in key variables such as population and technology, policy measures employed, and how and if the benefits of abatement are included (Weyant 2000). As a result, economic evaluations of greenhouse gas reductions for the U.S., for example, range from identifying net economic benefits from reductions greater than that required by the Protocol to those suggesting that meeting the targets would produce great economic hardship (Weyant 2000).

Grubb (1999), while noting that the literature has under-examined the issue, offers several political reasons for the apparent preference for emissions trading over comparable economic tools, such as a carbon tax, noting that economic principles suggest that a tax could be more effective. Firstly, emissions permits create assets for participating firms, which is politically preferable to imposing taxes. Secondly, national governments have flexible choices in distributing permits, such as between auctioning and allocations, which entails prospects for creating domestic political advantages. Thirdly, Grubb argues that greenhouse gas permits are more likely to fall within the ambit of environmental agencies, as opposed to tax policies that are the domain of financial agencies and which are usually less sympathetic to the task of emissions reduction. Contests for the institutional control of emission taxes between government agencies, he notes, are avoided in this way.

Having established the background to the Kyoto mechanisms, the key components of emissions trading and the CDM are briefly described below. Joint Implementation is a relatively minor aspect of the Kyoto mechanisms, both in terms of the quantities of emissions at stake and in interest to negotiators and interest groups, and is not covered here. Carbon sinks are added to this section because they are linked conceptually and have been part of the FCCC negotiating process over the mechanisms.

Emissions trading, the Clean Development Mechanism, and carbon sinks

Under the Kyoto Protocol's Article 17, national parties can purchase emissions reductions undertaken in another country that is able to meet its own reduction targets through the 'trading' of those emissions. Trading of national allowances to emit greenhouse gases has emerged as the basic architecture of the international climate change policy, namely a cap and trade system using 'rights to pollute.' In an idealized form, as developed nations' domestic actions lowered their emissions there would be vigorous trading as a means to reaching or surpassing their individual targets, and the collective cost would be as low as the efficiency of the trading system enabled. However, the practice of emissions trading will be quite different and herein lays the controversy of the system, generated by a quirk in the composition of Annex B.

A cursory examination of national greenhouse gas emissions since the baseline year reveals the basic appeal of emissions trading, namely the greenhouse gas emissions consequences of economic decline and persisting stagnation of the Former Soviet Union and Eastern Europe. Despite some economic recovery since their collapse, overall the Annex 1 economies in transition collectively were only 70 percent of the 1990 emissions by 1999 (i.e., 1.25 gtC/ annum in 1990, 0.85 gtC in 1999; see Bolin and Kheshgi 2001). In general terms, Russia is currently about a third below its 1990 levels and Ukraine about half. Come the full operation of the trading season, therefore, Russia and the Ukraine will have abundant goods for sale, although estimates of their potential emission credits vary: Yamin et al. (2001) suggest 120 million tons of carbon (mtC), Vrolijk (2000 in Metz et al. 2001) estimate 350 million tons, and Victor et al. (2001) offer several scenarios that range from 12 to 1100 million tons becoming available, with more estimates still as varied.

As indicated above, greenhouse gas emissions in the majority of Annex B nations continue to grow, making the task of meeting their reduction targets in eight to twelve years time 'challenging.' Policy-makers and a number of research institutes are casting a predatory eye on the emission credits of Russia and the Ukraine, knowing that these will be vital for reducing their greenhouse gas accounts. Purchase of these allowances is now taken as granted as being a major, if not the primary, source of emissions reduction by the U.S., the world's largest greenhouse gas emitter. Kopp and Anderson (1998), for example, considered that the U.S. could meet some 56 percent of greenhouse gas reduction commitment through such means. In the OECD's GREEN model, unrestricted emissions trading would bring the average OECD costs of abatement down to a third of those restricted by 'supplementarity,' with the telling outcome that the former would assume the bulk of the OECD's emissions reduction obligations (Yamin et al. 2001).

Using the CDM proposals, a device of the Protocol's Article 12, Annex B nations can invest in emission reduction projects in developing nations and claim the resulting greenhouse gas reductions (as 'certified emissions reductions'). Emission reductions will have to be certified which aims to ensure that emissions savings are measured, verified, and additional to domestic abatement activity by the Annex B nation. An executive board will oversee the activity, which will be responsible to the Conference of the Parties.

Investments in projects in developing nations offer potentially some of the lowest cost options for emissions reduction for the developed nations of Annex B nations. Recipient nations can benefit from the influx of investment and technology, and there is provision in the Protocol that projects undertaken support sustainable development objectives.

Proponents of the CDM have the support of many economic studies of its potential effects describing its ability to greatly lower greenhouse gas abatement costs, effectively bringing them close to zero and boosting income to selected non-Annex 1 nations (see Yamin et al. 2001: 192). Further studies have suggested that without the Kyoto mechanisms, it is the developing nations that will be most harmed by the developed world's efforts to reduce greenhouse gas emissions. Such findings reflect the economic effects of reduced earnings by the oil and gas exporting nations if developed nations reduce importations of their products, a loss that the mechanism could offset to some extent. With the first CDM projects approved, on landfill gas capture and a hydroelectric scheme, the rush of activity is now under way, with significant entrepreneurial initiatives across the developing world and a new breed of specialist services being created to develop and propose projects.

Although emissions trading and the CDM have been controversial, the issue of carbon sinks is further complicated by scientific uncertainty over some of its most basic components. Human activity directly influences the carbon cycle in two major ways, through the combustion of fossil fuel which releases carbon emissions to the atmosphere, and through land management, which influences both carbon releases and carbon sequestration in soils and vegetation. Land use and land use management activities can manipulate the store of carbon 'sinks,' whereby nations can increase the carbon store and count these levels in their national greenhouse gas inventories to offset greenhouse gas emissions (as allowed under Protocol articles 3.3, 3.4, 6, and 12). Considerable skepticism has surrounded the carbon sinks issue since its appearance as a possible component of the Protocol, not least of which came from scientific sources. Resolution of the role of sinks as a response to the climate change problem has been complicated by scientific uncertainty over central aspects relevant to the policy architecture. Consistently and reliably measuring the store, rate of accumulation, and fluxes of carbon in these biological stores has proved difficult and there are great variations across different ecological formations. IPCC produced a *Special Report on Land Use, Land Use Change and Forestry* (IPCC 2000b) which contained estimates of the potential sinks within categories and global regions, but the authors reported many persistent basic uncertainties.

Uncertainty over the absolute values of the carbon sink and its associated fluxes would not be a core problem if the values were small, however; the relative size of the carbon sink could be enormous, depending how the specific definitions applied. Noble and Scholes (2001) estimated the sinks under various articles of the Protocol, calculating that were carbon sinks for afforestation, reforestation, and deforestation to conform to the IPCC guidelines, there would be about 100 million tons of carbon a year available for offsets; other provisions potentially offer an even greater amount. For example, the *U.S. Greenhouse Gas Inventory* (1990–1997) (EPA 1999) reported that the net carbon sequestration from U.S. forests in 1997 was 208 million tons of carbon equivalent, which would have equaled 14 percent of total U.S. emissions for fossil fuel combustion. Nabuurs et al. (2000) analyzed various interpretations of the afforestation, reforestation, and deforestation, and found that most of the industrialized nations could exceed their greenhouse gas reduction commitments through afforestation, reforestation, and deforestation activities under some interpretations.

Determination of the carbon sinks and the inclusion in national inventories will be a major factor in many nations' greenhouse gas reduction circumstances. As Metz et al. (2001: 178) correctly observe, while the Kyoto Protocol targets are now fixed, the question of exactly how sinks will contribute to meeting those targets remains open. Negotiations have featured concerns over the permanence of sequestered carbon in land uses. Plainly, such stocks cannot be assumed to be relatively permanent; changes in land use, forest fire, the effects of future climate change, and other factors can quickly liberate sequestered carbon from its vegetative store to an aerosol form.

Carbon sinks are an allowable form of CDM under the Protocol, a decision that has generated both great interest as a potential source of project-based investments in developing nations, and great controversy over its potential effects in undermining emissions abatement and over the several technical issues of measurement and compliance. CDM projects may fail to satisfy sustainable development criteria; for example, indigenous forests converted to plantations of exotic species may satisfy sequestration objectives at the cost of ecological values. A major aspect of this debate concerns the potential of carbon sinks and other aspects of the Kyoto mechanisms to actively undermine the effectiveness of greenhouse gas abatement as a result of various activities that result in increased emissions, either through 'loopholes' in the system or 'gaming.' Collectively, this phenomenon is known as 'leakage,' namely carbon emissions that occur outside the provisions of the Protocol and thereby undermine its effectiveness. Such problems have led Richards and Anderson (2001) to suggest that the problems of carbon sequestration may be insurmountable, based on the difficulty of ensuring adequate measurement of individual projects and a range of implementation obstacles.

Liberal-democratic climate governance

Historical, practical, and ideological factors have made liberal democracy the theoretical ideal and pragmatic means for international cooperation on climate change. Underpinning these factors is the uniting theme of modernity.

Actions by states striving to protect existing economic and social conditions from future change and have sought solutions according with the prevailing social orthodoxy of liberal democracy, by applying technological solutions, managerial approaches that combine nation-state powers and market-based policy mechanisms, and utilizing the forces of globalization. Yet international cooperation or environmental protection doesn't come readily under liberal democracy. Liberal democracy's capacity to protect the interests of developing ations and ecological values in general has been inconsistent, at best. Under its existing goals, policy architecture, and international negotiating activities, priority has been given to the developed world's immediate interests in the international response to climate change. Efforts to organize an effective international response to climate change have necessarily encountered a novel set of challenges to nations' foreign and domestic policies, international institutions, and to civil society. Climate change puts the politics on modernity on trial.

Decisions to initiate the international responses to climate change reflect a general environmental awareness and the specific concerns and campaigns from both concerned scientists and environmental NGOs. As these activities began to coalesce into a formal UN initiative, developing world nations added their interests to the rationale for a response to climate change. Cost estimates of climate change impacts were available and part of the broader discourse, but states didn't base their response on a strict economic rationality, although such rationalizations have been expressed. Rather, international institutions developed as part of a broader international response to issues of global environmental justice, using the rationality of the precautionary principle.

Climate change represents that new class of environmental issues that are global in scale, understood scientifically, and whose resolution is far more technically and politically complex than local environmental justice issues involving a single political jurisdiction (see, e.g., Byrne et al. 2002). Ironically, although the recent risk of climate change is actually an old risk generated by the process that underpins the history of industrialization, but it epitomizes the new generation of environmental risks – its causes and responsibilities for blame are somewhat indeterminate, the risks are hard to perceive without science and remain highly uncertain, and there's no possibility for simple intervention or technological resolutions. Furthermore, these risks are highly differentiated and responses to the issue are made more difficult by constant changes in national and global economic and political factors. In resolving these issues, states are not only the loci for political contests over policy choices and perform essential services in order to maintaining the global capitalist economy, but are also self-interested economic parties by virtue of their place in national and international economies.

Climate change has been presented as an issue that determines political and institutional responses by liberal democracy. Within the graduation of these propositions is a continuum ranging from the generally accepted, such as the necessity for international cooperation to deal with emissions arising from all nations, to the use of global markets to implement response policies because the climate change problem is beyond the capacity of nation states acting on their own or in concert, to the highly contentious claims over the efficacy of the Kyoto Protocol emission reduction targets and timetable.

Nation states and international cooperation have been the focus for much of the scholarly discussion of over globalization and the diffusion of liberal democracy. As an international environmental agreement, the FCCC is an institution in tension with the interests of industrialized nation states, and those aspects of the globalizing economy promoting greenhouse gas emissions. Not only must the FCCC control state activity but also work against the momentum of a 'post-Fordist' force of globalizing capitalism wishing to use fossil fuels without environmental restraint. Abundant skepticism over the effectiveness of approaches such as the FCCC arises from at least two opposing camps: those favoring economic neo-liberalism and environmentalists wanting economic activities and economic interests restrained. For developed nations' domestic activity, ecological modernization has delivered a range of environmental restorative and protective initiatives through state and corporate cooperation, but such 'progress' has often had an uneasy relationship with economic globalization.

Proponents of liberal democracy consider globalization as the means for nations to eventually respond to pollution problems, albeit often accepting intermediate increases in pollutants and associated social costs as the 'price' of economic development. Globalization carries liberal democracy forward as an agent of both economic growth and democratic governance, according to this argument, empowering nations' attempts to address ecological problems. Environmentalists and ecological justice advocates believe global economic growth to be a destructive force. Local environmental protection can be undermined by cross-border pollution with the transport of wastes aided by either natural or social agents by the global relocation of pollution sources as a consequence of open trade between nations. Confidence in nation states' response to environmental justice issues is uneven because their performance has been so uneven regarding the generation of differences in exposure to environmental risk involving location, race, class, income, and other factors (see Byrne et al. 2002).

Ecological modernization features environmental 'improvement' through state cooperation with corporations and civil society, a strategy that enables states to retain their legitimacy, yet their ability to act independently is correspondingly lessened. Scientific and technical information is essential to resolving environmental problems and managing the environment, in which states both facilitate and consume such knowledge. A consistent critique from ecologism and some social critics is that ecological modernization produces 'scientism,' by turning political and social issues into technical problems. Efforts by states to depict their role as independent arbiters of neutral scientific advice have been readily undercut, diminishing both the state's legitimacy in environmental issues and public confidence in technical solutions.

Within the FCCC process are numerous expressions of these issues, as states have forged new international institutions to address problems beyond their individual capacities and cast resolutions that enshrine their necessary participation. Although these agreements amount to 'global governance,' they have been cast in ways that reflect the limitations of state capacities, as well as the contingencies of international negotiations. Design of the Kyoto mechanisms expresses compromises between the relationships states have with corporations within their boundaries, for which they are accountable (in an emissions counting sense) and a market-oriented policy architecture that allows global capitalism to facilitate carbon trading between firms. Such a division is symptomatic of an international agreement reliant on national policies as determined by each nation state in order to satisfy the FCCC and Kyoto Protocol goals, under which attempts in FCCC negotiations to impose policy preferences or priorities on states have been effectively resisted. Nation states do not exist in a simple, oppositional dichotomy with international institutions, as there are strong mutual dependencies between the two, nor are states the sole actors influencing this new form of governance.

Liberal democracy and global environmental governance

Global environmental governance emerges clearly in the age of environmentalism, although scholars have identified a plethora of relatively minor and obscure antecedents and precedents. 'Global environmental governance' is a new term capturing recent developments to resolve international and transnational governance problems of environmental management. 'Global governance,' as Lipschutz (1996: 1) states, replaces the notion of 'international governance' because these global politics involve "more than the interaction of states." Civil societies in many countries are involved, the governance is increasingly transnational, but is "articulated via a complex set of knowledge-based linkages, and at the same time, sensitive to differences among local places" (Lipschutz 1996: 1). Litfin stated of this development (1999: 359): "Thus, the greening of international relations has entailed a movement away from its traditional state-centric orientation."

From a historical perspective, this form of governance has grown in scope and ambition in response to ever-broadening ecological problems (especially those crossing national boundaries), disputes over natural resources and ecological services, and the revelations of ecological monitoring (e.g., Haas 1990a, 1990b; Hempel 1996; and Young 1997). Since WWII, and especially since the 1970s, there have been a plethora of environmental treaties attesting to the role for international cooperation. A wide array of environmental themes are subject to recent international agreements, including locations. regions, species, ecological processes, threatening processes and activities, resource use and pollution. Governance refers to establishing and operating social institutions, including rules, decision-making, and governing policies and does not imply 'government' (Young 1997: 5): "The general proposition that groups of interdependent actors can and often succeed in handling the function of governance without resorting to the creation of governments in the conventional sense is now well established."

Litfin (1999: 367–368) offered two observations on global environmental cooperation pertinent to this discussion, namely that mainly non-state actors have driven the rise of environmental agreements, and that efforts to improve the effectiveness of existing agreements often formally seek to expand the role of scientists, NGOs, industry, and international organizations. International environmental protection initiatives, however, should not be assumed to be preemptive or effective in restoring environmental values as "international cooperation has, for the most part, been too little and too late" (Litfin 1999: 367). Environmental conditions would undoubtedly been worse in the absence of global environmental governance initiatives, but nevertheless the global trend is that of declining conditions, of which the response to climate change is consistent and contributory.

Conceptually, global governance suggests a new form of governance, but it cannot be equated with national governance, or readily fitted to any of the usual categories of governance. Democratic theorist Dahl writes (1999: 929): "However, I suggest that we view international governments as systems of decision-making by political and bureaucratic elites that operate with a very high degree of autonomy, within limits set by charters, treaties, or other international agreements." In this sense, international governance involves largely self-regulating entities which evokes a classic issue of governance, that of accountability. Global governance, therefore, can be understood from two perspectives, as emanating from particular global institutions entities and as products of coalitions that reflect the circumstances and relationships of its nation state members.

Liberal-democratic themes have featured in the international responses to environmental issues since the outset. More often than not, these global environmental management initiatives aspired to goals of democratic political systems, international cooperation, and advocated selected use of economic instruments as a means to secure social and environmental goals. Democratic themes, principles, and goals can be found throughout a number of the key environmental conferences, documents, and processes that raised concerns about climate change, such as the UN Conference on Human Environment in 1972, the World Commission on Environment and Development, and the 1993 Earth Summit. Sustainable development, such as promulgated by the WCED and the Earth Summit, placed economic development, social justice, and environmental protection as inexorably connected goals and practices within a global capitalist economy (see, e.g.,

WCED 1987). Making the ideals of democracy and ecological protection tangible in policy form in these plans and agreements typically enlists the assistance of economic tools and concepts. Because these agreements engage capitalist nation states, environmental policies are 'fitted' to the economic interests of the participants. Debate over the apparent contradictions of applying capitalist institutions for ecological protection, such as raised in controversies over ecological modernization, globalization's effect on the environment, and sustainable development, have made little impression upon the UN's and developed nations' embrace of the liberal-democratic ideal.

Liberal democracy is usually depicted as the combination of three conditions or values. Firstly, there's democracy, usually in the form of 'representative democracy' involving an electorate, elections, and elective representatives to a legislative body, in which the majority passes laws. Secondly, there's a set of values or rights drawn from civil and natural rights, such as due processes of law, protection of minorities, freedom of expression, and so on. This 'liberal' element concerns limitations placed on government intervention in the lives of individuals (as derived from J.S. Mill's classic liberalism in *On Liberty*). Thirdly, there's the distinction between the state and civic society, which is enforced by internal and external checks on state power, by the influence of autonomous groups and interests, and by capitalism. Notwithstanding the debates over liberalism, liberal democracy can be reduced to those political and economic conditions that feature representative democracy and capitalism.

Modernity is closely tied to our understanding of liberal democracy. In the hands of some theorists, liberalism and modernity define each other; prominent liberal scholar Gray states (1986: 82):

> Liberalism – and most especially liberalism in its classical form – is the political theory of modernity. Its postulates are the most distinctive features of modern life – the autonomous individual with his concern for liberty and privacy, the growth of wealth and the steady stream of invention and innovation, the machinery of government which is at once indispensable to civil life and a standing threat to it – and its intellectual outlook is one that could have originated in its fullness only in the post-traditional society of Europe after the dissolution of medieval Christendom.

Political theorists differ widely over such claims, but there's little doubt that the developed world's governments, which are mostly liberal democracies (see Dahl 1998), laud liberal democracy as the ideal economic and political organization. Fukuyama (1992) stretched the case to its logical conclusion (following Hegel) with the controversial claim in *The End of History and the Last Man* that liberal democracy was not only an obtainable ideal, but marked the endpoint of social development.

Liberal democracy is undoubtedly the credo of the world of nation states and is promoted by the leading international institutions in the UN, OECD, IMF, GATT, World Economic Forum, and the World Bank. Driven by globalization, capitalism is arguably under its most ascendant phase in history (see Held et al. 1999), and it's inconceivable that any major global governance institution wouldn't reflect this condition. Regardless of their subject matter, recent global agreements increasingly feature market-related policies that in some form or, at least, reflect the global economy's influence. Associated in this way, a fundamental contradiction must be addressed, namely that unfettered capitalism and global markets will be ecologically destructive. Global environmental governance is therefore either a largely symbolic but empty effort to negate global market forces that's based on a false premise, or an accommodation of some kind.

FCCC as an instrument of global environmental governance

By any measure, the FCCC and Kyoto Protocol are highly complex matters of international law, environmental governance, and economic policy instruments, but the institutions of governance are relatively straightforward. Institutionally, the FCCC features a decision-making authority of participating nations in the COP, which has met somewhat annually since 1995. There are two 'subsidiary bodies:' one on Scientific and Technical Advice and the other on Implementation, additionally there are groups as created by the COP for special purposes, and a permanent Secretariat in Bonn.

As an effort at global environmental governance, the FCCC fits with a global version of ecological modernization, as it attempts to resolve the contradictions between the environmentally destructive capacity of capitalism using market restraints imposed by states through policy processes and informed by scientific advice (see, e.g., Glover 1999). Ecological modernization is not such a specific concept that it dictates a particular set of policy instruments, governance structures, and implementation approaches. Rather, we need to consider whether the features of the governance response to climate change captured in the global governance and liberal-democratic approach are consistent with ecological modernization. Usually, ecological modernization refers to nation-state conditions, but it also fits some international environmental agreements, including the FCCC. Included in the FCCC's ecological modernization attributes are that it reconciles routine functioning of developed states with environmental goals, namely climate 'stabilization.' Environmental sustainability is promoted as being compatible with existing systems of production and consumption. Further, the FCCC advocates and presumes 'techno-economic progress,' and tends to frame issues in terms of the natural sciences and monetary measurements. And finally, the climate change problem is treated as a managerial challenge, necessarily requiring experts and established authorities to assume leading roles in specific tasks for managing nature. While climate change has necessitated forming new institutions and reforming existing ones, such changes leave the basic global political, social, and economic orders in place.

Although Dahl and others might not regard global governance's democratic credentials highly, the FCCC exhibits democratic features in its organizational principles and procedures. Firstly, the Convention and Protocol negotiations purport to follow broad democratic approaches in their decision-making, with agreements reached through negotiation and voting by equal national representatives. Secondly, while the resulting agreements under the FCCC place a variety of obligations on participating parties, considerable formal limits are placed on the powers of the FCCC to influence individual states with policy instruments that allow both states and corporations freedom to determine policy choices. Thirdly, FCCC text carefully recognizes the economic rights of nations, aims to protect international economy activity, and recognizes that international economic markets' key role in global governance. Fourthly, the FCCC employs the 'Kyoto mechanisms' as economic policy instruments to enable nations to independently fashion least-cost emission reduction/sink enhancement strategies through international trading.

Holdren's (2002) *Democracy and Global Warming* is the most detailed and sophisticated examination of the implications of global warming for democracy and he points to the range of ways in which global warming influences democracy, both within the system of international governance and as consequential from the decisions arising from these processes. According to Holdren, there are many ways in which global warming can threaten the opportunities for democracy. As an institution, the FCCC attempts to 'govern without government,' for although new (international) social institutions have been established and are operating to resolve collective action problems amongst interdependent states, there are no new 'governments' to undertake these actions. Although nation states are often dealing with resource issues in these matters of global environmental governance, states are typically less concerned with notions of 'property rights' and more with 'sovereignty rights,' which in the case of climate change involves states exerting controls over the access to pollute the atmosphere with greenhouse gases (see, e.g., Young 1997). In effect, nations agree over their respective applications of sovereignty rights to determine property rights, providing substance to those such as Holdren concerned over the treatment of democratic ideals in this activity.

International relations and regime theory

Mainstream international relations uses 'regime theory' to interpret the new international environmental agreements. Facing problems of interdependence, the nation states respond with collective action initiatives based around 'regimes' restraining each participating state. "Regimes can be defined as sets of principles, norms, rules and decision-making procedures around which actor expectations converge in a given issue area " (Krasner 1983) and which govern the interactions of those actors around specific issues (Young 1997). Hence, a regime implies something greater than an organization or body of law, as it can include formal and informal agreements, and becomes an international institution of sorts. Studies applying regime theory are concerned with explaining regime formation, assessing and analyzing regime effectiveness, and determining regime influence on international and national institutions and activities (Greene 1996).

As Greene (1996) explains, regime theory emerged as a reaction to the 'neorealists" position by the 'institutionalists' to make a claim for the validity of international institutions as a force in world politics, a proposition now broadly accepted. Realism holds that nations follow self-interest above all else unless restrained by a supranational force, following individual goals of self-preservation. States expect other nation states to act according to their perceived self-interests, and therefore anticipate the worst outcomes from international relations. It follows that success is measured by outcomes and that intentions count for little (Morgenthau 1973). Yet because political results cannot be predicted on the basis of simple national military power and that state activity alone doesn't determine policy outcomes, understanding this new international dynamic involves the interdependence between states and the roles played by non-state actors (List and Rittberger 1992).

Liberalism, by contrast, considers that states can rise above self-interest and act in accordance with international law. Liberal and realist positions posit that the source of global environmental problems is either ad hoc trends or problems occurring between states. Liberal institutionalists assume the competency of the international system to resolve global environmental problems and that the 'international power structures' are "neutral" in their effects on the environment, so that the task of explanation is to describe state responses to such challenges (Paterson 2000).

Haas et al. (1993) propose that environmental protection must overcome three limitations: the difficulty of establishing a collective response amongst nations; developing adequate capacities within nations to respond effectively to environmental problems; and overcoming indifference to these problems. International institutions play a key role in addressing such problems. Collective action is made possible through the agency of international institutions where international negotiations can occur, who supply information and knowledge for decision-making, and provide monitoring and reporting which increases confidence for participating countries. International institutions can make available resources for nations without the necessary capital, technology, expertise, or information needed to respond to an environmental problem. In this way, inadequate domestic institutions are bolstered through international activity and Haas et al. (1993) describe the ways in which issue awareness is produced by international institutions, but note that other national activities are necessary for effective international awareness raising.

Regime theory reflects the values of liberal institutionalism, holding that the virtues of an international agreement can be assessed on institutional performance. For example, Wettestad (2001) identifies factors explaining the successful design of an international regime: access and participation procedures; rules for decision making; role of the secretariat; agenda structuring; organization of the science-policy 'interface;' and mechanisms for verification and compliance. Institutional performance is the rationale of bureaucracy, in which environmental problems are the core of a constellation of actors, interests, and other factors, but the identity of the regime is its crystalization in an institutional form. Regime performance is a measure of institutional performance. National circumstances feature strongly in Greene's (1996) account of the effectiveness of international environmental regimes. Those factors that influence regime effectiveness include the actors' interests and the distribution of coercive power, the capacity to effectively respond to the regime, the ability to monitor national activity, and the characteristics of the specific issue. By way of example, Greene approves of the FCCC on the basis of its 'pledge and review' approach to managing national greenhouse gas emissions.

However, regime theory doesn't adopt an idealistic view of the problems and difficulties of creating effective international agreement on environmental problems and identifies a number of limitations (Greene 1996; Susskind 1994; Susskind and Ozawa 1992; and Wettestad 2001). One set of problems derives from the international agreements themselves, which are largely ineffective in achieving their goals and frequently have a narrow scope. A second set of problems derives from the deficiencies in the convention–protocol approach that's become increasingly applied to UN environmental agreements. These lengthy processes dissipate much of the early political and public attention generated around the convention stage as the protocol stages wear on over the ensuing years. Politically, the process often comes to be driven and determined by the powerful states. Agreements reached are often deliberately vague in order to foster agreements between nations, producing the 'lowest common denominator' effect. A range of political views can be accommodated within regime theory therefore, and it should not be considered the exclusive domain of conservative thought; many of the limitations and failures identified by regime theorists are on the grounds of their failures to protect environmental values, foster international cooperation, and adhere to equitable and fair negotiation processes.

An international climate change regime

Many international studies explicitly describe the FCCC as an 'international climate change regime,' or implicitly do so by focussing on the elements of regime theory (e.g., Bodansky 2001a; Grubb et al. 1999; Molitor 1999; Oberthur and Ott 1999; and Soroos 1997). Research and scholarship into the international climate change regime is largely empirical or model based (see, e.g., Molitor 1999; Ramakrishna 1996). These studies form the prevailing and conventional view of international climate change politics, often produced by private and government research centers, and institutions with close relationships to those actively involved in the international negotiations.

Prominent amongst regime theory's concerns have been the formation of the FCCC institutions, the state's negotiation activities (especially in international meetings), FCCC and Kyoto Protocol 'policy architecture,' official procedures, and the economic evaluation of policy options. Climate change offers fertile ground for investigating its complexity and the divergent interests vying for influence, and of the possibilities for future changes. Further, as the international response has been so contentious and controversial, there are many opportunities for assessing and identifying normative alternatives. Both the FCCC institutions and regime scholarship share a broader concern with getting the system to work.

Collective action is regime theory's organizational theme and it depicts the response to climate change as sovereign states acting as self-interested parties driven to cooperation in order to avoid the inevitable (if uncertain) outcomes of non-cooperation. Scholarship to date is concentrated in three areas: 1) Institutional values and attributes of FCCC and Kyoto Protocol; 2) Climate change as a problem of collective national action; and 3) Policy architecture of the Kyoto Protocol, especially the Kyoto mechanisms. Nations have been effectively compelled into responding to the climate change issue internationally because of the FCCC. Consequently, proponents of the international climate change regime point out the necessity of the institution for organizing an international response, which has proved an overwhelmingly stronger response than notions of nations compelled only by self-interest. A key factor in the FCCC's institutional strength in organizing collective action has been its ability to generate, organize, and utilize climate change science and manage the scientific uncertainty issue by applying the precautionary principle, which individual nations would be less likely to apply. Regime theory also analyzes the abilities of the FCCC in establishing common policies, formulating innovative policies, setting monitoring and reporting standards and guidelines, and disseminating information on performance and compliance.

Regime theory identifies the limitations of the theory and practice of the FCCC as an institution. This convention–protocol model has its supporters, even amongst environmentalists, as each successive COP meeting offers opportunities to either recover lost ground or consolidate previous gains. Claims that the broad-scale interest and concern over climate change generated at Rio was dissipated during the decade of key negotiations has much backing, and accounts of national and NGO participants in these negotiations (regardless of their particular interests) are replete with exasperations and frustrations. By design, the convention–protocol model encourages deferring difficult issues. Almost by virtue of the time available, the COP process developed an institution of extraordinary complexity with many sections of the FCCC agreement covered by an array of sub-committees and specialized groups. Much of these group's activities have been to determine more exact meanings for FCCC phrases and concepts that were left deliberately vague and uncertain. It follows that the difficulty in reaching agreement over the Kyoto Protocol and why it took over a decade after the FCCC's ratification is partly attributable to the FCCC's institutional design.

A consistent feature of these regime studies is climate change's 'globality' – the diffuse sources of greenhouse gas emissions, climate change impacts' global reach, and the inescapability from global climate – that makes international collective action a defining necessity and the resultant institutions an agency for collective action. All nations produce greenhouse gases, so a system that fails to recognize the limitations of unilateral action in emissions reduction cannot succeed (because of 'free riders'), its followers claim. And all nations will suffer some global warming costs, although their magnitude and distribution is highly uncertain, so that individual national interests can only be served through international cooperation. Adaptation policies dealing with climate change impacts present a less compelling case for such cooperation, for national investments in adaptation will be largely confined to domestic investments largely disinterested in the actions of other states (i.e., adaptation policy concerns the equivalent of national 'private goods').

Set against the potential and necessity of the international climate change regime are those factors shaping national responses and relevant national circumstances that create a dynamic intending to maximize each nation's advantage in the regime process. Scholarship has focussed on the key negotiating protagonists, the U.S. and the E.U., in this regard, and the wider implications of international environmental agreements for national sovereignty. Concern over the excessive influence of the powerful nations in the FCCC processes has been consistent with suggestions of attempted U.S. hegemony (Porter and Brown 1996). Rowlands (2001) concluded that political power has been highly influential in the climate change negotiations and while the U.S. is a "crucial player," other states and non-state actors have also been highly influential. Except for U.S. supporters, there has been little empirical disputation of these claims, although views differ over the scale of U.S. success.

U.S. withdrawal from the Kyoto Protocol seemingly caught out many observers; some found in the COP-6 collapse signs of immanent failure of the entire regime. In any event, regime theory was not as disturbed as might appear by its withdrawal, as the U.S. proposed not unilateralism but the future release of a new plan for international action. Climate change isn't an issue that affords an obvious hegemonic dominance by a single nation.

Critics of the U.S. withdrawal and its proposed replacement for the Kyoto Protocol point to the institutional 'weight' of the existing scheme, asserting that an agreement bearing nearly every nation's signature is unlikely to be replaced in the near term (Begg 2002). Some commentators regard the U.S. return to the regime as inevitable, given its 'indispensibility.'

Within the climate change regime two competing worldviews vie to dominate the basic policy approach adopted: that of the E.U.'s managerialism through restraints on state and corporate emissions; and the U.S. advocacy for free market solutions. Some speculate that this difference is sytomatic of national ideologies. Bodansky (1994) claims that most governments saw climate change as a scientific and environmental, rather than an economic, issue – the exception being the U.S. Perceived neglect of economic concerns as a consequence of the U.S. EPA leading U.S. national responses to the development of the Montreal Protocol caused the Reagan administration to ensure that climate change negotiations avoided repetiting this outcome (Bodansky 1994). While other Western nations pursued more explicit environmental goals, the U.S. emphasized economic issues and pressed for further research to precede on-going policy formulation (Bodansky 1994).

Under the FCCC process, not only are the results strongly shaped by the most powerful states' interests, but a number of other characteristics also work against protecting environmental values and the interests of the less advantaged. Emission reduction targets set under the Kyoto Protocol and later agreements on carbon sinks exemplify how FCCC outcomes result from bargaining rather than efforts to meet the FCCC's objectives. Where agreements have are or are prospectively difficult, negotiations often tended to produce outcomes favorable to the majority of states by virtue of their modest goals, nowhere more so than the key clauses of the FCCC. However, the COP process also encourages nations to adopt fixed positions on matters of national interest and negotiate from these positions, often taking deliberations further away from resolving key problems. As a result, the scope of possible solutions begins with a narrow cast of choices and rapidly becomes defined around specific proposals.

Regime theory pays great attention to the details of the Kyoto mechanisms and sinks, comprising, as they do, the substantive aspects of the FCCC's climate change 'solution.' Accordingly, these studies record liberal democracy's expansion through the agency of global environmental governance, thereby constituting another dimension of economic and social globalization. Additional to regime theory's attribution of international institutions being at the center of the international response is its recognition of the role of international economic relations. Much concern has been expressed over the regime's effectiveness, especially over the provisions for emissions trading, the CDM, and carbon sink credits. In the case of 'hot air,' developing nations complained in the COP negotiations that developed nations were avoiding their emission reduction responsibilities and undermining the agreement's effectiveness (see, e.g., Agarwal et al. 1999, 2002). Counter-arguments by the regime's supporters offer that these are only short-term failings and are an acceptable compromise for securing a framework for emissions reduction with longer-term prospects for future increments in emission reduction targets (e.g., Metz 2001). Given such preoccupations of some regime theorists with formalizing the negotiations and agreements into a rational science, the descent into game theory was inevitable. Analyists have now produced a body of work that compresses the nation states into rational actions facing the prisoner's dilemma and some educators have used this work to simulate the international negotiations.

Limitations of the 'international climate change regime'

Criticisms of regime theory are best known from advocates of political economy and political ecology, but not exclusively so, as regime theory has also drawn fire because of its reliance on positivism, endorsement of international institutions, and prediliction for approving procedural successes whilst ignoring substantial failures in actual effectiveness. Political economy has a long-standing antipathy towards liberalism and liberal institutionalism and finds in regime theory the newest incantation of these inherent flaws (e.g., Paterson 1995; Saurin 1993, 1996, and 2001). Amongst regime theory's failings they identify is its political conservatism in accepting existing arrangements of state and corporate power (including global capitalist relations and economic globalization), the central role given to nation states, and an inability to recognize the social causes of an environmental crisis. Regime theory admits the roles played by non-state actors, but its central concerns are the nation states' conduct. Climate change is described as an emerging political issue to be resolved by specific institutions and organizational structures empowered by states, and how these led to the climate change regime's formation with distinct institutional forms. States are recognized as the key actors in these institutions and their interests, behavior, and strategies largely held to determine the resulting decisions and outcomes. Scientific inputs are recognized as essential, but are only rendered significant and of utility by the decisions and actions of states.

In effect, the climate change regime is depicted as "international public regulation" (Saurin 2001). As such, regime theory is pluralistic, being largely concerned with the goal of ensuring that the international agreement operates as well as possible within the accepted confines of existing social and economic 'realities.' For example (Bodansky 2001b):

> But long term progress in developing more stringent abatement measures will depend primarily on extralegal factors – the resolution of scientific and economic uncertainties; the development of technologi-

cal and policy solutions; and ultimately, the crystallization of popular and political will at the national and international levels.

Fulfilling the FCCC's goals would essentially satisfy regime theory's analytical role, as the nation states would have modified their activities as required by the agreement.

It follows that many FCCC critics favoring stronger protection of social and environmental values, especially those from developing nations and advocates of ecological justice, raise issues that fall outside the regime theory's routine ambit. Thematically, much of regime theory can be linked to international law, wherein the essential matters are legalistic in scope and intent, whereas the critiques of regime theory are more generally motivated by broader political and philosophical challenges to the status quo. Such political criticism questions those themes that regime theory accepts, such as the legitimacy of nation states, the values expressed by climate change science, the social and economic causes of greenhouse gas emissions, the involvement and influence of non-state actors, and the equity and fairness of the existing distribution of national wealth and power. Concentrating on the activities of states and the FCCC as an institution, regime theory doesn't take into account the myriad non-nation state factors that have been influential at the global scale but originating at the sub-national level and at the global scale, such as globalization.

Indivisable from the climate change regime is the epistemic role played by climated change science; indeed, it could be said that the role of each is to supply legitimacy to the other. Close to the surface of the climate change regime's rationale are claims of its 'scientific' character, bringing together state and non-state actors in a cause that transcends mere national self-interest and in which science assumes the role of the universe discourse. Critically, the very process that deemed it essential that resolving the climate change problem required a rational regime based on scientific understanding marginalized calls for greater equity and ecological protection. Elites in the international community of nations and in climate change science effectively empowered each other. Within regime theory we cannot find the tools for the task of self-analysis, and to identify such influences as ideology, economics, culture, or politics, we must turn elsewhere. As Jasanoff said of science in international regimes (1996: 174): "The widespread belief that *scientific* knowledge can only advance the cause of global *environmental* policy seems but an unproblematic instantiation of the more pervasive modernist dogma."

Political economy of the FCCC

Political economy understands the social condition as arising historically through material relationships that impart a systemic view of the ways in which economic and political interests interact. As a mode of inquiry, political economy deals mostly with forming a critique of the dominant social and economic arrangement of modern life, that of capitalist industrial society. Capitalist society is directed towards the accumulation of capital through productive processes that ultimately are founded on the exploitation of natural resources and human labor, although in contemporary times the location wealth creation and its ultimate sources can be distant, obscure, and fragmented. Successful capitalism requires a number of social institutions for ensuring order in markets and in society. Social institutions serve several essential functions in capitalist society and all major institutions are, by definition, serving this goal, including the law, government, family, technology, and education. Political economy identifies the ways in which these institutions interact and reinforce each other. In effect, the state responds to the needs of capital by maintaining the necessary institutional infrastructure of the market, private property, and the money system, as well as promoting capital's 'general interests' (such as economic growth and capital accumulation).

Within the uniformity of capitalist industrial society is the uneven distribution of its benefits, which political economy aims to describe and to ascribe to the character of capitalism. Differences within capitalist society can assume many forms, such as in income, health, education, safety, housing, and environmental risks. Political economy identifies how differences are manufactured through the economic and political systems' operation. Accordingly, corporate actions and interactions with the state are critical. Governments and the apparatus of the state, such as its political system, legal and regulatory powers, and controls over the media, empower corporate activity. Governance and corporate activity are bound into the reproduction of capitalist relations and political economy analyzes how this occurs. Such analysis is not bounded by scale, being applicable to wherever the means of producing wealth and political power finds expression and is applicable to dealing with international issues. Under environmentalism's influence, political economy examines the influence of capital and political power on natural entities and processes, exposing how the organization of industrial society utilizes the natural world.

Political economy is the basis for several climate change studies (e.g., Byrne and Rich 1992; Newell and Paterson 1998; Paterson 1996), and has been implicitly or partially involved in a great many other inquiries. At the basis of these analyses is a historical materialism, directed at the activities of corporations and state actors involved in fossil fuel production and use and entails a rejection of regime theories' tenets of states as unitary actors and that states and markets operate relative independently. Newell and Paterson (1998) argue that, as a result of the power of corporate power and influence, the (developed) state's responses to climate change have been weak. However, they also detect rivalries emerging in the corporate sector regarding climate change and these offer possibilities for alliances with environmentalists and other groups.

Activities of the state

Modern states have a vital role in the process of capital accumulation, especially relating to climate change. Paterson (1996) asserts that these states, essentially for reasons involved in building and maintaining themselves, have embarked on systematic programs of capital accumulation and he sees this occurring through state investments that generate wealth and other benefits and to boost household incomes, which makes greater funds available for the state via taxation. Meeting taxes increasingly means citizens' participation in the cash economy, so that increasing proportions of the population are effectively employed in the service of state needs. Economic development since the Industrial Revolution has centered on the unrestrained combustion of vast quantities of low-cost fossil fuels without regard to their social or ecological consequences, a process impossible without state action and support.

States of the developed world have benefited immensely from the 'carbon economy' and the interests of the two are closely tied. Public energy resources, notably coal, oil, and gas, are often state 'property,' as states control their extraction, processing, transport, and use, have power over their export and importation, own or direct all or part of energy systems in electricity, gas, and oil, as well as plan, fund, and facilitate and plan economic development that impinges on energy systems. Industrial states regard the fossil fuel supply as being national strategic importance, sometimes culminating in international conflicts (see, e.g., Yergin 1991). Standing behind the energy sector, in an economic sense, are myriad energy-dependent industries that states also often accord high regard. Corporations, as the predominant agent for organizing capital, gain great power within state decision-making. States benefit from corporate activity in the energy sector generally and effectively operate as corporate entities in the energy sector. Accordingly, the states' role is complex, marked by tensions and contradictions in encouraging and regulating corporate activity befitting their role as supporter of the market system, as well as benefactor of economic activity and supporter of broader national economic performance, combined with being major economic actors in their own right, with a vested interest in national and international policy.

GDP growth has been the de facto metric used by influential negiators in assessing policy options. Such a concern links to two dimensions that Newell and Peterson (1998) identify in which FCCC negotiations have presented domestic economic growth as a primary goal: firstly, in those differences between the developed and developing world regarding overall development inequities and greenhouse gas emissions specifically; and secondly, the divisions between nations dependent on either exporting or consuming fossil fuels and those with reasons to limit greenhouse gas (such as scarce domestic fossil fuel resources). As Newell and Paterson (1998: 693) conclude: "Strong networks of mutual dependency thus exist between the state and the energy sector."

Energy industries are vital to industrial states and their vigorous expansion fits with capitalism's general capitalistic appetite for growth. Within capitalist nations, economic growth is synonymous with national economic health; prolonged decline in GDP defines economic recession and depression. As for nations, so too for individual firms: growth is usually the primary source of increased profit maximization. Hence, the state and firm operate symbiotically: states requiring expanding national economies and firms requiring states to ensure such conditions. If economic growth is threatened by environmental protection measures, then both the state and corporations are likely to be provoked. Government planners' assumption that expanding energy use is a precondition for economic growth has been prevalent in developed nations in the post-WWII era. States have directed their efforts accordingly, encouraging and enabling continual expansion in energy consumption. Energy consumption reductions, as the dictates of the climate change discourse require, are frequently viewed as inimical to economic growth by state and firm alike. Within government, trade, industry, and energy agencies enjoy greater influence over national policy than environment agencies, and corporations enjoy a closer relationship with this former group (Newell and Paterson 1998). Policy debates have found states united in the belief that even modest efforts to limit carbon dioxide emissions will substantially erode national GDP. Thus (Newell and Paterson 1998: 693): "The interest of 'capital-in-general' has thus become synonymous with promoting the interests of fossil energy companies."

Comparatively, the world's richest nations contribute the greatest volume of carbon dioxide emissions, have the greatest volume of emissions per unit of GDP, and have the highest per capita emissions. Commentators have pointed favorably to these nations' efforts in improving energy efficiency, especially since the oil crises of the 1970s, and taken this as signifying the proper working of the global economy. However, since the 1970s there has also been a growing disparity in energy efficiency between core and periphery nations, with an increase amongst the former and a decrease in the latter (Roberts and Grimes 1997). One explanation is that the relocation of industrial capacity, notably manufacturing, and capital flows to the developing world has caused the carbon dioxide/GDP ratio to rise in those nations. Consequently, the developed world benefits from this transfer and can invest in less polluting industries. Grimes and Kentor (2003: 270) find that "*dependence on foreign capital accelerates* the rate of growth of CO_2 emissions in less developed countries." They offer that foreign investment in less developed countires is concentrated in energy-consuming industries, that the lengthening of commodity chains has increased overall transport energy use, energy efficiency of production is poor in the developing world, and foreign investment may be less likely for pollution controls in developing nations (where regulation and enforcement tend to be weaker than in richer nations). International efforts for reducing greenhouse gas emissions must immediately confront not just the economic implications of such action, but the state and corporate interests vested in continuation of a global system of fossil fuel energy production that sustains industrialization. As Paterson (1996) notes, policy in response to the FCCC at the national and international level has framed the issue of greenhouse gas reductions that accepts international capitalism in its current form, but with the necessity for maintaining economic growth.

Maintaining capitalism's dynamic demands continual market expansion by creating new commodities, by converting social and natural phenomena into commodity forms (i.e., the process of 'commodification'). State intervention is usually the only reliable means for restraining this expansion and even these controls are not always effective. Social convention, taboos, and religious dictates have proved relatively weak in restricting market expansion, although these may slow the process. Nature's bounty has proved particularly attractive as sources of capital; nation states assume control over natural resources within (and below and above) their boundaries and with state and economic powers negotiating over the commercial exploitation of natural resources. Applying the critique of capitalism to the international climate change regime takes the obvious formulation, based on the notion that climate change threatens a valuable natural service and a great number of assets and natural services, and that the FCCC was created to control access to the atmosphere as a sink for greenhouse gas emissions. Further, the atmosphere's capacity to accept greenhouse gas pollutants has been made into a commodity through the Kyoto mechanisms, in the form of carbon emission credits. An additional commodity is that of credited carbon storage, so that components and processes of the global carbon cycle are partitioned into fungible commodity units.

In a related way, developed states are a major facilitator in displacing industrialism's ecological costs into other jurisdictions. Under globalization, heavy and toxic industries with their polluting outputs have been 'migrating' to the developing world for many years, driven out by environmental protection laws and drawn to lower establishment and production costs. Exporting the wastes of rich nations for disposal in developing nations is now restricted by international regulation, yet pollution of commons resources has only been restricted through international agreements on specific locations and substances. Obviously, the FCCC fits this category in its efforts to restrict developed states from facilitating the pollution of the atmosphere and having the resultant costs distributed disproportionably to the developing world. Critics of the Kyoto mechanisms have argued that emissions trading and other measures perpetuate the developed states' ability to maintain a global economic advantage, evading the costs of emissions reduction, and continuing to displace the costs of the fossil fuel energy system onto poorer nations, future generations, and the environment (Agarwal and Narain 1991).

Corporate activity is driven by the profit motive and where this coincides with environmental protection, the interests of capital are satisfied. 'Market rationalizing' or 'free market' environmentalists approach environmental problems by attaching market values to market externalities, so that firms' decisions reflect something of the environmental value that otherwise goes unrecognized and is therefore allowed to deteriorate. Profit maximization is lowered by such measures, but if applied equally, all firms are theoretically equally disadvantaged. Following the artificial separation of commercial activity from its ecological consequences, profit maximization from fossil fuel combustion enabled its environmental consequences to be ignored. Subsequent attempts to value the benefits of reducing greenhouse gas emissions – such as through carbon taxes – resulted in corporations and their lobbyists putting up fierce resistance (see, e.g., Leggett 2000; Levy and Egan 1998). A major aspect of the case of corporations was that cutting greenhouse gas emissions meant reducing profits or losing international competitiveness.

Capitalist states create systemic social differences marked by hierarchies and political economy is concerned with how economic hierarchies validate the other hierarchies within the state. For scholars such as Paterson (1996), the structures of domination within states connect with those giving rise to the human domination of nature. Verifying such hierarchies empirically can be difficult, but political economy identifies several instances of the influence of elite political and economic groups. Political economists have claimed that national climate change policies, both domestic and in terms of international relations, reflect specific corporate and general economic interests far more than environmental or other concerns. Rather than deny such claims, many national policies exhibit this influence openly as evidence of their 'economic responsibility.'

Internationally, the states' activities have also produced distinct hierarchies as evidenced in the FCCC negotiations and policy architecture. Rejecting deep and effective emissions reductions, the developed nations have opted for modest targets, which implicitly accept some degree of global warming whose effects will most impact on poorer nations. Accordingly, political economy offers a critique centered on capitalism's role, which culminates in a belief that the FCCC is an instrument not for protecting the global climate, but for protecting global capitalism.

National influence and economic power

Fulfilling in practice the ideals of democracy that it espouses is a perennial burden for the UN and this challenge extends to its climate change activities. National circumstances and capacities vary greatly and the FCCC recognizes this in having the developed countries take the lead in emissions reductions, an equity-based rationale that gave the OECD group the prominent role. And, as the FCCC's history reveals, developed nations have dominated proceedings and the resulting outcomes greatly reflect their collective interests (e.g., Grubb et al. 1999; Oberthür and Ott 1999). As the world's economically and politically dominant nation, the influence and interests of the U.S. have been at the forefront in FCCC negotiations.

Nation-state influence accords with its economic and political power, as do national state groupings. In negotiations, the major powers exert their influence in establishing their positions and expectations; their concerns form the agenda. This forms one of the norms of the process and it largely occurs without comment. Analysis of the negotiations frequently begins with establishing the U.S. position and arranging the other nations' according to their response. Although official UN daily briefings and press releases from the COP meetings emphasize the contribution of an array of nations, these only serve to highlight the gap between the opportunity to contribute and the *realpolitik* of the final decisions arising from the deliberations.

State economic and political power is expressed in other ways. Within the negotiations, for example, the size of the national delegation varies greatly and this affects a nations' ability to participate and exert influence. Each COP features an array of technical meetings, side events, meetings of specialized bodies, and several sessions operating throughout the day and evening. Developed nations send large delegations; for example, even although it wasn't an 'official participant' at COP-6 *bis* and COP-7, the U.S. sent over one hundred officials; delegations of several dozen is common for Annex 1 parties. In contrast, many developing nations have delegations of one or two members to represent large national populations; some poor nations are without representation entirely. National delegations provide technical support for their negotiators, so that without access to technical information and experts, many aspects of the proposals at each Conference of the Parties cannot be understood or interpreted. This affects both the preparation prior to the meetings, assessing options and changes during the event, but also participation in IPCC and Subsidiary Body activities. Nations with larger technical and research capacities also benefit from the accumulating experience in complex policy issues. Developing nations have sought assistance from NGOs to counter this disadvantage, but this hardly adds to the independence of these parties.

Corporate activities

Corporations and their agents enjoy privileged access to, and influence with, state entities through formal and informal channels. This role derives from their economic significance and expertise (Newell and Paterson 1998: 684): "in helping governments to define realistic response strategies within appropriate time-frames and based on best available technology." Formulation of the U.S. *National Energy Policy* (NEPD 2001), for example, revealed how close the links between the G.W. Bush administration and fossil fuel industry were, including appointing corporate lobbyists and employees to administrative posts, corporate financing of elected candidates, and including corporation-suppled text into the document (see, e.g., van Natta 2002a,

2002b). Examples from the E.U. and U.S. demonstrate the victories of industry in lobbying to stymie progressive climate change policy initiatives (Gelbspan 1997; Leggett 2000; and van den Hove et al. 2002). Environmental group Transnational Resource and Action Center (Bruno et al. 1999) characterize industry's tactics on climate change as 'deny, delay, divide, dump, and dupe.'

But amongst the fossil fuel and associated firms, the response to climate change is not that of universal opposition. Corporations have made climate change plans, invested in climate change responses, monitored their activities, set greenhouse gas abatement targets, assessed climate change risks, and a range of other activities. A report by the Investor Responsibility Research Center (Cogan 2003) on 20 of the world's largest firms' response to climate change reveals the range of corporate responses. U.S. electric utilities have invested heavily in refurbishing their older coal-fired power stations and U.S. petroleum companies (e.g., ChevronTexaco, ConocoPhillips, and ExxonMobil) continue to concentrate on oil and gas development, in contrast to a number of European firms (e.g., BP and Royal Dutch/Shell) who are investing in renewable energy and are generally far ahead of their U.S. counterparts. Other large companies have shown a variety of responses, from those with comprehensive approaches to climate change, such as Alcoa and DuPont, to those doing little, such as Daimler-Chrysler and General Electric.

Oft-cited examples of repressive corporate influence are the specially formed groups to oppose public policy initiatives. Best known is the (now defunct) Global Climate Coalition that comprised many key corporations and associations, including the American Petroleum Institute, Amoco, Arco, Philips, Texaco, DuPont, Dow Hydrocarbons, Shell, BP, Association of International Automobile Manufacturers, Motor Vehicle Manufacturers Association, American Electric Power Service Corporation, American Mining Congress, Edison Electric Institute, and the National Coal Association. Groups such as these instructed and liaised with the sympathetic delegations at various FCCC and IPCC negotiations, especially OPEC (notably Saudi Arabia and Kuwait) and the U.S. and other national governments (Gelbspan 1997; Leggett 2000). Key members of these lobby groups were former senior members of the U.S. Presidential administrations of Reagan and George Bush (Gelbspan 1997; Leggett 2000).

Few official records acknowledge corporate influence on international and national climate change policy positions, although evidence is abundant of this effect. That some of the world's largest corporations involved in fossil fuel and related industries, such as the top 122 corporate carbon producers producing 80 percent of global fossil fuel carbon emissions (NRDC et al. 1999), have a political interest in climate change negotiations is self-evident. Their activities have included questioning IPCC science, conducting media campaigns, forming alliances with nations (notably OPEC states), advancing policy positions, and stifling the implementation of existing policies. Tactics of these delegations was (and remains) to frustrate, filibuster, and generally impede progress in the FCCC and IPCC processes. Overt examples of direct corporate input into the FCCC policy process are not difficult to find: the Global Climate Coalition supplied text to national delegations, including the U.S., for inclusion as official national input that subsequently made its way into FCCC policy.

Former Scientific Director of Greenpeace International's Climate Campaign, Leggett, in *The Carbon War* (2000), and the aforementioned Gelbspan (1997) produced accounts of the influence of corporations on international and national climate change policy. Many of the revelations about the so-called 'carbon club' of corporate interests have become common knowledge and the formerly clandestine character of the identity of the industry lobbyists, their corporate supporters, and their tactics during and between FCCC and IPCC meetings by being reported in the popular press. However, a full description of their activities is unlikely to become public knowledge.

State and corporate interests

Political economy identifies the influence of political and economic power in domestic and international climate change policy, but few scholars depict its influence as absolute as even under the hegemony of the industrial capitalist states there are sites of resistance and sources of challenge. Political economy does not hold that the interests of capital are homogeneous at the national and international levels, but rather it is 'capital-in-general' that the state advances, which favors particular firms or interests along the way. Overall, however, it is clear that modern states have favored fossil fuel industries extensively. These industries have been central to the 'Fordist' era economies and the transition to 'Post-Fordism' has seen the coal, oil, and automobile industries retain a prominent role as dynamic sectors in global capital accumulation.

Within capitalist economies, therefore, are competing interests that can alter the direction and scope of the economy, such as through changing labor practices and the introduction of new technologies, but axiomatically do not seek to disturb the economic system. Accordingly, climate change has prompted challenges to the fossil fuel industries by the insurance industry, renewable energy industries, and the nuclear power industry. Political economy suggests that the relatively minor impact these industries is not related to the strength or rationality of the case, but is attributable to their minor economic and political stature. Given the fossil fuel industries are both capital-intensive and generally resistant to change, the transition away from fossil fuels has advanced little.

Reluctant and tardy domestic action by developed nation states in moving towards a low-carbon economy accords with the interests of states and the global economy as viewed by political economy. In basic terms, action on climate change is simply against the interests of powerful firms and the state's own 'corporate' interests, and the costs of climate change are reckoned to be minor according to the dictates of their economic rationale, so the failure of high-profile initiatives to reduce emissions, such as the U.S. Clinton administration's attempt to introduce a carbon tax, are unsurprising. Similar explanatory factors account for the relatively weak response by developed nations to reduce emissions at the international level, as nation states and corporations have generally been successful in developing soft and short-term emission reduction targets.

Economic and state interests are closely interwoven in the climate change issue. For example, commentators have noted the U.S. G.W. Bush's administration's unusually close ties to U.S. oil and gas industries: the President, Vice-President, and the majority of the cabinet worked in the industries and/or have a financial interest, and the administration's election campaign in 2000 received considerable financial support from these sources (Down to Earth 2002: 6). Unquestionably, the Middle East's oil reserves have shaped U.S. and other OECD nation's foreign policy, with some attributing the recent war in Kuwait and the U.S. invasion of Iraq to rationales based on those nations' oil resources. Under political economy, it follows that national governments would be opposed to actions that threaten the interests of these industries, notably any measures to lower fossil fuel consumption. And the rise of the Kyoto mechanisms and the process of commodification of greenhouse gas emissions through the FCCC policy architecture conform closely to the ideals of a capitalist system for pollution control. Obviously, any market-based approach to pollution control strengthens the substance of a capitalist economy by creating assets in pollution trading, but these markets also serve to extend the legitimacy to an extended realm of state powers.

Limits of political economy

Despite its strength in explaining the key actors' actions and providing an account for the major contours of the climate change response, certain historical and contemporary aspects of the response are either not well captured by political economy, or are at odds with its assumptions. Some of these limitations arise from political economy's materialist approach to environmental issues. Although political economy has identified environmental problems as an outcome of capitalism's contradictions (see, e.g., the eco-Marxist interpretations of J. O'Connor 1998, 1994), it is difficult to claim that global warming has yet presented itself as significant damage to national and international economies, so that in a material sense there is high uncertainty about current climate change losses. Historically, political economy's account of global warming is strong its attribution of greenhouse gas emissions to capitalist economics, but somewhat weaker in addressing emissions from the former national practitioners of 'actually existing socialism.' Whereas many political opponents of greenhouse gas emissions direct their attention to industrial practices, political economy has been more concerned with economic practice and less vigorous in its critique of industrialization processes. Rowlands (2001) concedes that many of the historical materialist approaches describe the activities and positions of corporations and aspects of debates between the North and South. However, he considers that corporations are not as unified in their response to climate change as political economy suggests, pointing to the differences in views between coal and gas corporations, and allowing that many North–South debates don't adhere to the dictates of political economy.

Analysis of the policy actions at the nation-state scale where the connections between corporate influence and the political are immediate is suited to political economy, whereas in the international arena, explanations of outcomes have to take into account the influence of nations and national groupings that do not always match their economic status and the interests of capital-in-general, which is more nebulous. Political economy has demonstrated that the Kyoto mechanisms promote commodification, reinforce global capitalism, promote the interests of those nations most empowered by economic and strategic advantages, and exacerbate difference and inequalities at the national and international scale – but this critique is not set against any alternatives. Adoption by the FCCC of a policy architecture featuring the Kyoto mechanisms fits a rationale that vested interests are maintaining existing relations within global capitalism and applying capitalist tools to this end, yet many details of the arrangements can't be reduced to the dictates of a dominant economic and political interest. For example, political economy has yet to explain the negotiating differences between the E.U. and U.S., both of which have similar economic interests and an economic rivalry.

Political economy readily identifies the social injustices of the industrial state under capitalism and the workings of the global economy, but it does not readily critque industrialism itself. Such a limitiation is redolent of debates within eco-Marxism and eco-socialism concerning the question of whether either doscourse offers an alternative to industrial modernity. Within the ambit of social injustice, political economy is insightful, but efforts to extend the concepts of justice to a broader ecological field find policial economy largely limited to instrumentalist valuations of natural resources and ecostsyem services. Relatedly, discourses concerned with the influence of symbols and resrepresentations are beyond the materialst outlook of political economy; indeed, political economy dismisses such debates as ephemeral and counter-productive. As discussed later on, in a world in which public issues and political discourse are increasingly mediated through symbols, electronic media, publicity campaigns, and related phenomena, the influence of these forms of information and influence cannot be readily dismissed. In effect, in facing the problems of modernity and climate change, the limits of political economy are exposed.

Searches for ecological justice in the greenhouse

Although political ecology passes unrecognized by conventional international relations, it best captures the ethical dimensions and ecological justice components of the climate change debate. This is hardly surprising for, as Saurin (1996) states, international relations has largely ignored the principal scholars around the world writing about social, political, and economic conditions because they are largely unconcerned with the state system. One critique of international relations takes issue with the discipline's rationale and methods, attacking its attempts to produce findings akin to positive science, its empiricism, and its attempts at behaviorism (Neufield 1995). On the problem of global environmental politics, Hovden (1999) argues that the positivism and instrumental rationality of regime theory prevents it from adopting a critical approach on environmental thought, making it unlikely to be able to engage effectively with environmental concerns.

For understanding the developments in climate change politics, political ecology is vital for examining the ethical dimensions at the center of many critical debates. One way to understand the ethical claims for social justice and ethical treatment of the environment is through ecological justice. This relatively new term has been taken up by a number of environmentalists and ecologism's followers as it more fully embraces the broadening of the notions of justice to explicitly include environmental values (see Chapter 1). Low and Gleeson (1998) suggest that ecological justice is the extension of justice to include future human generations, non-human life, and ecological processes and entities. Christopher Stone, Holmes Rolston, and other aforementioned environmental philosophers also examined the issues surrounding giving non-human interests standing in decisions about the environment and offer ways to bring environmental ethics into environmental problems.

Political ecology and climate change

Political ecology presents another alternative to conventional analyses of the FCCC, and while sharing many of the criticisms made under political economy, political ecology expresses a number of additional and unique insights. Two aspects of political ecology's inquiry are of particular interest: firstly, the implications of the FCCC process and outcomes for ecological justice, which extend greatly beyond the usual conceptions of justice (and democracy); and secondly, the applications of the 'commons' concept to the global atmosphere. Much of the political ecology approach is built around the concept of the global commons or more specifically, the atmospheric commons (see, e.g., Volger 1995).

Developing world representatives, notably Brazil's Miguez and Argentina's Estrada-Oyuela (see, e.g., Pinguelli-Rosa and Munasinghe 2002), and AOSIS members, have pressed the claims of disadvantaged nations in the FCCC using ethical arguments and grounded specific propositions on them.

After a slow start, there are now a welter of scholarly and analytical works dealing with the ethical issues, many coming after the basic features of the Kyoto Protocol were fixed. Agarwal and Narain (1991), Grubb (1995), Byrne (1997), Shue (1993, 1995, and 1999), and others have raise ethical concerns over the atmosphere's treatment and developing nations' fate under the FCCC. Several authors pick up these themes following the U.S. rejection of the Kyoto Protocol, notably Brown (2002), Speth (2004) and Singer. Singer (2004: 134–142), one of the few philosophers to venture forth, uses the Kyoto decision as one element in his 'ethical assessment' of the President; Singer finds the President's conduct and rationale, unethical.

Not that political ecology enjoys an exclusive claim to ethical argumentation; for several alternative conservative approaches to the FCCC policies employ arguments based on 'fairness,' such as from the Pew Center on Global Climate Change (e.g., Claussen and NcNeilly 1998) and the World Resources Institute (e.g., Baumert et al. 2002). Ethical issues also underlay the critiques of the ways in which the possible costs and benefits of climate change have been assessed, especially the applications of these reckonings as the basis for decisions for setting emission reduction totals. In several aspects of the climate change debate, ecological justice is contesting basic questions over climate change policy with expressions of economic rationality.

Economic rationality's central place in the climate change debate is consistent with the economic concerns of nation states, the interests of corporate entities, and the relationship between the two. Economic rationality has underpinned much FCCC reasoning, approaches, and decisions. Such is the dominance of economic rationality that much of it passes without notice; economism is the norm of FCCC activity within its liberal democratic frame. Political ecology's critique of economism has been directed at two of its major implications: firstly, the costs of potential climate change impacts are relatively low and those of moderate and greater greenhouse gas emissions reduction are high, on which rests the economic rationale of the necessity, scale, and timing of emissions abatement; secondly, the Kyoto mechanisms are efficient, effective, and efficacious. Informed by the values of ecological justice, political ecology examines economic rationality in terms of its social and environmental effects.

Some scholars reject the central place of these debates, arguing that this activity is distracting and counter-productive to ecological justice. Jamieson (1992), for example, writes of the limitations of seeing climate change as a science issue and using assessments based on economics, concluding that such managerial responses will ultimately fail. Economic efficiency is but one value, he claims, and economics but one means of representing human motivation, and is an inaccurate and incomplete one at that. Furthermore, economic studies cannot evaluate all possible impacts and courses of action; the breadth of these impacts across the globe will be enormous, involving non-monetarized societies and a poorly understood global economy; and the potential impacts are poorly understood. Tellingly, Jamieson presages his discussion of several ethical issues (1992: 146): "However, the most fundamental reason why management approaches are doomed to failure is that the questions they answer are not the ones that are the most important and profound." Political ecology has attempted to redress this failing.

Assessing the economic costs and benefits of climate change

Allowing that an expression of power in polical processes is to set the subjects and terms of debate and to control the arenas in which debate occurs, the developed nations that shaped the FCCC have drawn strongly on economic rationality in formulating their policy preferences. As we indicated above, the treatment of assessing the effects of climate change and particularly the costs of reducing greenhouse emissions has been at the center of debates since the outset of the institutional response. Within the developed world's liberal democracies, economic rationality has held that these costs were measurable and could guide policy decisions for emissions abatement. That key political actors believed that only modest emission reductions were economically rational was fundamental in determining the FCCC and Kyoto Protocol's targets and timetables for emissions reduction.

Nordhaus' economic studies (e.g., 1977, 1991a, 1991b, 1992, 1993, and 1994) have proved highly influential in the on-going debate (see, e.g., IPCC working group III reports), many of which featured a prescience on emerging policy questions combined with a steady orthodoxy in approach. Optimality in climate change assumes that form most familiar to conventional economics, for as Nordhaus (1991a: 149– 50) explains, the optimal degree of greenhouse gas reduction occurs where "the marginal costs of control are equal to the discounted marginal damages from climate change," so that level of emissions control depends on the costs of reductions, the "damage to human societies," and rate at which the future is discounted. On these assumptions a considerable edifice of economic research has been erected. An early and widely-cited estimate was that of Nordhaus (1991), who calculated that a 60 percent reduction in U.S. carbon emissions would cost the U.S. US$309 billion annually and yield a benefit of US$55 billion. Using the DICE model, Nordhaus (1993) later calculated the optimal emissions reduction effort, concluding that only modest decreases were justified.

No less an authority than the IPCC Working Group III (2001c, Chapter 8) gave the cost of carbon dioxide stabilization in the atmosphere at 450 ppm at US$2.5–18 trillion, at 550 ppm at US$1–8 trillion, and at 650 ppm at US$0.5–2 trillion (by way of scale, US$18 trillion approaches the size of the 1990 global economy). Given the magnitude of these sums, it is hardly unexpected that U.S. President G.W. Bush and the U.S. Congress members have repeatedly cited the high economic costs of Kyoto compliance as a primary rationale for U.S. withdrawal from the FCCC process. Clearly, companies and their agents in the fossil fuel and related industries have invested greatly in having appropriate research conducted and in publicizing research findings suggesting high economic costs arising from Kyoto Protocol compliance (and these economic studies have formed part of the outputs of the science skeptics). Although the IPCC is charged with resolving such matters of research, the findings in Working Groups II and III have usually held close to orthodox economics and have been criticized accordingly.

However, findings of prohibitive costs have often been disputed, both within the economics community and, of course, by environmental NGOs. Many economic studies have calculated the costs of reducing greenhouse gases as being so high as to be politically unacceptable to the world's richest nations. Repetto and Austin's (1997) literature review and analysis for the World Resources Institute of 162 outcomes from 16 different models gave a good indication of economic research up to that time. Most of the studies examined the effects of a carbon tax, or similar device, on the U.S. economy as GDP losses. Obviously a great number of assumptions are made about critical factors (such as the carbon dioxide target, the time taken to reach such targets, the use of tax revenues in the economy, and so on). In summarizing the results, Repetto and Austin (1997) state that the worst-case scenario for meeting a 30 percent reduction in carbon dioxide by 2020 would cost the U.S. economy 3.3 percent of GDP, and the best-case an improvement of 2.5 percent. Critical choices in modeling were identified to account for the spread in results, such as the choice between general equilibrium models and macroeconomic models, whether associated non-climate benefits were included, the place of emission trading, and whether costs of climate change impacts were included. Model outcomes, as expected, reflected critical assumptions.

A more recent study from a key government agency provides further results. In response to a request by the U.S. House's Committee on Science, the Energy Information Administration (EIA 1998) conducted a study into the costs of the U.S. meeting its Kyoto Protocol target by carbon dioxide emissions only and without participating in international emissions trading. EIA found that such an effort would reduce U.S. GDP by 4.2 percent, a result that was partially attributed to the high short-term adjustment costs. If such actions were taken over a timeframe extending to 2020, the overall costs fall to 0.8 percent of GDP, being virtually negligible at the end of the timeframe (EIA 1998). Barker and Ekins (2001) note that these latter assumptions are quite unrealistic; the Protocol refers to a suite of greenhouse gases and allows emissions trading.

Further emphasizing the way in which these economic models respond to differing inputs can be found in the 1999 special edition of *The Energy Journal*. Comparing the effects of carbon taxes required to lower greenhouse gas emissions in a range of studies reveals widely varying outcomes in tax rates and GDP costs. In reviewing these modeling efforts of the potential costs of the Kyoto Protocol, Barker and Ekins (2001) concluded that the studies giving high costs are either incorrect or reflect critical economic assumptions which include the costs of policy mistakes, such as hasty introductions, excluding the Kyoto mechanisms, and choosing worst-case assumptions and parameters. Hamilton (2001) is similarly critical of the unrealistic assumptions in the controversial economic model used by the Australian government that suggested high economic costs of a carbon tax in that country, which were instrumental in Australia's decision to join the U.S. in rejecting ratification of the Kyoto Protocol.

Not all economic studies indicate the high costs of emission abatement; of particular interest are those examining the potential benefits from specific technologies and practices. Studies of the economic savings of increased energy efficiency and energy conservation in the U.S. using existing techniques and technologies have demonstrated considerable economic savings (e.g., Bailie et al. 2003; DOE 1997; IWG 2001; WEA 2000). Primarily through efficiency improvements to the U.S. electricity system, for example, a 25 percent reduction over the business-as-usual scenario is possible by 2020 (Bailie et al. 2003). IPCC (1996c, 2001c) concluded from its reviews of the research that 10–30 percent energy efficiency gains over current levels were possible in many places without costs or with savings and that applications of the highest-efficiency energy systems could yield efficiency gains of 50–60 percent. Because many such applications have immediate or very short payback periods, investments in such energy savings nearly always produce reduced greenhouse gas emissions at low costs or profits, as confirmed by virtually all studies. Reductions of total energy consumption of these magnitudes apply to all consumptive scales (household, firm, community, region, state, and nation) and across the sectors of the economy. A large number of studies have demonstrated that the barriers to greater energy conservation and energy efficiency of such 'no regrets' measures are not primarily economic.

Despite these wide differences in estimates of reducing greenhouse gas emissions, usually dealing only with carbon dioxide, there are some common findings. Developed industrial economies' energy consumption per unit of economic activity tends to fall over time, so that although total consumption is likely to continue growing, energy 'intensity' decreases. As an economy increases its energy efficiency and its greenhouse gas emissions per unit of economic activity fall, the costs of further efficiency gains usually to increase. Savings in economies with relatively high energy-efficiency, such as Japan, are more expensive compared with the returns accruing from improvements in low energy efficiency economies, such as Australia, Canada, and the U.S. Further reductions in greenhouse gas emissions require more extensive conversion to lower emitting sources of energy or alternative ways to meet needed energy services. Renewable energy technologies present a more complex and particular problem, being highly dependent on local circumstances. Those least expensive local renewable energy sources are frequently economically competitive with local conventional fossil fuel sources. Several studies have suggested the technical feasibility of preventing a doubling of atmospheric greenhouse gas levels from the pre-industrial level (these are discussed in Chapter 5). Scenarios under these studies emphasize end-use energy efficiency, substituting gas for coal, and rapid uptake of renewable energy (see, e.g., Azar and Schneider 2002). Longer-term strategies involve the use of energy systems featuring 'carbon-free energy technologies.'

Economic evaluations considering low-cost national greenhouse gas reductions, inexpensive energy efficiency and energy conservation measures, and cheaper forms of renewable energy are seemingly overwhelmed by the costs of economic transformation. Several factors are involved. Azar and Schneider (2002) point to differences between the 'bottom-up' models of engineers and physicists focusing on energy use and efficiency, and the 'top-down' models favored by economists who identify the repair of energy inefficiencies as larger than the costs of those inefficiencies. Studies of national economics deploy models of the whole economy, making the treatment of specific aspects of induced changes highly influential across the economy. Often the models simulate a carbon tax as the policy tool to reduce greenhouse gas emissions, which depresses overall economic activity and the extent of this loss of GDP depends greatly on how the model treats the resultant tax revenues. Time also becomes critical in determining the degree of the 'shock' to the economy of new taxes, the impacts of which diminish proportionally. Treatment of future technological change prompted by policy changes is frequently neglected. Another of the 'boundary' problems concerns decisions of whether the energy sector would bear the entire burden of emissions reduction and the point to which non-energy sources of emissions would be abated, and the measures thereby employed. Although conventional economic models purport to assess national economies, typically any environment benefits arising from particular actions are ignored. Ancillary environmental gains from such actions, such as improved human health arising from reduced air pollution, are beyond the bounds of the analyses. Theoretically, there are no barriers to the including in economic models any measurable variables with economic value. In practice, however, economic modeling usually draws its boundaries around those services, commodities, and relationships that exist in readily identifiable markets.

Grubb (1990) points out that climate change is not a threshold issue or discrete problem, so with rapid global warming now inevitable, climate change impacts may be non-linear in relation to emissions. Therefore, he concludes (1990: 88): "Any contribution to reducing emissions is therefore valuable, and the earlier it is taken the more valuable it will be." Azar and Sterner (1996) examine the effect of the treatment of time in greenhouse studies that advocate minimal emissions abatement, such as those of Nordhaus. They identify four problematic aspects of Nordhaus' work: 1) a time preference that heavily discounts future costs; 2) omission of any reckoning of possible severe risk to millions of people in the future; 3) pessimism over the effectiveness and adoption of cost-effective energy efficiency and renewable energy technologies; and 4) assumptions that climate change will be gradual and without catastrophic risk. Further, the authors highlight an ethical implication in Nordhaus' assumptions, namely that his cost–benefit approach assumes that benefits will be re-distributed to those who bear the costs, an unlikely outcome in the real world. In other words, although continued high emissions are justified as being economically optimal, the method is blind to the differential allocations of costs and benefits between communities. Further, because climate change impacts stretch so far into the future, models that ignore future costs place the burdens the current generation's decisions onto future generations. If a discount rate for estimating future costs reflects future impacts, then as Azar and Sterner (1996) calculate, making severe emissions cuts in the short term becomes economically optimal.

Chapman and Khanna (2000) identify another worrying aspect of several 'pessimist' studies, echoing an earlier controversy suffered by the IPCC. Many studies presume very low or negative costs of abatement in developing countries and high costs in developed countries (e.g., Harmaide and Boland 2000; McKibben et al. 1999), so that the goal of economic efficiency is best served by concentrating abatement in developing countries, leaving the richest nations and those having produced the bulk of historical emissions with a lesser abatement burden. As Chapman and Khanna (2000) argue, even where research has identified nations where immediate technological switches are economically attractive, such changes have not taken place, indicating that 'other cost' factors are operating. Closer examination at the case study level indicates the assumptions that developing country costs are close to zero to be false, so that focussing on such nations as part of a global strategy to reduce emissions would be mistaken.

It may be, however, that even the least optimistic economic models offer encouragement for emissions abatement, depending on how the results are understood. Azar and Schneider (2002) demonstrate that even high levels of costs for emission abatement (five percent annual global income) become tiny against the expected growth in the global economy over the next century using the assumptions of the 'pessimistic' economic models. On this basis they argue that low stabilization targets can be met within a rapidly growing economy and that average growth rates of the global economy over the next century would ensure that strict emissions reduction measures would average out to less than one-tenth of a percent annually.

Prominent in the Australian and U.S. national leader's rationales for rejecting Kyoto, voiced for domestic audiences, was the threat of employment losses resulting from joining the agreement. Within the domestic popular media such claims received little scrutiny and appeared to have found tacit support from business and labor leaders. That environmental protection axiomatically produces negative economic effects is a commonly held view, despite evidence cases where tighter environmental regulations increase employment (e.g., OECD 1997). Addressing the climate change policy and employment linkage, McEvoy et al. (2000) hold that initatives in improving energy efficiency and increased renewable energy use will create jobs.

Political ecology addresses the values embedded in economic rationality and the presumptions that such rationality should form the dominant advice heeded by policy-makers. Although NGOs and other critics of the economic models suggesting that climate change is insufficiently dangerous to warrant any significant social response point to the low values given to developing nations and the environment, such criticism risks validates the logic of economic models by implying that the social and ecological losses can be economically evaluated. Azar editorialized (2000: 233): "In the case of climate change, we have by now become used to economists claiming to have found the optimal level of CO_2 emissions." Value-laden assumptions, such as the value of life in rich and poor countries, of nature, of future values, and of "low probability high impact events," states Azar (2000), are often "concealed in a seemingly value neutral language." Reducing all values to economic currency is, of course, economism, a confining rationality and one favored by vested interests in social and economic hierarchies.

Yet, the FCCC does not itself always subscribe to the economic orthodoxies it champions. One of the justifications for using price instruments in preference to setting a fixed quantity on global emissions, according to environmental economics, is the assumption of low damage costs. If this assumption is proven false, and there are strong reasons for regarding it skeptically, then sensitivity analysis can be employed to determine at what emissions reduction level price instruments should be abandoned and quantity restrictions taken up. IEA (2002: 36–37) suggests that if emission cuts of greater than 40 percent were required, then quantity restrictions should be imposed. According to these environmental economics, the market-based measures within the policy architecture should be removed, as the level of emissions reduction required for stabilization exceeds 40 percent. To date, little attention has been directed at this point: orthodox economic thought supports quantity limits on emissions in order to avoid dramatic future climate changes.

Political ecology, the Kyoto mechanisms, and carbon sinks

Disagreements over economic issues have driven much of the national political dynamics of the responses to the international climate change agreements and those at the international scale over the market-based policies of the Kyoto mechanisms and the carbon sinks issues. These arguments have ranged across several planes, from the practical to the ethical, and from the symbolic and strategic. Objections to emissions trading by political ecologists are obvious; through their acquisition of greenhouse gas emission credits, developed nations are obviated of the need for that amount of domestic abatement. Richer nations are afforded an advantage by virtue of being able to purchase the emissions made elsewhere. Furthermore, as a result of the difference between the Protocol's emission assignments and actual emissions, unrestricted emission trading is likely to allow total emissions to rise. Purchase of emissions credits not achieved through domestic action is known in climate change jargon as 'hot air' trading. This seemingly violates the Kyoto Protocol's requirement that such purchases must be 'supplementary' to domestic action. Rather than being a means to reduce emissions cheaply, emissions trading offers to become a policy device to meet the Protocol targets cheaply and possibly fostering increased actual emissions while purporting to do the iopposite (Byrne and Glover (2000) term these "virtual reductions").

Through the COP process, the argument over emissions trading centered on whether trading should be restricted in some way so as to prevent nations taking advantage of the available credits and avoiding real emissions reduction through domestic action. Central to the COP-6 negotiations was the clause in the Kyoto Protocol requiring the Kyoto mechanisms to be supplemental to domestic efforts by Annex B nation's domestic greenhouse gas abatement programs. In effect, the ensuing debate concerned setting limits on the extent to which the Kyoto mechanisms could be used as credit; the E.U. and developing nations sought a 50 percent limit on national reductions comprising savings under the Kyoto mechanisms, while the U.S. and the 'umbrella' group sought unrestricted credit. Given the quantity of emission credits likely to become available, and their potential economic value, there was a great deal at stake.

Arguments by Metz et al. (2001) in favor of trading (or rather, for not linking trading to supplementarity) include: 1) 'hot air' has in effect been 'purchased' at the cost of those collapsed economies; 2) 'hot air' trading would attract a normal price, subject to supply and demand; 3) both the U.K. and Germany have benefitted from non-climate-related policies that lowered emissions since 1990, thus benefitting from their own version of 'hot air;' 4) 'hot air' represents a unique condition unlikely to be replicated in future budget periods; 5) caps on 'hot air' will not alter nations' 'banking' of emissions, as allowed under the Protocol; 6) trading lays the foundation for a future scheme in which developing nations could fully participate; and 7) 'hot air' sales will finance Russian and Ukrainian modernization. Valid as many of Metz's points are, they seemingly concede the basic concern of the environmentalists that emissions trading will increase the gross output of Annex B emissions by that amount of purchased 'hot air.' Illustrative of the difficulties of creating a emissions market among nations is how the original objective of lowering emissions becomes tangled with other interests, such as allowing nations to profit from emission credit sales, the acceptance of short-term failure as the basis for success in the longer term, and allowing incidental emission reductions to have equivalent values to those resulting from investment.

In many respects, the CDM is the thorniest of the three Kyoto mechanisms. Contrasted with emissions trading, where the controversy surrounds the implications of a single set of transactions, CDM is contentious at the fine scale. Several aspects of the mechanism have been contentious, none more so than determining the eligibility of potential projects that ensures that they contribute to sustainable development and are supplemental to Annex B domestic emissions abatement, so as to comply with the Protocol.

COP negotiations reflect, at least partially, how national circumstances can determine the response to the CDM to a greater extent than the emissions trading issue, with developing nation blocks breaking rank over proposals concerning the former. National negotiating views range broadly; some developing nations have sought projects that promote 'de-carbonisation;' the E.U. seeks a relatively 'narrow' definition of acceptable projects centered on the theme of energy and emissions; the U.S. and other developed nations favor a less restrictive regime. Prospects for 'leakage' appear high in the case of CDM projects, and higher than for emissions trading (Bollen 1998 in Yamin 2001), as both host and financier nation have a vested interest in exaggerating the project's emission saving. And because the site of 'leakage' is in a non-Annex B nation, it would go unreported in Annex B greenhouse gas inventories.

Projects under the CDM are a form of development aid and hence engage several aspects of this discourse, a factor that further complicates both practical and symbolic significance of competing proposals. Metz et al. (2001) and others identify the role of the CDM in facilitating, via exogenous technological inputs, developing nations along a path of ecologically sustainable development. Yamin et al. (2001) consider that the CDM could offset adverse economic impacts on developing nations resulting from Annex 1 nations responses to meet the Protocol.

Carbon sinks were one of the major issues that finally brought COP-6's first meeting undone. Objections to the use of carbon sinks by environmentalists are their substitution for emissions reduction (see, e.g., Fern 2000; WWF 2000). There are several aspects to this complaint, whereas much of the recent COP negotiations have focussed merely on the allowable quantities of carbon sinks, not their validity as a policy measure. Some environmentalists favored carbon sinks as a means to bolster other conservation objectives, particularly forest protection and biodiversity, in the early days of the negotiations. However, some environmentalists are skeptical of the effects of carbon sinks. Allowances for forest sinks (Annex Z) reflect negotiating outcomes, not environmental values. Measurement of carbon sinks (and associated carbon fluxes) has proved difficult, making the assessment and compliance aspects of national performance problematic. Encouraging enhanced carbon sinks could generate ecological damage, such as the effects of inappropriate afforestation. Carbon sinks are a temporary measure, as terrestrial storage can be transformed through vegetation changes, fire, climate change, and other factors that release carbon to the atmosphere. Political ecologists have pointed out that counting sinks amounts to deferring emissions, shifting the task of reduction into the future to be borne by others.

Political ecology's critique of economic commons approaches

One critical way of considering the atmosphere is as constituting a 'commons,' comprising a public resources and source of resource services accessible to the community (including the 'global community') on a shared basis. Such resources are usually considered to be finite, but possibly renewable, so that consumption by one member of community necessarily reduces the remaining stock at that time or permanently. Commons resources can assume many different forms, from the obvious natural resources of land, minerals and fuels, fresh and marine waters, to the less obvious ecosystem services, and resources such as genetic information and cultural knowledge. Many commons values can be derived from a single resource, such as the atmosphere that provides essential gases for much of life, climate services, waste reception, and for aesthetic and spiritual uses.

Different disciplines approach commons from different perspectives. Economics has long been concerned with commons resources, although usually deploying different terminology. In depicting the atmosphere as a global commons, for conventional economic thinkers, its most obvious feature is its 'open access' character, wherein the resource itself is amenable to unlimited use. Certain attributes of the atmosphere, as the climate change issue demonstrates all too clearly, are quite limited in the level of use they can sustain; 'open access' implies not an unlimited resource, but merely one whose access is requires collective action to control. Furthermore, the value of atmospheric commons is diminished by additional exploitation.

Regime theorist Young (1997) observes of problems of international environmental commons, such as the climate system, that there are three basic approaches for governance: 1) enclosure by extending national property rights; 2) supranational or world government; and 3) codes of conduct analogous to commons management in small-scale societies. Under the liberal democracy of the FCCC, global emissions are being controlled through a system of emission allowances and national targets, easily falling into the category of a property rights system. And it is precisely this approach that advocates of political ecology reject; further, many proposals of this group resemble commons management along communal lines.

Liberal democratic and ecological modernization advocates regard the atmospheric commons in economic and governance terms and rationales. Regarding the theme of equity, Soroos justifies its place in climate change negotiations thus (1997: 232): "Equity is an especially important consideration issue in the negotiation of international agreements because states that are not satisfied with the fairness of a proposed treaty will be reluctant to become signatories and ratifiers and be bound to its provisions." Liberal democracy requires that nations, acting in mutually agreed ways, allow the allocation of the use of the atmosphere in ways that satisfy international agreement. Through the global market established under the policy architecture of the Kyoyo Protocol, this allocation converts the atmosphere's use into commodity form (through emission permits), and utilizes market activity to ensure the most economically efficient distribution.

Soroos (1997), for example, argues for the atmosphere to be treated as a global commons and considers key issues being how to allow the greatest possible use of the resource, making the management scheme economically efficient, and whether the approach meets a test of equity between users, including future potential users. To date, the FCCC has worked steadily towards the commodification of the atmosphere by firstly establishing a series of policy instruments by which greenhouse gases and sequestered carbon in managed ecosystems are made into commodities and traded through the various Kyoto mechanisms. In this sense, the FCCC facilitates trading atmospheric pollution allowances as part of a scheme of national greenhouse gas accounting, by which access to pollute the atmospheric commons is regulated. Market advocates can envisage a clear destination from this path; Barnes (2001) argues in *Who Owns the Sky?* that atmospheric protection will be best served by an allocation of personal entitlements, a global trading system, and a global trust, and a distribution of income from the sale of permits to polluters. More orthodox economic approaches endorsing market theory haven't extended consumer sovereignty to the extent of Barnes, but rather consider that a 'post-Kyoto' agreement could governments and corporations with a fairly free rein in a global market of greenhouse gas commodities (e.g., Victor 2001).

Alternative understanding of commons emphasize their social dimensions, so whereas conventional economics discerns pollution as the unavoidable consequence of an absent or insufficient market system with property rights, those concerned with social values tend to examine the pollution as a systemic social failure with widely varying explanations. Further, this notion of a commons lends itself to consider environmental phenomena as being embedded in social and natural systems in complex and integrated ways, as opposed to the unitary valuation provided by economic perspectives. From political ecology and the values of ecological justice a very specific and important aspect of the climate change debate has emerged, namely the issue of per capita emission allocations in the context of establishing a global atmospheric commons.

Few others have gone to the extreme of Barnes, but there has been great attention given to economic refinements of the existing system. Less imaginatively and subject to greater research attention are economists' concerns over the arbitrary character of the existing national emission targets and proposals for an international per-GDP allocation approach. These economically rational approaches align the quantitative burden of emissions reduction with national wealth. For example, the Pew Center proposed an allocation system that used national GDP, along with two other criteria.

Nation states have assumed the atmosphere to be an internationally shared property subject to cooperative management agreements. To the title of *Who Owns the Sky?* the answer is: a coalition of nation states. Whatever sort of commons the atmosphere might have been prior to the FCCC, it has been drawn into the embrace of governance via the agency of the UN's articles of collective ownership. Such is the legitimacy of nations that such a transformation sat comfortably with the role of the nation state and international community of nations; in a world of legal arrangements, property law precedes property ownership, and here the UN wrote the law.

Advocates of ecological justice find the assumptive legitimacy of nations in appropriating the atmosphere offensive. As a commons, the atmosphere is theoretically available to all peoples in perpetuity, and by extension under ecological justice, it's a resource to be shared with ecology. As national property, access and use of the commons is determined by nations, which triggers an array of questions over justice.

Political ecology and the atmospheric commons

Three broad issues characterize debates over commons resources: firstly, dividing the spoils; secondly, allocating responsibility for the commons' care; and thirdly, the functing of the social institution that allocates the rewards and protects the resource. Approaches to international commons resources are often confined to issues of allocation and this will be subject to greatest disputation, but the other two issues invariably emerge. Considering the atmosphere as a commons is particularly complicated. Shue (1993) identifies several key equity issues: distributing the global warming prevention costs; distributing the climate change impacts costs; and allocating rights to emit greenhouse gas emissions, to which he adds the 'procedural' issue of how much national economic status should be a factored into decisions. Of these issues, debate has been concentrated on a single, albeit broad, question about the allocation of the rights to pollute. Other issues of protecting the global atmospheric commons, such as setting long-term targets for emissions abatement, and over the legitimacy of the global liberal-democratic system of state governance under the FCCC, are gaining greater attention, largely driven by the discourse of political ecology. And, as discussed elsewhere, questions of the construction of knowledge are essential for such issues as determining how to manage a particular commons resource sustainably, which for global climate change involves scientific knowledge and the role of epistemic communities.

Ethical concerns underly much of political ecology's approach to climate change politics and assume a more prominent role in shaping views about policies than the official FCCC processes. Treating the mitigation task as that of managing a global atmospheric commons, political ecology frames policy approaches of the Kyoto mechanisms not in economic terms of efficacy and efficiency, but as equity concerns. As Metz (2000), Shue (1993), and others describe, climate change evokes international, national (i.e., social), and intergenerational equity, to which Byrne and Glover (2000) and other followers of ecological justice add an ethical responsibility for nature. Already there have been a number of studies into equity and climate change, exploring a range of principles and approaches to equity: convergence of emissions, environmental protection, market allocations, property rights, polluter-pays, utilitarian, egalitarian, ability to pay, 'Rawlsian justice,' and others (IPCC 2001c).

Within the FCCC, specific articles incorporate equity issues, notably the recognition of equity as a basis for the protecting the climate system for present and future generations (in Article 3.1), the differentiated emission abatement commitments between developed and developing countries (in Articles 4.1–4.5), the flexibility offered to the economies in transition (in Article 4.6), taking developing countries into account when implementing policies, including those dependent on fossil-fuel exports (in Articles 4.8–4.10). Yet this basis in equity leaves much open to interpretation, as the variety of equity principles suggest and the subsequent development of the Kyoto Protocol demonstrate. There is also the difference between principles and practices: environmental NGOs have found that some distance opened up between the FCCC intentions and the actual Kyoto Protocol policies.

Economic approaches to equity in climate change policies have emphasized 'burden sharing' between developed nations considering egalitarian, 'ability to pay,' sovereignty, and economic circumstances when setting emissions reductions targets under the Kyoto Protocol. Political ecology approaches have stressed two aspects to equity: firstly, setting overall emission reduction targets that aim for greater protection of future generations and ecological values; and secondly, equity between nations. Broadly, political ecology inspires emissions targets that aim for stabilization of atmospheric greenhouse gases at lower levels than are likely under the current regime and for allocations of greenhouse gas emission rights that culminate in an equal share for all persons. Developing nations put forward approaches for per capita national emission calculations in early negotiation sessions under the FCCC (notably by Brazil), but these proposals were not accepted (see, e.g., the explanations offered by Agarwal et al. 1999 and La Rovere 2002). Political ecologists have continued to pursue these approaches however, producing now both official recognition of the goal within the FCCC, a number of concrete proposals, and interest in the research community.

Many environmentalists have advanced environmental justice arguments in proposing equity-based approaches to the atmospheric commons (e.g.,

Agarwal and Narain 1991, 1999; Byrne et al. 1998; and Meyer 2000). Rejecting the approach of the FCCC and Kyoto Protocol, these authors suggest that the atmosphere has been a degraded open-access resource to which property rights are now being assigned by the regime. Their concerns express two themes: firstly, that the dominance of developed nations in the FCCC is determining the rules of access to the atmosphere in a manner prejudicial to their own interests; secondly, this course places the entire project of global greenhouse gas abatement in jeopardy. Bound into this linkage is the challenge that the FCCC must somehow overcome both an ideological impediment in the form of its own idealized goals of democratic participation and that of building a regime that satisfies its own stated objectives (i.e., those of the FCCC).

Indian NGO the Centre for Science and Environment and the London-based Global Commons Institute have proposed per capita allocation systems based on what the Institute co-founder Meyer calls 'contraction and convergence.' Meyer (2000) proposes that all nations should converge on a uniform per capita carbon dioxide emission rate at which atmospheric greenhouse gas concentrations are stabilized, which entails great reductions by citizens of high-emission nations and slight increases by those inhabiting the lowest emission nations. Per capita levels are pegged at the population levels of the base year, neutralizing any allocations benefits gained by allowing population to rapidly increase. Several studies have proposed systems for calculating equitsable emission allocations. For example, Byrne et al. (1998) applied the per capita concept to a reckoning of each nation's emissions for the six Kyoto Protocol gases and a stabilization target of returning to present emissions by 2050, and determined a global per capita average (fixing national populations at their 1990 levels). From this mean value, a system of 'debtor and creditor' nations was established according to whether nations fell above or below the per capita 3.3 tons of carbon dioxide equivalent per annum allocation. As described above, this entails significant reductions for developed nations and modest increases for most developing nations.

Certainly, the per capita approach has gathered some momentum, with eminent climate scientist Bolin (Bolin and Kheshgi 2001) making the objective the centerpiece of greenhouse gas reduction strategies for the U.S. *Proceedings of the National Academy of Science.* Equity has been an issue within the FCCC negotiations and is part of the FCCC in several places, and calls for its adoption by the FCCC process are increasingly prominent. That developed nations are responsible for the bulk of greenhouse gas emissions is acknowledged in the FCCC Preamble, which states that "per capita emissions in developing countries are relatively low and that a share of global emissions originating in developing countries will grow to meet their social and development needs." Article 3.1 of the FCCC states: "The parties should protect the climate system for the benefit of present and future generations of humankind, on the basis of equity and in accordance with their common but differentiated responsibilities and respective capabilities."

What does equity imply in the consideration of the atmosphere as a global commons? Soroos (1997) identifies four possible strategies for managing commons: 1) voluntary restraint; 2) regulation; 3) partition (equivalent to privatization); and 4) creation of a single public enterprise (equivalent to socialization) – the latter two of which he deems inappropriate. However, the system that has emerged contains features of both regulation (as emission reduction targets and timetables under the Kyoto Protocol) and as privatization (through the Kyoto mechanisms). Further, none of these options necessarily feature equity.

One critical issue for equity is that raised by the FCCC preamble, namely that the developed nations bear the responsibility for the bulk of the anthropocentric greenhouse gas emissions to date and will take the lead in reducing emissions. Some commentators described this as an expression of the 'polluter pays' principle, wherein equity implies that developed nations will lower their emissions and developing nations will increase theirs. Yet, as our preceding account describes, the FCCC departed from this principle somewhat by loosening the notion that the greatest polluters would make the greatest sacrifices and by falling short of the commitment to offer greatest support to those nations most vulnerable to the impacts of climate change.

Questioning sovereignty

Environmentalists generally oppose globalization for its facility to accelerate global resource harvesting, environmental damage, and erosion of indigenous cultures and rights (see, e.g., Mander and Goldsmith 1996; Sachs 2000) and political ecology attempts to orient the FCCC process towards ecological justice and to counter the FCCC's integration into the global economy. This process of globalization has implications for the nation-state system, although commentators' interpretations differ greatly. Political ecology's critique of the FCCC process and outcomes is directed at its failings in democracy, fairness, and environmental protection; however, the critique hasn't often questioned the nation states' primary role in the FCCC. Notably, one of political ecology's primary contributions to the debate – the per capita emission allocations concept – is based on the global system of nation states. As discussed in Chapter 5, some environmentalists are skeptical about the construction of the 'global' in climate change politics, but this only partly impinged on the explicit role of nation states.

International relations theory highlights the contribution of non-state parties in the formation of international environmental agreements, especially the role of science and its institutions (Haas 1990a, 1990b, 1992; Litfin 1994). Contributions from these 'epistemic communities' supplement the states' activities in essential ways, but bolstering the rational-technocratic approach typical of these agreements has not resulted in a discourse that includes the multiplicity of actors and interests implicated in global environmental change. As Lipschutz and Conca argue (1993: 328), " … the dominant discourse overlooked some emerging patterns of social interaction that may contain hopeful alternatives for 'managing' our environmental futures, albeit in forms very different from those the dominant discourse offers." Given orthodox international relations' fixation with nation states, it's to be expected that much recent scholarship considers whether the rise of 'global governance' adds to, or detracts from, state sovereignty as states are subject to new external constraints but simultaneously exert new authority over previously ungoverned realms of the natural world and global activities. As a political and legal article of the nation state, sovereignty is coming to have both a domestic and international expression under international environmental agreements that both extends 'outward' to the global and reaches 'downward' to connect local circumstances to global issues. State authority is therefore being shifted away from the nation state to both global and local spheres (see Litfin 1993).

An alternative view to the state and the state system as enablers and facilitators of global environmental agreements holds that the states drive environmental destruction, especially the competition between states in economic and military aspirations. If the states don't directly foster environmental damage then, some scholars argue, they still cause harm by preventing effective action when environmental issues don't match the scale of states (being beyond states or of local scale) (e.g., Hempel 1996). Another line of reasoning popular in environmental politics holds that state authority has dis-empowered local communities in responding to environmental action (e.g., Dryzek 1987). Many alternatives have been considered in this light, but prompted by concerns that local communities may not consider the global implications of their actions, some scholars have argued for versions of world federalism in which authority is divided between several levels, from the global to the local (Eckersley 1992; Gare 1995). This debate questions the extent to which the modern states' environmental failures can be ameliorated by international institutions, and how the interests of civil society and ecological justice can find expression in global environmental institutions (Christoff 1996).

Kuehl's (1996) work is instructive on this question of how ecopolitics defies the assumptions over state definitions of territoriality, on which conventional international relations are built. Insisting on notions of governmentality and sovereignty in a world where national boundaries are frequently rendered obsolete by global environmental problems and where the major actors, such as NGOs and global agents of capital, operate without nation-state restraints cannot provide insights into these issues. Particularly useful in Kuehl's analysis is its recognition that environmental problems confound governance powers of states within nation borders as well as the efforts to express sovereignty over extra-territorial issues.

Several implications for the role of the nation state in climate change politics emerge from these inquiries. Firstly, nation states cannot and have not represented all interests in climate change politics, especially those advocating ecological justice. It may be that states consistently strive for such representation as an ideal, but political practice shows nations bringing only a narrow set of interests to the international negotiating tables. Secondly, nation states have exercised their political powers within the FCCC to secure their interests to the detriment of competing states and non-state interests and, arguably, to the FCCC as a whole (such as through the 'lowest common denominator' effect). Thirdly, nation states' and national economies' interests are tied and states accord economic performance a very high priority. Environmental advocates are required, therefore, to contest the global economy and individual states' economic motivations. Accordingly, it remains difficult for any global climate agreement to be free of the global economic system, thus ensuring a constant tension between environmental protection and economic gain within its policy architecture. Fourthly, nation states control the access to the FCCC processes and restrict the decision-making authority on key issues to themselves. International relations studies of climate change consistently reflect this condition in which the state is an object subject to outside interactions with other states and internal interests from domestic politics.

Environmentalists haven't canvassed, in any substantial manner, systematic alternatives to the nation-state-based climate change regime. In practice, a great array of climate change activity in reducing emissions by cities, regions, provinces, corporations and institutions, and other entities is under way. While much of this activity is supported by national governments, a portion occurs without this encouragement. Efforts under political ecology at reform are apparently bifurcated between political campaigns to influence nations and those pursuing greenhouse gas mitigation and other responses outside the national sphere, largely based on promulgating existing policies and practices. Strategically, the reformer's agenda either works with nation states or works around nation states. Revolutionary approaches reject the status quo of the climate change regime and consider options such as global emissions reductions plans that don't use nation states, campaigns based on that relatively small number of corporations responsible for the bulk of the world's emissions, carbon labeling schemes for internationally traded goods, and per capita emissions reductions according to income rather than nationality.

That nation states work in collusion to protect the interests of the nation-state system requires little explanation, however, but this need not obviate asking whether the recognition of a global problem mechanically denotes a resolution based in international cooperation between nation states. Ultimately, the claims of ecological justice are such that environmentalists must come to question the presumptive authority of the nation state in addressing climate change. Such skepticism will directly confront traditional and regime-based concepts based on the claimed necessity for collective national action to ensure individual national compliance. It may be that environmentalists become broadly persuaded that the existing FCCC approach is sufficiently capable of reform so as to eventually satisfy the demands of ecological justice, but to date the debate remains marked by an on-going division between reformers and revolutionaries.

5 Global environmental management of climate

As a crisis created by human activity, the problem of climate change has been formulated as another natural phenomenon subject to the aspirations of human management. Driven by the twin incentives of protecting future human welfare and limiting future environmental losses, the cause of environmental management is necessarily responding to a global environmental system facing imminent damage from human activity. Modernity could have no purer expression than the aspiration to manage the global climate system. In a world of burgeoning international environmental agreements, the decision to adopt a global perspective was routine, logical, and depicted as act of environmental responsibility. Yet little scholarly attention has been directed towards the question of the international climate change response as an effort of global environmental management.

International responses to address the causes of global warming face a disjuncture between international institutions required for international cooperation and the national and local scales where most action to reduce greenhouse emissions is required. Concern over global warming is generally expressed over specific impacts at the regional, national, and local scales and far few voices have been raised in defense of the global climate system. Collective interests and actions are assembled through international cooperation and international climate change institution of the FCCC. This 'global interest' is assembled from collective nation states' determination of what constitutes a global interest to them. Accordingly, the identity of that global interest can be interpreted far more widely than the oft-cited 'global problem requiring a global response' cliché suggests.

A more contentious problem concerns the rationality of attempting global climate management. Under the existing international approach, this issue is a technical or scientific challenge, the desirability and the feasibility of which is viewed skeptically by political ecology. Given that environmental management is essential to industrial society, economic growth, and other aspects of modernity, the question of the capacities and potential of modernity is bound into the issue of global climate management. Human inability to achieve such management brings forth therefore, not only the undesirable effects of global warming, but also expresses the failure of the modern project's defining attributes. This issue has two dimensions; firstly, that social management will accomplish global climate management, namely the re-orientation of industrial society to operate effectively without using energy derived (predominantly) from fossil fuels. Secondly, this goal will be realized through national entities acting cooperatively. Scientific knowledge and liberal democratic governance are essential for these tasks and they too are being tested by this trial.

Suggesting that the FCCC's goal is global climate management could elicit complaints that this exaggerates the FCCC's role and purpose, as the institution doesn't explicitly pursue manipulation of any component of the climate, but is essentially directed against an atmospheric pollutant. However, the FCCC's purpose is to manipulate atmospheric chemistry so as to attempt to control the risks of certain future climatic outcomes. That the function of the agreement is to slow and then stabilize the production of a pollutant that is currently being released with few restraints does not lessen its intention to impose a deliberate condition on the atmosphere by transforming the world's economies by regulating a global pollutant.

A longer-term program of global carbon management is also being considered in the scientific realm, indicating something of the scale and scope of future policy questions. Long-term sequestration of carbon on land (such as in deep wells) and in the deep oceans has been considered as an additional strategy for addressing climate change. For a period in the early 1990s there was considerable interest in the possibility of fertilizing the open oceans with iron with the intention of boosting its biological capacity to take up and sequester carbon (phytoplankton growth can be stimulated by increasing the iron content of ocean waters). Resolving the problem of atmospheric pollution by greenhouse gases by polluting the oceans eventually foundered both on practical grounds, ecological concerns, and persistent scientific uncertainties, although IPCC (2001b) reports that experimentation continues. More recently, UNESCO's International Oceanic Commission established an advisory panel on carbon dioxide to address the issue of oceanic carbon sequestration; at this time the concept remains controversial. Nuclear power displacing fossil fuel electricity generation remains a perennial favorite in some quarters, with much state support, while its implausibility in any strategy to lower overall energy use is generally overlooked (e.g., Pacala and Socolow 2004). Although perhaps the most audacious of the 'geo-engineering' proposals is that of increasing the earth's albedo through such means as increasing aerosols, reflective balloons, and mirrors in space; IPCC (2001b) concluded that the issues of risk, politics, and ethics would need to be resolved, as if that were possible.

Growing threats and expanding goals

Negotiations over the 'targets and timetables' in the FCCC and Kyoto Protocol have taken up much time and energy in the efforts to develop the

FCCC as a system for global climate management. However, the predominant governance issue has been establishing the policy architecture and only a minor aspect of which concerns determining the FCCC's long-term goal that remains un-quantified and qualitatively, only slightly more defined. Debates over national emission targets and commitment periods have focused almost entirely on the short term.

Global climate management through emissions targets

Today's international policy response to climate change is but the most recent manifestation of the interest in controlling, or at least influencing, the weather and climate. Aspirations to control weather and climate have long been part of human experience and pursued through various strategies and technologies and, in the modern era, subject to scientific investigation. Although we now consider intentional climate modification as largely fanciful, it was the subject of serious scientific research and experimentation for much of the twentieth century, including proposals to create continental inland seas and to remove Arctic ice (Lamb 1977). Further, there is a long history of research into the relationship between human activities at the local or broader scales can influence weather, especially concerning land cover changes.

Environmental management of the climate, for climate research purposes, has centered on the notion that improved climate prediction will enable societies to respond optimally to future weather and climate and to avoid its worst effects. With the advent of climate change and the international response, opportunities for grandeur are again presented. What distinguishes the FCCC from previous efforts more than anything else is scale; until now, global environmental management was not previously attempted for climate or any other natural phenomena. In an irony that has hardly gone unnoticed, while the goal of climate management was largely diminishing in credibility in scientific circles, human activity had been altering the climate as a consequence (albeit unintended) of its energy and other industrial production systems. Within the international response to climate change, as the reaction to the crisis of climate change, is a nascent atmospheric and global climate management system: the controlling agent is the atmospheric concentration of global greenhouse gas emissions, the objective is to prevent dangerous interference with the climate system, and the instrument of control is the FCCC. One obvious limit of such management regime's scope is the extent to which human activities can be controlled and organized, but within this necessary perimeter is the option for environmental management of the climate and the composition of the atmosphere. A vital codicil to this aim is the assumption that the rate and general 'trend' of a warming atmosphere will, in fact, respond to the deliberate changes to atmospheric greenhouse gas levels in predictable ways. In other words, we assume the atmosphere and global climate are manageable.

Individual scientists, environmentalists, and environmental groups began calling for action on climate change in the early to mid-1970s, as described above. Fossil fuel combustion was clearly the culprit in global warming, but the scientific discourse had offered little prescriptive advice on short or long-term emissions reductions. A critical asymmetry was emerging in the science and policy realms; science could define the general dangers of global warming occurring and of its potential broad-scale impacts but could not advise on what level of emissions would keep climate 'safe,' and the policy makers in nations promoting emissions reduction were only considering short-term goals. It follows that the first calls for addressing the risks of global warming from the scientific community did not produce anything in the way of quantitative goals for emissions reduction, the times by when these goals should be achieved, or specific suggestions for the distribution of this burden.

International response

Once the climate change issue registered in international awareness in the late 1980s, an array of international meetings took up the cause of calling for national and UN action. In 1987, the Villach/Bellagio Conferences called for an international treaty for reducing greenhouse gas production and in 1988 the UN General Assembly adopted Resolution 45/53, *Protection of the Atmosphere for Present and Future Generations of Mankind*, marking the UN's first statement on the need for a multilateral agreement on atmospheric protection (Molitor 1999). During the period when the UN passed Resolutions 43/53, 44/207, and 45/212 between 1988 and 1990 to protect the global climate and initiate the FCCC, there were dozens of meetings of the UN, UNEP, European Community, national governments, and non-governmental organizations addressing climate change. This phase of multifaceted international lobbying greatly diminished when the FCCC process began, although now in the wake of the Kyoto Protocol's ratification, European and other regional activity has increased.

Despite the number of meetings, the range of issues canvassed, and the variety of viewpoints, there was relatively little produced to guide long-term emissions reduction in this phase prior to the FCCC. Many governmental and non-governmental meetings alike avoided any statements on this subject, including the 1989 Langkawi Declaration on the Environment of the Commonwealth Heads of Government Meeting, the 1989 Male' Declaration on Global Warming and Sea Level Rise, the 1990 International Conference on Global Warming and Climate Change: African Perspectives, and the 1990 Ministerial Conference of Developing Countries on Environment and Development. NGO meetings, such as the 1989 International Conference on Global Warming and Climate Change: Perspectives from Developing Countries and the 1989 Conference on the Global Environment and Human Response: Towards Sustainable Development, similarly offered no targets or timetables for greenhouse gas emissions abatement.

Short-term emission reduction targets were set, however, by a few highly influential meetings although the subject of long-term goal of stabilization received scant attention (see Table 5.1). As would occur throughout the climate change negotiations, decisions reached on critical issues in one meeting would often become established as negotiating benchmarks for subsequent meetings of different organizations. Such a phenomenon appears to suggest that in some circumstances early acceptance of a decision becomes the status quo of unexpected robustness, especially in the absence of wider international concern. General and unspecified calls for greenhouse gas reductions were made definite when the 1998 Toronto Conference recommended immediate action: "An initial global goal should be to reduce CO_2 emissions by approximately 20 percent of 1988 levels by the year 2005;" and for "Stabilizing atmospheric concentrations of CO_2 is an imperative goal. It is currently estimated to require reductions of more than 50 percent from present emission levels." As Brenton (1994: 166) notes, this was "the first widely endorsed quantitative proposal to tackle climate change."

At Noordwijk, the Ministerial Conference on Atmospheric Pollution and Climate Change supported the Toronto target, as did the First World Climate Conference of 1990. European Community environment ministers met in Luxembourg in 1990 and agreed to a goal of stabilizing carbon dioxide

Table 5.1 Summary of Selected International Meetings on the Environment or Climate and the Treatment of Greenhouse Gas Emission Reduction Targets.

Meeting	Type	Year	Recommended Emissions Reductions
World Conference on 'The Changing Atmosphere: Implications for Global Security'	Non-governmental meeting	Toronto, 1988	Short term: 20% from 1988 by 2005 Long-term: stabilization
Ministerial Conference on Atmospheric Pollution and Climate Change	International conference	Noordwijk, 1989	Long-term: stabilization
European Communities. Climate Change Policy–Council Conclusions	European Community	1990	Short-term: 1990 levels by 2000 Medium term: Consider targets for 2005 and 2010
First World Climate Conference	International conference	Geneva, 1979	Short-term: 1990 levels by 2000
Second World Climate Conference	International conference	Geneva, 1990	No target or timetable

emissions at 1990 levels by the year 2000 which, as Molitor (1999: 222) stated, was "a target that would have far-reaching implications for the upcoming negotiations." Shortly after, the Second World Climate Conference was held, but its concluding Ministerial Declaration conspicuously didn't include any emissions reduction timetables or targets (Jager and Ferguson 1991).

Following the Second World Climate Conference negotiation began on the FCCC. Negotiations under the International Negotiating Committee concluded in February 1992 without an agreed emissions reduction target or timetable. Delegations from European Community member countries were unsuccessful in obtaining U.S. agreement to a stabilization target of 1990 levels by 2000. Attendance of U.S. President George Bush at the Rio conference was secured on the text of the climate change convention being without any commitments to greenhouse gas reduction targets (Porter and Brown 1996).

Throughout this process, the proposition that the developed nations who historically bear the responsibility for elevated atmospheric carbon dioxide would take the lead in global abatement was a prominent theme. Eventually this concept became institutionalized under the FCCC's 'differentiated abatement responsibilities' in Article 3.1. Achieving atmospheric stabilization will ultimately require action by all nations, developed and developing alike, to reduce global emissions, but the entry of the non-Annex 1 nations was deferred until a later phase of the FCCC. In 1995, the industrialized world accounted for about 73 percent of global carbon dioxide emissions and, under business-as-usual scenarios, it will take until 2035 for the industrialized and developing world to have equal outputs (UNDP 2000: 92). Discussion of this issue has occurred at the COPs and has played strongly in the domestic debate in the U.S. and elsewhere, but no clear indication exists as to when or how developing nations will participate in emissions abatement under the FCCC. Through the COPs, powerful developing nations India and China refused to participate if set emissions limits by the process. Restricting commitments for controlling greenhouse gas emissions to the industrialized nations obviated the need for developing nations' inclusion in negotiations over targets and timetables. So although greenhouse gas releases from developing nations were significant and forecast to increase, these nations were a "potential veto coalition" and their omission made strategic sense to those hoping to secure agreement on emissions reduction (Porter and Brown 1996).

Of course, the debate over the distant goal of stabilization carries with it the potential for great contemporary political differences. Those seeking to delay or avoid emissions reduction will favor high levels of stabilization simply because the higher the level the more distant it becomes and the greater the delay available before emissions reductions are necessary. For example, to endorse a 1000 ppmv carbon dioxide stabilization target would not require any emissions abatement to occur until late this century, around

2090 (IPCC 2001a). Conversely, a stabilization target of 450 ppmv would require global emissions to be reduced by 15–25 percent below the 1990 levels by 2050 (IPCC 2001a), implying the need for immediate action. However, stabilization at any level necessitates long-term greenhouse gas emissions to be in equilibrium in the global carbon cycle, namely that there be no net increases in global atmospheric concentrations, so that emissions and sequestration are balanced.

Long-term goals of the FCCC

Several key aspects of the FCCC are creatively ambiguous and none more so than the goal of the FCCC itself (UN 1999):

> The ultimate objective of this convention and to any related legal instruments that the Conference of the Parties may adopt to achieve, in accordance with the relevant provisions of the Convention, the stabilisation of greenhouse gases concentrations in the atmosphere at a level that would prevent dangerous interference with the climate system. Such a level should be achieved within a time-frame sufficient to allow ecosystems to adapt naturally to climate change, to ensure that food production is not threatened and to enable economic development to proceed in a suitable manner.

Definition 1 in Article 1 of the FCCC offers the following (UN 1999):

> Adverse effects of climate change means that changes in the physical environment or biota resulting from climate change which have significant deleterious effects on the consumption, resilience or productivity of natural and managed ecosystems or on the operation of socio-economic systems or on health and welfare.

Despite its greater specificity, this qualifier does little to circumscribe "dangerous" in this context. Many have remarked on the impossibility of making tangible such a goal. Suffice to observe that although stabilization is a relatively clear concept, the objective could hardly be less precise as to the desired level of stabilization. Moreover, the terms employed cannot be translated into any unequivocal quantity and nor is the objective any lucid on when this should be achieved. Several ecological and scientific terms feature in the FCCC text ("ecosystems,' "adapt," and "sustainable") suggestive of a scientific identification of the point at which ecosystems suffer significant losses. Although science might assist in such a task, the concepts involved are open to wide interpretation and the scale of such investigations specified only as "ecosystems," which is almost a scale-independent concept. Arguably, only the provision that economic development must "proceed" lends itself into ready translation into the continuance of international GDP growth; ecosystem "adaptation" to climate change is particularly elusive in ecological terms (see, e.g., IPCC 2001c). All that is currently unequivocal about the FCCC's ultimate goal is that atmospheric greenhouse gas concentrations will be stabilized and at a level that may be defended on ecological grounds

O'Neil and Oppenheimer (2002) directly address the FCCC's criteria on ecosystem adaptation using coral reefs, and large-scale discontinuities to the climate system using disintegration of the West Antarctic Ice Sheet and shutting or slowing down the thermohaline circulation. Avoiding dangerous interference they offer implies restricting global warming to 1°C above the 1990 baseline to protect corals, to 2°C to protect the Ice Sheet, and to 3°C to ensure the functioning of the thermohaline. Referring the warming ranges associated with stabilization of carbon dioxide at 450, 550, and 650 ppmv in the IPCC's third assessment report they note that coral reefs cannot be protected even at the lowest of these targets (where the warming range is 1.2–2.3°C). These authors make a case for urgent emission cuts, using a carbon cycle model, by pointing out that delaying meeting the Kyoto target until 2020 "risks foreclosing the option of stabilizing concentrations at 450 ppm." Many policy debates, notably in Europe, consider a 2°C warming to define the FCCC's goal.

Nature, of course, knows no 'danger' but only change. Climate change (anthropocentric) has doubtlessly already greatly altered the course of nature, adding to those other human influences that express human status as a major evolutionary cause. (Indeed, Crutzen and Stoemer (2000) dubbed this phase of the planet's development the "Anthropocene.") It might be debated that human climate interference has long been an agent of change to natural systems and, despite whatever action is taken to reduce climate change, future impacts from historic emissions will change ecological and values. "Dangerous" in this context cannot refer to the possibility of risks and losses to existing or future ecological and social systems, for this is now assured, but can only be understood in terms of magnitude of the loss of natural and social values and to human responsibility as the agent of their destruction.

Contemplating long-term stabilization

A variety of rationales have been put forward in favor of setting long-term goals for stabilization. Identifying the pathways of global emissions terminating in a stable atmospheric concentration of greenhouse gases at a nominated time makes tangible the goals of emissions reduction and stabilization targets. Resolution of the global carbon cycle provides an unavoidable accountability for greenhouse gas emissions, and, correspondingly for official sources, demarcates the realm of scientific knowledge from the decisions of political institutions for the setting stabilization targets. Short-term targets can be measured against long-term goals, providing a means to calibrate progress. Long-term targets can assist in shaping policies and decisions that have long-lived effects, especially in such areas of investment in plant, technology, and infrastructure, where contemporary choices have greenhouse gas emission implication for decades or longer. Hasselmann et al. (2003: 1924) argue: "Binding commitments to meet short-term emission targets must therefore go hand in hand with clearly defined strategies to achieve substantially more stringent reductions in the longer term." Associated with short-term policies are their effects in shaping technology choices and research directions, thereby becoming an agent of technological change, which is clearly critical for any transition to a future global low-carbon economy. Also essential for longer-term change is exerting influence over social choices and decision-making, whereby long-term targets can assist in promoting climate change goals, creating awareness, and mobilizing political interest and activity.

Following the lead of the Toronto Conference, the FCCC identified stabilization as a long-term goal for greenhouse gas concentrations (albeit set at an indefinable level). Recently, several nations have adopted longer-term emissions goals: the E.U. has set 550 ppmv for carbon dioxide concentrations; similarly, the U.K.'s Prime Minister Tony Blair announced the goal of a 60 percent reduction of emissions by 2050 and a stabilization of concentrations at 550 ppmv; while Sweden has set 550 ppmv for the six Kyoto Protocol gases.

Emissions rates and global warming are tied, and any consideration of a dangerous rate of warming is an evaluation of emission levels, so that moderate to high levels of emissions in the immediate future exclude the opportunities to contain the rate and ultimate level of global warming at modest levels. Stabilization of carbon dioxide levels at contemporary or somewhat higher levels (say, 450 ppmv) necessitates almost immediate and drastic reductions in emissions; failure to do so means that higher levels of warming are unavoidable. By way of calibrating the effects of different stabilization targets, IPCC (2001c) reports that a 450 ppmv carbon dioxide stabilization target would be associated with a mean global warming of 1.4–4^{0}C, a 550 ppmv stabilization with 1.5–4.5^{0}C warming, and 1000 ppmv stabilization with a warming above 4.5^{0}C, which would cause large-scale global changes. Whatever "dangerous" may come to mean, there can be little doubt that the failure to greatly arrest global emissions will produce sufficient global warming to meet almost any interpretation of the term.

Yet, the longer-term stabilization task proffers similar problems to those of setting short-term emission reductions. In the absence of any guidance from the FCCC there has been variation in both targets for stabilization and of stabilization levels. As described above, stabilization of atmospheric concentrations of greenhouse gases can only occur a considerable time after greenhouse gas emissions are stabilized, and the eventual level of atmospheric stabilization depends on the rate and extent of the reduction in emissions. Stabilization of greenhouse gases in the atmosphere will take

100–300 years following stabilization of emissions, and global temperatures taking a similar period (IPCC 2001d). Sea-level rise will continue for centuries to millennia after emissions are stabilized and before equilibrium is reached (IPCC 2001d).

Some indication of the stabilization task is that a target for the year 2100 for current concentrations implies accumulated global emissions over the century of 300–430 gigatons of carbon; on an annualized basis this is 2.7–3.9 gigatons a year – about 45–60 percent less than today's emissions (Azar and Sterner 1996). Stabilization at this level implies radical change to the world's energy system. Set against existing global conditions where emissions continue to increase and are forecast to do so in the absence of strong preventative action, stabilization implies increasing absolute and relative levels of emissions reduction in the future. Continuation of Business-as-Usual trends emissions, therefore, makes the stabilization goal increasingly difficult. Estimates of future emissions so far into the future are so tendentious as to make the exercise entirely questionable; for example, IPCC (2001d) emission scenarios suggested that global emissions range from below 5 to around 30 gigatons of carbon per annum by 2100, seemingly including virtually any future other than catastrophe.

In many respects, IPCC science has influenced negotiations about stabilization through its (basically arbitrary) selection of key parameters for modeling of emissions and the global carbon cycle. For example, most IPCC models consider stabilization at 2100 and accordingly this has become a commonly discussed time-frame for stabilization and has been frequently adopted by environmentalists. Similarly, the IPCC used stabilization targets for carbon dioxide (equivalents) of 350, 450, 550, 650, and 750 ppmv (see, e.g., IPCC 1996a) and policy discussions have focussed on these values. Currently, officials are disinterested in the values at either end of the scale, noting that we have already passed 350 ppmv and that, without action, long-term emissions will probably reach 750 ppmv.

Within the resulting range, those more sympathetic to environmental values obviously favor the lower value of 450, while those less concerned favor 550 or 650 ppmv for various reasons, such as relative costs and benefits, and feasibility. Note that the IPCC's 2001 Synthesis Report (2001d) in presenting the economic costs for different stabilization goals has 450 ppmv as the lowest value. Many scientific modeling exercises of global warming and impacts studies use 550 ppmv as a goal, that being conveniently two times the pre-industrial level. Although trivial, that 550 lies in the middle of the discussed range cannot be dismissed as a possibly influential factor if negotiators settle on a stabilization target. Obviously, 350 ppmv is the stabilization level considered most likely to associated with less environmental damage, that being the lowest level of the range under discussion.

Considering the long-term stabilization issue invigorates one particularly vexed aspect of the FCCC negotiations – setting targets for developing nations. Developing nations continue to base their economic development on fossil fuel pathways and the exploitation of fossil fuel reserves. In China's case, both environmentalists and conservatives seeking a convenient rationale are concerned about this nation's growing appetite for fossil fuels (e.g., Aldhous 2005). At present, targets only apply to developed nations and few other non-Annex 1 nations have voluntarily agreed to lower emissions. While the rationale and justification for adopting this course of action are described above, the FCCC has arguably fallen short of achieving global management of global greenhouse gas emissions. Furthermore, the performance to date in transferring resources and technology to developing nations to foster a high energy-efficiency and low-greenhouse gas emitting economic development is poor. Within the FCCC negotiations, the cause of setting targets and time-tables and for having developed nations take the lead in emissions reductions have been compatible positions held by the E.U. and many developing nations and opposed, most prominently, by the U.S. Any decisions to persuade the developing nations to accept limits on their emissions threaten to break these negotiating accords, and may partially explain why long-term issues of stabilization are contrary to the current agenda of those parties most likely to be concerned with stabilization.

Reducing global greenhouse gas emissions through climate change policy

There are many aspects to the FCCC's global management plans, but overwhelmingly the task is to reduce greenhouse gas emissions associated with the energy sector. As described above, the basic approach to reducing emissions from fossil fuel combustion is identical with energy policy reform directed at reducing energy consumption and to shifting away from oil and gas to less environmentally harmful alternatives and to renewable energy. Energy policy reform received its impetus in response to the 1970s 'oil crises,' when the essential parameters of reform were identified in technical, policy, and institutional realms. Greenhouse gas emissions reduction policy has largely fitted with this general area of policy development and has revitalized a change agenda that had in many respects been faltering due to privatization and deregulation initiatives in many developed nations. Examining international reviews of climate change policy, such as conducted by the International Energy Agency (e.g., IEA 2001), confirms that, as a generalization, national climate change policy is largely energy policy reform. Therefore, identifying the immediate policies to reduce greenhouse gas emissions was a relatively straightforward task and most policies recycled existing energy policies on energy conservation, improving energy efficiency, and modestly renewable energy (see, e.g., IEA 1992).

Failures to lower the rate of national greenhouse gas emissions, therefore, are not the outcome of insufficient knowledge about the functioning of energy system and of options for its improvement. National climate change policies have not managed to reverse the general trend of increasing greenhouse gas emissions (see, e.g., Höhne et al. (2005) for a recent summary of the G8's performance), although there have been successes at the state, sub-state, corporate, and city jurisdictions. For example, the NGO, International Council for Local Environmental Initiatives 'Cities for Climate Protection' program records the successful actions of cities and counties around the world. Several European cities have comprehensively addressed the issue, several U.S. states and cities have Executive Orders on energy efficiency and greenhouse gas emissions abatement (including New Jersey, New York, and Maryland), and a few major corporations have also reduced emissions as part of their own climate change programs (Cogan 2003, EPA 2002, and Rabe 2002). Progressive European and U.S. cities have provided the lead in effective climate change policy, often building on long-standing programs addressing energy and planning problems. As a result, the range of city and state performance in addressing climate change has become very great indeed, albeit with a few leaders and the majority showing modest performance, at best.

Despite the wealth of technical knowledge and accumulated experience around the world, formulating and implementing effective climate change policies is difficult. Policies to reduce carbon dioxide emissions from fossil fuel consumption, regardless of the degree of their strategic focus, are necessarily responding to a diffuse set of emission sources. Climate change policies to reduce emissions often feature hundreds of individual components addressing a multitude of specific sources spread across entire economies, landscapes, and jurisdictions. Forecast and analysis of such policies is challenging and often evokes key political issues concerning governance, distribution of costs and benefits, and political and economic interests. Determining the effectiveness of policy initiatives requires detailed monitoring and evaluation by experts.

Because fossil fuel combustion is essential to industrial societies, actions to reduce emissions strike at aspects central to their economies, confronting the inertia of large, established systems of energy production, transfer, and consumption. Energy systems in the industrialized world are characterized by the slow turnover of their stock and are generally resistant to rapid change. 'Carbon lock-in' is a term some commentators employ to describe the effect of policies and practices that reinforce the industrial economy's reliance on fossil fuels (Unruh 2000). Although climate change policies to reduce national emissions are largely considered in the context of developed nations, the question of avoiding or negating the carbon lock-in effect applies equally to developing nations. Conventional theories of economic development usually promote industrialization as the development path for lesser developed nations (e.g., World Bank 2000a, 2000b), which translate into increasing fossil fuel consumption (and empirically, national income is the dominant variable in explaining cross-national differences in carbon dioxide emissions; see Neumayer 2002). As the *World Energy Outlook* assured (UNDP et al. 2000: 117): "To summarise, no serious global shortage of energy resources is likely during at least the first half of the 21st century. Reserves of traditional commercial fuels – oil, gas, and coal – will suffice for decades to come." In the case of coal, the sufficiency will endure for more than 220 years based on current production (UNDP et al. 2000: 117).

Simple changes in energy consumption can be misleading from an environmental perspective as introduced substitutes of energy or materials in unmeasured aspects of production process can positively suggest reduction in energy consumption. Measures of embodied energy offer a way to avoid this impression by giving more inclusive accounts of the energy budget of a commodity, service, or activity (as energy and material intensity). Studies of the energy flows within economic systems have a direct conceptual link to ecological research of Howard Odum and others, and to pioneering studies in Russia and elsewhere in the early twentieth century. Although most approaches to reducing emissions focus on improving energy efficiency, energy conservation, and fuel switching at end points of consumption, energy budgets offer more comprehensive insights into energy as a dynamic phenomenon within the economy. Energy budgets are likely to become essential diagnostic tools in the quest to move to low or very low carbon economies in order to identify low emission approaches in an economy-wide context and avoid substituting end-use gains at the emissions expense of other areas.

Calculations of energy intensity, typically based on the energy required to produce each unit of national GDP, are used to assess energy systems performance. Historically, the developed nations have shown long-term continual improvement in deriving national output from energy (UNDP et al. 2000). A similar measure is that of carbon intensity, wherein the carbon dioxide emissions per unit of economic activity are assessed, and which usually matches national trends in energy intensity, as influenced by national circumstances. Trends in carbon intensity to date reflect decisions about fossil fuel use, although in the future we assume national climate change policies will play an increasing role.

One key aspect in this issue is the identification of the so-called 'decoupling' of energy use and economic growth in developed countries, wherein the former tight association between increasing energy use and increasing GDP has been loosened, with economic growth proceeding with proportionally lower energy inputs. Scholars have found this development encouraging, as it proffers that the transition to a more energy efficient and lower greenhouse gas-emitting global economy is already under way. But opinion is divided on this matter, as increasing energy and carbon efficiency has also been accompanied by absolute increases in energy use and greenhouse gas production, and disguised by rapidly increasing GDP, leading some commentators to regard efficiency increases skeptically (e.g., Herring 2000). Whether or not developing nations will be able to 'leapfrog' to the higher efficiency energy consumption as their GDP increases and avoid replicating the industrialized world's early inefficiencies will be a major factor determining the pathway of future global emissions.

Part of the variation in estimates of the costs and difficulty of reducing emissions stems not only from differing assumptions and interpretations of the extent of inertia in the broader energy system, but also to the extent to which embodied energy is taken into account. Within the energy sector itself, many capital stock components are both expensive and long-lived, notably power stations, transformers, transmission lines, and pipelines. Aspects of the built environment may last even longer, such as buildings, infrastructure, transport systems, and urban density. Furthermore, individual components exist within resilient social systems in which decisions, such as those concerning infrastructure, are restrained by social norms, practices, and expectations. Nowhere is the limitation of social systems better exemplified than in urban design and transportation, wherein preferences for low-density suburbs and the phenomenon of urban sprawl dictate the economics of transportation choices over long periods.

Other aspects of energy use are readily amenable to short-term improvements in efficiency, conservation, and fuel switching, and face relatively few social, economic, or technical barriers. A great number of household appliances, and commercial and industrial equipment have a relatively short lifetime and are amenable to replacement by higher-energy efficiency alternatives (IWG 2001) and there are many options available in the energy sector (e.g., Bailie et al. 2003). Climate change policies have tended to concentrate on these shorter-term initiatives, many of which have immediate or very short payback periods. Where greenhouse gas emissions reductions occur in the developed nations they are primarily the result of policy initiatives incidental to climate change policy (and usually driven by longer-standing policy goals, such as energy conservation or economic policy). Often these policies are minor in scale and economic cost, and, politically, readily acceptable. Several compendiums of national climate change activity are available, but there are relatively few efforts at assessing policy performance.

Cutting greenhouse gas emissions to meet the goal of atmospheric stabilization for most locations in developed nations goes well beyond the experience or goals of contemporary climate change policy, as it will necessarily involve energy systems based largely on renewable energy sources with low greenhouse gas emissions. Most developed nations have only a small percentage of their energy derived from renewable energy (WEA 2000). Although renewable energy sources have been identified, at least two great barriers remain to be overcome: firstly, renewable energy can only be fully effective if existing levels of energy consumption are greatly lowered; and secondly, public policy makers must be committed to provide renewable energy with the scale of support that fossil fuels have historically received.

Global climate management

Under the approach of ecological modernization, the task of reconciling social activity and resulting ecological damage becomes a management assignment in which nature–society relations are managed scientifically by state authority in processes involving a range of interest groups. Evidence for the success of this approach at the national level has been amply demonstrated. Ecological modernization (which embraces sustainable development) has also brought success in resolving international environmental problems, albeit mixed with numerous failures and disappointments. Sustainable development has been derided as a means to continue economic development at the expense of environmental values, but as Lafferty (1996) and others have suggested, sustainable development has been the rubric for many environmental success stories. To dismiss sustainable development as mere rhetoric is to effectively deny that any environmental restoration has occurred since, say, the WCED (1987).

Ecological modernization holds that modern states have reacted to the ecological crisis and local environmental problems through re-orientation of the industrial productive process, whilst retaining the basic social and economic structures of liberal democracy. Accordingly, in responding to environmental problems, the state assumes the responsibility for addressing the issue, either through changing its own actions or imposing changes on corporations. These changes involve institutional changes, such as agencies empowered to monitor and protect the environment, legal and regulatory changes pertaining to he environment, and symbolic changes indicating the state's awareness of key issues. Improvements in ecological indicators in the developed world, such as air and aquatic pollution in the large cities, are attributed to ecological modernization. In this sense, the powers of the modern industrial state exhibit evolutionary development, expanding its purview of necessary market regulation, and responding to the environmental concerns of citizens and political organizations. Normal processes and activities of industrial life are compromised through state action, but not to the extent to disturb its economic necessity or viability. Nation-state recognition of climate change and its acknowledging the need for reduced greenhouse gas emissions fits well with ecological modernization. But for fully realized ecological modernization, there must be action by the state. For climate change, the results of initiatives taken can be most readily assessed by their impact of the level of greenhouse gas emissions, and on this basis the trend of increasing emissions in most OECD nations suggests ecological modernization is not under way.

Ecological modernization and global climate management

All the efforts to create and implement the FCCC are in effect a response to risk, and the goals of the FCCC express the desire to manage these potential dangers. Nation states acting cooperatively have determined that global warming is a risk, albeit largely without agreement as to the exact dimensions of this risk. That the course of liberal democracy has assumed the priorities of global capital and nation-state interests and sought to implement the FCCC in ways that generate capital in preference to meeting the objectives of the FCCC doesn't detract from the FCCC's original goals.

Risk management is inherent in the rationale of the precautionary principle on which the FCCC is founded, holding that precaution is more prudent than unlimited risk-taking.

Liberation from fear over the dangers of the natural world was central to the Enlightenment. Yet, through the efforts to diminish such dangers as part of the overall development of modernity, new and novel ecological dangers have become its signature. Under the Enlightenment, social action is guided by moral imperative and risk is revealed by technology. An immediate conclusion is that nature is indeed imposing a risk on humanity and the ecological entities and features that society values, so that nature is 'beyond human control.' Modern society seeks, therefore, to contain these dangers and to bring nature back under control. Efforts to manage climate change risks are more complex that this formulation suggests for many reasons, including the role that human activity has played in creating the climate change crisis. Those dangers of climate change are not those of indifferent and independent natural processes, but a product of human activity, which vests the responsibility for the risks of global warming firmly in a social context.

Beck's thesis (1992, 1995, 1997, and 1999) of the 'risk society' is a key theoretical development in the concept of ecological modernization, and highly applicable to climate change. Risk society recognizes a linkage between science and modern state in the face of increasing risks, especially those generated by the environment. As actual and perceived risks continue to increase, democratic societies seek protection from their effects. Science becomes transformed from being one of the principal sources of risk generation to its role in identifying, assessing, and devising ways of neutralizing these risks. Modern states' preoccupation with securing the conditions for the growth of industrial output and economic expansion becomes re-oriented in risk societies in response to social demands. Political interests are re-oriented towards a more complex and circumspect condition, where they must assume the role of social 'risk managers.' Part of risk society is akin to a post-industrial condition, wherein developed nations shift their attention increasingly to 'quality of life' issues, having satisfied material needs to the brink of satiation. Again, fitting climate change into a context of risk is straightforward. Unrestricted global warming endangers society and it follows that industrial society will direct science and rational ecological management to the task of bringing the level of risk into the realm of the acceptable. Efforts to curb industrial activity that endangers society are supported, states undertake international cooperation, science is supported by states in an effort to understand the dangers of climate change and to help in designing measures to alleviate and anticipate climate change's attendant dangers.

In one sense, the regime has satisfied part of the task set by risk society, namely the use of science to identify a course of remediative action, the cutting of greenhouse gas emissions. Unfortunately, this scientific advice carries some caveats: there is no assurance available on whether cutting emissions will actually prevent those changes to climate already initiated or how emissions levels relate to the risks of a changed climate. As discussed above, this problem is reflected in the uncertainty over climate change impacts. Even if science has fulfilled its part of the risk society bargain, governance has yet to do so. National governance experiences to date have demonstrated that economic devastation is a highly reliable means of lowering emissions quickly, while the FCCC's market-based policy to reduce emissions is fraught with uncertainty.

As befits modern society, constructing climate change risks in the FCCC has been an exclusive role for science. Up to now, the task of defining the risks at hand has not been particularly fruitful. Science has not been able to reduce or contain these risks; indeed, even the task of describing the risks of climate change has not been fulfilled. Evidence for the limitations of science is revealed in the political debates over how these risks were generated, what they are, and what level of effort is justified in efforts to manage these dangers. One key construction to the central question of greenhouse gas reductions has been that developed nations have sought ways to reduce fossil fuel consumption by promoting economic growth through new avenues. Institutional reform of this type is the essence of ecological modernization and much of sustainable development leaves technological and political structures in place as environmental problems are resolved.

Globalization

Globalization is the processes by which social relations around the world are becoming increasingly connected, with the barriers of time and space being ever diminished, combined with a social awareness that this change is occurring. Much attention given to globalization deals with economic relationships and those cultural influences resulting from increasing interconnections involving developments in information and communication technologies. Many other factors also foster and promote globalization, which include scientific knowledge of the global condition and international environmental agreements, such as those of the FCCC. In brief, therefore, globalization influences the FCCC and is also a product of the FCCC. Conceptually, globalization runs through the three themes of our analysis (science, governance, and environmental management) and could be covered in each chapter, but for the purposes of brevity, a number of key points can be addressed simultaneously here.

Although global environmental governance is not commonly considered as being related to globalization (indeed, few popular texts on globalization identify environmental issues), this occurrence is an essential component of the globalization process, notably in supplying much of its legitimacy. A series of global governance initiatives and global institutions in the World Bank, WTO, IMF, NAFTA, and others serve to create and promote a global economic market. Environmental protection seeks to protect environmental values at the local, national, and international scales and in sustainable development we find an approach that explicitly links both the expansion of economic relations and environmental protection (WCED 1987). Globalization, from the perspective of sustainable development, is a process that embraces global economic growth and growth in global environmental protection.

Advocacy for globalization in explicit terms emanates from the political right and indeed many of its arguments derive from long-established free-trade shibboleths. Environmental concerns have been dismissed or ignored by this group. While such views are not generally dismissed by the developed nations and key international institutions, these nations and organizations have tended to adopt an ecological modernization approach, although their rhetorical commitment has usually exceeded that of their actions. Key institutions such as the World Bank (1999, 2000a, 2000b), World Economic Forum, World Business Council on Sustainable Development (2001), and others (e.g., WRI et al. 2002) all recognize the ecological foundations of economic activity and the associations between development, global poverty, and environmental protection. Generally, the approach of these groups is to find ways to accommodate economic globalization with these social and environmental goals that leave the fundamental extant political and economic practices in place. Central to these practices are conventional economic development and growth and promotion of liberal democracy as an ideal type. Sustainable development holds forth the promise that environmental repair and remediation can be made part of routine globalization, so that globalization's ideal type comprises not only economic development and democratic governance, but also environmental protection.

Ecological modernization rejects simple economic determinism and laissez-faire economics, implying that economic globalization can only be acceptable given that its outcomes are compatible with environmental protection. This legitimization is founded on several grounds, several of which have recourse to research findings and empirical bases. One of the strongest arguments is that richer economies are usually in better environmental conditions than poorer economies, especially when comparisons are made within the spectrum of industrialization. Partly this is attributed to economic transformation from the industrial economy to the 'post-industrial,' with the concomitant switch from a manufacturing to a service orientation. As society generates wealth, it has an increasing capacity to invest in environmental remediation, so it follows logically that environmental damage incurred through industrialization can be remediated from the fruits of capital accumulation. Research findings of selected variables confirm this association in some circumstances, giving rise to the generalized 'environmental Kuznets curve' (EKC) (a u-shaped response of environmental quality to rising income) (Grossman and Krueger 1995; Seldon and Song 1994). Globalization offers the promise of increases in wealth that, in the wisdom of the World Bank, UN, and others, will lead to improved environmental conditions and according an increase in human welfare.

Despite the empirical basis of the 'environmental restoration through wealth creation' thesis, its opponents have discredited the concept. Such has been the extent of rejection of the EKC by the ecological economics community that this position partly defines the school; certainly prominent ecological economists have derided the concept, finding it highly conditional, misleading, and simply erroneous (e.g., Arrow et al. 1995; Ayres 1995; de Bruyn et al. 1998; and Suri and Chapman 1998). Where environmental problems are isolated and amenable to technological solutions of low cost, then conditions of increasing wealth can be associated with successful remediation. When such ecological 'repairs' are affected under conditions of increasing income, laissez-faire advocates attribute causation to the benefits of economic growth. Critics of economic growth paradigms find the association largely coincidental with social changes such as political activity by social groups and environmental NGOs, the level and competency of governance, and the efficacy of political responsiveness. Accordingly, what the advocates of the EKC imply is the outcome of economic variables, its critics counter that any correlation is the outcome of the role of political and governance factors which are partially and occasionally captured by indirectly related economic factors.

Closer inspections of the reasons behind environmental restoration further undermine the alleged benefits of globalization's promotion of economic growth. Environmentalists point out that the restoration of ecological values follows the process that necessarily degraded them, so that industrialization overall reduces environmental qualities. Further, restoration of single attributes of environmental quality don't amount to restoration of ecosystems, or can permanent losses of species, processes, or ecosystems ever be 'undone' by technology or social organization. Ecological economists such as Robert Ayres, Robert Costanza, and Michael Common have rejected the conventional economic assumption that all goods and services can effectively be substituted for each other once all is rendered into economic value. Analysis by ecological economists has also questioned the character of the environmental benefits produced by economic growth, as these may reflect the benefits of relocating wastes, polluting activities, and industrial plants to places and jurisdictions outside the area where the benefits are being recorded (i.e., 'exporting pollution'). Similarly, environmental benefits may result from the imposition of social and environmental costs that are not considered in the assessment in a process of substituting one ecological value for another.

Globalization and climate change

Scholars and activists alike have paid almost no attention to the connections between globalization and climate change (some notable exceptions being Barkin 2003 and Retallack and Sobhani 2001). Despite this lack of interest, there are a number of issues worthy of closer examination. One important dimension is globalization's effect on increasing global greenhouse gas emissions that occurs through a variety of channels as it accelerates and extends the activities and practices inimical to global climate protection (see Grimes and Kentor 2003; Roberts et al. 2003 and Roberts and Grimes 1997). International development agencies, international banks and financial institutions, and national governments promote conventional neo-liberal models of national economic development based on primary resource harvesting, industrialization, and fossil fuels energy systems. Consequently, economic growth not only continues in the developed nations, but developing nations are following a pattern of economic development that increases their contributions to global greenhouse gas emissions given the role of fossil fuels (Podobnik 2002). Consumption of energy-intensive goods and services is increasing with the associated rises in greenhouse gas emissions, although critically much of developing world manufacturing is for mass consumption in OECD export markets (Grimes and Kentor 2003; Roberts and Grimes 1997). Modernization through globalization is also transforming traditional practices, such as agriculture, into models of production involving greater applications of fossil fuel energy sources. Global emissions from transport are also increasing as a consequence of greater volumes of international trade.

Another dimension of globalization's influence is the design and operation of the FCCC and Kyoto Protocol. One obvious feature of the atmosphere from an economic perspective is its universal distribution, thus being immediately amenable for consideration as a globally dispersed commercial opportunity. Ecological modernization's goals of reforming state and market activity are consistent with the FCCC's use global markets and market-based policies to assist in implementing its goals. Primarily achieved through the aforementioned Kyoto mechanisms of the Kyoto Protocol, these policies to reduce greenhouse gas emissions fit into the global economy of international trade. Carbon credits will be traded within established markets as routine commodities and several firms have already been established in anticipation of a burgeoning global market. Considering the volume of hot air available in the first commitment period, the potential value of carbon trading appears high. So prevalent in elite quarters are the perceived advantages of global markets that the concept of international trading of carbon credits was established early in the negotiating activity.

Ecological modernization strategies for harnessing the global economy under globalization have as their longer-term goal the global transition of the energy base of industrial society away from the reliance on fossil fuel. Through policies that mix public and private sector initiatives, the FCCC will seek a global change to the near universal model of development through industrialization based on fossil fuel consumption. Accordingly, the FCCC's strategies must embrace the possibilities inherent in globalization, whereby greater social and economic connectivity can assist in the spread and adoption of this alternative development path. For this reason, its advocates argue, the FCCC has consistently considered the economic aspects of its policies, so as to produce an accord between nations and corporations in policies directed towards global activity. Indeed, the FCCC's commitment to globalization may be suggested by its greater attention given to activities between actions in the global economy than in activities occurring within national boundaries.

Furthermore, there may be other transformations and trends within the broader global economy helpful to the goals of the FCCC. For example, Ehrlich and Brunello (2001) identify several features they consider may greatly improve the efficiency of energy use, including the substitution of information for energy in certain production processes, the general trend in developed economies to falling energy intensity in economic activity, improvements in energy management, and the transition to less carbon-intensive technologies. Within the U.S. energy sector, for instance, renewable energy use has outgrown fossil fuel use growth rates, partly facilitated by broader economic changes, such as privatization and utility deregulation.

An emerging dialogue in the wake of the U.S. withdrawal from the FCCC process involves using various international trade approaches, models, and techniques for controlling greenhouse gases, openly seeking to replace global environmental governance with that of international trade regulation. Even within the U.S., the northwestern states have been developing a carbon emissions trading system (known as the 'Regional Greenhouse Gas Initiative'). Aspects of this approach overlap with the suite of proposals to more explicitly establish national greenhouse gas emission reductions according to reduction cost criteria, sometimes described euphemistically as 'national circumstances.' While these latter arguments concerning national circumstances are increasingly popular with market advocates, any rationale that trade negotiations offer a successful model for agreement between nations for achieving an absolute standard, such as the absence of national economic subsidies, lack credence. Given the gestation for the WTO was essentially the entire latter half of the twentieth century, it might well be argued that the trade negations could learn from the more rapid progress of the FCCC process.

Political and economic interests in global climate management

Climate change studies employing political economy have tended not to examine the goal of environmental management per se, but have provided two vital sources of critique on the issues of globalization, global environmental management, and climate change. Firstly, the claims of the environmental benefits of economic growth – the key rationalization of ecological modernization under globalization – have been seriously undermined.

Secondly, political economy has identified a rationale to explain a set of causal explanations for the FCCC's basic goal setting based in economic and political interests. Political economists have highlighted the current global reporting of social and environmental conditions, especially those examining the trends of recent decades. UN and World Bank data reveal that the era of globalization has not yielded universal gains in income or environmental conditions; in fact, the gap between rich and poor widened. Under the reporting of the institutions promoting economic growth, it appears that the project of globalization has failed to meet its own expectations.

Political economy identifies some of the causes for the inability to change the course of the fossil fuel economies, including the costs of reducing emissions; costs of structural change and technological development; and political implications of confronting major stakeholders in the political process, especially corporations. Ecological modernization is necessary to ensure the ecological legitimacy of globalization, as is the claim of liberal democracy that economic development is concomitant with expanding democratic freedoms. Yet both these rationalizations stand in contrast to the empirical findings that cast considerable doubt on the claims that globalization is rendering a world with greater democratic freedoms or arresting the decline in ecological values (see, e.g., World Bank 2000a; UNDP 2000; and UNDP et al. 2000, 2001). And both the conventional development path and ecological modernization are modernization paradigms, in which the goals, pathway, and means of transformation of the social world and society–nature relations concern modernity.

Despite these commonalities, political economy and ecological modernization regard globalization quite differently, which has several implications for the FCCC. Ecological modernization opposes unrestrained market forces and seeks to reconcile capitalism with social goals, and therefore finds in globalization both hope and risk. As explained above, the potential for global market forces to produce low-cost and efficient means to reduce emissions is expected to facilitate the global effort of emissions reduction. By way of contrast, political economy (and political ecology) identifies in globalization the tendency for the ecologically and socially destructive capacities of global capitalism to be unleashed on those nations and communities least well defended by suitable social, political, knowledge, and judicial institutions. If the global climate is to be protected, then forces that promote economic growth based on the fossil fuel model of industrialization and the push to mass consumption societies must be opposed. Under political economy, it is contradictory and counterproductive to support the very economic forces in globalization that increase the problem of fossil fuel combustion the FCCC is charged with reducing. Essentially, the critical issue becomes whether the forces of globalization can be marshaled around the goals of a low-carbon global economy having being so embedded with the promotion of the fossil fuel model of development. To date, there is little evidence of such a radical transformation occurring.

Critiques from political ecology

Views of global climate management under political ecology vary. Political ecology includes those seeking to reform the existing emissions reduction approach the Kyoto Protocol emission targets in order to satisfy the environmental protection goals of the FCCC. There are others skeptical or rejecting of the goal of global climate management, a position not readily compatible with reform approaches. Resistance to the 'global' appellation is not denial of the planetary character of the issue, but a contestation over its meaning and attendant political implications.

'Ecologically sustainable' emissions targets

Political ecology rejects the FCCC emission targets as ineffectual for protecting the global climate because the reductions sought are simply too meager. Comparing the targets of the Kyoto Protocol of around 5 percent by 2008–2012 with that of the 60 percent reduction, environmental groups have argued that the modesty of the FCCC Kyoto Protocol is such that the exercise is both ineffectual and pandering to state and corporate interests. Environmental groups and advocates have been consistent in their call for greatly accelerated programs of emissions reduction in the developed world and for the FCCC to foster stringent reduction targets far exceeding those of the Kyoto Protocol's first commitment period. Advocacy of 'ecological' emissions targets has formed a core belief of this group. Those giving a high priority to environmental values seek reductions to achieve stabilization of atmospheric concentrations in the shortest time possible and at the lowest levels possible.

Environmentalists hold that their contributions are efforts to be true to the goal of the FCCC, i.e., the quest for stabilizing atmospheric greenhouse gases to prevent ecological loss, but the claim could be made that they're implicitly subscribing to ecological modernization and the goals of global climate management. However, accepting political modernization shouldn't be axiomatically assumed to be conservative, for the environmentalists seek emissions reduction to a level where radical social change is unavoidable. Considerable differences exist between different groups in the preferences for a stabilization level, ranging from returning to pre-industrial levels, to maintaining present values, to allowing higher levels (typically expressed as two and three times the pre-Industrial concentrations). Many environmentalists and advocates have used a set of IPCC estimates (1990a and 1996a) that atmospheric stabilization at present levels by 2050 would require global emissions reductions of around 60 percent of current levels (see, e.g., Byrne et al. 1998). If developed nations take the lead in emission reductions, as the FCCC prescribes, then this group would require deeper cuts. Stabilization of atmospheric concentrations through such emission targets is sometimes referred to in the shorthand of 'climate stabilization targets' and 'ecologically sustainability targets' (although future continuation of global climate stability cannot be assured by a return to current atmospheric concentrations of greenhouse gases and continued global warming is highly certain).

Environmentalists argue that the Kyoto Protocol's modest targets are far less than could be achieved by a dedicated effort to apply known policy settings and available technologies, a claim that has considerable technical support. Emissions reductions of the order suggested by the 'ecologically sustainable rate' cannot be readily accommodated within the existing energy systems of the developed world. Critics of such ecological targets refer to economic claims of the type already described that suggest high costs of extensive emission reductions. Most economic evaluations are of emission cuts of the magnitude set by the Kyoto Protocol; reductions of 60 percent or more entail such fundamental changes as to make cost estimation difficult. Importantly, such criticisms often overlook the path dependency of today's choices. Continued global emissions growth not only escalates the future magnitude of the reductions needed to meet any of the canvassed stabilization targets, but also makes the types of technological, economic, political, and social changes that ecologically sustainable rates would more difficult, because a set of policy choices that are only available in the present are closed off.

Resistance to the global

In the era of modern science, the unitary identity of the planet is accompanied by the expanding awareness of the influences of planetary-scale ecological processes and, in more contemporary times, of their vulnerability to human violation. Equally modern is the political construction of a terrestrial world divided by national territories and zones, and of oceans and polar extremities subject to peculiar rules derived from agreements between nations. Ecological processes and entities not readily confined by national designs of sovereignty, such as watercourses, migratory species (including our own), and air-borne pollutants, are the subject to ever-increasing rule and regulation in agreements between nations and involving international bodies. Similarly global are the activities of social organizations, from corporations to non-governmental organizations.

Many hold that environmental consciousness is a product of the images of earth from space, or at least partly so, and certainly these views of 'spaceship earth' became commonplace in the literature and policies of ecological awareness. From the perspective of space, much environmentalism proffered an impulse of totalizing protection, indifferent to the local and desiring of action global in scale. Interestingly, the international dimensions of many environmental problems from this era onwards demanded responses that could accommodate pollution that crossed national borders, resolve problems that affected many nations simultaneously, and facilitate coordinated national action. International environmental action takes many forms consistent with a world of nation states: international bodies (e.g., UNEP, UNDP, and UNESCO), international agreements (e.g., conventions and treaties on the Antarctic, biodiversity, desertification, endangered species, hazardous materials, tropical timber, and whales), and international laws and policies (e.g., the Law of the Sea).

That agreements between nations should eventually become global represents the culmination of a simple, if uneven, spread of international relations through the modern era. Many rationales drive the agreements for cooperation between states, such as economic, political, cultural, and strategic motivations. Global environmental agreements, however, are somewhat different to arrangements governing aspects of social life because they feature controls over components of the global environment. Liberal-democratic assumptions about nations' roles and actions (and their international bodies) are extended from social subjects to matters of nature. Exemplifying these assumptions is the legitimacy of commodifying natural goods and services by nation states within and beyond existing borders and current times, diverting and containing ecosystem processes and entities for human use, manipulating the environment to reduce hazard and risk to human health and capital, imposing environmental dangers across national borders, and altering genetic materials. Foremost amongst these assumptions is that of the world as a 'global environment.'

As several commentators have described, such as Yearly (1996) and Jasanoff (1996), the universality of the discourse of science is essential in defining the global. Not only has science revealed the world as a world, but the information it supplies that leads to the acceptance of this revelation is also itself a global discourse of sorts. Science is frequently identified as 'dis-covered' information about the natural world, so that scientific revelations of global conditions are simply truths about the natural conditions (i.e., the 'positivist' view of knowledge). As such, science is held to be unique as a universal discourse and therefore uniquely capable of revealing what is 'global' in the world. Only science can determine scientific claims about global identity, so that only science can assess scientific claims to 'globality.'

Decisions about managing the global environment that depend on science policy are the outcome (and mutual influence) of science and political action. Positivists present environmental policy decisions as the result of a rational process to fit scientific findings into institutional settings, and whose efficacy can be scientifically assessed. It follows that decisions about inquiries into the global environment, scientific knowledge of the global environment, and the application of scientific knowledge to decisions to manage the global environment all come to be stamped with the imprimatur of scientific knowledge and method. Within this rational/bureaucratic/positivist perspective of environmental policy, political decisions are secondary to the role of science, for policy is designed to yield scientifically supported outcomes.

Global environmental management, therefore, is identified with many virtues. Environmental problems extending across national borders or requiring international cooperation are understood scientifically and subject to scientific management solutions, in which science's 'disinterest' in political values ensures that global management will be perceived as politically neutral. Policies and programs can be assessed on scientific criteria and in light of their performance, adjusted as necessary so as to meet the scientific objectives. Epistemic communities represent the embodiment of the virtues of their subject and can be entrusted with formulating and assessing global management programs. International institutions embody the epistemic community's ideals and represent international cooperation and consensus around the core mission of scientific management. There is a logical appeal that nature be managed by 'science,' acknowledging that social problems require management approaches sensitive to social difference and political realities.

'Global,' therefore, is a particular way of considering nature, nation states, governance, and ecological problems. By implication, the 'global' designation carries an array of values and claims about science, international environmental institutions, and epistemic communities. As raised in earlier chapters, the positivist views of science and governance are deeply flawed explanations, and these critiques extend into these positivistic perspectives on the construction of global environmental management. It follows that rather than being the only way to consider widespread or diffuse ecological problems, both the depiction of nature and of nations at the planetary scale and in the global sense represents a particular social construction. Furthermore, political values and judgments are expressed within the concept of global environmental management, as revealed by several analysts.

Shiva (1993) laments the rise of the global environmental issues for several reasons. Firstly, there is disenfranchisement of local action, for as a consequence of defining problems as 'global,' global solutions are implied, whereby local initiatives and action are excluded or devalued. Secondly, the promotion of narrow interests and strategies occurs with greatly reduced conventional restrictions applied to local initiatives. By virtue of the 'global' appellation, a particular set of interests achieve political dominance under the rationale that they represent a universal interest, thereby escaping many conventional means of social and political accountability. Thirdly, in addressing global environmental issues there is often the false assumption that global actions are more democratic than non-global actions. Promoters of global approaches assume that the global is atop a hierarchy of democratic practices to which the lower orders are considered subservient.

Shiva evokes a democratic ideal in identifying the association of global environmental management with a systematic loss of political influence at the sub-global level and the corresponding expansion of narrow interests. In such charges, Shiva finds identifying the global environmental problem as inimical to the interests of ecology and civic society, and presumably advantageous to corporations and nation states. If this is the case for climate change then it is testimony to the powers of these groups to turn a program that was initiated by environmentalists and civic society to protect ecological values to their advantage. Accounts of the rise of contemporary environmentalism record the early identification of global problems and the need for concerted international action, such as the 1971 UN Man and the Biosphere Program, the 1972 UN Conference on the Human Environment, and the seminal work of the Club of Rome. International environmental agreements followed these initial activities with increasing frequency, supported by a wide array of environmental groups.

Space does not permit exploration of the rationale of environmentalism in supporting global-scale environmental management, other than to identify some possible leads. Dobson (2000) identifies several relevant themes in his account of environmental political thought, notably, ecologism's belief in the universality of its ideology (i.e., an appeal to all social identities) and the green movement's engagement in liberal-democratic governance processes, which includes that conducted at the global scale. Perhaps also, environmentalists have simply frequently subscribed to modernist beliefs in the necessity of global environmental management as the 'natural' policy choice based on a belief in its effectiveness.

Political values in global climate management

Political ecology remains generally skeptical of the environmental claims made for globalization's benefits, specifically that global resource use and waste generation has accelerated under increased global trade; that increasing national wealth produces both environmental improvements and deterioration; environmental improvements generally result from NGO activity, democratic governance, research and scientific knowledge, and legal mechanisms, and from not general economic variables, such as increasing income; and actions to improve environmental conditions often occur at the expense of another environment. As revealed by emissions trading, the use of the global market has allowed corporations to profit and nations to lower the inventory of greenhouse gas emissions, without having to change actual emissions in any way. Global greenhouse gas management has involved full engagement with the global economy and has served corporate interest at the expense of environmental conditions and values. Political ecology finds that any system of global environmental management based in the global economy is placing environmental values into a direct competition with the profit orientation of the market. Since environmental protection is a function primarily vested in governance, integration with the global economy necessarily requires constant vigilance to ensure that corporate interests don't subvert the mechanisms of governance. Byrne and Yun (2000), for example, find that the liberal-democratic approaches to climate change through the FCCC process axiomatically pursue the goals of global markets, which logically must work against the interests of global environmental protection.

Defining climate change as a global management issue for nations and specific institutions immediately evokes a political construction marked by those legitimately authorized to manage the climate and those excluded. Empowered by this self-appointed responsibility for global climate management, this group defines the problem, controls the relevant knowledge processes required for management, develops suitable policy architecture, and carries out policy implementation. Part of this arrangement's rationale is presented as the rationality of responding to the characteristics of the global climate problem. Critics of the FCCC process and outcomes contest the deterministic character of defining climate change in this way, arguing that the cause of global environmental protection disguises the motivations of vested interests.

Yearly identifies global heterogeneity as one reason for questioning the world as being of universal character, considering the differentiation of the impacts of global environmental problems in different locales and the variation in socio-economic circumstances, "talk of global 'challenges' and calls for united global responses can be seen as misleading and tendentious" (1996: 79). In depicting climate change as a global issue, it is assumed that there is much commonality in responding to the issue, when clearly interests vary greatly between and within nation states. Calls for responding to such problems globally, writes Yearly (1996), can be taken as claims for the interests of select nations, as exemplified in the international climate change response.

If the FCCC reflects the interests of powerful nations and corporations, then the depiction of the role of environmental management will produce a system with a distribution of costs and benefits prejudicial to these interests. Shiva suggested that globalization of environmental issues follows this logic, so that those responsible for creating problems evade detection and the blame is transferred to communities "that have no global reach." Under the construct of global climate management by liberal-democratic interests, the developed world uses the concept to secure access to atmospheric resources and the economic benefits that accrue from fossil fuel combustion. Concomitant with this aspect of globalization is the strategy to ensure the costs of future climate change impacts are shared across the world's nations. Ross (1991: 14) explored the international climate change initiatives as an instance of global environmental management, built on scientific systems of knowledge "governed by the new corporate logic of planetary management," noting that: "While these developments are clear evidence of the political and economic impact of ecology at the highest levels of decision-making, there are reasons to be wary of a distributive systems with such an Olympian perspective."

A number of environmentalists have raised similar points more generally and with global warming specifically, typically concentrating on the management of global commons resources. For Ross (1991: 15), the "budgetary way of looking at the world ... is continuous with the scientific perspective of quantitatively dominating the physical world. Having demonstrated the human influence on the atmosphere, it follows that the system requires human management." Redclift (1995) notes that environmental management is suggestive of mastery of nature and control over the environmental consequences of human behavior. Complicit in such management is the protection of economic interests in the era of globalization (Ross 1991: 15):

> As the economic scope of capitalism enters into its truly global phase, it is clear that this logic of reckoning inputs against outputs is entirely complicit with its interests of the new global investors, a spectrum that runs from the small-time players on the futures market, so heavily determined by the effect of local meteorological fluctuations on food commodities, to the earth-movers and shakers at the World Bank, whose efforts to profitably shape the future of the multinational economy are equally dependent on regional climate stability.

Accordingly, the regulation of greenhouse gas emissions is also an opportunity "for regulating the physical world that did not exist hitherto." Making atmospheric management complicit and necessary for successful global capitalism, it follows that much management efforts are replete with the same problems produced by these economic relations. A basic contradiction of capitalism is evoked, in Ross's view, by seeking regulatory control to protect the atmosphere in order to meet the objective of allowing the climate system to revert to a self-regulating form. As Ross states (1991: 16):

> The crusade to keep the whole world "free" for liberal capitalism is currently in lockstep with the campaign to "free" the climate from human influence. History suggests to us that both definitions of "freedom" are shot through with the lowest form of irony.

Global climate management as 'scientism'

Although arising from intense political negotiations between nations, corporations, interest groups, and others expressing differing political values and positions, the business of global climate management is officially presented as a rational, technical matter guided by scientific knowledge. By characterizing climate change as a challenge to scientific knowledge and international cooperation, it is assumed that the usual barriers of 'irrationality,' such as vested national interests, market failures, and political scheming, block the rational path to global management. Such a view holds that the imperative of protecting the planet can only get under way when the FCCC process resolves these problems and impediments to rational planetary management. Political ecologists find in such technical rationality expressions of 'scientism' writ on a planetary scale.

Morgan et al. (1999) exemplify the critique of those concerned with the reduction of global climate management to a rational exercise of knowledge and expertise. They identify a systemic limitation in conventional policy analysis of global environmental change, including assumptions about the natural world that climate change impacts under consideration are manageable, are of modest uncertainty, and are amenable to management. Applying economic rationality in this system also requires a number of assumptions about the climate change problem that political ecology finds problematic, including that cslimate change impacts can be valued marginally (i.e., the assumption that the environmental system is linear), that these values can be identified and taken as static, and that conventional exponential discounting can capture future preferences (Morgan et al. 1999).

Climate management at the global scale determines the need for particular understandings of the natural and social world that render both amenable to social control, namely science, and particular forms of social organization, national cooperation, and international institutions to both produce scientific knowledge and the means for governance. In effect, critics of scientism find that in rendering the climate change problem in terms of increasing complexity, urgency, seriousness, and political divisiveness, because of its global character, the role of science, technology, and rational management increases in its appeal. Having secured technical rationality as indispensable for protecting the world's future from the dangers of climate change, the major challenges are technical problems. Political differences and interests are not lost in the cause of building a system of planetary management, but those dominant interests are effectively 'subsumed' into matters of rational management. IPCC oversight, for example, of the ways in political and economic entities encourage emissions is not accidental in the views of political ecology, but reflects how emissions reduction issues are made 'technical' and become useful for protecting those groups benefitting most from the existing emissions production.

Efforts to manage the atmosphere represent, for some political ecologists, the final frontier of managerialism. Ross (1991) is particularly concerned over Revelle and Seuss's (1957) depiction of global warming as a global experiment. However, the adoption of the metaphor of the experiment has also been used as an expression of concern that takes the form of a failed or misconceived trial. For example, the Toronto Conference Statement (WMO 1989): "Humanity is conducting an unintended, uncontrolled, globally pervasive experiment whose ultimate consequence could be second only to global nuclear war." Such an "experimental attitude," writes Ross (1991: 18), " ... especially when it takes the whole planet for its laboratory, becomes a form of constructive power that reshapes the world in a different image, detaching it from meaning and value, and delivering it up to the rationality of technical description and control." And the form of control that has been exerted has been expressed through the FCCC process that has empowered both national states and the global economy.

6 Conclusion
Climate change and ecological postmodernity

Modernity and ecologism

History suggests that the strength, legitimacy, social support, and rationale of social institutions are tested by crises, either generated from within or imposed from without. In contemporary times, environmentalism has emerged as a critique identifying the degradation of environmental values and the ecological systems that support life as a major social problem, giving voice to the 'environmental crisis.' Placed in this context, environmentalism's critique of various environmental crises besetting the modern world challenges modernity in several ways. Tested is modernity's ability to respond to losses of environmental values in order to fulfill its goal of ensuring social progress and, further, whether modernity can be maintained as the dominant means to understanding and organizing the social world and its relations with nature.

Within environmentalism is the more revolutionary body of thought, namely 'ecologism,' that offers potentially greater challenges to modernity through its defining interests in setting ecological limits on human activity, recognizing the intrinsic values of the environment, and addressing social alienation from nature. 'Ecological justice' is taken here as the ethical foundation of ecologism, as it seeks to extend the realm of justice from the conventional preoccupation with individuals and social phenomena so as to become an agency for reforming nature–society relations. Essential to this goal is ecological justice's recognition of the interests of future generations, ecological entities, and ecological processes and it offers a means to respond to the environmental losses resultant from developing and ever-expanding industrial society under capitalist economics. As modernity and industrial society are now effectively identical, the cause of ecological justice is fundamentally in contention with modernity. Climate change and the international and national policy responses have been subject to extensive research, investigation, and scrutiny and although many studies have assessed the international response to climate change and 'tested' the prevailing approach and its underlying assumptions, these inquiries and assessments are predominantly bounded within modernity. Climate change is conventionally evaluated from a variety of different political and interest perspectives that accept the tenets of modernity. A contrary view is that the climate change crisis and the international response challenge modernity.

Postmodernity and environmental thought

Through their initial periods of conceptual development, the philosophies of environmentalism and postmodernity neither acknowledged each other nor admitted to sharing mutual ground, and have usually been regarded as being irrelevant to each other. Even those aspects of environmentalism and postmodernity sharing a common rejection of modernity have had seemingly little in common, having arisen from widely divergent sources, been preoccupied with different concerns, issues, and conceptualizations, and following quite distinct trajectories. Environmentalists responding to postmodern writings have generally depicted its major contributions as irrelevant to the political imperatives of arresting the destructive passage of industrialism. Whilst from the other perspective, postmodern thought, as developed and promulgated in philosophy and cultural studies following and incorporating post-structuralism, largely ignored the ecological crisis; certainly, the seminal works of Baudrillard, Derrida, Foucault, and Lyotard are devoid of references to environmentalism.

Yet, there have been select postmodernists who examined the ecological crises and, following the general wave of postmodern interest in the social sciences, an array of environmental scholars embracing and exploring postmodernism and environmentalism. Researchers and scholars dealing with environmental issues in ecology, ethics, feminism, history, international relations, philosophy, politics, science studies, sociology, spirituality, and other fields have explored issues of modernity and postmodernity. Although it may seem a crude duality, environmental though can be divided according, not to its response to postmodernity, but as to its position on modernity. Either side of this cleavage are environmentalists working to modify modernity's assault on ecology through reform and those for whom environmental protection and routine industrial society are essentially incompatible. Environmental discourses grounded in modernity and pursuing reform agendas include sustainable development, market rationalism, and democratic rationalism, while radical political ecology, social ecology, environmental justice, animal liberation, eco-feminism, bioregionalism, and eco-theology are irreconcilable with key aspects of modernity.

An ecologically defined postmodernity

If postmodernity's broader relationship with environmentalism has been predominantly one of neglect and that postmodernity legitimates relativism, then its critics are correct in arguing that postmodernity must be inimical to ecological justice. In place of this argument is offered an understanding of modernity that takes nature–society relationships as essential, wherein postmodernity can then be understood and defined as an environmental condition and does not need to resort to relativism. Ecological justice is central to this view of nature–society relations and accordingly constructs an interpretation of postmodernity at odds with interpretations of postmodernity that present it as an endorsement of a 'hyper-modernity.'

Three linked arguments are offered for defining postmodernity in ecological terms. Firstly, following ecologism, culture cannot be defined independently of nature–society relations. Even those aspects of culture considered in purely social terms, such as language, art, or economics cannot be regarded as artifacts completely isolated from nature. Modernity has used scientific knowledge in positivism, evaluation of natural resources and services through capitalism, and other devices to manage nature for human ends based on the assumption that culture was separable from nature. Yet through this activity, few social restraints have been placed on exploitation of the natural world, with the inevitable consequence that numerous environmental crises have resulted, fostered by modernity's creed of unlimited economic growth, so that progress is being defined without reference to environmental consequences and other manifestations of the disregard of the ecological basis of society. Modernity's essential characteristics are therefore indivisible from its environmentally destructive tendencies. In this respect, ecologism is reflected in the approaches of human ecology in so far as modernity's efforts to alienate society from ecology are deemed to be misleading, harmful to society and nature, and ultimately false. Our understanding of the social condition necessarily refers, ultimately, to material conditions in ecology.

Furthermore, advances in technology have enabled the reach of human interest to extend into the processes by which natural values are created, so that in a metaphorical and actual sense modern society has sought not to harvest the seed, but to re-design its genetic code. Climate change, as described above, finds this interleaving of natural and human systems is such that the two influences cannot now be separated in terms of their climatic effects, and that future global climate will feature anthropogenic influences. Consequently, the modern formulation of nature separate from society has been rendered redundant by virtue of the failings of the abstract divisions that made the concept of autonomous nature feasible.

Secondly, and following on from above, is that modernity cannot reproduce nature. Not only is modernity's use of science, social organization, and environmental management based on, and designed to extend, a perception of a separate nature, but carries forward the notion that these social capacities can replace nature when needed or desired. Ecologism rejects modernity on this ground. Although some natural goods and services can be replicated by science, degraded ecological values repaired by social actions, and natural values stimulated by accident or social choice, this falls well short of being able to create the entities or processes of nature. Critical to modernity has been the role of substituting the artificial for the natural, such as the approach of conventional economics that substitutes present ecological losses for future social gains. In ecology, natural information is unique and contextural and cannot be replaced by artificial means, so that the losses of natural values through human activity based on modernity are permanent.

Thirdly, if society cannot be divorced from ecology and modernity is ecologically destructive, and that those ecological losses cannot be undone through the basic tenets of modernity (i.e., positive scientific knowledge, social organization through liberal democracies, and environmental management), then modernity's exclusive claims for always ensuring social progress seem to be without an ecological foundation. Whilst at the small scale the effects of modernity are often obscure, localized, or perhaps little different from the impacts of pre-modern cultures, claims for the loss of modernity's legitimacy on ecological grounds are seemingly exaggerated. At the scale of global environmental crisis, the effects of modernity are effectively maximized, representing the collective impacts of myriad small-scale issues, the loss or permanent diminution of resources or ecosystem services of global significance, and the environmental effects of modernity *intoto*. Modernity moves to respond to these crises, but they arise and persist at a greater rate than they can be addressed; the possibilities for progress continually recede into the future, whilst the impacts of past mistakes continue to be manifest in the present.

Of course, defining nature in the postmodern era creates some special problems. Evernden (1992) adroitly exposed the problems of defining the natural through ecology and using this knowledge as a referent for determining the extent of human influence in the natural realm and as a benchmark for environmental protection and restoration. Foremost of these problems is the construction of ecology itself for, as Evernden argued, legitimate competing theories of ecology can be used to justify nature as seeking harmony and balance as equally as for it being chaotic and competitive. Environmental protection on the grounds of maintaining natural conditions, and ecological restoration aimed at returning to these conditions, are therefore fraught with interpretive difficulties.

Climate change and the limits of modernity

Limits of positive science

Modernity holds positive scientific knowledge as the primary means for understanding the natural and social dimensions of climate change and constitutes the only reliable tool for their management. Social studies of science have, however, identified a number of limitations in the positivist view in environmental management and, further, there are a number of developing nations' critics dissatisfied with the way science has been developed and applied in climate change politics and policy. These criticisms have been directed widely and cover the methods, institutions, priorities, participants, and political and moral values of existing climate change science, especially as embodied and presented by the IPCC. Many of the issues raised by political economy are endorsed by political ecology. Modern climate change science may have its roots in the flowering of the scientific age and the plethora of competing theories and speculations, but its modern genesis effectively derives from the application of 'big science' in quest of military advantage in the Cold War. In this sense, climate change knowledge reflects these particular nation-state interests and, at one time at least, was developed to service those interests.

Contemporary climate change science has become an enormous enterprise and, without exaggeration, could be depicted as a major research industry involving, as it does, billions of U.S. dollars in expenditure, a great number of research institutions and tens of thousands of researchers. Political economy would hold that such an industry operates in accordance to the directions set by its sources of income (nation states and nation-state-funded international institutions) and its own interests. Science might protest that many of its participants are motivated by person ideals about knowledge and environmental protection, but political economy is typically scornful of sentiments that decry self-interest.

Constructivists and other critics endorse many aspects of political economy, finding that climate change science not to be neutral as the positivists espouse, but rather reflects particular political interests (notably those of the developed world, prestigious institutions, 'experts,' military objectives, and corporate goals). Critics of constructivism identify a wider and more fundamental set of limitations and problems with positivist science, including the primacy of scientific rationality. Central to the positive role ascribed to climate change science (via the IPCC) is that of the rational policy model, depicting science providing factual inputs for the formulation of policies by administrators and officials (operating under political guidance provided by the FCCC outputs and processes). Positivist linkages between policy-making and science are found to be more rhetorical and symbolic than actual, leading constructivist critics to conclude that the overwhelming amount of climate change science outputs have been irrelevant to policy formulation. Further, constructivists discount the existence of 'neutral facts,' and identify 'value-laden knowledge' as the outputs of science. Some supporters of the rational policy model have conceded the absence of a tight correspondence between science and policy, by maintaining that science informs policy 'heuristically,' to which constructivists have responded that this allows both that 'big science' is unnecessary and admits the essential role of political judgments by scientist and policy-maker alike.

Central to many criticisms of positive climate change science is the charge of 'scientism,' for which there are a number of empirical exemplars. Much of this debate centers of the IPCC's functions and activities, which has generally treated all dimensions of the climate change issue as matters of positive science. As a result, IPCC science has offered few insights into the social dimensions of climate change and these have been primarily through economic analysis, the conclusions of which have been laden with political and moral judgments inimical to the values of ecologism (such as the findings that it is not economically efficient to greatly reduce greenhouse gas emissions to protect climate-threatened environmental values). 'Official' science has neglected social issues, especially for poorer nations and communities, and locations and values likely to be harmed by climate change impacts. Nowhere is this charge of neglect more acute that in the relative lack of progress in impacts assessment and adaptation preparations under the current IPCC approach. Critics' charges, especially from developing nations, that the 'official' climate change science has neglected the pressing climate change information needs of poorer nations have credence. Claims that the endeavors of the 'big science' enterprise have been largely disinterested in the values associated with local communities, endangered and at-risk species and ecosystems, and the broader social and political impacts are readily validated.

Although largely undeveloped in legitimate science to date, but with the potential for future controversy, is the IPCC's monopoly over the science considered by the FCCC. On the surface, this charge is almost absurd given the scale and range of material embraced by the IPCC, so that few scientific developments can be said to have escaped its notice, for in this sense it is highly efficient, even-handed, and broad-ranging in its coverage of scientific findings. Yet the IPCC determines what constitutes 'legitimate' science, of which crucial aspects are disputed by civil society. For example, one avenue of criticism against the IPCC is directed at the hierarchy of knowledge the IPCC employs, with the dominance of the general circulation models, and speculation that a more varied, flexible, and dynamic model of research could be used to generate a knowledge base better suited to meeting the social needs for knowledge. Such a revised knowledge base could address the risks of future climate 'surprises' more satisfactorily, the results of which could create a case for greater urgency for action by the FCCC in reducing greenhouse gas emissions. Public controversy over climate change science, fed by fossil fuel corporations' revenue, has been a chimera that has attempted to erode the legitimacy of conventional climate change research while a more fundamental questioning over the priorities of conventional science has been largely unexplored.

Limits of liberal-democratic governance

Collectively, most of the criticism of the liberal-democratic governance conforms to political ecology, and thereby envelops many aspects of political economy. In general, political economy finds that the FCCC is essentially an instrument and process designed to meet the needs of nation states, corporations, and 'capitalism in general.' Political ecology identifies an additional set of limitations and problems with the FCCC-designed system of governance being put in place, especially those controversial aspects of its policy architecture featuring market-based policy instruments. By drawing attention to the sources of greenhouse gases, the wide variation in national per capita emissions from current emissions and from accumulated historical emissions has been made part of the official international discourse on climate change. With only eight nations responsible for over half current global greenhouse gas emissions and over 70 percent of Annex I emissions from four nations, the FCCC's depiction of greenhouse gas emissions as necessarily a 'global' problem has been questioned.

Although knowledge of climate change as a problem of the natural sciences has been rejected as 'scientism,' the use of economic studies to inform the policy positions of the developed world has been particularly contentious. Conservative economic studies by government agencies, international agencies, and research centers produced an array of findings attesting to the high economic costs of emissions abatement and to the low economic impacts of forecast warming. Armed thus, most developed nations' governments were able to act 'responsibly' in agreeing to weak emission reduction targets and formulating national strategies that usually extended policy reform no further than that already embodied in existing policy platforms, predominantly in the energy sector. Political ecologists rejected these economic studies in citing a plethora of value judgments and assumptions that ascribed minimal, if any, worth to the loss of ecological values, the effects on developing nations, or the burdens to be borne by future generations.

Under the FCCC and the Kyoto Protocol, only the developed nations are subject to agreed reductions in greenhouse gas emissions, effectively placing the future of the global climate in the control of the governments of these nation states. Essential to the global climate change management system being established is the set of policy instruments designed to fit the climate change response into the global economy. These 'Kyoto mechanisms' feature a means for the developed nations under the greenhouse gas emissions reduction requirements of the Protocol to trade their emissions in commodity form as credits and have further opportunities to develop credits by investing in approved projects in developing countries using the CDM. Political ecology rejects these mechanisms on ideological, ethical, and pragmatic grounds. While some critics find the FCCC's treatment of emissions as tradable commodities ethically abhorrent, others offer that the concessions to developed nations are excessive to the extent that the emission abatement targets are reduced to token levels. These latter issues express a skepticism over whether such a market will assist in reducing emissions, suggesting that it will be prone to inefficiency and corruption, become driven and directed by market interests, and create a policy regime where matters of process, rule-making, and enforcement take precedent over basic issues of reducing emissions as quickly as possible. Cited as evidence for some of these claims is the phenomenon of 'hot air,' whereby some nations can trade emission credits that accrue by virtue of historical circumstances unrelated to climate change policy, and yet count these as genuine emissions reduction and can be sold for substantial gains (i.e., hundreds of millions of U.S. dollars). Similarly, the CDM has been criticized, complaints including that its projects are those that would have occurred in the absence of the policy, so that no genuine emissions reductions occur.

Further evidence that the key policies of the Kyoto Protocol are contrary to the goals of climate protection is offered by the critiques of the Protocol's acceptance of carbon sequestration as an additional form of emissions credit for the Annex 1 group. Carbon sequestration by soils and ('natural') vegetation can be counted as emission 'offsets,' whereby a vulnerable and temporary component of the global carbon cycle is credited in an identical manner as a permanent reduction in anthropogenic greenhouse gas emissions. Although the use of carbon sinks as equivalents of emissions reduction, the measure effectively further reduces the need for developed nations to actually reduce emissions. A further point of concern with the Protocol's global carbon market is that an apparent disjuncture has emerged with the withdrawal of the U.S. from the treaty without any corresponding restrictions on that nation's participation in the global carbon trading market. Consequently, it is now possible for the carbon emissions trading scheme to operate fully and effectively, generate profits for trading firms, and not to contribute to any significant lowering of greenhouse gas emissions. Indeed, to date, there is no evidence that climate change policy at the national level has in fact led to reduced emissions in the developed world, as those few national emissions reductions that have occurred are the result of other factors and circumstances.

Other problems identified with the Protocol include the absence of a clear connection between the immediate emission reduction targets and the long-term goal of the FCCC, the absence of a methodology to determine individual national commitments, an unconvincing enforcement and compliance system, the apparent neglect of the impacts and adaptation aspects of climate change, and on-going uncertainties over the costs of compliance.

Limits of global climate management

Global climate management is the overall goal of the FCCC, ostensibly for the protection of human and natural interests. As such, the goal embodies and expresses both the role of science as a form of knowledge about the climate change problem and its solutions, and also the role of global governance by which the interests of nation states and the global economy can be brought together to organize an international response to climate change. By emphasizing the global dimension of the climate change problem, the international scale has become dominant and the definition of the global interest vested in the activities of the nation states involved in the FCCC, particularly those dominating the FCCC process and vested with greenhouse gas emission reduction responsibilities. Under the guise of 'global' interests, critics claim that the FCCC has been constituted so as to best serve those parties that most influenced its creation and design – developed nations operating under the guidance of liberal democracy and the aspirations set by a neo-liberal global economy. Consequently, the opportunities for contributions from civil society and lesser-developed nations are obviated, with the accompanying assertion that the democratic component of liberal democracy has been systematically neglected in the practices and the outputs of the FCCC.

A number of other issues also contest for attention in this theme, but one of great contention is that of greenhouse gas emission reduction targets and timetables. Presently, the current targets for developed nations under the Kyoto Protocol to be reached by the period 2008–2012 amount to a little over 5 percent below their 1990 collective output, from which must be subtracted the effect of the Kyoto mechanisms and sink allowances, which may be sufficient to soften the target to having to equal 1990 emissions. Such a meager official target suggests that the FCCC process is unlikely to generate a set of emission reduction targets that would greatly or quickly lower global emissions, given the manner of its operation and the political forces in play. Further, there is the absence of any clear long-term goal for greenhouse gas concentrations set by the FCCC. Given that the FCCC itself sets no quantifiable goal for atmospheric concentrations of greenhouse gases and the Kyoto Protocol is concerned with emission targets, there currently is no long- or short-term stabilization target. Under the Kyoto Protocol and the current global emission rates, the efforts to manage the future levels of greenhouse gases appear unlikely to be successful and there is considerable ambiguity as o how such success might be assessed.

Alternative pathways for responding to climate change

Although the preceding description and analysis has demonstrated the limits and limitations of modernity's response to climate change, alternative approaches that partly or wholly lie outside the boundaries of modernity are only partially developed at this time. It is possible to identify a number of features within the critiques and alternative approaches to climate change canvassed in preceding chapters as being possessed of the potential to escape or at least transcend the limitations of the contemporary international response. Modernity and its alternatives in ecological postmodernity can, therefore, be formed into contrasting types (such as shown in Table 6.1).

Beginning with the issue of knowledge formation, a 'discursive' science could overturn the monopoly of narrow interests dominating the existing system of scientific knowledge production, thereby allowing the entry of a

Table 6.1 Contrasting the characteristics of modernity and ecological postmodernity in the international response to climate change.

Modernity	Ecological Postmodernity
Positive science	Discursive science
Liberal-democratic governance	Ecological justice
Global environmental management	Commons/'Lifeworld'

greater variety of values and interests known to be at stake in climate change. Including communities, underdeveloped nations, and environmental NGOs in the scientific knowledge addresses the goal of better aligning representation within science with the composition of civil society. Determining how to reconcile state and corporate interests with those of civil society within such an approach to science remains uncertain.

Additional to the participants in science are the issues pertaining to the forms of knowledge produced, and a discursive science would evoke a 'loosening' of the current research priorities and approaches. Efforts to break the 'monopoly' of 'big science' involve questioning, if not always rejecting, its existing priorities, methods, approaches, and outputs. Such a task may well involve breaking free of the political forces that have shaped the science to date, and forging a greater response to recognized problems as established by the participants. Moving away from the general circulation model hierarchy under the present system, for example, means that greater attention can be given to such areas as low-carbon economy for industrial nations, alternative economic development pathways for developing nations, addressing the social transition uncertainties, protecting the most vulnerable communities and ecological values/entities.

In replacing liberal-democratic governance in the climate change response with ecological justice, there would be myriad changes. A critical issue is that of the extent to which the existing capitalist global economy would be compatible with an 'ecologically just' approach to climate change. To date, there has been relatively little consideration of these implications, although several contributions from political economy suggest that global environmental protection is incompatible with global capitalism. Under political ecology there have been a number of specific suggestions made for reform under the FCCC. For example, if governance is to reflect a more inclusive representation of social and environmental interests in climate change than currently exists under the FCCC, then a range of 'non-state' parties must be involved. Such a change would see the addition of environmental NGOs and other aspects of civil society. But governance would not necessarily become sympathetic to ecological justice, or respond effectively to its agenda, merely through changes to the membership of the governing bodies. As climate change governance occurs at the confluence of nation-state interests and economic globalization, finding a new course for action necessitates breaking free of these currents and this involves changes in the existing FCCC and Kyoto Protocol policy architecture.

An effective approach to governance will necessarily feature moving away from the climate change response as an international agreement that legitimates the expansion of liberal-democratic principles, provides a means of commodifying the global atmosphere, strengthens the nation states, and boosts the process of globalization which necessarily favors those states and corporations with greatest economic strengths. Global environmental governance appears essential to ensure international cooperation and coordination. Yet, hegemonic aspirations of the part of powerful states have to be taken into account, as the position taken by the U.S. in rejecting the Kyoto Protocol demonstrates the environmental damage that can be organized by powerful nation states acting independently. Clearly, an agreement of nation states must be effective and this effectiveness assessed by the extent of change in state behavior in meeting the goals of the agreement.

However, depicting the agreement for global governance that axiomatically is considered in terms of the nation state is limited. Automatic placement of nation states as the locus for all policy responses presumes that the sum of nation states represents 'global' interests. Alternative possibilities for organizing a global response have been considered and, especially in the context of the global economy, the international regulation of the firms most responsible for greenhouse gas emissions must be examined. Furthermore, non-state interests need to be brought into the governance system, especially those that represent environmental interests and disadvantaged groups. One modest but necessary means for moving towards this goal would be greater efforts to operate the FCCC in a manner that accords more closely to the principles of democratic governance, and to move away from the present model where the outcomes are largely determined by a few influential states.

Accordingly, the architecture of climate change policy must be disengaged from its involvement in global capital and economic globalization, by rejecting greenhouse gas emissions trading and accreditation schemes in particular and the commodification process of carbon in general. Changes to the policy architecture would find such current features as international emissions trading, international emission accreditation schemes, and various burden-sharing initiatives removed on the basis that their operation invariably leads towards market optimization and away from ecological justice. Alternative strategies could be adopted, with strategic priorities directed towards the world's largest polluting nations or, alternatively, against those corporations responsible for the bulk of the world's emissions.

In place of the FCCC goals for global environmental management are those of 'ecologically sustainable targets' that seek emissions reductions leading to stabilization of the atmospheric concentrations of greenhouse gases. Environmental advocates seeking to maximize protection of environmental values argue for stabilization levels at current concentrations or closer to those existing prior to the Industrial Revolution, which necessitates commitment to great social change during the coming centuries. Considering the atmosphere as a global atmospheric commons is an alternative policy approach that offers a means to equitably allocate the rights to greenhouse gas emissions between the world's peoples (within national boundaries) that can be combined with emissions reduction targets seeking rapid and substantial lowering in the 'per capita allocation' approach.

Under the FCCC, many aspects of overall nature–society relations are not only inimical to ecological justice, but also appear to embody ambiguity to the point of irrationality. One clear change to nature–society relations in climate change would be to set a clear and unequivocal target for climate change policy, which at the moment does not exist. Both long and short targets are needed for greenhouse gas reductions and these need not be inflexible, permanent, and universal, but could indicate to the global community exactly what is being required. Preparations for adaptation to the inevitable climate change impacts could be advanced far more than the minimal state of current policy and planning, given that climate change is inevitable. Indeed, the protection of the values identified under ecological justice demands that such measures take place.

Coda: ecological postmodernity

Reviews of the work of selected environmental theorists found that changes in nature–society relations can be used to define the emergence of the postmodern condition, although interpretations differ widely as to why this is so, what it means, and what this condition portends. Climate change is a crisis not only of contemporary times but of one of indefinite reach whose social and ecological losses now cannot be averted, but at best only mollified. Changes in the global climate and the potential for permanent and profound changes to social and ecological values as a consequence of human activity mark a division in the history of human relationship with nature. Compelled to respond, a community of nations has sought to bring the causes of the problem under control and to prepare for the inevitable effects into a system of global management. This international climate change regime, as it is often labeled, has come to embody the ideals and practices of modernity. Climate change thus tests modernity in ways and at a scale that appears without precedent in the environmental realm.

Presented before the communities of the world is a struggle not between corporations and civil society, nor between the developed and developing world, nor even between the protection and despoilation of nature, but all these struggles embodied in a larger contest, that of between modernity and its potential ecological successor. In the international efforts to address climate change, nature–society relations have arrived at a social condition wherein a key aspect of industrial society, namely its nature–society relations, produces a paradox and a crisis whose resolution lies beyond or outside modernity. Climate change has placed the global community in a contra-diction because the crisis demands a response that will feature contributions of scientific knowledge, international governance, and global environmental management, yet these features of modernity that define the FCCC have manifestly failed. Defining a postmodern condition does not, therefore, imply abandoning modernity entirely, but living in a paradoxical relation-ship between retaining aspects of modernity and moving beyond their restraints. It follows that these essential institutions of modernity need to be recast in ways consistent with the philosophy of ecologism that necessarily entails moving beyond modernity.

Postmodernity, whatever other meanings it evokes or represents, can be used to describe a more fundamental shift in the trajectory of human affairs, namely the demise of the ability to know, govern, and manage the global environment according to the dictates of modernity – hence the expression of 'ecological postmodernity.' It may be that 'postmodern' is now too laden with other meanings and attendant controversies to also carry this environmental definition of social conditions without confusion and that some new term is needed to denote this era.

Climate change expresses the unintended consequences of the modern project in which there is nothing natural left in the global atmosphere; humanity lives in and breathes an atmosphere that's an artifice of industrial activity and, consequently, the global climate is also now beyond nature. Humanity has obviously not created the atmosphere, but has indelibly made its future part of our future, so that in a systemic fashion we cannot return this global ecological system to the conditions prior to the Industrial Revolution. In this manner, humanity has gone beyond local and regional landscape change or its effects on individual species and communities to cul-minate in global ecological process changes. Essentially, the response to the dilemma of the social and environmental costs for which society is respon-sible has been to direct the same project that created the problem to its redress. Yet the repairs being attempted through ecological modernization are not working and cannot be made to work. In seeking to control the global climate it is clear that society is past the boundary of what modernity can achieve – there is a postmodern nature in which postmodern society now lives. Postmodernity is an ecological condition wherein modernity has become bankrupt as a sole form of knowledge, social organization, and society–nature relations. As we now live under a postmodern sky and in a postmodern climate, we must put down the modern tools of global envir-onmental management and search for more appropriate instruments for understanding, organizing, and considering our social relations with nature.

References

Agarwal, A. and Narain, S. (1991) *Global Warming in an Unequal World: A Case of Environmental Colonialism*, New Delhi: Centre for Science and Environment.

Agarwal, A., Narain, S. and Sharma, A. (2002) 'The global commons and environmental justice – climate change,' in J. Byrne, L. Glover and C. Martinez (eds.) *Environmental Justice: Discourses in International Political Economy*, New Brunswick, NJ and London: Transaction Books.

——(eds.) (1999) 'Boiling point: The United Nations Framework Convention on Climate Change/Kyoto Protocol,' Chapter 1 in *Green Politics: Global Environmental Negotiations*, New Delhi: Centre for Science and Environment.

Agrawala, S. (1999) 'Early science–policy interactions in climate change: Lessons from the Advisory Group on Greenhouse Gases,' *Global Environmental Change*, 39, 2: 157–169.

——(1998a) 'Context and early origins of the Intergovernmental Panel on Climate Change,' *Climatic Change*, 39, 4: 605–620.

——(1998b) 'Structural and process history of the Intergovernmental Panel on Climate Change,' *Climatic Change*, 39, 4: 621–642.

Agrawala, S. and Anderson, S. (1999) 'Indespensibility and indefensibility? The United States in the climate treaty negotiations,' *Global Governance*, 5: 457–482.

Aldhous, P. (2005) 'China's burning ambition,' *Nature*, 435, 30 June: 1152–1154.

Almond, B. (1995) 'Rights and justice in the environment debate,' in D.E. Cooper and J.A. Palmer (eds.) *Just Environments: Intergenerational, International and Interspecies Issues*, London and New York: Routledge.

Anderson, P. (1998) *The Origins of Postmodernity*, London and New York: Verso.

Anderson, T.L. and Leal, D.R. (1991) *Free Market Environmentalism*, Boulder, CO: Westview.

Andreae, M.O., Jones, C.D. and Cox, P.M. (2005) 'Strong present-day aerosol cooling implies a hot future,' *Nature*, 435, 30 June: 1187–1190.

Arrhenius, S. (1908) *Worlds in the Making: The Evolution of the Universe*, New York: Harpers.

——(1896) 'On the influence of carbonic acid in the air on the temperature of the ground,' *The London, Edinburgh, and Dublin Philosophical Magazine and Journal of Science*, 41, 251: 236–276.

Arrow, K., Bolin, B., Costanza, R., Dasgupta, P., Folke, C., Holling, C.S., Jansson, B.-O., Levin, S., Maler, K.-G., Perrings, C. and Pimental, D. (1995) 'Economic growth, carrying capacity, and the environment,' *Ecological Economics*, 15, 2: 91–95.

Ashman, K.M. and Baringer, P.S. (eds.) (2001) *After the Science Wars*, London and New York: Routledge.

Atkinson, A. (1991) *Principles of Political Ecology*, London: Belhaven Press.

Ausbel, J.H. (1983) Annex 2: Historical note, in National Research Council, *Changing Climate: Report of the Carbon Dioxide Assessment Committee*, Washington, DC: National Academy Press.

Ayres, R.U. (1995) 'Economic growth: Politically necessary but *not* environmentally friendly,' *Ecological Economics*, 15, 2: 97–99.

Azar, C. (2000) 'Economics and distribution in the greenhouse,' *Climatic Change*, 47, 3: 233–238.

Azar, C. and Schneider, S.H. (2002) 'Are the costs of stabilizing the atmosphere prohibitive?,' *Ecological Economics*, 42, 1–2: 73–80.

Azar, C. and Sterner, T. (1996) 'Discounting and distributional considerations in the context of global warming,' *Ecological Economics*, 19, 2: 169–185.

Bailie, A., Bernow, S., Castelli, B., O'Connor, P. and Romm, J. (2003) *A Path to Carbon-Dioxide-Free Power: Switching to Clean Energy in the Utility Sector*, Tellus Institute and The Center for Energy and Climate Solutions.

Balling, R. (1992) *The Heated Debate: Greenhouse Predictions versus Climate Reality*, San Francisco, CA: Pacific Research Institute for Public Policy.

Barber, J.P. and Dickson, A.K. (1995) 'Justice and order in international relations: The global environment,' in D.E. Cooper and J.A. Palmer (eds.) *Just Environments: Intergenerational, International, and Interspecies Issues*, London and New York: Routledge.

Barker, T. and Ekins, P. (2001) *How High are the Costs of Kyoto for the US Economy?*, Tyndall Centre for Climate Change Research, Working Paper 4.

Barkin, J.S. (2003) 'The counterintuitive relationship between globalization and climate change,' *Global Environmental Politics*, 3, 3: 8–13.

Barnes, P. (2001) *Who Owns the Sky? Our Common Assets and the Future of Capitalism*, Washington, DC, Covelo, CA, and London: Island Press.

Barnett, J. (2003) 'Security and climate change,' *Global Environmental Change*, 13, 1: 7–17.

——(2001) *The Meaning of Environmental Security: Environmental Politics and Policy in the New Security Era*, London: Zed Books.

——(2000) 'Destabilizing the environment–conflict thesis,' *Review of International Studies*, 26, 2: 271–288.

Barnett, T.P., Pierce, D.W. and Schnur, R. (2001) 'Detection of anthropogenic climate change in the world's oceans,' *Science*, 292, 13 April: 270–274.

Baudrillard, J. (1996) *The System of Objects*, London and New York: Verso.

——(1990) *Cool Memories*, London and New York: Verso.

——(1981a) [1973] *For a Critique of the Political Economy of the Sign*, trans. C. Levin, New York: Telos Press.

——(1981b) *Simulations*, trans. P. Foss, P. Patton, and P. Beitchman, New York: Semitext(e).

——(1975) *The Mirror of Production*, trans. M. Poster, St. Louis: Telos Press.

Bauman, Z. (1991) *Modernity and Ambivalence*, Cambridge, UK: Polity Press.

Baumert, K. (ed.) (2002) *Building on the Kyoto Protocol: Options for Protecting the Climate*, Washington, D.C.: World Resources Institute.

Baxter, B. (1999) *Ecologism: An Introduction*, Washington, DC: Georgetown University Press.

Beck, U. (1999) *World Risk Society.* Cambridge, UK: Polity Press.

——(1997) 'Global risk politics,' in M. Jacobs (ed.) *Greening the Millennium? The New Politics of the Environment*, Oxford, UK and Malden, MA: Blackwell.

——(1995) *Ecological Politics in an Age of Risk*, Cambridge, UK: Polity.

——(1992) *Risk Society: Towards a New Modernity*, London: Sage.

Beck, U., Giddens, A. and Lash, S. (eds.) (1994) *Reflexive Modernization: Politics, Tradition and Aesthetics in the Modern Social Order*, Cambridge, UK: Polity.

Beder, S. (1997) *Global Spin: The Corporate Assault on Environmentalism*, Dartington: Green Books.

Begg, K.G. (2002) 'Implementing the Kyoto protocol on climate change: Environmental integrity, sinks and mechanisms,' *Global Environmental Change*, 12, 4: 331–336.

Bello, W. (1992) *People and Power in the Pacific: The Struggle for the Post-Cold War Order*, San Francisco, CA: Food First Books.

Bello, W. and Rosenfeld, S. (1990) *Dragons in Distress: Asia's Economic Miracle in Crisis*, San Francisco, CA: Food First Books.

Benedict, R. (2001) 'Striking a new deal on climate change,' *Issues in Science and Technology*, Fall: 71–76.

Benko, G. and Strohmayer, U. (eds.) (1997) *Space and Social Theory: Interpreting Modernity and Postmodernity*, Oxford, UK: Blackwell.

Bennett, J. and Chaloupka, W. (eds.) (1993) *In the Nature of Things: Language, Politics and the Environment*, London: University of Minnesota Press.

Benton, T. (ed.) (1996) *The Greening of Marxism*, New York: Guildford.

Benton, T. and Redclift, M. (1994) 'Introduction,' in M. Redclift and T. Benton (eds.) *Social Theory and the Global Environment*, London and New York: Routledge.

Berger, P.L. (1977) *Facing Up to Modernity: Excursions in Society, Politics, and Religion*, New York: Basic Books.

Berger, P.L., Berger, B. and Kellner, H. (1974) *The Homeless Mind: Modernization and Consciousness*, Harmondsworth, UK: Penguin Books.

Berger, P.L. and Luckman, T. (1966) *The Social Construction of Reality: A Treatise in the Sociology of Knowledge*, New York: Doubleday.

Bertens, H. (1995) *An Idea of the Postmodern: A History*, London and New York: Routledge.

Best, S. and Kellner, D. (2001) *The Postmodern Adventure: Science, Technology, and Cultural Studies at the Third Millennium*, New York and London: Guildford Press.

——(1997) *The Postmodern Turn*, New York and London: Guildford Press.

——(1991) *Postmodern Theory: Critical Interrogations*, New York: Guildford Press.

Blanchard, O. and Perkaus, J.F. (2004) 'Does the Bush administration's climate policy mean climate protection?,' *Energy Policy*, 32, 18: 1993–1998.

Blühdorn, I. (2000) 'Ecological modernization and post-ecological politics,' in G. Spaargaren, A.P.J. Mol, and F.H. Buttel (eds.) *Environment and Global Modernity*, London, Thousand Oaks, CA, and New Delhi: Sage.

Bodansky, D. (2001) 'The history of the global climate change regime,' in U. Luterbacher and D.F. Sprinz (eds.) *International Relations and Global Climate Change*, Cambridge, MA and London: MIT Press.

——(1994) 'Prologue to the Climate Change Convention,' in I.M. Mintzer and J.A. Leonard (eds.) *Negotiating Climate Change: The Inside Story of the Rio Convention*, Cambridge, UK and New York: Cambridge University Press.

Boehmer-Christiansen, S. (2000) 'Differentiation since Kyoto: An exploration of Australian climate policy in comparison to Europe/UK,' *Energy and Environment*, 11, 3: 343–354.

——(1997) 'A winning coalition of advocacy: Climate research, bureaucracy and 'alternative' fuels,' *Energy Policy*, 25, 4: 439–444.

——(1994a) 'Global climate protection policy: The limits of scientific advice – Part 1,' *Global Environmental Change*, 4, 2: 140–159.

——(1994b) 'Global climate protection policy: The limits of scientific advice – Part 2,' *Global Environmental Change*, 4, 2: 185–200.

——(1993) 'Science policy, the IPCC and the climate convention: The codification of a global research agenda,' *Energy and Environment*, 4, 4: 362–407.

Boland, J. (1994) 'Ecological modernization,' *Capitalism, Socialism, Nature*, 5, 3: 135–141.

Bollen, J.C., Gielen, A. and Timmer, H. (1999) 'Clubs, ceilings and CDM: Macroeconomics of compliance with the Kyoto Protocol,' *Energy Journal*, Special Issue: The Costs of the Kyoto Protocol: A Multi–model Evaluation: 177–206.

Bolin, B. (1998) 'The Kyoto negotiations on climate change: A science perspective,' *Science*, 279, January 16: 330–331.

——(1994) 'Science and policy making,' *Ambio*, 23, 1: 25–29.

Bolin, B., Döös, B., Jäger, J. and Warrick, R.A. (1986) *The Greenhouse Effect, Climate Change, and Ecosystems*, Chichester, UK: John Wiley and Sons.

Bolin, B. and Kheshgi, H.S. (2001) 'On strategies for reducing greenhouse gas emissions,' *Proceedings of the National Academy of Science*, 98, 9: 4850–4854.

Bookchin, M. (1995) *The Philosophy of Social Ecology: Essays on Dialectical Naturalism*, Montreal, New York, and London: Black Rose Books.

——(1986) *The Modern Crisis*, Philadelphia, PA: New Society Publishers.

——(1971) *Post-Scarcity Anarchism*, London: Wildwood House.

Borgmann, A. (1999) *Holding on to Reality: The Nature of Information at the Turn of the Millennium*, Chicago, IL: University of Chicago Press.

——(1995) 'The nature of reality and the reality of nature,' in M.E. Soule and G. Lease (eds.) *Reinventing Nature? Responses to Postmodern Deconstruction*, Washington, DC and Covello, CA: Island Press.

——(1992) *Crossing the Postmodern Divide*, Chicago, IL: University of Chicago Press.

Bouton, K.A. (1999) *The Political Economy of Acceptable Risk: The Case of Global Warming*, unpublished Ph.D. thesis, School of Urban Affairs and Public Policy, University of Delaware.

Boykoff, M.T. and Boykoff, J.M. (2004) 'Balance as bias: Global warming and the US prestige press,' *Global Environmental Politics*, 14: 125–136.

Braun, B. and Castle, N. (eds.) (1988) *Remaking Reality: Nature at the Millennium*, London and New York: Routledge.

Bray, D. and von Storch, H. (1999) 'Climate science: An empirical example of postnormal science,' *Bulletin of the American Meteorological Society*, 80, 3: 439–455.

Brenton, T. (1994) *The Greening of Machiavelli: The Evolution of the International Environmental Politics*, London: Earthscan.

Briggs, A. (1959) *The Age of Improvement 1783-1867*, London: Longman.

Broecker, W.S. (1987) 'Unpleasant surprises in the greenhouse?,' *Nature*, 328, 9 July: 123–126.

——(1997) 'Thermohaline circulation, the Achilles heel of our climate system: Will man-made CO_2 upset the current balance?,' *Science*, 278, 28 November: 1582–1588.

Broecker, W.S., Peteet, Dorothy M. and Rind, D. (1985) 'Does the ocean-atmosphere system have more than one stable mode of operation?,' *Nature*, 315, 2 May: 21–25.

Brown, D.A. (2002) *American Heat: Ethical Problems with the United States' Response to Global Warming*, Lanham, MD: Rowman and Littlefield.

Brunner, R.D. (1996) 'Policy and global change research: A modest proposal,' *Climatic Change*, 32: 121–147.

Brunner, R.D. and Klein, R. (1999) 'Harvesting experience: A reappraisal of the U.S. Climate Change Action Plan,' *Policy Sciences*, 32, 2: 133–161.

Bruno, K., Karlinger, J. and Brotsky, C. (1999) *Greenhouse Gangsters vs. Climate Justice*, San Francisco, CA: Transnational Resource and Action Center.

Bryson, R. and Murray, T.J. (1977) *Climates of Hunger: Mankind and the World's Changing Weather*, Madison, WI: University of Wisconsin Press.

Bugnion, V. and Reiner, D.M. (1999) *A Game of Climate Chicken: Can EPA Regulate Greenhouse Gases Before the U.S. Senate Ratifies the Kyoto Protocol?*, MIT Joint Program on the Science and Policy of Global Change, Report no. 57.

Burton, B. and Rampton, S. (2002) 'Thinking globally, acting vocally: The international conspiracy to overheat the earth,' *PR Watch.org*, Volume 4, 4. Available at: http://www.prwatch.org/prwissues/1997Q4/warming.html. Accessed 23 April 2002.

Bush, President G.W. (2001a) 'Text of a letter from the President to Senators Hagel, Helms, Craig, and Roberts,' *Press Release*, The White House, March 13.

——(2001b) 'Remarks by the President on climate change,' *Press Release*, The White House, Office of the Press Secretary, June 11.

Bush, V. (1945) *Science, the Endless Frontier*, Washington, DC: US Government Printing Office.

Byrne, J. (1997) *Equity and Sustainability in the Greenhouse: Reclaiming our Atmospheric Commons*, Pune, India: Parisar.

Byrne, J. and Glover, L. (2000) *Climate Shopping: Putting the Atmosphere up for Sale*, TELA Series No. 5, Melbourne, Australia: Australian Conservation Foundation.

Byrne, J., Hadjilambrinos, C. and Wagle, S. (1993) 'Distributing costs of global climate change,' *IEEE Technology and Society*, 13, 1: 17–24.

Byrne, J., Martinez, C. and Glover, L. (2002) 'A brief on environmental justice,' in J. Byrne, L. Glover and C. Martinez (eds.) *Environmental Justice: Discourses in International Political Economy*, New Brunswick, NJ and London: Transaction Books.

Byrne, J. and Rich, D. (1992) 'Toward a political economy of global change: Energy, environment and development in the greenhouse,' in J. Byrne and D. Rich (eds.) *Energy and Environment: The Policy Challenge*, New Brunswick, NJ: Transaction Publishers.

Byrne, J., Wang, Y.-D., Lee, H. and Kim, J.-D. (1998) 'An equity- and sustainability-based policy response to global climate change,' *Energy Policy*, 26, 4: 335–343.

Byrne, J. and Yun, S.-J. (2000) 'Efficient global warming: Contradictions in liberal democratic responses to global environmental problems,' *Bulletin of Science, Technology and Society*, 19, 6: 493–500.

Cahoone, L. (1996) 'Introduction,' in L. Cahoone (ed.) *From Modernism to Postmodernism: An Anthology*, Malden, MA: Blackwell.

260   References

Cain, M.L. (1983) 'Carbon dioxide and the climate: Monitoring and a search for understanding,' in D.A. Kay and H.K. Jacobson (eds.) *Environmental Protection: The International Dimension*, Totowa, NJ: Allanhead, Osmun and Co.

Calder, N. (1974) *The Weather Machine*, New York: Viking.

Callicott, J.B. (1999) *Beyond the Land Ethic: More Essays in Environmental Philosophy*, Albany, NY: State University Press of New York.

——(1994) *Earth's Insights: A Survey of Ecological Ethics from the Mediterranean Basin to the Australian Outback*, Berkeley, CA, Los Angeles, CA, and London: University of California Press.

Cantrill, J.G. and C.L. Oravec (eds.) (1996) *The Symbolic Earth: Discourse and the Creation of Our Environment*, Lexington, KT: The University Press of Kentucky.

Carpenter, C. (2001) 'Business, green groups, and the media: The role of NGOs in the climate change debate,' *International Affairs*, 77, 2: 313–328.

Carson, R. (1962) *Silent Spring*, Boston, MA: Houghton Mifflin.

Castree, N. and Braun, B. (eds.) (2001) *Social Nature: Theory, Practice, and Politics*, Malden, MA and Oxford, UK: Blackwell.

Cerney, P.G. (1999) 'Globalization and the erosion of democracy,' *European Journal of Political Research*, 36, 1: 1–26.

Chapman, D. and Khanna, N. (2000) 'Crying wolf: Why economists don't worry about climate change, and should,' *Climatic Change*, 47, 3: 225–232.

Cheney, J. (1989a) 'Postmodern environmental ethics: Ethics as a bioregional narrative,' *Environmental Ethics*, 11, 2: 117–134.

——(1989b) 'The neo-stoicism of radical environmentalism,' *Environmental Ethics*, 11, 4: 293–325.

Christianson, G.E. (1999) *Greenhouse: The 200-Year Story of Global Warming*, Harmondsworth, England: Penguin.

Christoff, P. (1996) 'Ecological citizens and ecologically guided democracy,' in B. Doherty and M. de Geus (eds.) *Democracy and Green Political Thought: Sustainability, Rights and Citizenship*, London and New York: Routledge.

Churchill, R. and Freestone, D. (eds.) (1991) 'Appendice 24: Noordwijk Declaration on Atmospheric Pollution and Climate Change, adopted at the Ministerial Conference on Atmospheric Pollution and Climate Change, Noordwijk, Netherlands, 5–7 November 1989,' in *International Law and Global Climate Change*, London, Dordrecht, and Boston: Graham and Trotman and Martinus Nijhoff.

Claussen, E. and McNeilly, L. (1998) *Equity and Global Climate Change: The Complex Elements of Global Fairness*, Washington, DC: Pew Center on Global Climate Change.

Climate Change Science Program (CCSP) (2003) *The U.S. Climate Change Science Program: Vision for the Program and Highlights of the Scientific Strategic Plan*, report by the Climate Change Science Program and the Subcommittee on Global Change Research. Washington, DC: U.S. Climate Change Science Program.

Cogan, D.G. (2003) *Corporate Governance and Climate Change: Making the Connection*, A CERES Sustainable Governance Project Report, Washington, DC: CERES and Investor Responsibility Research Center.

Cohen, S., Demeritt, D., Robinson, J. and Rothman, D. (1998) 'Climate change and sustainable development: Towards dialogue,' *Global Environmental Change*, 8, 4: 341–371.

Common, M. (1995) *Sustainability and Policy: Limits to Economics*, Cambridge: Cambridge University Press.

Commoncause (2002) *Chart I: Total PAC and Soft Money Contributions from Members of the Global Climate Coalition.* Available at: www.commoncause.org/publications/hot/chart1.html. Accessed 23 April 2002.

Commoner, B. (1966) *Science and Survival*, New York: Viking Press.

Condorcet, A.-N. de (1795) [1955] *Sketch for a Historical Picture of the Progress of the Human Mind*, trans. J. Barraclough, New York: Noonday Press.

Conley, V.A. (1997) *Ecopolitics: The Environment and Poststructuralist Thought*, London and New York: Routledge.

Cortner, H.J. (2000) 'Making science relevant to environmental policy,' *Environmental Science and Policy*, 3, 1: 21–30.

Croll, J. (1875) *Climate and Time in their Geological Relations: A Theory of Secular Changes of the Earth's Climate*, New York: D. Appleton.

Cronon, W. (1994) 'Cutting loose or running aground?' *Journal of Historical Geography*, 20, 1: 38–43.

Crutzen P.J. and Stoemer, E.F. (2000) 'The "Anthropocene", ' *Global Change Newsletter*, 41 (May): 17–18.

Dahl, R.A. (1999) 'The shifting boundaries of democratic governments,' *Social Research*, 66, 3: 915–931.

——(1998) *On Democracy*, New Haven, CT: Yale University Press.

Dalby, S. (2002) *Environmental Security*, Minneapolis, MN: University of Minnesota Press.

Daly, H.E. (1996) *Beyond Growth: The Economics of Sustainable Development*, Boston, MA: Beacon Press.

Dansgaard, W., White, J.W.C. and Johnsen, S.J. (1989) 'The abrupt termination of the Younger Dryas event,' *Nature*, 339, 15 June: 532–533.

Darwin, C. (1859) *On the Origin of the Species by Means of Natural Selection, or the Preservation of Favoured Races in the Struggle for Life*, London: John Murray.

Deleuze, G. and Guattari, F. (1988) *A Thousand Plateaus: Capitalism and Schizophrenia*, trans H. Massumi, Minneapolis, MN: University of Minnesota Press.

Demeritt, D. (2001) 'The construction of global warming and the politics of science,' *Annals of the Association of American Geographers*, 91, 2: 307–337.

——(2000) 'The new social contract for science: Accountability, relevance, and value in USA and UK science and research policy,' *Antipode*, 32, 3: 308–329.

——(1994) 'Ecology, objectivity and critique in writings on nature and human societies,' *Journal of Historical Geography*, 20, 1: 22–37.

Demeritt, D. and Rothman, D. (1999) 'Figuring the costs of climate change: An assessment and critique,' *Environment and Planning A*, 31, 3: 389–408

Department of Energy, United States (DOE) (1997) *Scenarios of US Carbon Reductions: Potential Impacts of Energy Technologies by 2010 and Beyond*, Washington, DC.

de Bruyn, S.M., van den Bergh, J.C.J.M. and Obschoor, J.B. (1998) 'Economic growth and emissions: Reconsidering the empirical basis of environmental Kuznets curves,' *Ecological Economics*, 25, 2: 161–175.

de Moor, A.P.G., Berk, M.M., den Elzen, M.G.J. and van Vuuren, P.D. (2002) *Evaluating the Bush Climate Change Initiative*, RIVM report 728001019/2002.

Derrida, J. (1976) *On Grammatology*, trans. G. Spivak, Baltimore, MD: Johns Hopkins University Press.

Dessai, S., Adger, W.N., Hulme, M., Turnpenny, J., Köhler, J. and Warren, R. (2004) 'Defining and experiencing dangerous climate,' *Climatic Change*, 64, 1–2: 11–25.

Dobson, A. (2000) *Green Political Thought*, 3rd edn, London and New York: Routledge.

——(1996) 'Democratising green theory: Preconditions and principles,' in B. Doherty and M. de Geus (eds.) *Democracy and Green Political Thought: Sustainability, Rights and Citizenship*, London and New York: Routledge.

Doherty, B. and de Geus, M. (1996) 'Introduction,' in B. Doherty and M. de Geus (eds.) *Democracy and Green Political Thought: Sustainability, Rights and Citizenship*, London and New York: Routledge.

Down to Earth (2002) 'From the barrel of oil,' October 31.

Dryzek, J.S. (1997) *The Politics of the Earth: Environmental Discourses*, Oxford, UK: Oxford University Press.

——(1987) *Rational Ecology: Environment and Political Economy*, Oxford, UK: Basil Blackwell.

Durkheim, E. (1984) *The Division of Labor in Society*, trans. W.D. Halls, New York: The Free Press.

——(1950) *The Rules of Sociological Method*, New York: The Free Press.

Eckersley, R. (1992) *Environmentalism and Social Theory: Towards an Ecocentric Approach*, London: UCL Press.

Edwards, P.N. (1996) 'Global comprehensive models in politics and policymaking,' *Climatic Change*, 32, 2: 149–161.

Edwards, P.N. and Schneider, S.H. (2001) 'Self-governance and peer review in science-for-policy: The case of the IPCC Second Assessment Report,' in C.A. Miller and P.N. Edwards (eds.) *Changing the Atmosphere: Expert Knowledge and Global Environmental Governance*, Cambridge, MA: MIT Press.

Egenhofer, C. and Cornillie, J. (2001) *Reinventing the Climate Negotiations: An Analysis of COP6*, CEPS Policy Brief Number 1, Brussels: Centre for European Policy Studies.

Ehrlich, E.M. and Brunello, A.J. (2001) 'The new economy: Implications for climate change policy,' in E. Claussen (ed.) *Climate Change: Science, Strategies, and Solutions*, Leiden, Boston, and Köln: Brill.

Ehrlich, P.R. (1989) 'The limits to substitution: Meta-resource depletion and a new economic-ecological paradigm,' *Ecological Economics*, 1, 1: 9–16.

Energy Information Agency (EIA) (1998) *Impacts of the Kyoto Protocol on the U.S. Energy Markets and Economic Activity*, SR/OIAF/98–03, Washington, DC.

Ellul, J. (1964) *The Technological Society*, New York: Vintage Books.

Elzinga, A. (1997) 'From Arhenius to megascience: Interplay between science and public decision making,' *Ambio*, 26, 1: 72–80.

Escobar, A. (1999) 'After nature: Steps to an autoessentialist political ecology,' *Current Anthropology*, 40, 1: 1–30.

——(1996) 'Construction nature: Elements for a post-structuralist political ecology,' *Futures*, 28, 4: 325–343.

——(1995) *Encountering Development: The Making and the Unmaking of the Third World*, Princeton, NJ: Princeton University Press.

Esty, D.C. (1994) *Greening the GATT: Trade, Environment, and the Future*, Washington, DC: Institute for International Economics.

Esty, D.C. and Mendelsohn, R. (1998) 'Moving from national to international environmental policy,' *Policy Sciences*, 31, 3: 225–235.

European Union, The. Environment Council (1998) *Press Release. Community Strategy on Climate Change – Council Conclusion, Appendix 1*, 16 June, Luxembourg.

Evernden, N. (1992) *The Social Creation of Nature*, Baltimore and London: The Johns Hopkins University Press.

Fern (2000) *Sinking the Kyoto Protocol: The Links Between Forests, Plantations and Caron Sinks*, Moreton-on-Marsh, UK: Fern.

Fleming, J.R. (1998) *Historical Perspectives on Climate Change*, New York and Oxford, UK: Oxford University Press.

Foucault, M. (1978) *The History of Sexuality*, New York: Pantheon Books.

——(1977) *Discipline and Punish: The Birth of the Prison*, New York: Pantheon Books.

——(1973a) *The Birth of the Clinic: An Archaeology of Medical Perception*, New York: Pantheon Books.

——(1973b) [1965] *Madness and Civilization: A History of Insanity in the Age of Reason*, New York: Vintage Books.

Freestone, D. (1991) 'The precautionary principle,' in R. Churchill and D. Freestone (eds.) *International Law and Climate Change*, London, Dordrecht, and Boston: Graham and Trotman and Martinus Nijhoff.

Fukuyama, F. (1992) *The End of History and the Last Man*, New York: The Free Press.

Funtowitcz, S.O. and Ravetz, J.R. (1994) 'Emergent complex systems,' *Futures*, 26, 6: 568–582.

——(1993) 'Science for the post-normal age,' *Futures*, 25, 7: 739–755.

——(1992) 'The emergence of post-normal science,' in R. von Schomberg (ed.) *Science, Politics, and Morality*, Dordrecht: Kluwer Academic Publishers.

Gallagher, R. and Appenzeller, T. (1999) 'Beyond reductionism,' *Science*, 284, 2 April: 79.

Gare, A.E. (1995) *Postmodernism and the Environmental Crisis*, London and New York: Routledge.

Gelbspan, R. (2004) *Boiling Point: How Politicians, Big Oil and Coal, Journalists and Activists are Fueling the Climate Crisis – and What We Can Do to Avert a Disaster*, New York: Basic Books.

——(1997) *The Heat is On: The High Stakes Battle Over the Earth's Threatened Climate*, New York: Addison-Wesley Publishing.

Giddens, A. (1976) *New Rules of Sociological Method*, London: Hutchinson and Co.

Glacken, C.J. (1967) *Traces on the Rhodian Shore: Nature and Culture in Western Thought from Ancient Times to the End of the Eighteenth Century*, Berkeley, CA, Los Angeles, CA, and London: University of California Press.

Glover, L. (1999) 'Atmosphere for sale: Inventing commercial climate change,' *Bulletin of Science, Technology and Society*, 19, 6: 501–510.

Gough, C. and Shackley, S. (2001) 'The respectable politics of climate change: The epistemic communities and NGOs,' *International Affairs*, 77, 2: 329–345.

Gottfried K. and Wilson, K.G. (1997) 'Science as a social construct,' *Nature*, 386, 10 April: 545–547.

Gray, J. (1986) *Liberalism*, Minneapolis, MN: University of Minnesota Press.

Greenberg, J.B. and Park, K.T. (1994) 'Political ecology,' *Journal of Political Ecology*, 1, 1: 1–12.

Greene, O. (1996) 'Environmental regimes: Effectiveness and implementation review,' in J. Volger and M.F. Imber (eds.) *The Environment and International Relations*, London and New York: Routledge.

Gribbin, J. (1990) *Hothouse Earth: The Greenhouse Effect and Gaia*, New York: Grove Weidenfeld.

——(1976) *Forecasts, Famines and Freezes?* New York: Walker.

Gribbin, J. and Gribbin, M. (2001) *Ice Age*, New York: Barnes and Noble.

Griffin, D.R. (ed.) (1998a) *The Reenchantment of Science: Postmodern Proposals*, Albany, NY: State University Press of New York.

——(1998b) *Spirituality and Science: Postmodern Visions*, Albany, NY: State University Press of New York.

Grimes, P.E and Kentor, J. (2003) 'Exporting the greenhouse: Foreign capital penetration and CO_2 emissions 1980–1996,' *Journal of World-Systems Research*, IX, 2: 261–275.

Gross, P.R. and Levitt, N. (1994) *Higher Superstition: The Academic Left and its Quarrels with Science*, Baltimore, MD: Johns Hopkins University Press.

Grossman, G.M. and Krueger, A.B. (1995) 'Economic growth and the environment,' *Quarterly Journal of Economics*, May: 353–377.

Grubb, M. (2001a) 'Cold shoulder in a hot climate: Climate change responses on the knife edge,' *Energy Policy*, 29, 11: 833–836.

——(2001b) 'Who's afraid of atmospheric stabilization? Making the link between energy resources and climate change,' *Energy Policy*, 29, 11: 837–845.

——(1999). 'The political context for emissions trading in the climate change negotiations,' in O. Hohmeyer and K. Rennings (eds.) *Man-Made Climate Change: Economic Aspects and Policy Options*, Heidelberg and New York: Physica-Verlag.

——(1995) 'Seeking fair weather: Ethics and the international debate on climate change,' *International Affairs*, 71, 3: 463–496.

——(1990) 'The greenhouse effect: Negotiating targets,' *International Affairs*, 66, 1: 67–89.

Grubb, M. and Depledge, J. (2001) 'The seven myths of Kyoto,' *Climate Policy*, 1, 2: 269–272.

Grubb, M., Vrolijk, C. and Brack, D. (1999) *The Kyoto Protocol: A Guide and Assessment*, London: Earthscan.

Grubb, M. and F. Yamin (2001). 'Climatic collapse at The Hague: What happened, why, and where do we go from here?' *International Affairs*. Volume 77 (2): 261–276.

Grundbransen, L.H. and Andressen, S. (2004) 'NGO influence in the implementation of the Kyoto Protocol: Compliance, flexibility mechanisms, and sinks,' *Global Environmental Politics*, 4, 4: 54–75.

Guardian (2001) 'A dirty business,' March 30.

Guattari, F. (2000) *The Three Ecologies*, trans. I. Pindar and P. Sutton, London and New Brunswick, NJ: The Athlone Press.

Guha, R. (2000) *Environmentalism: A Global History*, New York: Longman.

Gupta, J. (2001) *Our Simmering Planet: What to do about Global Warming?* London and New York: Zed Books.

Haas, P.M. (1992) 'Introduction: Epistemic communities and international policy coordination,' *International Organization*, 46, 1: 1–35.

——(1990a) Obtaining international protection through epistemic consensus, *Millennium: Journal of International Studies*, 19, 3: 347–364.

——(1990b) *Saving the Mediterranean: the Politics of International Environmental Cooperation*, New York: Columbia University Press.

Haas, P.M., Keohane, R.O. and Levy, M.A. (eds.) (1993) *Institutions for the Earth: Sources of Effective International Environmental Protection*, Cambridge, MA: MIT Press.

Habermas, J. (1971) *Knowledge and Human Interests*, Boston, MA: Jeremy Shapiro.

Hadjilambrinos, C. (1999) 'For richer and poorer? The role of science, politics, and ethics in the global climate change policy debate,' *Bulletin of Science, Technology and Society*, 19, 6: 521–531.

Hagel, Senator C. (2001) *Testimony*, U.S. Senate Commerce, Science and Transportation Committee Hearing on Climate Change, 1 May 2001.

Hajer, M.A. (1995) *The Politics of Environmental Discourse: Ecological Modernization and the Policy Process*, Oxford: Oxford University Press.

Halacy, D.S. (1978) *Ice or Fire? Can We Survive Climate Change?* New York: Harper and Row.

Hamilton, C. (2001) *Running from the Storm: The Development of Climate Change Policy in Australia*, Sydney: University of New South Wales Press.

Hansen, J.E. (1988) 'The greenhouse effect: Impacts on current global temperature and regional heat waves,' Prepared Statement, U.S. Congress and Senate Committee on Energy and Natural Resources, *The Greenhouse Effect and Global Climate Change*, Hearing, June 23, 100th Congress, 1st Session.

Hansen, J., Nazarenko, L., Ruedy, R., Sato, M., Willis, J., Del Genio, A., Koch, D., Lacis, A., Lo, K., Menon, S., Novakov, T., Perlwitz, J., Russell, G., Schmidt, G.A. and Tausev, N. (2005) 'Earth's energy imbalance: Confirmations and implications,' *Science*, 308, 3 June: 1431–1434.

Hansen, J., Johnson, D., Lacis, A., Lebedeff, S., Lee, P., Rind, D. and Russell, G. (1981) 'Climatic impacts of increasing atmospheric carbon dioxide,' *Science*, 213, 28 August: 957–966.

Hardin, G. (1968) 'The tragedy of the commons,' *Science*, 162, 13 December: 1242–1248.

Harmaide, B. and Boland, J.J. (2000) 'Benefits, costs, and cooperation in greenhouse gas abatement,' *Climatic Change*, 47, 3: 239–258.

Hart, D.M. and Victor, D.G. (1993) 'Scientific elites and the making of US policy for climate change research, 1957–74,' *Social Studies of Science*, 23, 4: 643–680.

Harvey, D. (1992) *The Condition of Postmodernity: An Enquiry into the Origins of Cultural Change*, Cambridge, MA: Blackwell.

Hasselmann, K., Latif, M., Hooss, G., Azar, C., Edenhofer, O., Jaeger, C.C., Johannseen, O.M., Kemfert, C., Welp, M. and Wokaum, A. (2003) 'The challenge of long-term climate change,' *Science*, 302, 12 December: 1923–1925.

Hassan, I. (1987) *The Postmodern Turn: Essays in Postmodern Theory and Culture*, Columbus, OH: Ohio State University Press.

——(1975) POSTmodernISM: A Paracritical bibliography,' in *Paracriticisms: Seven Speculations of the Times*, Urbana, IL: University of Illinois Press.

Healy, S.A. (1999) 'Extended peer communities and the ascendance of post-normal politics,' *Futures*, 31, 7: 655–669.

——(1997) 'Changing science and ensuring our future,' *Futures*, 29, 6: 505–517.

Hecht, A.D. and Tirpak, D. (1995) 'Framework agreement on climate change: A scientific and policy history,' *Climatic Change*, 29, 4: 371–404.

Held, D., McGrew, A., Goldblatt, D. and Perraton, J. (1999) *Global Transformations: Politics, Economics and Culture*, Cambridge, UK: Polity.

Helvarg, D. (1994) *The War Against the Greens*, San Francisco, CA: Sierra Club Books.

Hempel, L.C. (1996) *Environmental Governance: The Global Challenge*, Washington, DC: Island Press.

Henderson–Sellers, A. and McGuffie, K. (1999) 'Concepts of good science in climate change modelling,' *Climatic Change*, 42, 3: 597–610.

Herring, H. (2000) 'Is energy efficiency environmentally friendly?,' *Energy and Environment*, 11, 3: 313–325.

Hilgartner, S. (1997) 'The Sokal affair in context,' *Science, Technology, and Human Values*, 22, 4: 506–522.

Hobsbawm, E.J. (1969) *The Pelican Economic History of Britain, Volume 3: From 1750 to Present Day.Industry and Empire*, Harmondsworth, England: Penguin Books.

Hoffert, M.I., Caldeira, K., Jain, A.K., Harvey, L.D.D., Haites, E.F., Potter, S.D., Schlesinger, M.E., Schneider, S.H., Watts, R.G., Wigley, T.M.L. and Wuebbles, D.J. (1998) 'Energy implications of future stabilization of atmospheric CO2 content,' *Nature*, 395, 29 October: 881–884.

Hofricher, R. (ed.) (1993) *Toxic Struggles: The Theory and Practice of Environmental Justice*, Philadelphia, PA: New Society Publishers.

Holdren, B. (2002) *Democracy and Global Warming*, London and New York: Continuum International Publishing Group.

Homer-Dixon, T.F. (1999) *Environment, Scarcity, and Violence*, Princeton, NJ: Harvard University Press.

Höhne, N., Wartmann, S., and Graus, W. (2005) *WWF Climate Scorecards: Comparison of the Climate Performance of the G8 Countries*, Worldwide Fund for Nature: Gland, Switzerland.

Horgan, J. (1997) *The End of Science: Facing the Limits of Knowledge in the Twilight of the Scientific Age*, New York: Broadway Books.

Hovden, E. (1999) 'As if nature doesn't matter: Ecology, regime theory and international relations,' *Environmental Politics*, 8, 2: 50–74.

Ihde, D. (2002) 'How could we ever believe science is not political?,' *Technology in Society*, 24, 1–2: 179–189.

Illich, I. (1977a) *Limits to Medicine.Medical Nemesis: The Expropriation of Health*, Harmondsworth, England: Penguin Books.

——(1977b) *Energy and Equity*, New York: Harper and Row.

——(1973a) *Tools for Conviviality*, London: Calder and Boyars.

——(1973b) *Deschooling Society*, Harmondsworth, England: Penguin Books.

Intergovernmental Panel on Climate Change (IPCC) (2001a) *Climate Change 2001: The Scientific Basis.Contribution of Working Group Ito the Third Assessment Report of the Intergovernmental Panel on Climate Change*, J.T. Houghton, Y. Ding, D.J. Griggs, M. Noguer, P. van der Linden, X. Dai, and K. Maskell (eds.), New York: Cambridge University Press.

——(2001b) *Climate Change 2001: Impacts, Adaptation, and Vulnerability:Contribution of Working Group II to the Third Assessment Report of the Intergovernmental Panel on Climate Change*, J.J. McCarthy, O.F. Canziani, N.A. Leary, D.J. Dokken, and K.S. White (eds.), New York: Cambridge University Press.

——(2001c) *Climate Change 2001: Mitigation.Contribution of Working Group III to the Third Assessment Report of the Intergovernmental Panel on Climate Change*, B. Metz, O. Davidson, R. Swart, and J. Pan (eds.), Cambridge, UK: Cambridge University Press.

——(2001d) *Climate Change 2001: Synthesis Report. A Contribution of Working Groups I, II, and III to the Third Assessment Report of the Intergovernmental Panel on Climate Change*, R.T. Watson and the Core Writing Team (eds.), Cambridge, UK: Cambridge University Press.

——(2000a) *Emissions Scenarios: A Special Report of Working Group I to the Intergovernmental Panel on Climate Change*, N. Nakicenovic and R. Swart (eds.), Cambridge, UK: Cambridge University Press.

——(2000b) *Land Use, Land–Use Change and Forestry: An IPCC Special Report*, R.T. Watson, I.R. Noble, B. Bolin, N.H. Ravindranath, D.J. Verado, and D.J. Dokken (eds.), Cambridge, UK: Cambridge University Press.

——(1997a) *Stabilization of Atmospheric Greenhouse Gases: Physical, Biological and Socio–economic Implications*, IPCC Technical Paper 3. J.T. Houghton, L.G. Meira Filho, D.G. Griggs, and K. Mas (eds.), Geneva, Switzerland: IPCC.

——(1997b) *Implications of Proposed CO2 Emission Limitations*, IPCC Technical Paper 4, J.T. Houghton, L.G., Meira Filho, D.G. Griggs, and M. Noguer (eds.), Geneva, Switzerland: IPCC.

——(1996a) *Climate Change 1995: The Science of Climate Change*, J.T. Houghton, L.G. Meira Filho, B.A. Callender, N. Harris, A. Kattenberg, and K. Maskell (eds.), Cambridge, UK: Cambridge University Press.

——(1996b) *Climate Change 1995: Impacts, Adaptations and Mitigation of Climate Change: Scientific–Technical Analyses*, R.T. Watson, M.C. Zinyowera, and R.H. Moss (eds.), Cambridge, UK: Cambridge University Press.

——(1996c) *Economic and Social Dimensions to Climate Change*, J. Bruce, H. Lee, and E. Haites (eds.), Cambridge, UK: Cambridge University Press.

——(1994) *Climate Change 1994: Radiative Forcing of Climate Change and An Evaluation of the IPCC IS92 Emission Scenarios*, J.T. Houghton, L.G. Meira Filho, J. Bruce, H. Lee, B.A. Callander, E. Haites, N. Harris, and K. Maskell (eds.), Cambridge, UK: Cambridge University Press.

——(1992) *Climate Change 1992: The Supplementary Report to the IPCC Scientific Assessment*, J.T. Houghton, B. Callander, and S.K. Varney (eds.), Cambridge, UK: Cambridge University Press.

——(1990a) *Climate Change: The IPCC Scientific Assessment*, T.J. Houghton, G.J. Jenkins, and J.J. Ephraums (eds.), Cambridge, UK: Cambridge University Press.

——(1990b) *Impacts Assessment of Climate Change: Report of Working Group II*, W.J. Tegart, G.W. Sheldon, and D.C. Griffiths (eds.), Canberra, Australia: Australian Government Publishing Service.

——(1990c) *The IPCC Response Strategies – Report of Working Group III*, Covelo, CA: Island Press.

Interlaboratory Working Group on Energy–efficient and Low-Carbon Technologies (IWG) (2001) *Scenarios of U.S. Carbon Reductions: Potential Impacts or Energy Technologies by 2010 and Beyond*, Washington, DC: US Department of Energy.

International Energy Agency (IEA) (2002a) *CO$_2$ Emissions from Fuel Combustion: 1971–2000*, Paris: OECD/ IEA.

——(2002b) *Beyond Kyoto: Energy Dynamics and Climate Stabilisation*, Paris: OECD/IEA.

——(2001) *Dealing with Climate Change: Policies and Measures in IEA Member Countries*, Paris: OECD/IEA.

——(1992) *Climate Change Policy Initiatives*, Paris: OECD/IEA.

Jacobs, J. (1961) *The Death and Life of Great American Cities*, New York: Random House.

Jacoby, H. and Reiner, D.M. (2001) 'Getting climate policy on track after The Hague,' *International Affairs*, 77, 2: 297–312.

Jager, J. and Ferguson, H.L. (eds.) (1991) 'Conference Statement: Second World Climate Conference,' Geneva, November 7, 1990, *Proceedings of the Second World Climate Conference*, Cambridge, UK: Cambridge University Press.

Jameson, F. (1991) *Postmodernism, or, The Cultural Logic of Late Capitalism*, Durham, NC and London: Duke University Press.

Jamieson, D. (1992) 'Ethics, public policy, and global warming,' *Science, Technology, and Human Values*, 17, 2: 139–153.

Jasanoff, S. (1996) 'Science and norms in global environmental regimes,' in F.O. Hampson and J. Reppy (eds.) *Earthly Goods: Environmental Change and Social Justice*, Ithaca, NY and London: Cornell University Press.

——(1992) 'Science, politics, and the renegotiation of expertise at EPA,' *OSIRIS*, Second Series, 7: 195–217.

Jasanoff, S. and Wynne, B. (1998) 'Science and decisionmaking,' in S. Rayner and E.L. Malone (eds.) *Human Choice and Climate Change: Volume 1: The Societal Framework*, Columbus, OH: Batelle Press.

Jencks, C. (1987) *The Language of Post–modern Architecture*, New York: Rizzoli.

Jones, M.D.H. and Henderson-Sellers, A. (1990) 'History of the greenhouse effect,' *Progress in Physical Geography*, 14, 1: 5.

Jones, P.D., Wigley, T.M.L., Folland, C.K., Parker, D.E., Angel, U.K., Lebedeff, S. and Hansen, J.E. (1988) 'Evidence for global warming in the past decade,' *Nature*, 332, 28 April: 790.

Karl, T.R. and Tremberth, K.E. (2003) 'Modern global climate change,' *Science*, 302, 5 December: 1719–1723.

Kellogg, W.W. (1987) 'Mankind's impact on climate: The evolution of an awareness,' *Climatic Change*, 10, 2: 113–1136.

——(1978) 'Global influences of mankind on the climate,' in J. Gribbin (ed.) *Climatic Change*, Cambridge, UK: Cambridge University Press.

Khor, M. (1993) 'Economics and environmental justice: Rethinking North–South relations,' in R. Hofrichter (ed.) *Toxic Struggles: The Theory and Practice of Environmental Justice*, Philadelphia, PA: New Society Publishers.

Kopp, R.J. (2001) 'An analysis of the Bonn agreement,' *Weathervane*. Available at: Resources for the Future website: http://www.waethervane.rff.org/features/feature134.htm. Accessed 12 September 2001.

Kopp, R.J. and Anderson, J.W. (1998) *Estimating the Costs of Kyoto: How Plausible Are the Clinton Administration's Figures?*, Washington, DC: Resources for the Future.

Korppoo, A. (2002) 'Russian ratification process. Why is the rest of the world waiting?,' *Climate Policy*, 2, 4: 387–393.

Krasner, S.D. (1983) 'Structural causes and regime consequences: Regimes as intervening variables,' in S.D. Krasner (ed.) *International Regimes*, Ithaca, NY: Cornell University Press.

Kuehls, T. (1996) *Beyond Sovereign Territory: The Space of Ecopolitics*, Minneapolis, MN: University of Minnesota Press.

Kuhn, T.S. (1970) *The Structure of Scientific Revolutions*, 2nd edn, Chicago, IL: University of Chicago Press.

Kumar, K. (1995) *From Post-Industrial to Post–Modern Society: New Theories of the Contemporary World*, Oxford, UK: Blackwell Publishers.

——(1988) *The Rise of Modern Society: Aspects of the Social and Political Development of the West*, Oxford, UK and New York: Basil Blackwell.

——(1978) *Prophecy and Progress: The Sociology of Industrial and Post-- IndustrialSociety*, New York: Penguin Books.

Lafferty, W.M. (1999) 'The pursuit of sustainable development – concepts, policies and arenas,' *International Political Science Review*, 20, 2: 123–28.

——(1996) 'The politics of sustainable development: global norms for national implementation,' *Environmental Politics*, 5, 2: 185–208.

Lamb, H.H. (1982) *Climate, History and the Modern World*, London and New York: Menthuen.

——(1977) *Climate: Present, Past and Future*, London: Methuen.

Lashof, D.A. and Tirpak, D.A. (eds.) (1990) *Policy Options for Stabilizing Climate Change*, New York, Washington, DC, Philadelphia, PA, and London: Hemisphere.

Leggett, J. (2000) *The Carbon War: Global Warming and the End of the Oil Era*, Harmondsworth, UK: Penguin.

Levitus, S., Antonov, J.I., Wang, J., Delworth, T.L., Dixon, K.W. and Broccoli, A.J. (2001) 'Anthropogenic warming of the earth's climate system,' *Science*, 292, 13 April: 267–270.

Levitus, S., Antonov, J.I., Boyer, T.P. and Stephens, C. (2000) 'Warming of the world ocean,' *Science*, 287, 24 March: 2225–2229.

Levy, D.L. and Egan, D. (1998) 'Capital contests: national and transnational channels of corporate influence on the climate change negotiations,' *Politics and Society*, 26, 3: 337–361.

Lipietz, A. (1995) 'Enclosing the global commons: Global environmental negotiations in a North–South conflictual approach,' in V. Bhaskar and A. Glyn (eds.) *The North, the South and the Environment: Ecological Constraints and the Global Economy*, Tokyo, New York, and Paris: United Nations University Press, and London: Earthscan.

Lipschutz, R.D. (1996) *Global Civil Society and Global Governance: The Politics of Nature from Place to Planet*, Albany, NY: State University of New York Press.

Lipschutz, R.D. and Conca, K. (1993) 'The implications of global ecological interdependence,' in R.D. Lipschutz and K. Conca (eds.) *The State and Social Power in Global Environmental Politics*, New York: Columbia University Press.

List, M. and Rittberger, V. (1992) 'Regime theory and international environmental management,' in A. Hurrell and B. Kingsbury (eds.) *The International Politics of the Environment*, Oxford: Clarendon Press.

Litfin, K.T. (1999) 'Constructing environmental security and ecological interdependence,' *Global Governance*, 5: 359–377.

——(1994) *Ozone Discourses: Science and Politics in Global Environmental Cooperation*, New York: Columbia University Press.

——(1993) 'Eco–regimes: Playing tug of war with the nation-state,' in R.D. Lipschutz and K. Conca (eds.) *The State and Social Power in Global Environmental Politics*, New York: Columbia University Press.

Lovins, A.B. (1977) *Soft Energy Paths: Toward a Durable Peace*, San Francisco, CA: Friends of the Earth International.

Lovins, A.B., Lovins, L.H., Krause, K., and Bach, B. (1981) *Least-Cost Energy: Solving the CO2 Problem*, Andover, MA: Brick House.

Low, N. and Gleeson, B. (1998) *Justice, Society and Nature: An Exploration of Political Ecology*, London: Routledge.

Lyotard, J.-F. (1993) *Toward the Post–Modern*, R. Harvey and M. S. Roberts, New Jersey and London: Humanities Press.

——(1984) *The Postmodern Condition: A Report on Knowledge*, Minneapolis, MN: University of Minnesota Press.

Lubchenco, J. (1998) 'Entering the century of the environment: A new social contract for science,' *Science*, 279, 23 January: 491–497.

Luke, T.W. (1997) *Ecocritique: Contesting the Politics of Nature, Economy, and Culture*, Minneapolis, MN and London: University of Minnesota Press.

Mander, J. and Goldsmith, E. (eds.) (1996) *The Case Against the Global Economy and for a Turn Toward the Local*, San Francisco, CA: Sierra Club Books.

Marcuse, H. (1972) [1964] *One Dimensional Man*, London: Sphere Books.

Martell, L. (1994). *Ecology and Society: An Introduction*, Cambridge, UK: Polity Press.

Martin, P. (2000) 'With mastery as our aim . . . ,' *Environmental Science and Policy*, 3, 1: 15–16.

Marx, K. (1906) *Capital: A Critique of Political Economy*, F. Engels (ed.), New York: The Modern Library.

Marx, L. (1996) 'The domination of nature and the redefinition of progress,' in L. Marx and B. Mazlish (eds.) *Progress: Fact or Illusion?*, Ann Arbor, MI: University of Michigan Press.

——(1994) 'The environment and the "Two Cultures" divide,' in J.R. Fleming and H.A. Gemery (eds.) *Science, Technology and the Environment*, Akron, OH: The University of Akron Press.

Mashood, E. (1995) 'Temperature rises in dispute over costing climate change,' *Nature*, 378, 30 November: 429.

Mashood, E. and Ochert, A. (1995) U.N. Climate Change report turns up the heat,' *Nature*, 378, 9 November: 119.

Mastrandrea, M.D. and Schneider, S.H. (2001) 'Integrated assessment of abrupt climatic changes,' *Climate Policy*, 1, 4: 433–449.

Mazur, A. and Lee, J. (1993) 'Sounding the global alarm: Environmental issues in the US national news,' *Social Studies of Science*, 23, 4: 681–720.

McEvoy, D., Gibbs, D.C. and Longhurst, J.W.S. (2000) 'The employment implications of a low–carbon economy,' *Sustainable Development*, 8, 1: 27–38.

McGuffie, K. and Henderson-Sellers, A. (1997) *A Climate Modelling Primer*, 2nd edn, Chichester, UK: John Wiley and Sons.

McIntosh, R.J., Tainter, J.A. and McIntosh, S.K. (eds.) (2000) *The Way the Wind Blows: Climate, History, and Human Action*, New York: Columbia University Press.

McKibben, B. (1989) *The End of Nature*, New York: Random House.

McKibben, W.J., Ross, M.T., Shackleton, R. and Wilcoxen, P.J. (1999) 'Emissions trading, capital flows and the Kyoto Protocol,' *Energy Journal*, Special Issue: The Costs of the Kyoto Protocol – A Multi Model Evaluation: 287–333.

Meadows, D.H., Meadows, D.L., Randers, J. and Behrens, W. (1972) *The Limits to Growth*, London: Pan.

Merchant, C. (1980) *The Death of Nature: Women, Ecology, and the Scientific Revolution*, San Francisco, CA: Harper & Row.

Metz, B. (2001) 'International equity in climate change policy,' *Integrated Assessment*, 1, 2: 111–126.

Metz, B., Berk, M., Kok, Marcel T.J., van Minnen, J.G., de Moor, A. and Faber, A. (2001) 'How can the European Union contribute to a COP–6 agreement?' *International Environmental Agreements: Politics, Law and Economics*, 1, 2: 167–185.

Meyer, A. (2000) *Contraction and Convergence: The Global Solution to Climate Change*, Foxhole, Dartington, Totnes, Devon: Green Books for The Schumacher Society.

Michaels, P.J. (1992) *Sound and Fury*, Washington, DC: Cato Institute.

Michaels, P.J. and Balling, R.C. (2000) *Satanic Gases: Clearing the Air about Global Warming*, Washington, DC: Cato Institute.

Midgley, G.F., Hannah, L., Millar, D., Rutherford, M.C., and L.W. Powrie (2002) 'Assessing the vulnerability of species richness to anthropocentric climate chngae in a biodiversity hotspot,' *Global Ecology and Biogeography*. Volume 11, 6: 445–451.

Milbrath, L.W. (1989) *Envisioning a Sustainable Society: Learning Our Way Out*, Albany, NY: State University of New York Press.

Molitor, M.R. (1999) 'The United Nations climate change agreements,' in N.J. Vig and R.S. Axelrod (eds.) *The Global Environment: Institutions, Law and Policy*, Washington, DC: Congressional Quarterly Incorporated.

Morgan, M.G., Kandlikar, M., Risby, J. and Dowlatabadi, H. (1999) 'Why conventional tools for policy analysis are often inadequate for problems of global change,' *Climatic Change*, 41, 3–4: 271–281.

Morgenthau, H. (1973) [1948] *Politics Among Nations: The Struggle for Power and Peace*, 5th edn, New York: Knopf.

Moss, R.H. (1995) 'Avoiding 'dangerous' interference in the climate system,' *Global Environmental Change*, 5, 1: 3–6.

Müller, B. (2004) 'The Kyoto Protocol: Russian Opportunities,' *Briefing Note*, prepared for 'Russia and the Kyoto Protocol: Issues and Challenges' Meeting at RIIA, 17 March, London: The Royal Institute of International Affairs.

Mumford, L. (1970) *The Pentagon of Power*, New York: Harcourt Brace Jovanovich.

——(1967) *Myth of the Machine: Technics and Human Development*, London: Secker and Warburg.

——(1934) *Technics and Civilization*, New York: Harcourt Brace and Company.

Myers, S.L. and Revkin, A.C. (2003) 'Russia to reject pact on climate, Putin aide says,' *New York Times*, 3 December.

Myerson, G.J. (2001) *Ecology and the End of Postmodernity*, Duxford, UK: Icon Books.

Nabuurs, G.J., Dolman, A.J., Verkaik, E., Kuikman, P.J., van Diepen, C.A., Whitmore, A.P., Daamen, W.P., Oenema, O., Kabat, P. and Mohren, G.M.J. (2000) 'Article 3.3 and 3.4 of the Kyoto Protocol: Consequences for industrialized countries' commitment, the monitoring needs, and possible side effects,' *Environmental Science and Policy*, 3, 2–3: 123–34.

Næss, A. (1973) 'The shallow and the deep, long–range ecology movement: A summary,' *Inquiry*, 16: 95–100.

National Academy of Sciences (NAS) (2001) *Climate Change Science: An Analysis of Some Key Questions*, Washington, DC: National Academy Press.

——(1991) *Policy Implications of Greenhouse Warming*, Washington, DC: National Academy Press.

National Energy Policy Development Group (NEPD) (2001) *National Energy Policy*, Washington, DC: US Government Printing Office.

National Environmental Trust (NET) (2002) *First in Emissions, Behind in Solutions: Global Warming Pollution from U.S. States Compared to more than 150 Developing Countries*, Washington, DC: NET.

National Research Council (NRC) (2002) *Abrupt Climate Change: Inevitable Surprises*, Washington, DC: National Academy Press.

——(2001) *Climate Change Science: An Analysis of Some Questions*. Washington, DC: National Academy Press.

——(1983) *Changing Climate: Report of the Carbon Dioxide Assessment Committee*, Washington, DC: National Academy Press.

——(1979) *Carbon–dioxide and Climate: A Scientific Assessment*, Washington, DC: National Academy of Sciences.

——(1977) *Energy and Climate*, Washington, DC: National Academy of Sciences.

Natural Resources Defense Council, Union of Concerned Scientists, and U.S. Public Interest Research Group Education Fund (NRDC et al.) (1999) *Kingpins of Carbon: How Fossil Fuel Producers Contribute to Global Warming*, New York: NRDC.

Nature (2001) 'Editorial: 'Problems with the president,' 410, 29 March: 499.

Neufeld, M. (1995) *The Restructuring of International Relations Theory*, Cambridge, UK: Cambridge University Press.

Neumayer, E. (2002) 'Can natural factors explain any cross-country differences in carbon dioxide emissions?,' *Energy Policy*, 30, 1: 1–12.

Newell, P. (2000) *Climate for Change: Non–State Actors and the Global Politics of Greenhouse*, Cambridge, UK and New York: Cambridge University Press.

Newell, P. and Paterson, M. (1999) 'A climate for business: Global warming, the state and capital,' *Review of International Political Economy*, 4–5, Winter: 679–703.

Noble, D.F. (1977) *America by Design: Science, Technology, and the Rise of Corporate Capitalism*, New York: Oxford University Press.

Noble, I. and Scholes, R.J. (2001) 'Sinks and the Kyoto Protocol,' *Climate Policy*, 1, 1: 5–25.

Nordhaus, W.D. (2001) 'The ghosts of climates past and the specters of climate change future,' *Science*, 294, 9 November: 1283–1284.

——(2000) *Warming the World: Economic Models of Global Warming*, Cambridge, MA: MIT Press.

——(1995) 'The ghosts of climates past and the specters of climate change future,' *Energy Journal*, 23, 4–5: 269–282.

——(1994) *Managing the Global Commons: The Economics of Climate Change*, Cambridge, MA: MIT Press.

——(1992) 'An optimal transition path for controlling greenhouse gases,' *Science*, 258, 20 November: 1315–1319.

——(1991a) 'To slow or not to slow: The economics of the greenhouse effect,' *The Economic Journal*, 101, 6: 920–937.

——(1991b) 'The cost of slowing climate change: A survey,' *Energy Journal*, 12, 1: 37–65.

——(1977) 'Economic growth and climate: The carbon dioxide problem,' *The American Economic Review*, 67, 1: 341–346.

Nordhaus, R.R., Fotis, S.C., and Van Ness Feldman (1998) *Analysis of Early Action Crediting Proposals*, Washington, DC: Pew Center on Global Climate Change.

Norgaard, R. (1994) *Development Betrayed: The End of Progress and a Coevolutionary Revisioning of the Future*, London and New York: Routledge.

Norton, S.D. and Suppe, F. (2001) 'Why atmospheric modeling is good science,' in C.A. Miller and P.N. Edwards (eds.) *Changing the Atmosphere: Expert Knowledge and Environmental Governance*, Cambridge, MA and London: MIT Press.

Oakerson, R.J. (1992) 'Analyzing the commons: A framework,' in D.W. Bromley (ed.) *Making the Commons Work: Theory, Practice and Policy*, San Francisco, CA: Institute for Contemporary Studies Press.

Oberthür, S. and Ott, H.E. (1999) *The Kyoto Protocol: International Climate Policy for the 21st Century*, Berlin and New York: Springer.

O'Connor, J. (1998) *Natural Causes: Essays in Ecological Marxism*, New York: Guildford Press.

——(1988) 'Capitalism, nature, socialism: A theoretical introduction,' *Capitalism, Socialism, Nature*, 1, Fall: 11–38.

O'Connor, M. (ed.) (1994) *Is Capitalism Sustainable?Political Ecology and the Politics of Ecology*, New York: The Guildford Press.

Oelschlaeger, M. (ed.) (1995) *Postmodern Environmental Ethics*, Albany, NY: State University of New York Press.

O'Neil, B. and Oppenheimer, M. (2002) 'Dangerous climate impacts and the Kyoto Protocol,' *Science*, 296, 14 June: 1971–1972.

O'Neil, R.V. and Kahn, J.R. (2000) 'Homo economus as a keystone species,' *Bioscience*, 50, 4: 333–337.

Oppenheimer, M. and Boyle, R. (1990) *Dead Heat: The Race Against the Greenhouse Effect*, New York: Basic Books.

Oreskes, N., Shradaer-Frechette, K., and Belitz, K. (1994) 'Verification, validation, and confirmation of numerical models in the earth sciences,' *Science*, 278, 4 February: 641–646.

Organization for Economic and Cultural Development (OECD) (1997) *Environmental Policies and Employment*, Paris: OECD.

Ostrom, E. (1990) *Governing the Commons: The Evolution of Institutions for Collective Action*, Cambridge: Cambridge University Press.

Paarlberg, R.L. (1999) 'Lapsed leadership: U.S. international environmental policy since Rio,' in N.J. Vig and Axelrod, R.S. (eds.) *The Global Environment: Institutions, Law and Policy*, Washington, DC: Congressional Quarterly Incorporated.

Pacala, S. and Socolow, R. (2004) 'Stabilization wedges: Solving the climate problem for the next 50 years with current technologies,' *Science*, 305, 13 August: 968–972.

Parmesan, C. and Yohe, G. (2003) 'A globally coherent fingerprint of climate change impacts across natural systems,' *Nature*, 421, 2 January: 37–42.

Passacantando, J. (1999) 'How industry combats efforts to protect our climate,' in J. Scherff (ed.) *The Piracy of America: Profiteering in the Public Domain*, Atlanta, GA: Clarity Press.

Passmore, J. (1974) *Man's Responsibility for Nature: Ecological Problems and Western Traditions*, New York: Scribner.

Paterson, M. (2000) *Understanding Global Environmental Politics: Domination, Accumulation, and Resistance*, London: Macmillan.

——(1999a) 'Green political strategy and the state,' in B.N. Fairweather, S. Elworthy, M. Stroh, and P.H.G. Stephens (eds.) *Environmental Futures*, New York: St. Martins Press.

——(1999b) 'Overview: Interpreting trends in global environmental governance,' *International Affairs*, 75, 4: 793–802.

——(1996) *Global Warming and Global Politics*, London and New York: Routledge.

——(1995) 'Radicalising regimes? Ecology and the critique of IR theory,' in A. Linklater and J. Macmillan (eds.) *Boundaries in Question: New Directions in International Relations*, London: Macmillan.

Paterson, M. and Grubb, M. (1992) 'The international politics of climate change,' *International Affairs*, 68, 2: 293–310.

Pearce, F. (1989) *Turning up the Heat: Our Perilous Future in the Global Greenhouse*, London: Paladin Books.

Pepper, D. (1996) *Modern Environmentalism: An Introduction*, London and New York: Routledge.

——(1993) *Ecosocialism: From Deep Ecology to Social Justice*, London and New York: Routledge.

Phylipsen, G.J.M., Bode, J.W., Blok, K., Merkus, H., and Metz, B. (1998) 'A triptych sectoral approach to burden differentiation: GHG emissions in the European bubble.' *Energy Policy*, 26, 12: 929–943.

Pielke, R.A. (2000a) 'Policy history of the US Global Change Research Program: Part I. Administrative development,' *Global Environmental Change*, 10, 1: 9–25.

——(2000b) 'Policy history of the US Global Change Research Program: Part II. Legislative process,' *Global Environmental Change*, 10, 2: 133–144.

Pinguelli–Rosa, L. and Munasinghe, M. (eds.) (2002) *Ethics, Equity and International Negotiations in Climate Change*, Cheltenham, UK and Northampton, MA: Edward Elgar.

Podobnik, B. (2002) 'Global energy inequalities: Exploring the long–term implications,' *Journal of World-Systems Research*, VIII, 2: 252–274.

Polanyi, K. (1944) *The Great Transformation*, New York: Rinehart.

Pollard, S. (1971) *The Idea of Progress: History and Society*, Harmondsworth, UK: Penguin.

Ponte, L. (1976) *The Cooling*, Englewood Cliffs, NJ: Prentice-Hall.

Porter, G. and Welsh Brown, J.W. (1996) *Global Environmental Politics*, 2nd edn, Boulder, CO: Westview Press.

Postman, N. (1993) *Technopoly: The Surrender of Culture to Technology*, New York: Vintage Books.

President's Science Advisory Council (1965) *Restoring the Quality of our Environment: Report of the Environmental Pollution Panel*, Washington, DC: The White House.

Proctor, J.D. (1998) 'The meaning of global environmental change: Retheorizing culture in human dimensions research,' *Global Environmental Change*, 8, 3: 227–248.

Proctor, R.N. (1991) *Value-Free Science? Purity and Power in Modern Knowledge*, Cambridge, MA and London: Harvard University Press.

Rabe, B.G. (2002) *Greenhouse and Statehouse: The Evolving State Government Role in Climate Change*, Arlington, VA: Pew Center on Global Climate Change.

Ramakrishna, K. (1996) 'Building an effective climate regime,' in O.R. Young, G.J. Demko, and K. Ramakrishna (eds.) *Global Environmental Change and International Governance*, Hanover, NH and London: University Press of New England.

Ramanathan, V., Cicerone, R.J., Singh, H.B. and Kiehl, J.T. (1985) 'Trace gas trends and their potential role in climate change,' *Journal of Geophysical Research*, 90: 5547–5566.

Ravetz, J.R. (1999) 'What is post-normal science?' *Futures*, 31, 7: 647–653.

Ravetz, J.R. and Funtowicz, S. (1999) 'Post–normal science – an insight now maturing,' *Futures*, 31, 7: 641–646.

Redclift, M. (1995) 'Values and the global environment,' in Y. Guerrier, N. Alexander, J. Chaste, J., and M. O'Brien (eds.) *Values and the Environment: A Social Science Perspective*, Chichester, UK: John Wiley and Sons.

Redclift, M. (1998) 'Dances with wolves? Interdisciplinary research on the global environment,' *Global Environmental Research*, 8, 3: 177–182.

Redclift, M. and Sage, C. (1998) 'Global environmental change and global inequality: North/South perspectives,' *International Sociology*, 13, 4: 499–516.

Reilly, J., Stone, P.H., Forest, C.E., Webster, M.D., Jacoby, H.D. and Prinn, R.G. (2001) 'Uncertainty and climate change assessments,' *Science*, 293, 20 July: 430–433.

Repetto, R. and Austin, D. (1997) *The Costs of Climate Protection: A Guide for the Perplexed*. Washington, DC: World Resources Institute.

Report on the Study of Man's Impact on Climate (SMIC) (1971) *Inadvertent Climate Modification*, Cambridge, MA: MIT Press.

Rescher, N. (1999) *The Limits of Science*, rev. edn, Pittsburgh, PA: University of Pittsburgh Press.

Retallack, S. and Sobhani, L. (2001) 'The impact of economic globalization on global climate,' *Transactional Associations*, 3: 157–165.

Revelle, R. (1985) 'Introduction: The scientific history of carbon dioxide,' in E.T. Sundquist and W.S. Broeker (eds.) *The Carbon Cycle and Atmospheric CO2: Natural Variations Archean to Present*. Geophysical Monographs 32, American Geophysical Union, Washington, DC.

Revelle, R. and Suess, H.E. (1957) 'Carbon dioxide exchange between atmosphere and ocean, and the question of an increase of atmospheric CO_2 during the past decades,' *Tellus*, 9, 18: 18–27.

Revkin, A.C. and Seelye, K.Q. (2003) 'Report by the E.P.A. leaves out data on climate change,' *New York Times*, June 19.

Richards, K. and Anderson, K. (2001) 'The leaky sink: persistent obstacles to a forest carbon sequestration problem based on individual projects,' *Climate Policy*, 1, 1: 41–54.

Roberts, J.T. and Grimes, P.E. (1997) 'Carbon intensity and economic development 1962–91: A brief exploration of the environmental Kuznets curve,' *World Development*, 25, 2: 191–198.

Roberts, J.T., Grimes, P.E. and Mandale, J.L. (2003) 'Social roots of global environmental change: A world–systems analysis of carbon dioxide emissions,' *Journal of World-Systems Research*, IX, 2: 277–315.

Rolston, H. (1988) *Environmental Ethics: Duties to and Values in the Natural World*, Philadelphia, PA: Temple University Press.

——(1985) 'Duties to endangered species,' *Bioscience*, 35, 11: 718–726.

Root, T.L., Price, J.T., Hall, K.R., Schneider, S.H., Rosenzweig, C. and Pounds, J.A. (2003) 'Fingerprints of global warming on wild animals and plants,' *Nature*, 421, 2 January: 57–60.

Rorty, R. (1979) *Philosophy and the Mirror of Nature*, Princeton, NJ: Princeton University Press.

Rosa, E.A. and Dietz, T. (1998) 'Climate change and society: Speculation, construction and scientific investigation,' *International Sociology*, 13, 4: 421–455.

Ross, A. (ed.) (1996) *Science Wars*, Durham, NC and London: Duke University Press.

——(1991) 'Is global culture warming up?' *Social Text*, 28: 3–30.

Roszak, T. (1995) *Ecopschology: Restoring the Earth, Healing the Mind*, San Francisco, CA: Sierra Club Books.

——(1992) *The Voice of the Earth*, New York: Simon and Schuster.

——(1978) *Person/Planet: The Creative Disintegration of Industrial Society*, Garden City, NY: Anchor Press/Doubleday.

——(1972) *Where the Wasteland Ends: Politics and Transcendence on Post-Industrial Society*, Garden City, NY: Doubleday.

Rowlands, I.H. (2001) 'Classical theories of international relations,' in U. Luterbacher and D.F. Sprinz (eds.) *International Relations and Global Climate Change*, Cambridge, MA and London: MIT Press.

Roy, R. (1997) 'The twilight of science – last of the gods,' *Futures*, 29, 6: 471–482.

Sachs, W. (1999a) *Planet Dialectics: Explorations in Environment and Development*, London and New York: Zed Books.

——(1999b) *Post-Fossil Development Patterns in the North*, Wuppertal Papers, 95: Wuppertal Institute, Germany.

——(1996) 'Neo-development: "Global ecological development," ' in J. Mander and E. Goldsmith (eds.) *The Case Against the Global Economy and for a Turn Toward the Local*, San Francisco, CA: Sierra Club Books.

——(1994) 'The blue planet: An ambiguous modern icon,' *The Ecologist*, 24, 5: 170–175.

——(1993a) 'Global ecology and the shadow of development,' in W. Sachs (ed.), *Global Ecology: A New Arena of Political Conflict*, Atlantic Highlands, NJ: Zed Books.

——(ed.) (1993b) *Global Ecology: A New Arena of Political Conflict*, Atlantic Highlands, NJ: Zed Books.

——(1992) *The Development Directory: A Guide to Knowledge as Power*, London: Zed Books.

——(1991) 'The story of a dangerous liaison,' *The Ecologist*, 21: 252–257.

Sachs, W., Loske, R. and Linz, M. (1998) *Greening the North: A Post–Industrial Blueprint for Ecology and Equity*, London: Zed Books.

Sagan, C. (1983) 'Nuclear war and climate catastrophe: Some policy implications,' *Foreign Affairs*, Winter, 1983/84: 257–292.

Sagan, C. and Turco, R. (1990) *A Path Where No Man Thought: Nuclear Winter and the End of the Arms Race*, New York: Random House.

Sale, K. (1985) *Dwellers in the Land: The Bioregional Vision*, San Francisco, CA: Sierra Club.

Saloranta, T. (2001) 'Post–normal science and the global climate change issue,' *Climatic Change*, 50, 4: 395–404.

Saurin, J. (2001) 'Global environmental crisis as the 'disaster triumphant': The private capture of public goods,' *Environmental Politics*, 10, 4: 63–84.

——(1996) 'International relations, social ecology and the globalisation of ecological change,' in J. Volger and M.F. Imber (eds.) *The Environment and International Relations*, London and New York: Routledge.

——(1993) 'Global environmental degradation, modernity and environmental knowledge,' *Environmental Politics*, 2, 4: 46–64.

Schneider, S.H. (2001) 'What is 'dangerous' climate change?' *Nature*, 411, 3 May: 17–19.

——(1990) *Global Warming: Are We Entering the Greenhouse Century?* San Francisco, CA: Sierra Club Books.

——(1976) *The Genesis Strategy: Climate and Global Survival*, New York: Plenum.

Schneider, S.H. and Londer, R. (1984) *The Coevoltion of Climate and Life*, San Francisco, CA: Sierra Club Books.

Schumacher, E.F. (1974) *Small is Beautiful: A Study of Economics as if People Mattered*, London: Sphere Books.

Schwartz, P. and Randall, D. (2003) *An Abrupt Climate Change Scenario and Its Implications for United States National Security*, report commissioned by the U.S. Department of Defense.

Scott, D., Jones, B., Audrey, J., Gibson, R., Kay, P., Mortsch, L., and K. Warriner (eds.) (2000) *Climate Change Communication*, Proceedings of an International Conference, June 22–24, Kitchner-Waterloo, Ontario, Canada.

Seitz, F., Jashrow, R. and Nierenberg, W. (1989) *Scientific Perspectives on the Greenhouse Problem*, Washington, DC: George C. Marshall Institute.

Seldon, T.M. and Song, D. (1994) 'Environmental quality and development: Is there a Kuznets curve for air pollution emissions?' *Journal of Environmental Economics and Management*, 27, 2: 147–162.

Sell, S. (1996) 'North–south environmental bargaining: Ozone, climate change, and biodiversity,' *Global Governance*, 2: 97–118.

Shackley, S. (1997) 'The Intergovernmental Panel on Climate Change: consensual knowledge and global politics,' *Global Environmental Change*, 7, 1: 77–79.

——(1995) 'Global climate change: The natural construction of a science–policy domain,' *Science and Public Policy*, 22: 218–230.

Shackley, S. and Wynne, B. (1996) 'Representing uncertainty in global climate change science and policy: Boundary–ordering devices and authority,' *Science, Technology and Human Values*, 21, 3: 275–302.

——(1995) 'Integrating knowledges for climate change: Pyramids, nets and uncertainties,' *Global Environmental Change*, 5, 2: 113–126.

Shiva, V. (1999) 'Ecological balance in an era of globalization,' in N. Low (ed.) *Global Ethics and the Environment*, London and New York: Routledge.

——(1998) 'Development, ecology, and women,' in J.S. Dryzek and D. Schlosberg (eds.) *Debating the Earth: The Environment Politics Reader*, Oxford: Oxford University Press.

——(1997) *Biopiracy: The Plunder of Nature and Knowledge*, Boston, MA: South End Press.

——(1993) 'The greening of the global reach,' in W. Sachs (ed.) *Global Ecology: A New Arena of Political Conflict*, London: Zed Books.

Shue, H. (1999) 'Global environment and international inequality,' *International Affairs*, 17, 3: 531–545.

——(1995) 'Ethics, the environment and changing international order,' *International Affairs*, 71, 3: 453–461.

——(1993) 'Subsistence emissions and luxury emissions,' *Law and Policy*, 15, 1: 39–59.

——(1992) 'The unavoidability of justice,' in A. Hurrell and B. Kingsbury (eds.) *The International Politics of the Environment: Actors, Interests, and Institutions*, Oxford, UK: Oxford University Press.

Singer, P. (2004) *The President of Good and Evil: The Ethics of George W. Bush*, New York: Dutton.

Singer, S.F. (ed.) (1989) *Global Climate Change: Human and Natural Influences*, New York: Pergamon House.

Smart, B. (1996) 'Postmodern social theory,' in B.S. Turner (ed.) *Social Theory*, Cambridge, MA: Blackwell.

Smith, D.N. (2001) 'The stigma of reason: Irrationalism as a problem for social theory,' in K.M. Ashman and P.S. Baringer (eds.) *After the Science Wars*, London and New York: Routledge.

Sokal, A.D. and Bricmont, J. (1998) *Fashionable Nonsense: Postmodern Intellectuals' Abuse of Science*, New York: Picador.

Soroos, M.S. (1997) *The Endangered Atmosphere: Preserving a Global Commons*, Columbia, SC: University of South Carolina Press.

Soulé, M.E. (1995) 'The social siege of nature,' in M.E. Soulé and G. Lease (eds.) *Reinventing Nature? Responses to Postmodern Deconstruction*, Washington, DC: Island Press.

Soulé, M.E. and Lease, G. (eds.) (1995) *Reinventing Nature? Responses to Postmodern Deconstruction*, Washington, DC: Island Press.

Spaargaren, G., Mol, A.P.J. and Buttel, F.H. (2000a) 'Introduction: Globalization, modernity and the environment,' in G. Spaargaren, A.J.P. Mol and F.H. Buttel (eds.) *Environment and Global Modernity*, London, Thousand Oaks, CA, and New Delhi: Sage.

——(eds.) (2000b) *Environment and Global Modernity*, London, Thousand Oaks, CA, and New Delhi: Sage.

Spengler, O. (1937) *The Decline of the West*, New York: Alfred A. Knopf.

Speth, J.G. (2004) *Red Sky at Morning: America and the Crisis of the Global Environment*, New Haven, CT: Yale University Press.

Spretnak, C. (1997) *The Resurgence of the Real: Body, Nature, and Place in a Hypermodern World*, Reading, MA: Addison-Wesley.

——(1991) *States of Grace: The Recovery of Meaning in the Postmodern Age*, San Francisco, CA: HarperCollins.

Spretnak, C. and Capra, F. (1984) *Green Politics: The Global Promise*, New York: Dutton.

Stark, J.A. (1995) 'Postmodern environmentalism: A critique of deep ecology,' in B.R. Taylor (ed.) *Ecological Resistance Movements: The Global Emergence of Radical and Popular Environmentalism*, Albany, NY: SUNY Press.

Stavins, R.N. (1997) *Policy Instruments for Climate Change: How Can National Governments Address a Global Problem?* Discussion Paper 97–11, Washington, DC: Resources for the Future.

Stent, G. (1978) *Paradoxes of Progress*, San Francisco, CA: W.H. Freeman.

Stolzenburg, G. (2001) 'Reading and relativism: An introduction to the science wars,' in K.M. Ashton and P.S. Baringer (eds) *After the Science Wars*, London and New York: Routledge.

Stone, C.D. (1987) *Earth and Other Ethics: The Case for Moral Pluralism*, New York: Harper & Row.

Study of Critical Environmental Problems (SCEP) (1970) *Man's Impact on the Global Climate: Report of the Study of Critical Environmental Problems*, Cambridge, MA: MIT Press.

Suri, V. and Chapman, D. (1998) 'Economic growth, trade and energy: Implications for the environmental Kuznets curve,' *Ecological Economics*, 25, 2: 195–208.

Susskind, L.E. (1994) *Environmental Diplomacy: Negotiating More Effective Global Agreements*, New York: Oxford University Press.

Susskind, L.E. and Ozawa, C. (1992) 'Negotiating more effective international agreements,' in A. Hurrell and B. Kingsbury (eds.) *The International Politics of the Environment: Actors, Interests, and Institutions*, Oxford, UK: Oxford University Press.

Tainter, J.A. (2000) 'Global change, history, and sustainability,' in R.J. McIntosh, J.A. Tainter, and S.K. McIntosh (eds.) *The Way the Wind Blows: Climate, History, and Human Action*, New York: Columbia University Press.

Thiele, L.P. (1997) *Thinking Politics: Perspectives in Ancient, Modern, and Postmodern Political Theory*, Chatham, NJ: Chatham House.

Thomas, C.B., Cameron, A., Green, R.E., Bakkenes, M., Beaumont, L.J., Collingham, Y.C., Erasmus, B.F.N., de Siqueira, M.F., Grainger, A., Hannah, L., Hughes, L., Huntley, B., van Jaarsveld, A.S., Midgley, G.F., Miles, L., Ortega-Huerta, M.A., Peterson, A.T., Phillips, O.L., and Williams, S.E. (2004) 'Extinction risk from climate change,' *Nature*, 427, 8 January: 145–148.

Tickell, C. (1977) *Climate Change and World Affairs*, Cambridge, MA: Harvard Studies in International Affairs.

Time (2001) Greenhouse issue, 23 April.

Tokar, B. (1997) *Earth for Sale: Reclaiming Ecology in the Age of Corporate Greenwash*, Boston, MA: South End Press.

Toulmin, S. (1990) *Cosmopolis: The Hidden Agenda of Modernity*, Chicago, IL: University of Chicago Press.

Trainer, T. (2001) 'The "de-materialization" myth,' *Technology in Society*, 23, 4: 505–514.

Turton, H. and Hamilton, C. (2001) *Comprehensive Emissions per Capita for Industrialized Countries*, Canberra, Australia: The Australia Institute. Available at: http://www.tai.org.au/latest1_files/Percapita.shtml

Tyndall, J. (1863) 'On radiation through the earth's atmosphere,' *The London, Edinburgh, and Dublin Philosophical Magazine and Journal of Science*, 4: 200–207.

Ungar, S. (1995) 'Social scares and global warming: Beyond the Rio convention,' *Society and Natural Resources*, 8: 443–456.

——(1992) 'The rise and (relative) decline of global warming as a social problem,' *The Sociological Quarterly*, 33, 4: 483–501.

Unruh, G.C. (2000) 'Understanding carbon lock-in,' *Energy Policy*, 28, 12: 817–830.

United Nations (1999) *Framework Convention on Climate Change*. Available at: www.unfccc.de/resource/conv/conv

——(1998) *Report of the Conference of the Parties on Third Session, Held at Kyoto From 1to 11 December, 1997.* FCCC/CP/1997/7/Add.1.

United Nations Development Programme (UNDP) (2000) *Human Development Report 2000*, New York and Oxford, UK: Oxford University Press.

United Nations Development Programme, United Nations Department of Economic and Social Affairs, and World Energy Council (UNDP et al.) (2000) *World Energy Assessment: Energy and the Challenge of Sustainability*, New York: UNDP.

United Nations Development Programme, United Nations Environment Program, World Bank, and the World Resources Institute (UNDP et al.) (2001) *World Resources 2000–2001: People and Ecosystems: The Fraying Web of Life*, Washington, DC: World Resources Institute.

United States Energy Information Agency (EIA) (2000) *Annual Energy Outlook 2001*, U.S. Department of Energy. Available at: www.eia.doe.gov/oiaf/aeo

United States Environment Protection Agency (EPA) (2002) *Partnerships and Progress. EPA State and Local Change Program: 2001 Progress Report*, Washington, DC: EPA 430-R-02-002.

——(1999) *United States Greenhouse Gas Inventory, 1990–1997*, Washington, DC.

United Nations Framework Convention on Climate Change Secretariat (2001). *Synthesis and Assessment Report of Greenhouse Gas (GHG) Inventories Submitted in 2000*. UNFCCC Document: FCCC/WEB/SAI/2000.

United Nations Framework Convention on Climate Change Secretariat (2003) *Kyoto Protocol Status of Ratification*. Available at: http://www.unfccc.int/resource/kpstats.pdf. Accessed on 24 January 2003.

——(2002) *Press Release: Kyoto Protocol receives 100th ratification*, Bonn, 18 December.

Van den Hove, S., Le Menestrel, M. and de Bettignies, H.-C. (2002) 'The oil industry and climate change: Strategies and ethical dilemmas,' *Climate Policy*, 2, 1: 3–18.

van Natta, D. with Banerjee, N. (2000a) 'Bush policies have been good to energy industry,' *New York Times*, Sunday April 21.

——(2000b) 'Many made the move from the industry to the administration,' *New York Times*, Sunday April 21.

Venturi, R. (1966) *Complexity and Contradiction in Architecture*, New York: Museum of Modern Art.

Venturi, R., Brown, D.S. and Izenour, S. (1972) *Learning from Las Vegas*, Cambridge, MA: MIT Press.

Victor, D.G. (2001) *The Collapse of the Kyoto Protocol and the Struggle to Slow Global Warming*, Princeton, NJ: Princeton University Press.

——(1995) 'On writing good histories of climate change and testing social science theories,' *Climatic Change*, 29, 4: 363–369.

Victor, D.G., Nakicenovic, N. and Victor, N. (2001) 'The Kyoto Protocol emission allocations: Windfall surpluses for Russia and Ukraine,' *Climatic Change*, 49, 3: 263–277.

Vig, N.J. (1999) 'Introduction: Governing the international environment,' in N.J. Vig and R.S. Axelrod (eds.) *The Global Environment: Institutions, Law and Policy*, Washington, DC: Congressional Quarterly Inc.

Virilio, P. (2002) *Open Sky*, London: Verso.

Vitousek, P.M., Ehrlich, P.R., Ehrlich, A.H., and Matson, P.A. (1986) 'Human appropriation of the products of photosynthesis,' *Bioscience*, 36, 6: 368–373.

Vitousek, P.M., Mooney, H.A., Lubchenco, J., and Melillo, J.M. (1997) 'Human domination of the earth's ecosystems,' *Science*, 277, 25 July: 494–499.

Volger, J. (1995) *The Global Commons: A Regime Analysis*, Chichester, UK: John Wiley and Sons.

von Neumann, J. (1955) 'Can we survive technology?' *Fortune*, June: 106–108, 151–152.

Vrolijk, C. (2001) 'Meeting Report: President Bush might have done Kyoto a favour,' *Report of a discussion meeting organized by the Energy and Environment Programme of the Royal Institute of International Affairs 'Is Kyoto Dead?'* Chatham House, London, 25 April.

Wackernagel, M. and Rees, W.E. (1996) *Our Ecological Footprint: Reducing Human Impact on the Earth*, Gabriola Island, Canada: New Society Publisher.

Wall, D. (1994) *Green History: A Reader in Environmental Literature, Philosophy and Politics*, London and New York: Routledge.

Walther, G.-R., Post, E., Convey, P., Menzel, A., Parmesan, Camille, Beebee, Trevor, J.C., Fromentin, J.-M., Hoegh-Gulberg, O., and Bairlein, F. (2002) 'Ecological responses to recent climate change,' *Nature*, 416, 28 March: 389–395.

Waple, A.M., Lawrimore, J.H., Halpert, M.S., Bell, G.D., Higgins, W., Lyon, B., McMenne, M.J., Gleason, K.L., Schnell, R.C., Christy, J.R., Thiaw, W., Wright, W.J., Salinger, M.J., Alexander, L., Stone, R.S., and Camargo, S.J. (2002) *Climate Assessment for 2001*, Geneva, Switzerland: World Meteorological Organization.

Washington Post (2001) 'Editorial. About-face on warming,' March 15: page A24.

Weale, A. (1998) 'Politics of ecological modernization,' in J.S. Dryzek and D. Schlosberg (eds.) *Debating the Earth: The Environment Politics Reader*, Oxford, UK: Oxford University Press.

Weale, A. (1992) *The New Politics of Pollution*, Manchester, UK and New York: Manchester University Press.

Weber, M. (1930) [1904] *The Protestant Ethic and the Spirit of Capitalism*, London: Urwin University Books.

Weyant, J.P. (2000) *An Introduction to the Economics of Climate Change Policy*,

Weyant, J.P. and Hill, J.N. (1999) 'Introduction and Overview to Special Issue,' in J.P. Weyant (ed.) *The Costs of the Kyoto Protocol: A Multi-Model Evaluation*, Special Issue of *The Energy Journal*.

Weinberg, A. (1972) 'Science and trans-science,' *Minerva*, 10: 209–222.

Weiner, J. (1997) 'Global trade in greenhouse gas control,' *Resources*, 129, Fall. Available at: www.rff.org.resources-articles.

Weizsacker, E. von, Lovins, A. and Lovins, H. (1997) *Factor Four: Doubling Wealth-Halving Resource Use*, London: Earthscan.

Wettestad, J. (2001) 'Designing effective environmental regimes: The conditional keys,' *Global Governance*, 7, 3: 317–341.

Wharton Econometric Forecasting Associates (1998) *Global Warming: The High Cost of the Kyoto Protocol, National and State Impacts*, Eddystone, PA.

White, R.M. (1996) 'The nature of progress: progress and the environment,' in L. Marx and B. Mazlish (eds.) *Progress: Fact or Illusion?* Ann Arbor, MI: University of Michigan Press.

White, R.M. and Hooke W. (2004) 'Climate science, technology and politics: A tangled web,' *Technology in Society*, 26, 2–3: 375–348.

Wigley, T.M.L. (2001) 'The science of climate change,' in E. Claussen (ed.) *Climate Change: Science, Strategies, and Solutions*, Leiden, Boston, and Köln: Brill.

Williams, R. (1989) *Resources of Hope: Culture, Democracy, Socialism*, R. Gable (ed.), London and New York: Verso.

Winner, L. (1977) *Autonomous Technology: Technics-out-of-Control as a Theme in Political Thought*, Cambridge, MA: MIT Press.

World Bank (2000a) *World Development Report 2000/2001: Attacking Poverty*, New York: Oxford University Press.

——(2000b) *Energy Services for the World's Poor*, Washington, DC: World Bank.

——*World Development Report 1999/2000: Entering the 21st Century*, New York: Oxford University Press.

World Business Council on Sustainable Development (WBCSD) (2001) *The Business Case for Sustainable Development: Making aDifference Toward the Johannesburg Summit 2002 and Beyond*, Geneva, Switzerland: WBCSD.

World Commission on Environment and Development (WCED) (1987) *Our Common Future*, New York: Oxford University Press.

World Energy Assessment (WEA) (2000) *World Energy Assessment: Energy and the Challenge of Sustainability*, New York: United Nations Development Programme,

United Nations Development of Economic and Social Affairs and the World Energy Council.

World Meteorological Organization (WMO) (1989) *Proceedings of the World Conference on the Changing Atmosphere: Implications for Global Security*, WMO Doc. 710, Toronto, Canada, June 27–30.

——(1985) *International Assessment of the Role of the Carbon Dioxide and of Other Greenhouse Gases in Climate Variations and Associated Impacts*, Villach, Austria: WMO.

——(1979) *Proceedings of the World Climate Conference*, Rpt. No. 537, Geneva, Switzerland: WMO.

World Resources Institute, United Nations Environment Programme, and the World Business Council for Sustainable Development (WRI et al.) (2002) *Tomorrow's Markets: Global Trends and their Implications for Business*, Washington, D.C.: World Resources Institute.

World Wide Fund for Nature (WWF) (2000) *Make or Break for the Kyoto Protocol*, Gland, Switzerland: WWF.

Worster, D. (1994) *Nature's Economy: A History of Ecological Ideas*, 2nd edn, Cambridge, UK: Cambridge University Press.

Wynne, B. (1994) 'Scientific knowledge and the global environment,' in M. Redclift and T. Benton (eds.) *Social Theory and the Global Environment*, London: Routledge.

Yamin, F., Burniaux, J.-M. and A. Nentjes (2001) 'Kyoto mechanisms: Key issues for policy-makers at COP-6,' *International Environmental Agreements: Politics, Law and Economics*, 1, 2: 187–218.

Yamin, F. and J. Depledge (2004) *The International Climate Change Regime: A Guide to Rules, Institutions and Procedures*, Cambridge, UK and New York: Cambridge

Yearly, S. (1996) *Sociology, Environmentalism, Globalisation: Reinventing the Globe*, London: Sage.

Yergin, D. (1991) *The Prize: The Epic Quest for Oil, Money, and Power*, New York: Simon and Schuster.

Young, O.R. (1997) *Global Governance: Drawing Insights from the Environmental Experience*, Cambridge, MA and London: MIT Press.

——(1994) *International Governance: Protecting the Environment in a Stateless Society*, Ithaca, NY: Cornell University Press.

——(1989) *International Cooperation: Building Regimes for Natural Resources and the Environment*, Ithaca, NY: Cornell University Press.

Zimmerman, M.E. (1994) *Contesting the Earth's Future: Radical Ecology and Postmodernity*, Berkeley, CA: University of California Press.

——(1987) 'Feminism, deep ecology, and environmental ethics,' *Environmental Ethics*, 9, 2: 21–44.

Index